Programming Visual Basic
for Palm OS

Programming Visual Basic
for Palm OS

Matthew Holmes, Patrick Burton,
and Roger Knoell

O'REILLY®

Beijing · Cambridge · Farnham · Köln · Paris · Sebastopol · Taipei · Tokyo

Programming Visual Basic for Palm OS
by Matthew Holmes, Patrick Burton, and Roger Knoell

Published by O'Reilly & Associates, Inc., 1005 Gravenstein Highway North,
Sebastopol, CA 95472.

O'Reilly & Associates books may be purchased for educational, business, or sales promotional
use. Online editions are also available for most titles (*safari.oreilly.com*). For more information,
contact our corporate/institutional sales department: (800) 998-9938 or *corporate@oreilly.com*.

Editor:	Tim O'Reilly
Production Editor:	Claire Cloutier
Cover Designer:	Ellie Volckhausen
Interior Designer:	Melanie Wang

Printing History:

April 2002:	First Edition.

ISBN: 0-596-00200-9
[C]

Table of Contents

Part III.   Advanced Topics

Part IV.   Appendixes

Preface

This book provides comprehensive coverage of software application development for the Palm, using the Visual Basic (VB) language. In this book, we'll illustrate Palm development using a variety of software techniques, but we'll focus on a new Visual Basic compiler for the Palm: the AppForge Add-in for Microsoft Visual Basic.

This book shows you how to leverage your existing skills as a VB programmer into a new market and toolset. If you're a typical VB programmer with a decent understanding of GUI application development, you should be running code on the Palm within a day or two of reading this book.

In this book, we'll focus on high-level design and user-interface issues of building mobile handheld applications, not the intricacies of the Palm OS or the programming interface of yet another list view control. The entire appeal of developing in VB is that the programmer is insulated to some degree from the underlying hardware and operating system. Rather than provide another tutorial, the book will explain how VB programming for the Palm device is similar to VB development for Windows, and how it is different.

We'll cover all the techniques necessary for building a complete application. And we'll also address the larger concerns of the corporate software developer: data management, synchronization with internal networks and the Internet, integration with other Palm applications, and development of shared libraries, tools, and components.

Who Should Read This Book

This book is written for the corporate software developer who uses Microsoft Visual Basic to develop Windows applications and is interested in, or needs to develop for, the Palm. While the reader should have experience with the property-method-event model of VB programming, no familiarity with Palm products is assumed or required.

Some later chapters assume familiarity with C/C++, including COM. These chapters are intended for system-level programmers who need to go beyond the limits of VB to develop custom or shared components.

Others who will benefit from this book are software architects, middle-ware developers, and engineering managers who need to understand the strengths and limits of VB on the Palm, and how to integrate VB-based Palm applications into their corporate IT infrastructure or product offerings.

Organization of This Book

This book is structured into three sections. Developers new to the Palm should read at least the first three chapters in order; more seasoned programmers can dive into the later sections and chapters in pretty much any sequence.

Part I, Programming with AppForge

The first section covers Palm application development using the AppForge add-in for Microsoft Visual Basic: how to obtain and install a development environment, principles and techniques of user interface programming, and how to access the Palm's primary storage feature, its database.

Chapter 1, Introducing AppForge

This chapter introduces the basic software used throughout the book: the AppForge add-in for Visual Basic and the Palm OS Emulator. We look briefly at the architecture of AppForge. Then we cover obtaining and installing the necessary software components and walk through using AppForge to build a simple Palm application.

Chapter 2, Application Development

In this chapter, we focus on how to design and develop Palm applications. We introduce almost all the features common to Palm applications. The emphasis is on using AppForge *ingots* to create the user interface and leveraging the libraries provided by AppForge to access Palm native functions within Visual Basic.

Chapter 3, Palm Database Programming

In this chapter, we cover the Palm OS database manager and how it works. Then we show how to access the Palm database features via the AppForge PDB library. We also explain the AppForge database schema extensions, which free the developer from many bookkeeping chores normally associated with Palm database programming.

Part II, Data Connectivity

The second section covers moving techniques for moving local and network data into and out of the device: how to use the Palm Conduit Development Kit, how to develop applications that leverage the use of SQL data repositories, and how to access the Internet through the Palm.Net wireless infrastructure. This section covers a variety of development techniques: Microsoft VB on the desktop, AppForge VB on the Palm, and VBScript on the Web server. Because this section is data-centric, there is a fair amount of SQL as well.

Chapter 4, Conduit Development

This chapter covers building conduits using Microsoft VB and the Palm COM Conduit Development Kit. We show how to design a proper conduit, and we cover all the required interfaces and features that a conduit must implement. We also show how to interactively debug a conduit and how to use the HotSync Manager log.

Chapter 5, SQL Databases

This chapter shows how to develop data-intensive applications using Microsoft SQL Server. We demonstrate a variety of techniques, including preprocessing the data on the desktop and implementing on-device manipulation. The chapter also covers the AppForge Universal Conduit, which is used to automatically synchronize Palm and Microsoft ODBC-compliant databases.

Chapter 6, Web Clipping Applications

In this chapter, we cover web development using Palm's wireless Palm.Net functionality. Note that this is not WAP—these are full-featured HTML applications. We show how to integrate the Palm VII handheld into Microsoft web applications, and how to format HTML pages especially for the handheld. Special attention is paid to security for wireless devices.

Part III, Advanced Topics

The third section diverges a little from the VB mainstream and shows how to extend the reach of VB Palm applications using features accessible only to the C/C++ language. Topics covered include developing callable applications that access operating system internals and using shared libraries to package common functionality. An exciting feature of AppForge—Piedmont, a portable COM-based framework that extends AppForge itself—is covered as well. We also include a chapter on debugging techniques.

Chapter 7, Operating System Access

In this chapter, we look at how to use features of the Palm OS that cannot be accessed from the standard AppForge libraries. We build a complete fuser application that encrypts and decrypts Palm record databases using the DES libraries in the Palm OS.

Chapter 8, Shared Libraries

In this chapter, we look at extending an application's functionality through the use of shared libraries—units of reusable code that contain frequently used sets of functionality.

Chapter 9, Piedmont

This chapter covers the AppForge *Piedmont* Framework, which is a component development kit for handheld devices. We cover building system-level ingots, which are similar to Windows COM DLL servers, and we lay the foundation for U/I Ingots, which are similar to ActiveX controls.

Chapter 10, Debugging

This chapter covers some simple debugging techniques, such as using conditional compilation variables to optionally include or exclude debugging code. We show how to use the Palm Reporter tool to trace through a program. Finally, we provide sample code that logs information to a database for later analysis.

Part IV, Appendixes

The book concludes with two appendixes that provide some reference material.

Appendix A, Ingot and Enumeration Summary

This appendix enumerates the many properties and methods of the AppForge Ingots for the Palm OS.

Appendix B, DBSLib Sample Project Setup

This appendix provides detailed instructions on configuring the Metrowerks Code Warrior compiler to build shared libraries.

Required Software

This book covers a lot of ground, from straight Palm development to SQL to wireless Internet to C++ Ingot construction. As you might imagine, you are going to need a lot of software if you want to build and run all the applications in this book.

Microsoft Visual Basic 6.0

Almost any version (Enterprise, Professional, Learning) can be used. There is a specific service pack requirement documented on the AppForge web site (*http://www.appforge.com*). We use service pack 4.

AppForge 2.0 for Palm OS

This product is available for purchase or as a 30-day evaluation from the AppForge web site. There is a personal edition, which we do not recommend, as it lacks many of the features used in this book.

Palm Operating System Emulator 3.3

This freeware tool lets you test almost all your Palm code on the Windows desktop. Earlier releases will not work with AppForge 2.0.

Palm Desktop Software 4.01

This freeware software suite allows you to install software to real Palm hardware and to develop and test conduits for data synchronization. We use release 4.01, but most any version is acceptable.

Microsoft SQL Server 2000

Several of the applications in Chapters 4, 5, and 6 use SQL Server to demonstrate the use of relational data. We used the 2000 release, but 7.0 should work as well. If you want to use a different database manager, make sure it supports stored procedures.

Microsoft Internet Information Server (IIS) 5.0

We use IIS for the wireless applications developed in Chapter 6; IIS 4.0 is also adequate. If you use a different web server, make sure it supports a script environment that allows the creation of VB objects.

Metrowerks CodeWarrior for Palm OS Platform 7.0

We use this C++ compiler to develop the shared libraries and other advanced components in Chapters 7, 8, and 9.

Microsoft Visual C++ 6.0

We use this compiler to build and test AppForge components in Chapter 9 with normal VB on the Windows desktop.

Conventions Used in This Book

The following typographical conventions are used in this book:

Constant width

Indicates command-line computer output and code examples, as well as constants, variables, enumerations, objects, controls, menu options, menu titles, classes, and flow-control statements such as if.

Constant width bold

Indicates code input that a reader should type verbatim.

Italic

> Introduces new terms and indicates URLs, user-defined files and directories, commands, file extensions, filenames, directory or folder names, properties, methods, attributes, events, parameters, and UNC pathnames.

> This is an example of a note, which signifies valuable and timesaving information.

> This is an example of a warning, which alerts you to a potential pitfall in the program. Warnings can also refer to a procedure that might be dangerous if not carried out in a specific way.

How to Contact Us

We have tested and verified the information in this book to the best of our ability, but you may find that features have changed (or even that we have made mistakes!). Please let us know about any errors you find, as well as your suggestions for future editions, by writing to:

> O'Reilly & Associates, Inc.
> 1005 Gravenstein Highway North
> Sebastopol, CA 95472
> (800) 998-9938 (in the United States or Canada)
> (707) 829-0515 (international or local)
> (707) 829-0104 (fax)

You can also send us messages electronically. To be put on the mailing list or request a catalog, send email to:

> *info@oreilly.com*

To ask technical questions or comment on the book, send email to:

> *bookquestions@oreilly.com*

We have a web site for the book, where we'll list examples, errata, and any plans for future editions. You can access this page at:

> *http://www.oreilly.com/catalog/vbpropalm/*

For more information about this book and others, see the O'Reilly web site:

> *http://www.oreilly.com*

Acknowledgments

Collectively, we would like to thank our editors at O'Reilly: Tim O'Reilly, Troy Mott, Frank Willison, and Bob Herbstman. There many events during this project that we were sure signaled the end: blown deadlines, rewrites necessitated by new software releases from AppForge and Palm, the sad and demanding events of September 11th, and simple changes in the market. Through it all we were encouraged to stay the course, in particular by Bob and Troy. We also love the flying fish on the cover, and we thank the design department at O'Reilly for finding them.

This book benefited greatly from the efforts of our formal technical reviewers, Bob Holt and Neil Rhodes. Both caught many small and not-so-small errors; of course, we assume responsibility for any remaining errors. Neil, in particular, seemed almost omniscient. We also had the help of a longtime AppForge developer, John Bonin, who provided great feedback on the usability of the first three chapters. And there are many indirect contributors who posted remarks and comments to the user forums; we learned a great deal simply studying these postings.

Matthew Holmes

I would like to thank first my long-suffering family, particularly my beautiful and patient wife Liz and my children Jonathan, Molly, and Claire. They tolerated and encouraged this effort, providing many boosts when the going was difficult.

I've been fortunate to have a great number of managers who have provided the guidance, insight, and sometimes sobering advice over the past decade that made writing this book possible: Thomas Joost, Gary Kerr, Mike Wagner, Jim McClave, and John Casey stand out in this regard. I have also been fortunate to work with an eclectic group of developers on some wonderful—and some dismal—software products: Bob Kline, Curtis Jones, Todd Morris, Adam Blum, Kevin Smith, Brian Williams, Robb Butler, Bill Ericson, Bill Eisner, and Tony Tocci.

And special thanks go to Bob Walson, whose sure career guidance and personal example has been a blessing over the years.

Patrick Burton

I would like to thank my family for their support throughout this endeavor. Thanks especially to my wife Paula, who encouraged me and kept me on schedule when I was getting weary. Thanks to Matthew Holmes, who spearheaded this effort, and kept us focused amidst the ups and downs. Bob Holt at AppForge was an invaluable resource for getting us the latest beta releases of the software, and for providing technical guidance on my writing and sample code. I would also like to thank a number of colleagues with whom I have had the privilege of working, and who have inspired and influenced me along the way to writing this book: Pat O'Neill, Steve Wolter, John Palm, Phil Eichensehr, and Phil Muhlenkamp.

Roger Knoell

For me, this is my first book. It took a lot more time and effort to produce than I ever imagined. If it were not for the diligent support of my wife Christine, I would never have finished. Thanks also go to my children Alexa and Jenna for their understanding of why Daddy spent more time working on the book than playing with them. Thanks, of course, to my coauthors, our O'Reilly editors, the great people at App-Forge, and our technical reviewers, John Bonin and Neil Rhodes. I would like to also thank a few people who provided the inspiration over the years necessary to complete this book: Gordon Blankenship, Brett Johnson, Time Henderson, Mario Martins, Shelley Meredith, and my longtime friends Jack Baron and especially John Staudt.

I would like to dedicate my efforts on this book to my mom, Barbara, whose passing during this project, while very difficult, provided me with the determination to do the very best I could. Finally, special thanks to my dad and my three brothers Bob, Richard, and Kevin, for helping me through the rough times.

PART I

Programming with AppForge

CHAPTER 1

Introducing AppForge

Over the past five years, the Palm PDA has zoomed to prominence as the handheld device of choice for the consumer and the enterprise. In that time, the Visual Basic developer has been relegated to the sidelines—the Palm doesn't run the Microsoft Windows operating system, and its processor isn't based on a design from Intel. The available development tools mostly favored the C/C++ developer, or they required an individual or corporate investment in a proprietary scripting language.

All that changed when AppForge introduced its flagship product, a VB compiler for the Palm. AppForge calls its product a "family of visual software tools that enables virtually anyone to write engaging GUI software for non-PC computer devices." (In this chapter and throughout this book, when we mention AppForge, we mean the add-in for VB for Palm OS.)

AppForge is an add-in for Microsoft's Visual Basic. With AppForge, developers build applications that execute on the Palm PDA from within the native VB integrated development environment (IDE). Instead of compiling code into a Windows executable, AppForge generates a Palm Resource (PRC) file—roughly speaking, a program file.

From a practical perspective, this means that it is very easy to come up to speed with the AppForge tool. Developers can focus right away on forms and controls, events and procedures, without learning a new development environment.

In this chapter, we take a quick look at what it means to develop software for the Palm handheld device, which is very different from the Windows desktop. We provide an overview of the AppForge product—what it is and how it works. We cover installing AppForge onto a development system, and we explain how it integrates into the VB IDE.

After all that, we'll walk through getting a simple project up and running. Along the way, we'll touch on some things that are different from desktop VB development, such as cross-platform emulation tools and the user interface controls for the Palm.

Palm Software

If you are reading this book, the chances are high that you are new to Palm software development or to the AppForge product, or very likely both. Writing software for embedded devices—such as the Palm, the Pocket PC, or pagers like the RIM Blackberry—was once the exclusive territory of the professional C developer. Every bit was counted, and every screen pixel hoarded.

This approach is still important—you simply cannot write software for the handheld market as if it were the Windows desktop. Microsoft has been trying that for years with dismal results. Consumers and corporate users do not buy handheld devices for the quality of the Web browser; instead, they want focused tools that enhance personal productivity or enable key business processes, and they want applications that run quickly.

Look in a typical PDA, and you will see organizer software, notepad programs, diet and exercise planners, newsreaders, games and entertainment software, stock applications, and so on. In fact, one of the major reasons for the success of the Palm device is its thousands and thousands of quality software products.

All these successful applications share at least one common factor: they are focused on providing exactly what the user wants, and little else. They do not provide a feature list bloated with nice-to-have features; they do provide timely access to information that really matters—a telephone number, a stock quote, a photograph, or directions to the shopping center.

This book cannot tell you which features are critical to your users and your market—only you can do that. This book will, however, show you when and how to use the available Palm features to structure a program that works well on the handheld device.

If you are completely new to the Palm, you should stop right now and get a book on *using* the Palm handheld device. This will give you a better foundation for developing software that fits the Palm device. There are many important differences between desktop and Palm development that will force you to rethink the way software is engineered and used.

There is just no way around the fact that handheld devices are small. The Palm OS currently supports a screen that measures 160 pixels tall by 160 pixels wide. The majority of Palm devices have monochrome screens that can display four shades of gray, two of which are black and white.

By way of contrast, consider the font selection listbox in Microsoft Office's Word application. That single feature of Word is about 240 pixels wide by 270 pixels tall—over two and a half times the available screen size for an entire Palm application. Figure 1-1 shows the listbox with the Palm screen superimposed on it.

Figure 1-1. Sizes of Microsoft Word font selection listbox and Palm screen

The Palm device has no keyboard and no mouse—only a stick that functions as both. The stick is referred to as a stylus. Text entry is done in the Graffiti language—sort of a block alphabet—that the serious user will master. Novices will use the virtual keyboard and tap out their words one letter at a time. Even with practice, it is difficult to key in more than a dozen words per minute.

But there are also many advantages to working with the Palm PDA. The screen is touch-sensitive, which means that you can be very creative in how your application handles user input. The hardware buttons, particularly the scroll buttons, provide other opportunities for innovative input techniques. There are add-on keyboards available if your application relies on significant data input. And the screen limitations themselves impose a discipline—you should constantly consider why a certain feature needs to be on the screen, or if there is a more effective way to present it.

Many Windows applications are open and idle in the background for extended periods of time. The user can probably spare a few minutes to get some coffee while your application is opening files or running a data-mining query. Since the application might be open for several hours, these moments are insignificant over the course of a business day.

The Palm user, however, accesses an application such as the Address Book very frequently during the day, even though she may only use the application for a few seconds each time. Since the Palm runs only one program at a time, an application is always starting and stopping—an inordinate delay in either process can be excruciating. Your design must address response times, in particular how quickly the user can navigate and access the really vital functionality.

Here is something else to think about: most Windows applications are used on a stable desktop, with the user seated in a chair. Consider where the Palm device is most often used—the hand. The user might be in an elevator, or stopped at a traffic light. He is not going to wait 10 or 20 seconds for your splash screen to initialize—after all, the light might change.

Now consider the basic Palm device itself. Entry-level models have a 16 MHz central processor, 2 MB of memory, a couple of AAA batteries. This represents computing power that was nearly obsolete in the 1980s, when the Apple Macintosh was a fast machine. On the positive side, the device contains fully functional serial and infrared ports that offer standards-based communication with computers, cellular phones, and printers.

When designing software for the Palm, you must consider these factors if your application is to have the "Zen of Palm"—that combination of features and ease of use that can make the handheld so compelling.

Main Features of AppForge

Before we get down to installing AppForge, let's review the versions of the product. First of all, AppForge supports multiple handheld platforms: the Palm Computing Platform and the Microsoft Pocket PC. In this book, we are only going to cover App-Forge for the Palm OS. AppForge for the Palm comes in two flavors: Personal and Professional. We'll look at what comes with each edition, and how each is different.

Both editions ship with the AppForge Visual Basic add-in, which is the compiler.* Like Microsoft VB, compiled AppForge programs on the Palm require a runtime component to function—the Booster. This is the equivalent of Msvbvm60.dll, the Microsoft VB Runtime. The Booster for Palm OS is freely available for download and redistribution from the AppForge Web site.†

There are costs and benefits associated with the use of the AppForge Booster:

Execution speed
> Calling into another layer of code can impact performance. The performance penalty on a Windows machine is trivial, but it can be significant on the low-powered Palm PDA.

Code size
> The Booster is large—more than 350 KB of memory. Even though 8 MB of memory is more common now, this is still a big amount.

---

* Since the AppForge compiler runs on Windows, it is actually a *cross-compiler*—a program that produces executable code for a different runtime platform. This executable code can be targeted at either the Palm OS or the Pocket PC environments.

† The Booster for other platforms has a runtime fee, although you can download evaluation copies for development at no charge.

Shared code

If more than one AppForge application is installed on the Palm PDA, then there is an advantage to using the Booster, because library and common code is not duplicated between applications.

Maintenance

Bug fixes to the common functions in the Booster need only be distributed once to patch all AppForge applications on a Palm PDA.

The AppForge Booster consists of three core components that provide basic services analogous to the Microsoft Component Object Model (COM): *pCOM.prc*, *AFCore.prc*, and *ByteStream.prc*. These components must be installed on the Palm device in order to run any AppForge application. In addition, AppForge libraries and services are implemented in separate components; these are only necessary if your application uses their functionality. AppForge provides a detailed explanation of the components in the Booster in their Knowledge Base, available at *http://www.appforge.com*; see article number 010926-0000039.

Each edition of AppForge ships with a set of ingots. Ingots are like the *ActiveX* controls that you normally would drop on VB forms. AppForge includes a basic set of ingots that provide the functions of the VB intrinsic controls and some advanced ingots for other features.

 You cannot use the VB intrinsic controls on the Palm, nor can you use third-party ActiveX controls. The AppForge add-in will issue an error if you try to reference one of these controls in the VB editor.

Each edition includes a set of libraries that provide extra functionality to an application on the Palm PDA. These libraries offer functions similar to the Microsoft Win32 API, such as the ability to access databases or call other applications

Each edition also ships with a set of tools to help automate software development tasks outside of the VB IDE. One tool generates Palm database (PDB) files from a Microsoft Access database. This is useful because the Palm doesn't have a traditional filesystem—all persistent data for an application must be stored in a PDB file. Also included with some editions are programs that convert images and True Type fonts to AppForge's native format.

Ingots

As we said earlier, ingots are the AppForge equivalent of the VB intrinsic controls. In fact, ingots have a dual existence. When in the VB IDE, they are ActiveX controls, just like any other control in the toolbox. When running on the Palm, however, they are part of the Booster runtime.

When used in an application, ingots support most—but not all—of the properties of the Microsoft intrinsic controls. This makes a great deal of sense, as many of the graphical features of Windows do not exist on the Palm. And of course, there is a runtime penalty for supporting extra features that are simply too much overhead for the Palm PDA and its tiny CPU. We won't cover every unsupported or changed property in this book, but we will point out the important differences between Windows and the Palm.

For example, the command button on Windows supports several properties that govern how the button appears when it is pushed, disabled, or transparent. These properties are not supported in the corresponding AppForge ingot—they have no meaning on the Palm, and their sudden appearance in an application would be disconcerting to the user. And don't even think about drag and drop technology.

Overall, AppForge has struck a reasonable balance between supporting the native Palm interface style and providing the extra functionality that VB developers are used to having. Note that the different ingots are implemented by different components of the AppForge Booster. We present them in the following sections, grouped by Booster component.[*]

Basic ingots

The following ingots are implemented in *BasicIngots.prc*.

Form
> This is the familiar Form object.

AFButton
> This is a Palm-style command button, flat with rounded corners. There is no cancel or default property.

AFCheckbox
> This is a Palm-style checkbox, flat with an extended check mark.

AFComboBox
> This is a multimode Combo box. One mode supports the native Palm style, and two others support a more Windows-like appearance and behavior.

AFLabel
> This ingot implements the Label control.

AFListBox
> This is like the VB ListBox control. This control is used sparingly on the Palm because it is so space-intensive.

AFRadioButton
> This is a Palm-style radio button.

---

[*] When deploying your applications, you will only want to install those Booster components truly necessary to run, so that you can conserve memory on the Palm device.

AFShape
> This is like the VB Shape control. This is a useful ingot, because there is no support for the VB Line or Frame controls.

AFTextBox
> This is a Palm-style text box, complete with dotted lines in multiline mode.

AFTimer
> This is a standard timer. Like the VB timer, it measures intervals in milliseconds.

Enhanced ingots

These ingots are implemented in *EnhancedIngots.prc*.

AFGraphic
> This is similar to the VB Image or VB PictureBox, which have no corresponding Palm interface element. There is no control container support.

AFGraphicButton
> This is a graphical style command button that allows an image to be used instead of a textual caption. The button supports different states, such as disabled or down.

AFGrid
> This is like the MS Grid control, which is similar in function, but not in appearance, to the Palm table interface element. There is no data binding support for this or any other AppForge control.

AFHScrollBar
> This ingot implements a horizontal scroll bar. Professional only.

AFSlider
> This ingot provides a Palm-style slider control. Professional only.

AFVScrollBar
> This ingot implements a vertical scroll bar. Professional only.

Communications ingots

The following ingots are implemented in *DataCommIngots.prc*.

AFClientSocket
> This ingot is used to perform socket-based communications over a wireless or network connection. Professional only.

AFInetHTTP
> This ingot provides access to the native wireless Internet library on radio-enabled Palm devices (InetLib). Professional only.

AFScanner
> This is a special-purpose ingot for accessing the barcode hardware on the Symbol SPT1500 and 1700, as well as plug-in Springboard scanner modules for the Visor. Professional only.

AFSerial
> This ingot accesses the serial and infrared ports on the Palm device. It is similar to the VB Comm control.

AFSignatureCapture
> This ingot is used to record user handwritten signatures via the stylus. Professional only.

Multimedia ingots

These ingots are implemented in *MultimediaIngots.prc*.

AFFilmStrip
> This is like the VB Animation control, which has no corresponding Palm interface element.

AFMovie
> This ingot plays converted AVI movies. Professional only.

AFTone
> This ingot plays surprisingly good tones of a fixed frequency for a specified duration.

Libraries

The AppForge libraries also have a dual existence. When in the VB IDE, they are ActiveX servers, and all their features are available from the Object Browser. When running on the Palm, they are part of the Booster runtime. Because these libraries are integrated into the AppForge Booster, a new release of the Booster must be installed on the Palm PDA whenever AppForge adds or changes libraries. Of course, this is only true if your application needs to access those new features.

Here are the basic libraries that ship with all editions of AppForge (all implemented in *afExtLib.prc*):

PDB library
> This library provides functions that wrap the Palm OS database manager. This includes a schema capability that simplifies reading and writing fielded data records.

Numeric library
> This library provides a random number generator.

System library
> This library includes miscellaneous functions, such as the Palm username. It also provides a way to access extended keycodes on the Palm PDA.

Extended functions library
> This library provides a raft of functions for accessing or changing settings on the Palm PDA. This includes features like the Graffiti handwriting state and a listing of all the databases.

If you are new to Palm software development, it might surprise you to learn that inter-process communication is quite difficult on the Palm. This is because the Palm was designed as a single-tasking computer—the user is generally focused on one program, not sharing data between multiple windows.

The operating system doesn't provide direct support for dynamic data exchange or object linking. Instead, you invoke a Palm application as a sub-routine call, with a special launch code.* AppForge provides a library to support this capability:

Extensibility library
> This library is used to launch other Palm applications. Professional only.

You can also use this library to call functions in the Palm operating system. App-Forge has a sample application, *Fuser*, which demonstrates this capability. We'll look at the extensibility library in depth in Chapter 8. This library is implemented in *afPalmOS.prc*.

Utilities

AppForge provides a raft of utility programs to support application development. Many of the software aids that VB developers take for granted do not exist yet for the Palm. These AppForge utilities fill voids in the range of available software tools.

For example, there is no *Active Data Object* support on the Palm, so all record and database access must be coded by hand. This is similar to programming directly to the ODBC function specification. The AppForge Database Converter, however, not only converts an Access table to native Palm format, it also generates VB source code to read and write records in the converted database.† This is not quite object-oriented, but it is much better than rolling your own ADO or OLE-DB layer.

The following basic utilities ship with all editions of AppForge:

Database Converter
> This utility converts a single Microsoft Access table into a Palm database.

Graphics Converter and Viewer
> This utility converts BMP graphics to the AppForge format, a 4-bit monochrome image. Converted graphic files can be used with the Graphic, Graphic button, and Filmstrip ingots.

---

* Unfortunately, few applications publish their database formats or launch codes, so accessing other programs usually involves a reverse-engineering effort, or poring through the source code if it's available.

† It is important to note that the Database Converter only works with a single table at a time; you have to run the converter multiple times to process all the tables in an Access MDB file.

As with the libraries, AppForge provides some special-purpose utilities available only with the Professional Edition of the product:

Font Converter and Viewer
> This utility converts True Type fonts to the AppForge format. Converted fonts can be used with any ingots that have a Font property. Professional only.

Movie Converter and Viewer
> This utility converts AVI movie formats to the AppForge format. Converted movie files can be used with the Movie ingot. Professional only.

Universal Conduit
> This utility interfaces Palm databases to any ODBC-compliant data source, using the standard Palm HotSync technology. Professional only.

A conduit is software that replicates or synchronizes databases on the Palm with personal or corporate data on the desktop. As you will see in Chapter 4, developing a conduit is a significant amount of work. If your application data is in a relational or tabular format and doesn't require a lot of special-case processing, then the Universal Conduit can save a lot of effort. We address the Universal Conduit in Chapter 5.

Installing AppForge

There are a few prerequisites for installing and using the AppForge compiler. Most importantly, AppForge will only work with Microsoft Visual Basic 6. Fortunately, it will work with just about any flavor of VB—Learning/Working Edition, Professional Edition, or Enterprise Edition.

AppForge requires that Visual Studio Service Pack 4 be applied prior to installation. The service pack is freely downloadable from the Microsoft Visual Studio web site; this is a large download of more than 50 megabytes. AppForge includes the service pack on some of its CD-ROM distributions.

Most Palm users have a version of the Palm Desktop software installed on their computers. From the developer's perspective, the most important components of the Palm Desktop are the installation application and the HotSync manager, which install programs and databases on the Palm PDA. This is usually accomplished using the Palm cradle and a serial connection. The Palm Desktop is not required for development, although having it can simplify the compile-debug-test cycle. The latest version of the Palm Desktop software can be freely downloaded from the Palm web site: *http://www.palm.com/software/desktop/*.

If you don't have a Palm PDA, don't worry—we cover how to use the *Palm Operating System Emulator* (POSE) to run your Palm programs later in this chapter.

The Emulator is a Windows application that simulates the Palm PDA's hardware and software down to the last detail—even including the Palm VII radio.*

Installing AppForge itself is straightforward. There is a license screen that requires a registration key, which you should have obtained with your version of AppForge. If you downloaded an evaluation copy, you can install the software immediately, but you cannot run it until you receive a key from AppForge (usually via email). If you later purchase AppForge, you can apply the new license information from within the product; you do not need to reinstall.

After installation, all the AppForge tools are accessible from the Windows Start menu, as shown in Figure 1-2. We installed the Professional version of AppForge, so you may or may not have the same tools.

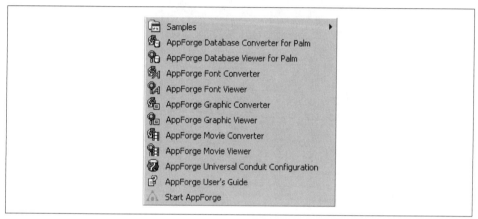

Figure 1-2. Windows AppForge menu

But the real beauty of AppForge is that most of your development is done from within the VB IDE. The ingots discussed earlier are integrated into the standard VB Toolbox, as shown in Figure 1-3.

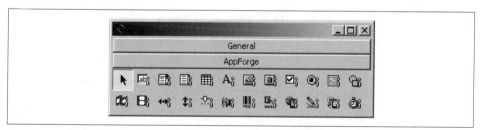

Figure 1-3. VB Toolbox with AppForge Ingots

---

* There are versions of the Emulator for the Macintosh and Linux platforms as well, but we will discuss the Windows version in this book.

Note that we added the AppForge tab to the Toolbox manually; this useful trick will help break us of the habit of dropping the wrong controls on the AppForge form.

The AppForge functionality that is specific to producing software for the Palm is combined into a single VB menu choice appropriately labeled AppForge. This menu, shown in Figure 1-4, deals mainly with configuring, compiling, and packaging program files, or accessing AppForge-specific help.

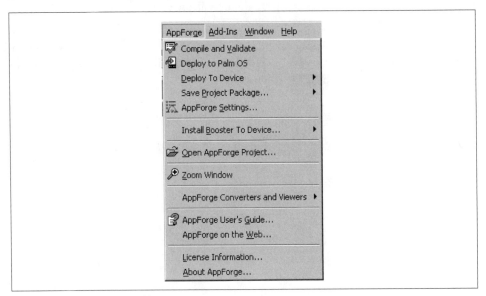

Figure 1-4. VB AppForge Add-In Menu

Of course, this special menu is only available when working on an AppForge project. We'll describe how to create an AppForge project in the next section.

Using AppForge

Now that the software is installed, let's look at how to build a Palm PRC program from within VB. Start by launching the VB IDE. Notice that there is now an AppForge project type available from the New Project dialog, as shown in Figure 1-5.

You might have to scroll the dialog a little to see the AppForge project icon, especially if you have a lot of other project types and wizards installed. Once you select AppForge, you will get another dialog asking you to select a runtime target—Palm OS or Pocket PC. Since this is a book about Palm software development, choose Palm OS.

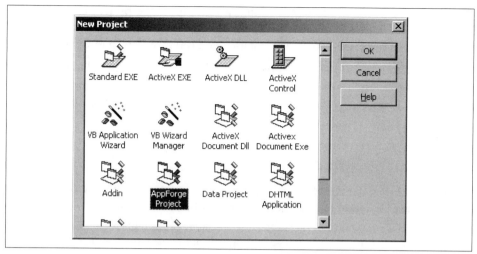

Figure 1-5. New AppForge Project

Alternatively, you can use the Start AppForge menu option that is accessible from the AppForge program group. This starts the VB IDE and brings up a history of recent Palm OS projects, as shown in Figure 1-6. Choose the New Project button, and once again select Palm OS as the runtime target.

Figure 1-6. AppForge project manager

The first thing you will see after creating a new AppForge project is a very small form. Get used to it—that's all there is on the Palm PDA. We'll look into the user interface issues imposed by the Palm's stark 160×160 pixel screen in Chapter 2.

We're going to build the simplest possible application, so add the following code to the usual Form1:

```
Option Explicit

Private Sub Form_Load( )

    MsgBox "Hello, Hand-held World!"

End Sub
```

Push F5 to run the program, and note that the form and message box come up. App-Forge projects—ingots, database libraries, and all—run almost as well on Windows as on the Palm. With judicious use of conditional compilation, this capability is a great debugging technique. Many of the AppForge tutorial projects use this idea, although we don't stress it in this book.

Configuring the Project

Before compiling, we need to configure the project. From the AppForge menu, select the AppForge Settings option. This brings up a dialog window to target a selected Palm device, configure the PRC file setting as necessary, and update any dependencies for the project. See Figure 1-7 for an example.

Note that this dialog supports two possible devices: Palm OS and Pocket PC. Select Palm OS. If you do not have the Palm Desktop software installed, you will see an error similar to that shown in Figure 1-8. This simply means that AppForge will not be able to install software directly to the HotSync manager.

The dialog supports two settings for the PRC file: the Creator ID and a profile for the Palm Desktop.* The Creator ID is a four-byte string that uniquely identifies an application and any associated databases. Enter a Creator ID of CH01 for this simple application. If you plan to distribute your applications, you must reserve a unique Creator ID with Palm. See "The Palm Creator ID" sidebar, later in this chapter.

The Dependency tab on the Project Setting window is used to identify any dependencies that the PRC will need during operation, such as:

- Associated PDB files
- Converted graphics, movies, or fonts

There are no dependencies for this simple application. We will discuss dependencies in greater detail in Chapter 2.

---

* The profile drop-down combo box will be disabled if the Desktop software is not installed.

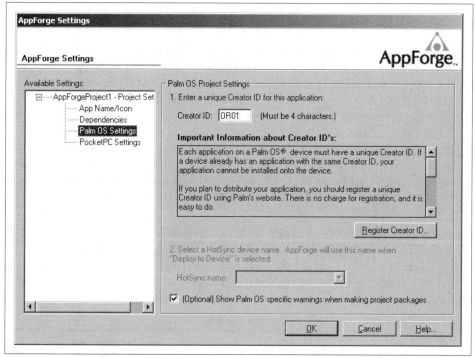

Figure 1-7. AppForge project settings

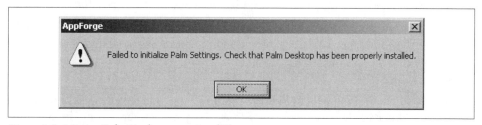

Figure 1-8. Missing Palm Desktop warning dialog

Compiling a Project

Before compiling with AppForge, be sure to save your project. The AppForge compiler is distinct from the VB compiler, and it only sees files—or file content—that have been saved to disk. Note that the Palm application name is taken from the VB project name, which you set from the VB Project → Properties menu option. We use the name Hello for this example.

Select Compile and Validate from the AppForge Add-In menu (which was previously shown in Figure 1-4). AppForge displays status information as it validates and compiles your project. All compilation errors in your project are displayed in a dedicated error window, which floats at the top of the screen. If an error has a line number,

The Palm Creator ID

The Creator ID is used to uniquely identify ownership of Palm applications and databases. All Palm databases have a Creator ID. In this sense, the Creator ID is very much like a Windows globally unique identifier (GUID). One major difference: Microsoft has distributed code that can—in theory—generate a GUID. Palm, however, requests that all Creator IDs be registered with a central repository.

You can do this with no fee at the Palm web site. The Creator ID registration page is *http://dev.palmos.com/creatorid*. This page provides some background information and allows the registration of new Creator IDs. After choosing a Creator ID, use the simple search engine to ensure that your Creator ID has not already been used. Then fill out the form and submit a request. The entire process takes just a few minutes.

Palm has reserved Creator IDs that consist solely of lowercase letters and numbers, such as abc1. Your Creator ID may use any combination of ASCII characters in the range of 32 to 127, as long as you use at least one uppercase letter—for example, AbC2.

You really only need to register the Creator ID if you plan to distribute your application. We haven't registered with Palm any of the Creator IDs that we use in the sample projects in this book.

double-clicking the error message opens the corresponding code module, and highlights the offending entity. This is a nice feature when sifting through a lot of open code windows, and much better than the VB compiler, which stops at the first error.*

The compilation process by itself doesn't produce a PRC file, unlike the VB *Make* command that builds an EXE file. Instead, compilation has validated the syntax of your AppForge project files and generated intermediate code, which is saved in the project directory.

The last step when building is to link the intermediate code into the PRC file. To do this, select either Deploy to Device or Save Project Package from the AppForge menu. Chose the first option if you have the Palm Desktop installed and you want the new program installed with the next HotSync. Choose the second option to save the PRC file locally. AppForge will combine the intermediate code; when that successfully completes, AppForge prompts for a directory to store the new PRC file. If you have a Palm PDA and the Desktop software, you can now install and run this PRC file as you would any other application.

Remember, to run an AppForge program, you must have the Booster on your Palm PDA. You can do this by selecting the Install Booster on Device menu choice. Note that the Booster requires initialization to function correctly. After it is installed, the Palm PDA will perform a soft reset, which will allow the Booster to configure itself.

---

* You can also compile your application for Windows using the traditional *File → Make EXE* commands. This is useful if you want to build a prototype or debug your logic right in Windows.

You can use the Upload Project menu choice to queue the application file for installation. If all went well and you chose the Deploy to Device option, you are prompted to synchronize the device to install the software.

At this point, the program and Booster are installed and ready to run on the Palm PDA. When launched, the application displays the simple message box, as shown in Figure 1-9.

Figure 1-9. Hello, Handheld World message box

Palm Emulator

If you don't have a Palm PDA, then you can run the application in the Palm Operating System Emulator. As implied by its name, the Emulator mimics the hardware and software of the Palm PDA.

If you study the various models of Palm PDA available on the market, you will notice that most share a common hardware base—the Motorola *Dragonball* chip, a touch screen, some buttons, infrared, and serial ports. What is different between the models is the memory architecture—the read-only memory, or ROM, and the operating system.

The Emulator can load different ROM images, allowing it to simulate any device in the Palm PDA family. And it can load different bitmapped *skins*, allowing the software to take on the appearance of any Palm PDA. See Figure 1-10 for an example of the Emulator configured as a Palm IIIc.

By using the Emulator, it is possible to develop and test many features of an application without ever uploading the PRC to a physical Palm PDA.

The Emulator software is freely downloadable from the Palm web site, *http://www. palmos.com/dev/tools/emulator*. There are several WinZip archives that need to be downloaded, one for the Emulator itself and another that contains the skins. Un-zip both the archives into the same directory; and be certain to use the subdirectory paths defined in the files.

You must use POSE version 3.3 or higher when testing AppForge programs. Earlier versions of POSE have bugs that prevent the AppForge Booster from running properly.

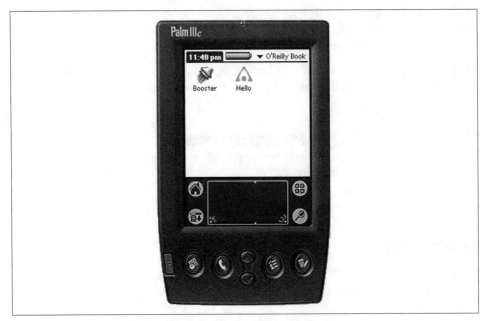

Figure 1-10. Emulation of Palm IIIc

At this point, the Emulator will not run because it is missing the ROM image file. Having the Emulator alone is like having a computer with no operating system. There are two ways to get ROM files:

- Download the ROM image from a Palm PDA. You must have an actual device to use this technique

- Get the ROM image from Palm. You must join the Palm OS Developer Program and sign a non-disclosure agreement

The first method is a little tricky; it requires the installation of a special ROM transfer application onto the Palm PDA. This is useful if you need to debug something, because by transferring the device ROM into the Emulator, an exact copy of the Palm PDA is made. Refer to the documentation that comes with the ROM transfer application for more details.

After you complete the legal paperwork for the Palm OS Developer program and are accepted into the program, you will be able to download various ROM images from the Resource Pavilion web site.*

Running *Emulator.exe* for the first time will open the New Session dialog, as shown in Figure 1-11. Select one of the ROM files previously downloaded from the Palm Alliance Pavilion.

---

* You can sign up at *http://www.palmos.com/dev/programs/pdp/join.html*. Be warned that the acceptance process often takes a day or more.

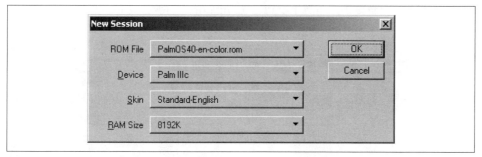

Figure 1-11. Emulator New Session dialog

The Emulator determines which device types are compatible with the chosen ROM. For example, if you select *Palm OS 3.5-en-color.rom*, the Emulator knows that the device can only be a Palm IIIc. Likewise, the Emulator knows which skins to use, based on information in the ROM. The RAM size selection allows you to control how much memory is in the simulated Palm PDA; any setting is fine.

Press OK to create a new emulator session. To save the session, select the Save As choice from the Emulator context menu.

You interact with the Emulator as if it were an actual Palm PDA—the Windows mouse even functions as a stylus! Substitute the mouse for a finger when pressing the four main buttons or the power switch. To change any settings, right-click anywhere on the Emulator to access a context menu with all settings and options.

There are several ways to install applications into an Emulator session. The simplest is to drag-and-drop a PRC file onto the Emulator. To run the sample application, drag it and the necessary Booster files into your session. Our simple application requires the following Booster files: *AFCore.prc*, *ByteStreamVM.prc*, *pCOM.prc*, and *BasicIngots.prc.*[*]

 After installing the Booster files, you must do a soft reset of the Emulator before running AppForge applications. This is easily done by bringing up the context menu and selecting the Reset option.

One of the features of the Emulator is to report dangerous application behavior. The AppForge Booster requires direct access to certain Palm system functions, such as processor registers and screen memory addresses usually controlled by the operating system. Occasionally you will see an error message from the Emulator when running AppForge applications.

---

[*] These files are located in the directory where you installed AppForge, in the *Platforms\PalmOS\TargetImage* subdirectory.

You can disable these messages from the Emulator context menu. Select Settings →
Debug Menu and then *unselect* the checkboxes, as shown in Figure 1-12.

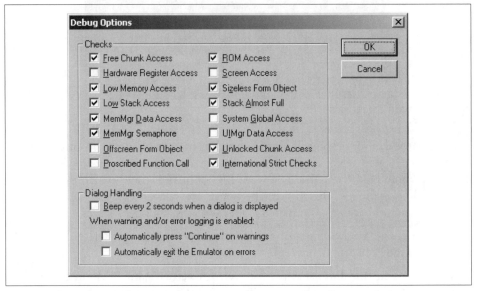

Figure 1-12. Emulator Debug Options screen

Note that the Debug Options screen changes between releases; don't worry if your
screen doesn't look exactly like Figure 1-12. We aren't going to explain every setting
for the Emulator in this book, since it is well documented by Palm. The Emulator
does have some special features that make it a great complement to testing only on
actual hardware.

The ROM images obtained from Palm contain debugging information for the Emula-
tor, allowing it to trap many kinds of programming errors. Other features include
Gremlins, a powerful application stress test, and Reporter, an application log tool.
We'll cover how to use the Emulator to test and debug applications in Chapter 10.

At this point, you can run the sample application in this chapter in the Emulator.
When running, you should see an "Hello World" screen like that shown earlier in
Figure 1-9.

Resources

In addition to the online documentation, the AppForge installation includes example projects, each of which highlights a specific AppForge feature or function:

Extensibility library
> Illustrates how to call another Palm application in AppForge to obtain system-
> specific information; professional edition only

Palm DB samples
> Illustrates how to read and write the native Palm application databases, such as the Address and To-do databases

PDB library
> Illustrates how to use most of the AppForge database library calls, including database and record manipulation and sorting

Recipes to go
> Illustrates how to build a large, multiform application that supports several databases with categories

Slide
> Illustrates simple graphical programming, using the traditional 15-piece puzzle

Unit converter
> Illustrates a data-driven application, using the AppForge Database Converter

Even after months of using AppForge, we still find ourselves coming back to the samples to review code snippets. In addition, there is a comprehensive tutorial that is nicely organized into lessons that cover almost all aspects of AppForge development.

The AppForge Developers Sector is an online resource that contains documentation, the knowledge base, and a code library. The knowledge base contains bug reports, fixes, and other technical articles. Of course, it is searchable. The code library contains example applications and techniques posted by both AppForge and members of the development community. See *http://www.appforge.com/dev/index.html* for details.

Two active user groups on Yahoo! are dedicated to AppForge development; one is moderated and one is completely open. See *http://groups.yahoo.com/group/appforge* for more information. AppForge actively monitors the lists as well, and will often provide clarification or support in this forum.

CHAPTER 2
Application Development

Creating Palm applications requires you to consider many different design aspects, as discussed in Chapter 1. The success of your applications, however, will ultimately ride on their usability by the end users, so it is important to understand both the style of a typical Palm application and how to achieve that using Visual Basic and AppForge.

This chapter will explain how to design and develop Palm applications that provide most or all the features common to other Palm applications. The emphasis is on using AppForge ingots to create your user interface and leveraging the libraries provided by AppForge, which give you access to many native Palm functions within Visual Basic. The chapter offers a building block approach, in which we will present several topics and then incorporate them into an application. Where appropriate, we will build on previous examples. However, the goal is to teach you specific concepts and not focus on building a large monolithic application by chapter's end. It is intended that the source code be generic enough that you can cut and paste code into your applications as you see fit. The source code and compiled versions of all examples presented in this chapter are available for download at *http://www.oreilly. com/catalog/vbpropalm/*.

User Interface Design

User interface design is one of the most challenging aspects of Palm programming. Creating a usable interface is the key to user acceptance; if an interface is too hard to work with, people won't use it.

There are many styles of Palm interfaces, especially for custom applications never intended for public distribution. However, style guidelines do exist for the Palm OS, just as they do for Windows programming. Palm has a programming design and style guide posted on their web site that covers some of the topics in this chapter.

Your applications should be designed to provide quick execution and data retrieval, to minimize data entry and provide selection lists where appropriate, to reduce the number of taps to navigate to key screens, and to find data quickly via sorts and filters.

Time is critical to Palm users, since they often need to keep up with external activities such as conversations while they look up an address, enter a new phone number, or jot down a quick note.

You also want your interface to operate in a similar fashion to other Palm applications, thus providing the user with a common look, feel, and operation. Let's review some of the basic user interface (UI) elements and how they can be used to achieve these goals.

Your basic application layout will usually have a title bar, an application workspace, and operation buttons along the bottom. This screen is sometimes referred to as the base screen. The following list provides more information about the elements in the base screen.

Title/information bar

You should put either the application name or some other pertinent information based on the application context in the upper left of the screen. Figure 2-1 shows the Palm scheduler application with the title set to the current day being viewed. This title changes based on the currently selected view format. This area could also be used for quick navigation controls (in this case, day and week navigation push buttons). This is also where an application menu bar will reside. Menus on the Palm are normally hidden to save space and are usually displayed by tapping the title bar tab or the silkscreen menu button. The typical height of the menu bar is 15 pixels.

Application workspace

The main thing to remember is to maximize space by using as much space as you can from edge to edge and top to bottom. The actual device screen has an unusable border frame that keeps your interface from looking crowded, even if the controls are right to the edge.

Operation buttons

Buttons placed along the bottom of the screen typically perform an operation on the data from the current view. The use of an ellipsis (...) to indicate a secondary entry screen is optional in order to save space. Button text should have at least one pixel between it and the button border.

There are several types of button styles: command, push (or toggle), and repeating. A command button is just that: it initiates a specific action when clicked, such as opening up a dialog window. Push buttons are usually associated with actions that are

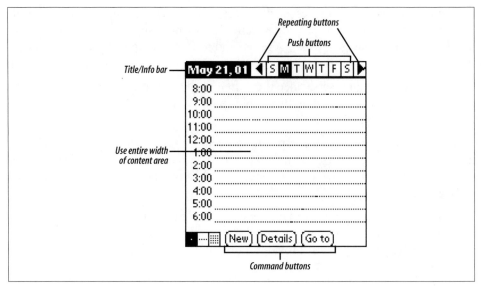

Figure 2-1. Basic window layout

mutually exclusive to each other, with only one active at a time. The active button in a push button group is usually highlighted or indicates in some manner that it is the current selection. For example, a collection of push buttons could each define a distinct data view for the user, of which only one can be active at a time. Repeating buttons perform a repetitive action when pushed. Scroll or increment buttons are examples of this style.

Buttons are usually left-aligned within the form. This is also the case for dialog windows in which standard buttons like OK, Cancel, Yes, No, Abort, Retry, and Ignore are aligned left to right.

Dialog windows have their own look and feel, which provide visual feedback to a user that this operation is modal. Normally, dialog windows should be sized to neatly contain the applicable controls, and dialog windows that are not full-sized are usually aligned along the bottom. However, AppForge currently does not *correctly* support forms smaller than the full screen size, which can overlap and be visible at the same time (more on this later), so use full-screen forms for your dialog windows. Figure 2-2 shows the key features of the dialog window.

Tip screens are normally triggered by the information icon located in the upper right corner of a dialog window. However, you may link to tip windows via the application menu or from the command and graphic buttons. Figure 2-3 shows a basic tip screen.

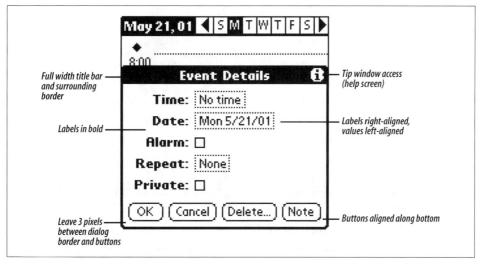

Figure 2-2. Dialog window layout

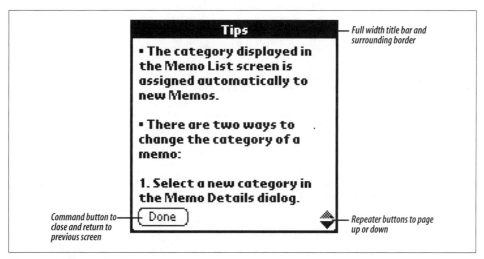

Figure 2-3. Tip window layout

Other Important Guidelines

There are many other principles to keep in mind when designing your application.

- Use command buttons for important tasks.
- Use push buttons to quickly change data presentation to better suit the needs of the user, especially when sorting or filtering data for easier access.

- Use pop-up lists instead of manual input when users have many options from which to select. Be cautious, however, to not create pop-up lists that are too long and require extended time to traverse.

- Avoid having too many buttons on the form, which could create clutter and confusion for the user.

- Avoid nesting dialog windows (in which a dialog calls another dialog, etc.) unless it is for an infrequently used functionality.

- Don't gray out unavailable menu items or controls; consider removing (i.e., hiding) them instead.

- Consider overloading the hard buttons if your application may benefit from it. (This could be the case with a game program.) Remember to always release control of these buttons when your application terminates.

- If possible (and desirable), allow for finger navigation by making buttons wide enough for clear recognition by the Palm OS. The calculator is a classic example.

- Create consistent default behavior when an application starts. For example, if the user's first action is to enter in some text, ensure that the cursor is active in the text control and ready for the user to start scribing.

- Minimize taps for navigation as much as possible.

Basic Application Layout Example

Our first application's purpose will be to set up a typical base window with a title bar and a command button. Our goals for this application are to:

- Introduce the Shape, Label, and Command button ingots
- Compile and run in Visual Basic
- Generate a PRC file and run it on a Palm device

Start by opening an AppForge project in Visual Basic. Your first form, like regular Visual Basic applications, will be autogenerated. What you will see is a form that's 160 × 160 pixels in size, with a blank title bar. Of course, Windows-style title bars do not exist in the Palm OS. This title bar is there to provide you with a means to drag the window around your desktop and close the form if you are test-running it in the Visual Basic IDE. This size and color of the title bar provide a common foundation for developing forms for the typical Palm or Pocket PC device that match the actual screen size of those devices. Change the name to frmBase.

The next step is to add a title bar that is common to almost all Palm applications. There are two methods to produce a title bar, custom or automatic. First, let's look at creating a custom title bar. There are only a few reasons why you may want to create your own custom title bar, and you'll most likely find that letting AppForge create it automatically will meet your needs. But it's worth a quick review just in case you do want to create your own. (Automatic title bar creation was introduced in AppForge version 2.0.) We are going to create our title bar by using a label and two Shape ingot controls. You may be wondering why you need to use so many controls, but remember, you are responsible for painting everything you see on the screen. As we stated previously, the standard height for a title bar is 15 pixels, so we can create our title bar using the following method. Other methods are possible, such as using a graphic ingot, but the method we'll use produces an exact replica of a title bar that has no overlapping controls (an issue discussed in the next section) and that takes up less memory that a graphic ingot and its associated external graphic.

The layout of the controls is shown in Figure 2-4.

Figure 2-4. Form title bar layout

Place a Label and two Shape ingots on the form as shown and make the changes shown in Table 2-1 to create your title bar:

Table 2-1. Custom title bar ingots and settings

Property	Shape 1	Shape 2	Label
Name	ShpTitleTop	ShpTitleBorder	LblTitleBar
Left	1	55	0
Top	−1[a]	13	2
Width	53	103	55
Height	2	2	14
Alignment			Center
BackColor			Black
Font			Palm5Bold
ForeColor			Background

[a] We place it offscreen by 1 pixel, since minimum height for a Shape ingot is 2 pixels.

That's really all there is to creating a custom title bar, but AppForge provides a quick and easy method to satisfy 99% of developers who just need a simple title bar. App-Forge uses the contents of the form's Caption property as the label for the title bar. It automatically sizes the title tab to fit the caption size and also creates the title bar border. Its size is always 15 pixels and you can still place controls on top of it (although you will get a warning at compile time). By default, a new form has an empty caption property, and leaving it empty signals AppForge not to create a title bar.

Why would you want a custom title bar? The simple answer is that you might need control over the title bar. Since a custom title bar is comprised of ingots, you can manipulate them as you would any other ingot. For example, you could "move" them as you scroll a form to keep their normal position, have them respond to events, or have them perform any other action you deem necessary based on the needs of your application. However, these situations are rare, and that is why App-Forge added the automatic title bar feature.

To complete your application, place another Label and Command Button ingot on the form and name them lblMessage and cmdShow, respectively. Change the button caption to Show. Finally, add the following code to the form:

```
Option Explicit

Private Sub cmdShow_Click( )
    lblMessage.Caption = "Hello HandHeld World!"
End Sub
```

That's it! We're now ready to test-run our application in Visual Basic. Push F5 to run the program, and click the Show button. Your message will display. It will look something like the screen shown in Figure 2-5.

Figure 2-5. The layout application

Since AppForge projects run on Windows just as they do on the Palm, this is a great debugging technique. However, certain processes, such as connecting to databases, have different call structures for each platform, so make judicious use of conditional compilation to take advantage this debugging capability. Many of the AppForge tutorial projects use this idea. A note of caution: what may run flawlessly in Visual Basic may not compile and/or run correctly in the Palm environment. This is due to the Palm environment's potentially limited or nonexistent support for certain Visual Basic language features. The best advice is to compile with AppForge often, and don't be surprised if you need to implement some workarounds. We'll cover language support later in this chapter.

Configuring, Compiling, and PRC Generation

As we discussed in Chapter 1, you must configure the application, compile it, fix any errors, and then generate the PRC file for upload to the Palm device or for installation on the Palm Emulator.

From the AppForge menu, select the AppForge Settings option. Select Palm OS Settings from the available setting list. Change the Current User as appropriate (based on your Palm Desktop configuration) and set the Creator ID to OR21.

 Thie AppForge Settings dialog box has a setting that allows you to register your Creator ID from within the VB IDE. Just click the Register Creator ID button, which will link you to the appropriate Palm registration form.

That's all there is to project configuration. We'll cover the ins and outs of application dependencies, names, and icons later, so disregard the rest of the settings for now and select OK. Select Compile and Validate from the AppForge menu. You should not receive any compiler errors, but if you do, they would be displayed at this time. If successful, select Save Project Package → Palm OS from the AppForge menu to generate the Palm application file.

At this point, the PRC file is ready for use. We can upload it to the Palm device by selecting Deploy To device → Palm OS from the AppForge menu or installing it into an open Palm Emulator session. The upload function from AppForge will take the PRC and any dependencies (like images or databases) and programmatically run the install function of the Palm Desktop using the User and Creator ID from the project properties. This places a copy of the files physically in the Palm user directory on the hard drive and informs the HotSync manager that new files are ready for upload.

To install files on the Palm Emulator, open a session and right-click on the emulator skin to access the context menu. Choose Install Application → Database and select the files to install, or simply drag and drop the desired files to load directly onto the emulator skin. Run the application to confirm correct operation by clicking the command button to display the hello message.

You've now successfully developed a Palm application using Visual Basic and AppForge. Let's look at the basic building block of an application, the ingot, and review the ingots introduced in this example.

What's an Ingot?

Ingots are specialized, reusable, ActiveX-like components and controls that are designed to operate in both the Windows and Palm environments. This is achieved through a platform-independent component object model called the Piedmont

Framework. Piedmont provides all the functionality necessary to operate on the Palm OS while bridging the gap to underlying COM services on the Windows OS. As you've seen from the sample application, ingots have a look, feel, and function similar to their Windows counterparts. It is important to note that standard Visual Basic controls cannot be used in AppForge projects, but ingots can be used in both. This makes them versatile controls if you find a need for them in desktop applications.

Common ingot attributes

Each ingot may have its own special purpose, but most share common traits.

Color

Many ingots have color-oriented properties such as *ForeColor* and *BackColor*. These properties take a long value in the form of &HBBGGRR where BB is blue, GG is green, and RR is red (e.g., green would be &H00FF00). You could also use the original AppForge grayscale color constants: Background (green or white, depending on the device), Light Gray, Dark Gray, and Black.

Fonts

The *FontName*, *FontSize*, *FontStyle*, and *FontColor* compose the total definition of the desired font. The *FontName* property expects the name of a valid, converted font. *FontSize* expects an integer for indicating the font size in pixels.* *FontStyle* can be four possible constants: Plain (0), Bold (1), Italic (2), Bold & Italic (4). *FontColor* is a long, as described previously. If you change any of these properties to create an invalid combination (i.e., the font doesn't exist), no text will be displayed. Also, if you dynamically change fonts at runtime, the compiler will not pick them up as a dependency. Add them manually via AppForge Settings → User Dependencies.

Text Alignment

For those ingots that display text, there is an *Alignment* property that allows for Left, Center, or Right alignment of the text; the default varies based on the ingot but is usually either Center or Left.

Almost every ingot has a *Left*, *Top*, *Width*, *Height*, *Tag*, *Index*, *Enabled*, and *Visible* attribute that operates exactly as in native Visual Basic.

Let's review the ingots used in our first application.

Command Button ingot

The Command Button ingot is the workhorse control in many applications. Its purpose is to provide the user with a triggering mechanism to execute or stop a task.

---

* Keep this is mind when you are converting TrueType fonts to AppForge Fonts, since TrueType fonts aren't based on width in pixels (i.e., size 12 TrueType font characters are larger than 12 pixels in width per character, so adjust accordingly). This does not apply to *Form*, the font size attribute that still uses points as the unit of measurement.

There are several key differences between the Palm command button and the Windows version, beyond the contrast in appearance.

- The *Appearance* property has three possible styles based on the target OS: Rounded (Palm OS), 3D (Windows), and Flat (Pocket PC). There is another style called Native that changes the style based on the OS the ingot is running, thus providing cross-OS compatibility.

- There are no *Cancel* or *Default* attributes, since these are not applicable in the Palm context.

Label ingot

The Label ingot is another control that is common to all applications. Its purpose is to label some data or controls, and it is not directly modifiable by users. It is also commonly used to display application status information at runtime.

The Label ingot supports the same font and color characteristics as does the Command Button ingot. It doesn't support the following characteristics available in the VB label control.

- *AutoSize* and *WordWrap* for variable length strings
- Transparency to other controls
- *UseMnemonic* to make the control act as shortcut-accessible
- Data binding or DDE targeting
- Right-to-left caption direction (for use with other languages)

Shape ingot

The Shape ingot is potentially the most commonly used ingot, since it is the primary mechanism to customize your interface. The Shape ingot also uses much less memory than the Graphic ingot, since the Graphic ingot requires an external graphic file.

- The Shape ingot cannot be transparent to other ingots. If *FillStyle* is set to transparent, it does not show overlapping control. It fills the shape using the color value from the *BackColor* property.

- The Shape ingot supports the Rectangle, Square, Oval, Circle, Rounded Rectangle, and Rounded Square types. However, unlike in VB, there is no Line ingot and therefore no way to draw a diagonal line. Lines can be drawn programmatically using the Graphic ingot, but the minimum area the control would take up is the bounding rectangle encompassing the two endpoints of the line. This could lead to a considerable number of overlapping controls and would certainly use lots of memory while most likely adding little value to your application.

Remember, ingots are designed to provide as much functionality and behavior as possible from their standard Windows counterpart, controls. However, the differences usually exist because there really is no direct functional or visual "translation" to a Windows control, or because this was left out on purpose to minimize the size (in bytes) of the control, ultimately affecting the size of the PRC generated.

Forms Management

When we talk about forms management, we really want to focus on understanding the altered use of Visual Basic form objects by the AppForge runtime known as the Booster. The Booster runtime consists of several PRC files that execute your Visual Basic code, which has been altered to operate as best as possible under the Palm OS.

With this in mind, it is important to understand what the Palm OS expects and how you, the programmer, will help the Booster achieve those expectations. There are clear, fundamental differences between Windows forms (VB forms running under the Windows OS) and AppForge forms (VB forms running under Palm OS). We'll discuss these differences in the following sections.

Form characteristics

AppForge forms are much simpler than Visual Basic forms for a good reason: they don't need all the functionality that a Windows form needs (even for basic operation).

Your basic Windows form requires support for border, title bars (which include the control box, caption, minimize, maximize, and close buttons), and a host of other functionalities, such as background images, font, and drawing support.

The AppForge form under the Palm OS requires much less functionality. Below is the total set of form properties, methods, and events supported by AppForge forms.

Properties
> BackColor, Caption, Enabled, ForeColor, Height, KeyPreview, Left, ScaleHeight, ScaleLeft, ScaleTop, ScaleWidth, StartUpPosition, Tag, Top, Visible, Width

Methods
> Hide, Move, Refresh, Show, Zorder

Events
> Activate, Click, Deactivate, Initialize, KeyDown, KeyPress, KeyUp, Load, QueryUnload, Resize, Terminate, Unload

As you can plainly see, this is a small subset of the properties, methods, and events supported by the Visual Basic form under Windows. This is simply because size and performance are the most critical aspects of any Palm application. To add support for other functionalities will ultimately affect both of these design traits. Of course, you may eventually need to add some unsupported functionalities in other ways (such as by using workarounds), depending on the needs of your individual application.

One of the most noticeable differences with the AppForge form, visually, is its size. As stated previously, Palm application forms are a maximum of 160 × 160 pixels. AppForge supports a larger-sized form (240 × 269) for the Pocket PC only. If you attempt to set the AppForge form *StartupPosition* to Manual and change the *ScaleTop* property, you will find that it will run Visual Basic, but will throw an AppForge compiler error telling you that the *ScaleMode* property must be set to Pixels, and a compiler warning that indicates the form may not be visible on the device. Since changing the size is only a warning, resetting the *ScaleMode* to Pixels, generating the PRC, and running on a Palm device will display a smaller form, as you specified. However, the form displays centered in the display area (or where you place it using the form's *Move* method) and will lock the application if you tap anywhere outside the smaller form. The answer is to make all forms full-sized.

Displaying forms correctly

As an AppForge developer, it is important for you to understand how to correctly code your forms for display. Any normal combination of the *Unload* or *Load* event, *Show* or *Hide* method, or the form's *Visible* property setting will correctly display forms under the Palm OS. Realize that setting a form's *Visible* property is equivalent to using the *Hide* or *Show* method.

When considering how to code a form's operation, remember the following principles.

- Only one form should be visible at any given time under AppForge. However, any number of forms may be loaded depending on available memory.
- You want to minimize the number of simultaneously loaded forms.

One AppForge form limitation that was alluded to earlier during our discussion of dialog windows was the correct display of forms smaller than full screen size. It appears that, although a form can be smaller and placed at a desired point on the screen, there is a problem with the form's input focus if the user taps outside the bounds of the smaller dialog form onto the underlying form. To avoid this problem, it's best to keep all forms full-sized.

Another thing to consider is the device *model*. If you are deploying an application to older model devices, such as the Palm III series, Heap memory is very limited.

Dynamic Heap memory is analogous to Windows RAM, which is used by running applications to store various data and resources. There are physical limits to Heap memory based on your OS version, despite how much overall free memory you have. These limits are listed in Table 2-2.

Table 2-2. Heap size versus OS version

Palm OS version	Maximum Heap size
3.0	96K
3.02, 3.1, 3.2, 3.3	128K
3.5 or greater	256K[a]

[a] As of version 3.5, dynamic Heap space is now sized based on the amount of memory available to the system: 64K for less than 2Mb, 128K for greater than or equal to 2Mb, and 256K for greater than or equal to 4Mb.

AppForge leverages the Palm stack and dynamic heap data structures as best as possible in order to maximize performance and efficiency. To achieve this, AppForge loads all forms and ingots on the dynamic heap, while placing all variables and function parameters on the stack. This approach allows the Palm Memory Manager to use smaller chunks of contiguous memory for each structure, thus improving performance, especially for large applications.

Threads of execution and events

Earlier versions of the AppForge Booster had two threads of execution while running in the Palm OS. The first thread was for the execution of code and the second was used to handle all form display requests. For example, code residing in a form's *Load* event might not have executed correctly before the form appeared because certain code might have required the form to be visible to execute. However, since version 2.0, the Booster has been changed to a single-threaded model so that event callbacks happened properly.

Applications running under AppForge operate identically to their Windows counterparts with respect to event handling. Code that triggers an event is immediately executed without waiting for the currently executing code block (function, subroutine, or event) to be finished.

The AppForge form doesn't support every event of the standard VB form, but it provides almost all that you will need for Palm applications. To receive the form's *KeyPress*, *KeyDown*, and *KeyUp* events, the form's *KeyPreview* property must be set to True. ioAlso, the device's built-in hard scroll up and down keys automatically generate *KeyDown* events. We will cover how to use and intercept all the hard and silkscreen keys, including Graffiti strokes, later in this chapter.

Finally, let's review a form's event life cycle to understand how code will be executed and in what order. See Figure 2-6 for a pictorial chart of the life cycle.

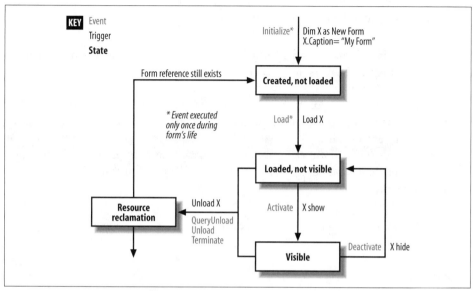

Figure 2-6. Form event life cycle

Initialize

This event is triggered on the creation of a new instance of the form. Upon completion of the event, the form is created but not loaded. Use this event to execute code you want to run before the form's *Load* event, such as initializing form-level variables.

Load

This event occurs before the form is made visible. Check to ensure that you don't run into any execution problems, as previously discussed. This is also your chance to perform any initialization of the form prior to it being displayed. It is a good place to open databases and retrieve records for initial viewing.

Activate

This event happens after the form is visible or receives focus. Place any code that is having problems running in the form's *Load* event here. *Activate* is not triggered by just loading a form; it must be visible to be triggered. This is a good place for code that updates ingots. Shifting code normally performed in the *Load* event to this event gives the appearance of faster performance, since the form appears quicker.

Deactivate

This event happens when focus is removed from the form, for example, by hiding a form and showing a new form. This event is not triggered before the *Unload* event.

QueryUnload

> This event provides an opportunity to perform any final actions before the *Unload* event occurs. It also allows you to cancel the *Unload* event, including determining how the unload was triggered.

Unload

> This event is used to unload a form from memory and reclaim any used memory from form-level variables and structures. There is more to this event than meets the eye, though. First, this event is *not* triggered automatically if you move focus to another application on the device. The *Unload* event must be explicitly called in order for the event handler to execute. In code, this would involve using the *Unload* statement. However, if you wish to have your application end gracefully when a user opens another application, you will need to intercept button calls and trigger the *Unload* event from there. We will cover button interception later in this chapter.

Terminate

> This event occurs when the form is destroyed in memory, such as when an application ends.

Form refreshing

Form ingots are normally refreshed automatically during periods of inactivity. Unlike the VB *Refresh* method, the effect of the refresh is not guaranteed to happen immediately. Visible ingots will get repainted, while non-visible ingots will force an update to the data associated with the ingot.

AppForge does not perform the refresh immediately in an effort to increase performance, but you can still force a refresh by using the *DoEvents* function. The *DoEvents* function executes all pending events under AppForge (on the Palm) as it does under Windows.[*] To force a refresh of a component, you need to execute a direct refresh of the component followed by a call to *DoEvents*. For example:

```
Form1.AFLabel1.Refresh
DoEvents
```

Using *DoEvents* will lengthen execution time, but it gives you the ability to perform other tasks while waiting for the lengthy operation. An example of this would be loading a grid control with a large amount of data. If you must have an application that takes an extended period of time to load a database/grid, incorporating some form of indicator that the application is working is prudent. This could be in the form of a status field change or a spinner animation (shown in Chapter 3, when we focus on databases). In any case, the indicator will not be updated without calls to *DoEvents*.

---

[*] This was not the case under AppForge 1.x, since calling *DoEvents* did not interrupt execution of code (say, a loop) to process pending message events.

Form scrolling

With the limited size of the application workspace, it makes sense that an important design consideration would be to create forms that are scrollable, if necessary. There are several methods of scrolling that we'll review in this chapter.

- Paging a form that is larger than 160 pixels (in either width or height)
- Scrolling a form that is larger than 160 pixels (in either width or height)
- Scrolling the controls on a form that is standard size (160 × 160 pixels)

The first two methods are easier to implement, since they don't involve per-ingot changes; they involve manipulating the *Top* property (or *Left* property for Horizontal scrolling). However, a note of caution: AppForge warns that this functionality, while working at present, is not guaranteed to work in future releases of AppForge.

The last method, while more involved, is supported since it manipulates the ingots on the form and not the form itself. The sample code shows a scrolling application to demonstrate the techniques described below.

Paging a large form

This is the simplest method and involves first developing a form with width, height, or a combination of both, in increments of 160 pixels. You can accomplish this by dragging the form boundaries out to the proper *ScaleWidth* and *ScaleHeight* properties.

 Changing these values in the Properties window does not resize the form, but instead changes the *ScaleMode* property to User mode.

Your mechanism for changing pages can vary greatly. The most common approach would be to place next and previous buttons or up and down arrow graphic buttons on each "form." The code to place behind these buttons is as follows:

```
'Vertical Paging
Me.Top = Me.Top + 160   'use for the Up (or Previous) Button
Me.Top = Me.top - 160   'use for the Down (on Next) Button

'Horizontal Paging
Me.Left = Me.Left - 160 'use for Left (or Next) Button
Me.Left = Me.Left + 160 'use for Right (or Previous) Button
```

Creating control arrays for the up and down buttons allows you to write the code only once for each procedure. It also allows you to check if you are at either end of the form by examining the control index parameter in the buttons click event.

```
Private Sub cmdNext_Click(Index As Integer)
    'move to next page unless this is last page
    If Index <> 2 Then Me.Left = Me.Left - 160
End Sub
```

```
Private Sub cmdPrev_Click(Index As Integer)
    'move to previous page unless this is first page
    If Index <> 0 Then Me.Left = Me.Left + 160
End Sub
```

To optimize the form and reduce the number of navigation button ingots, just create one set of buttons (up and down) and simply reposition them each time they are clicked. Figure 2-7 provides an example of a horizontally paging form.

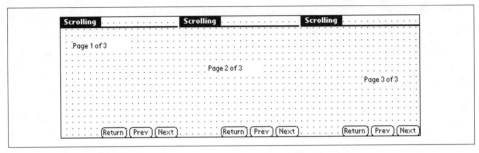

Figure 2-7. Paging form

Scrolling a large form

This method is similar to the paging example. It simply involves manipulating the *Top* and/or *Left* properties of the form, except that the increment is much less than 160 pixels, thus producing a scrolling effect. Scrolling large forms can get easier or harder depending on how much style and function you wish to implement in your application. For example, the form shown in Figure 2-8 keeps the entire title bar in place while scrolling the form. In reality, two things are happening: the form is shifted vertically and the ingots comprising the title bar are moved by the specified increment to keep them stationary.

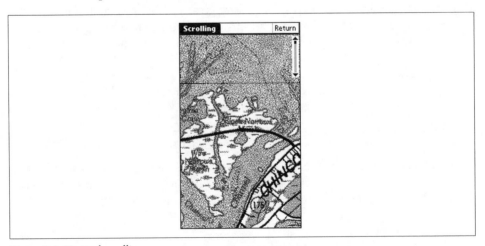

Figure 2-8. Vertical scrolling

The code to support this scrolling effect is:

```
Const MAX_UP As Integer = -80
Dim miCurrent As Integer

Private Sub ScrollDown(ByVal Amount As Integer)
    'only scroll form to point that you desire as defined by MAX_UP
    If Me.Top > MAX_UP Then
        Me.Top = Me.Top + Amount
        AdjustTitleBar -Amount
    End If
End Sub
Private Sub ScrollUp(ByVal Amount As Integer)
    'stop once top shape has return to home posititon
    If Me.Top + Amount <= 0 Then
        Me.Top = Me.Top + Amount
        AdjustTitleBar -Amount
    End If
End Sub
Private Sub AdjustTitleBar(ByVal Amount As Integer)
    'move controls to keep them stationary
    shpTitleBorder.Top = shpTitleBorder.Top + Amount
    lblTitleBar.Top = lblTitleBar.Top + Amount
    shpTitleTop.Top = shpTitleTop.Top + Amount
    cmdExit.Top = cmdExit.Top + Amount
    Vscroll.Top = Vscroll.Top + Amount
End Sub
Private Sub VScroll_Change( )
    'user clicked above scrollbar thumb
    If miCurrent > Vscroll.Value Then
        'is change large or small?
        If Abs(miCurrent - Vscroll.Value) > Vscroll.SmallChange Then
            ScrollUp Vscroll.LargeChange
        Else
            ScrollUp Vscroll.SmallChange
        End If
    Else
        If Abs(miCurrent - Vscroll.Value) > Vscroll.SmallChange Then
            ScrollDown -Vscroll.LargeChange
        Else
            ScrollDown -Vscroll.SmallChange
        End If
    End If
    'store current value
    miCurrent = Vscroll.Value
End Sub
```

MAX_UP is the desired amount of pixels from the bottom you wish the form to stop scrolling. The miCurrent variable stores the current value of the Scrollbar ingot. Let's take a quick look at the Scrollbar ingot that this example uses.

Scrollbar (horizontal or vertical) and Slider ingots

The Scrollbar ingots are very simple and are perfectly suited for form scrolling. The ingots differ only in their directional orientation. Their property, method, and even set is identical. They can take on one of two styles based on the *Appearance* property. They can be Borderless (Palm style) or Borders (Pocket PC style). There is also a Native setting that sets the appearance to match that of the native operating system. Visually, the ingot can change the background and the scroll thumb's color.

The Scrollbar ingot operates like its Windows counterpart. Simply set the desired bounding *Max* and *Min* values and adjust the default *SmallChange* (1) and *LargeChange* (10) properties as desired. A *Change* event is triggered for each tap of the scrollbar. As you can see from the preceding code segment, you will need to determine direction by comparing the value before the tap with the new value if direction is important. The ingot also doesn't indicate if the tap resulted in a large or small change, so you'll need to determine this on your own (as shown).

Another control that operates identically to the horizontal scrollbar ingot is the Slider ingot. The only major differences are in the Slider ingot's appearance attributes. The ingot can have several *Appearance* types: Pointer Up, Pointer Down, Rectangle (Pocket PC), and Rounded (Palm OS). These styles can all have a series of tick marks displayed next to the slider track. These ticks can be turned off if desired, and their frequency can be adjusted. Operationally, the only difference between the Scrollbar and Slider ingots is that the Slider ingot triggers a *SliderMoved* event that supplies an input parameter indicating the slider's new value. This is identical to the contents of the *Value* property.

Scrolling ingots on a normal-sized form

This method does not involve moving the form itself, but rather the ingots on the form. As you can expect, this method can become very tedious to code and maintain for forms with a lot of ingots, so use this method appropriately. This method is, however, guaranteed to work in future versions of AppForge, since we are not manipulating the form's *Left* and *Top* properties.

The form in Figure 2-9 contains only a few ingots, and a Scrollbar ingot is used to control the movement of the form.

The code is relatively simple. Making calls to the *ScrollForm* method shifts the ingots the appropriate amount and adjusts the scrollbar ingots.

```
Public Sub ScrollForm(ByVal Increment As Integer)
        'stop before top control reaches bottom OR
        'bottom control reaches top
        If (lblMsg(0).Top + Increment < 150) And _
           (lblMsg(2).Top + Increment > 20) Then
            AdjustIngots Increment
        End If
End Sub
```

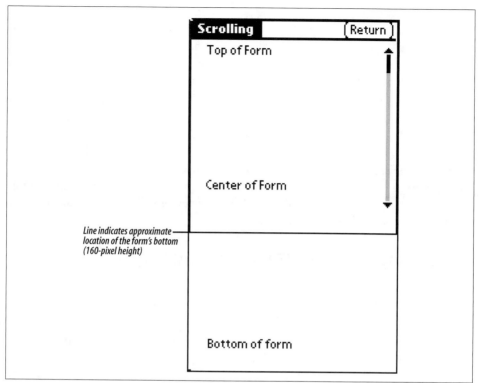

Figure 2-9. *Ingot scrolling*

The code for the scrollbar is identical to that shown in the last listing.

Control layering

The layering of ingots on a form at design time is identical to the process of layering controls in a Windows application. Every ingot on a form has not only an X or Y position, but also a position along the Z-axis, in what is called the form's Z-order. The *ZOrder* method can be manipulated at runtime to establish the ordering of the controls on the form. You can set an ingot's *ZOrder* implicitly at design time when placing the ingots on a form, by using each ingot's right-mouse context menu's Bring To Front and Send To Back commands.

Icons and title for Palm applications

Palm applications can have two distinct icons: one for the icon view and one for the list view of the main launcher window. The icons should be 22 × 22 pixels for the Icon view and 15 × 9 for the List view. AppForge does support color icons.

The Palm OS application icon title can be any length, but on average fits about 9 characters in Icon view and about 12 in the List view. The Palm application name and icon title are derived from the VB project object name, not the *Application Title* property nor the actual Visual Basic Project (.VBP) filename. Since the *Project* name property doesn't allow spaces, AppForge built in a way for you to get spaces into your deployed application name. Simply use an underscore (_) in the project name wherever you want a space and ensure that the Convert spaces in project name option is checked on the `AppForge Settings → App Name/Icon` dialog.

Finally, if you upload an application that is already physically deployed on your Palm device, but for which you've changed the *Project* name, then the new application will be a separate and distinct application reflecting the changes you've made. It will be linked to the original application record in the Palm's application database. This link is generated because the applications have the same Creator ID. Changing the ID for each application will ensure a separate entry for each application in the Palm's application database. Deleting the application from the device will remove all instances of the application, including all corresponding icons.

The Basic Application Layout Example, Continued

This example extends our first basic application to demonstrate how to display multiple forms, how to implement a menu system, and how to provide a template dialog and tip window for you to use in your own applications.

The new controls added in this example are the Graphic and Textbox ingots. The Graphic ingot is not just a graphic image container, it also provides you with a drawing area that you can leverage in your code to draw a variety of things, such as charts or graphs. The Textbox ingot is your primary textual input control and, as you will see, has quite a bit of functionality.

First, let's look at the application's two new forms, the dialog and the tip windows (shown in Figure 2-10). The dialog window is your primary mechanism to collect information from the user in a "modal" fashion, while the tip window provides textual help about the dialog window's (or application's) purpose or operation. Both window types provide a visual cue to the user with their distinctive title bars and form borders. AppForge does not support an autogenerated dialog title bar, so these must be custom-made for Shape and Graphic ingots.

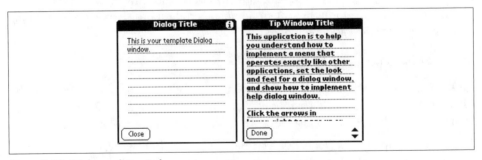

Figure 2-10. Dialog and tip windows

By convention, the dialog typically has an information icon in the upper righthand corner, signifying that a stylus tap will open a tip window (or some other means of displaying information). Tip windows generally have a text box with repeat buttons on the form. These buttons actually leverage the text boxes' inherent text paging capability.

Use the *Hide* method for the dialog form instead of unloading, since tip windows are generally open for a small duration and are not resource-intensive.

```
frmDialog.Hide
frmHelp.Show
```

Figure 2-10's tip window contains two repeat style buttons, the page up and page down buttons. These buttons simply repeat the action for each stylus tap. Each tap moves the text up or down, using the Textbox's *TopLine* and *TotalLines* properties.

```
'code for down button
txtHelpText.TopLine = txtHelpText.TopLine + 10

'code for up button
txtHelpText.TopLine = txtHelpText.TopLine - 10
```

Set the page increment to whatever you desire. Setting the *TopLine* property to a negative number or to a number greater than *TotalLines* does not cause an error, but sets *TopLine* to the first or last line, as appropriate.

Form menus

AppForge provides excellent menu support for the Visual Basic developer. To build a menu for any form, simply use the built-in Visual Basic menu editor off the Tools menu. Since Windows menus support some actions that Palm menus do not, it's important to understand what gets translated from the menu built through the menu editor.

- Menus can have as many top-level menu titles as desired, limited only by what is visible on the Palm device display. Menu items that are onscreen will still work.
- Menus can only be one level deep; they do not support any cascading sub-menus.
- There can be any number of menu items, limited only by what is visible on the Palm device display.
- Adding an accelerator (&) will display the stroke-character combination to invoke the menu item.
- AppForge does not recognize the *Shortcut*, *Checked*, *WindowList*, *NegotiatePosition*, and *HelpContextID* attributes.

Operationally, the menu works as follows:

- Tapping the application title bar tab displays the menu bar.
- Tapping a menu title displays the drop menu portion; subsequent taps hide it.

- Tapping a menu item invokes the appropriate functionality and hides the drop menu portion and menu bar in its entirety.

- Tapping on the form while the menu is visible hides the drop menu portion and menu bar in its entirety.

- Tapping the menu silkscreen button displays the menu bar; subsequent taps hide it.

The only special circumstance to remember when developing your menus is that top-level menu titles do not trigger events.

The menu shown in Figure 2-11 is a simple menu with one menu title (App) and a drop-down portion containing two menu items. Note that the menu items have a shift accelerator available. Simply performing the menu shift scribe brings up the command menu at the bottom of the form. Following it by the specified letter will trigger the menu item.

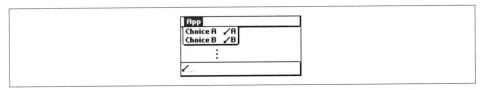

Figure 2-11. Example menu structure and command menu

Our end result is an application that can be used as a template for all future applications, whatever their size. Let's review the ingots that were added to this project.

Graphic ingot

The Graphic ingot is one of the most versatile ingots in the toolkit. This is because it not only can display a graphic image, but also can be used as a drawing surface at runtime to create a wide range of things, such as charts and graphs. It also can interact with a user's stylus taps by capturing the stylus coordinates.

The ingot's primary job is to display a graphic image. The image that the *Picture* property can be assigned is an AppForge Graphic (*.rgx*), a bitmap (*.bmp*), or a JPEG (*.jpg*). The RGX file is an AppForge proprietary format. AppForge provides a graphics conversion tool that converts bitmaps (BMP) to the AppForge Graphics (RGX) format. The converted files have the following limitations:

- They cannot exceed 64K in size (this includes raw BMP and JPG files).

- The conversion creates a monochrome image.

- The RGX file must reside in the same directory as the project source files. When AppForge creates the PRC file, it only looks in the project directory for the RGX files to bundle into the PRC, so no path should be specified in the *Picture* property or *PaintPicture* method.

Let's expand on the last point. When including graphics in an application, only the files specified by the ingot's properties will be included in the generated PRC file. In order to also include additional files assigned to ingots at runtime (i.e., by code assignment), you must manually include them. This is done from the AppForge Settings window.

On the User Dependencies tab, use the Add and Delete buttons to manually modify the dependencies list. The Automatic Dependencies tab shows the resources that have been found during a search of the project files for any *image* files assigned to ingots at design time.

Some points to remember about the Graphic ingots operation:

- The ingot will not auto-resize for a picture assigned at runtime.
- Issuing a refresh after changing the *Picture* property or invoking the *PaintPicture* method will force the image to refresh more quickly.
- Picture scrolling can be achieved using the *PaintPicture* method by manipulating the X and Y coordinate parameters instead of moving the entire control. Specifying negative coordinates is supported, and the image will be clipped appropriately if it is moved outside the ingot boundaries.
- *DrawCircle, DrawLine, DrawRectangle, DrawText*, or *SetPixel* will draw on top of any picture assigned to the ingot.
- The Graphic ingot is the only ingot that directly responds to stylus actions. These actions trigger the *MouseMove* and *MouseDown* events. These events occur before the *Click* event.
- The *Cls* method clears the ingot of all graphics.

AppForge color support

AppForge supports up to 24-bit color for all images assigned to ingots. However, with this capability come some caveats that you must heed if you want to see good performance on image loading:

- 1-, 2-, 4-, and 8-bit/pixel *monochrome* images (i.e., up to 256 shades of gray) will load the fastest. The RGX format is 2 bit/pixel, so its performance should be very good.
- Loading a color image on a monochrome device will increase memory use and display times, since the device must now convert and map every pixel's color to a grayscale value supported by the device. Consider deploying your application with a color and monochrome set of images displaying the appropriate image based on the device's color support.

- Image size will affect display time. Try to reduce the image size as best as possible for faster performance.

- The higher the color depth, the longer the image will take to load. For best load performance of *color* images, the optimal color depth is 8 bits, and the image should use the Netscape-safe Web palette.

The real performance hit comes from the color depth of an image. Palm uses its default color palette to display a provided image. If the colors from the image are not in the Palm palette, the Palm must then apply an algorithm to convert the palette, which runs against all pixels n the image for every color in the palette. (For 2-, 4-, or 8-bit color images, it only has to map every color, not every pixel.) This operation can take *tens* of seconds, depending on the color complexity of the image.

Needless to say, the best strategy is to use the Palm palette for your color images targeted for the device. Many graphics packages provide the Palm color palette, or you can load the Palm palette manually. But what if the Palm palette is not suitable for your image? Load your own! AppForge does not supply a method to load a palette for you, but it can be easily done by tapping into the AFCore library. What is required is an 8-bit color, 1 × 1 pixel bitmap, using your desired palette, that you will package with the application for upload to the device. You can then change the palette by calling the following procedure:

```
Public Sub LoadPalette(ByVal PaletteTemplate As String)
    Dim objShell As New CShell
    Dim objPaletteImage As CImage

    If (objShell.ScreenDepth = 8) Then
            Set objPaletteImage = objShell.LoadImage(PaletteTemplate)
            Set objShell.ScreenPalette = objPaletteImage.Palette
    End If
End Sub
```

Pass it the name of your palette file:

```
LoadPallete "MyPalette.bmp"
```

Now, the device is optimized for your images, and all images loaded from now on will use the newly loaded palette. You can switch to other palettes or back to the Palm palette at any time. The Palm palette bitmap template is available from AppForge Support at *http://support.appforge.com* and will also be posted on this book's web site.

Textbox ingot

The Textbox ingot is designed to provide most of the functionality of its Windows counterpart. The control provides a unique "lined paper" format and has some built-in methods to identify and set individual lines when multiple lines of text are present.

Keep the following points in mind:

- The Textbox ingot has the same font and color characteristics as the Command Button ingot.

- The entire text content can only have one font style (i.e., it is not a rich text box).

- The *DisplayableLines* method returns the total number of lines that will fit into a Textbox ingot. This number is determined by the ingot's selected size and font.

- Set the *PasswordChar* property to any desired mask character. The *Text* property still contains the actual text. Set the *PasswordChar* property and empty string to return the ingot to default behavior.*

- Use the *Top* property to set the specified line of text to be displayed at the top of the ingot. The *TotalLines* property returns the total number of lines in the ingot.

Language and Libraries Support

The Palm OS is considerably different from the Windows OS in many aspects. Its underlying structure, memory model, and data storage are radically different and require an "application abstraction layer" to provide easier access to the underlying OS. This abstraction layer is provided to the VB programmer via the AppForge libraries. These libraries provide access to native Palm OS functions, including complete support for creating and maintaining Palm databases.

There is considerable support for the VB language constructs. However, there also has been a conscious effort to increase application efficiency by limiting or eliminating (i.e., ignoring) certain aspects of VB by the AppForge compiler. There are many reasons for this, but they are related to the sheer fact that mobile handheld devices are limited by available power. Applications that require the device to perform resource-intensive processes, such as continually accessing RAM, will draw more power than usual. Another power-limiting factor is the use of slower processors to conserve energy. Consequently, some Windows features were either optimized to provide satisfactory response times or were eliminated altogether.

Visual Basic Language Support

In this section, we will cover the Visual Basic functionality that is not supported by the AppForge compiler.

---

* Palm discourages the use of masked characters for one obvious reason: you will not get immediate feedback that you correctly Graffiti-scribed the correct characters. Why bother when you can just as easily shield the device from possible onlookers?

Object support

AppForge *does* allow the creation of user-defined classes (i.e., class modules), using the *New* keyword in the *Dim* statement. You can also create object references to the libraries and ingots provided by AppForge, but you cannot create new ingots. No external references can be made to other objects and, as you may have guessed, the *CreateObject* method is not available (since it attempts to create an ActiveX object, which is obviously not supported by the Palm OS).

AppForge requires all objects to be early-bound. Even though AppForge supports the Object type, it does not allow you to directly call properties or methods of a generic object unless it is recast to the correct object. For example, let's say we have a class object, clsCalc, which has a method called *Square* that takes an integer and returns its squared value. The following code would generate an AppForge compiler error (but works fine in VB on the desktop):

```
Dim x As Object
Dim y As New clsCalc
Set x = y
x.Square 5
Set x = Nothing
Set y = Nothing
```

The compiler error indicates that the member function *Square* does not exist in IUnknown (the default object interface), since x was a late-bound object. Avoid this by ensuring that all objects are early-bound (as in the earlier Dim y statement). App-Forge also supports the use of the generic VB library control class, which, like the object class, is a generic class for all controls. However, only the extender properties and methods can be called with the Control type: *Top*, *Left*, *Height*, *Width*, *Move*, and *SetFocus*. Unlike the object class, an ingot cast to the control class can have the methods called directly:

```
Dim a As Control
Set a = AFButton1
a.Left = a.Left + 50
Set a = Nothing
```

There is also some limited support for control (ingot) collections. Controls in a collection can be accessed only through explicit use of the *Item* property. The *Count* property is also supported; however, as we've already discussed, AppForge does not allow the creation of controls at runtime. Therefore, the *Add* method is not supported. When accessing a control via the collection, only the extender functions are available (as described above). Finally, the *With* and *For-Each* constructs are not currently supported.

Limitations of ingots

Ingots cannot act as container classes for other ingots, as a frame does for a group of checkboxes in Windows, for example. Ingots also have no data awareness, whereas their Windows counterparts can have their source data derived from database queries.

Of course, you already know that most ingots differ from their Windows counterparts (when appropriate) by the subset of methods, properties, and events supported. These differences, however, are mainly due to the limitations of what can actually be implemented under the Palm OS, since it differs drastically from the Windows OS.

Drag-and-drop support is also not provided for ingots. It is unsure if AppForge will include this support in future versions, since it's not critical to making efficient applications. (It would also require significant overhead to track the status of drag-and-drop operations—something to avoid on handheld devices.)

Unsupported types and limitations

Currently, Decimal and Variants are not supported types.

User-Defined Types (UDTs) cannot be passed by value (must be by reference) or specified as a function's return type.

There are some unique issues with strings that pertain solely to operating on the Palm OS:

- Although string length is typically limited by available device memory, no string within AppForge may exceed 65,000 characters.
- Variable length strings are stored using heap memory.
- If any characters in variable-length strings require Unicode, all characters in the string are stored in Unicode format.
- Locally scoped strings are stored on the stack. Avoid creating large, fixed-length strings, since they would use considerable stack space.
- All characters stored in fixed-length strings are Unicoded.

Arrays

The biggest restriction is the lack of support for dynamic arrays. All arrays must be statically dimensioned arrays. AppForge made a conscious decision to not store any bookkeeping information about the array during runtime in order to increase speed and save memory. Since bookkeeping information is not stored, the *Lbound* and *Ubound* methods are not applicable. Array bounds must be positive and dimensioned with at least one element. Bounds checking at runtime was dropped to increase array access speed.

Finally, arrays cannot be passed as parameters to procedures or functions due to the lack of bookkeeping information. A convenient workaround is to define a UDT with the only member being the array and pass the UDT to the procedure by reference.

Arrays can consist of any supported types, including user-defined types and other static arrays.

Intrinsic user interaction

The familiar *MsgBox* method will produce a Palm message box when run on the device or in the emulator. However, it will produce a standard Windows message box when run under the VB IDE. The difference is that the method supports only two parameters: the *Prompt* and a subset of the button constants. The title of the message box is determined by the severity of the message. The *HelpFile* and *Context* parameters are unsupported.

The following button constants are available to customize your message box: vbAbortRetryIngnore, vbCritical, vbExclamation, vbInformation, vbOKCancel, vbOKOnly, vbQuestion, vbRetryCancel, vbYesNo, and vbYesNoCancel.

For those of you who like to pop up a quick InputBox, you're currently out of luck since it is not supported for some strange reason (although there's nothing from stopping you from making your own!).

Error handling

AppForge supports all variations of the VB On Error error handling statement. This includes the use of the Resume statement in error handlers. Error handling operates just as it does in VB, with one exception. If AppForge encounters a second error within an error handler, it returns execution to the last active error handler. (VB would throw a runtime error.) This is because AppForge resets the error state as soon as the error is caught.

Err.Raise is supported and operates as it does in VB, with one little twist. Under AppForge, a call to Err.Raise produces a specialized message box, as shown in Figure 2-12, if there are no remaining active error handlers.

Figure 2-12. Error Raise message box

The error message box can be customized by providing your own error number, source, and description. The title is based on the severity of the error.

AppForge has also defined a built-in compiler constant, APPFORGE, which you can use judiciously through your code to differentiate code that is to be run under the App-Forge Booster on the device or emulator or under the VB IDE. A classic use is in opening a Palm database that has two call signatures based on whether it is opening on Windows or on the Palm OS.

```
#If APPFORGE Then
    'open Device way
    x = PDBOpen(Byfilename, "MyDB", 0, 0, 0, 0, afModeReadWrite)
#Else
    'open Windows way
    x = PDBOpen(Byfilename, App.Path & "\MyDB", 0, 0, 0, 0, afModeReadWrite)
#End If
```

Events

Triggering an event under AppForge works the same as under Windows. Events are handled as soon as they are triggered. Events no longer have to wait for the currently executing procedure to complete, as they did in AppForge version 1.x.

Miscellaneous

There are many small nuances that we'll leave to you to discover. In the meantime, here are some other things to keep in mind:

There is no intrinsic context-sensitive help mechanism or the concept of a help file. Certainly a "context-like" help system can be created by changing a label or text box to display a value in a controls *Tag* property as the control's receive focus, but unless absolutely necessary, this should be avoided because it takes up valuable real estate. A better approach is to include a help option from the menu that displays a tip window with all the help information you want to show.

The Static keyword is not supported. This is because static variables will remain in memory for the entire time the application is open and thereby take up heap space, which is a valuable commodity.

AppForge supports a large number of Visual Basic's intrinsic functions. When functions are not supported, it's usually because they are not applicable to the Palm OS (such as functions dealing with PC filesystems) or simply because their convenience in Windows is not worth the overhead under the Palm OS.

However, there are some functions that would be useful and are unsupported. Spend time reviewing the AppForge documentation on what is and is not supported. You certainly don't want to waste time creating code around an approach that is not supported.

AppForge Library Support

AppForge has provided a set of libraries to gain access to the Palm OS, including other Palm applications.

Numeric and System libraries

The Numeric library's purpose is to contain math-related functions. Currently, the Numeric library supports only two methods: *RandomLong* and *SeedRandomLong*. Both are based on the underlying Palm OS random number functions.

Using *SeedRandomLong* with any number greater than zero will set the random generator to a random starting point. Setting *SeedRandomLong* equal to zero will reinitialize the generator.

Calling *RandomLong*(N), where N is the desired range from 0 to N-1, generates a random long value. Thus:

```
X = RandomLong(100) + 1
```

will yield a number between 1 and 100. Calling *SeedRandomLong* with the same number before each *RandomLong* call will continually yield the same set of random numbers, so set it once "per session." A session would be a series of calls to *RandomLong*. For example, setting the seed to 10 may yield 91,43,56,79,89 for each call to *RandomLong*. Calling *SeedRandomLong* again with 10 will yield the same set of numbers.

To help create a random seed, the System library contains a method called *TimerMS* that returns a long representing the number of milliseconds since the device was powered on. Continual calls to this method will return increasing numbers as long as the device is on.

This library will hopefully begin to fill with other useful methods in later versions of AppForge.

There are three other methods in the System library besides *TimerMS*. The *RegisterKeyCode* is used to hook into the Palm OS to receive the device's hard and silkscreen button activations created by the user. These methods take only one parameter, the desired *keycode*. Once hooked, the application can then catch the button activation via the Form's *KeyDown* event.

 You need to register the keycode only once in the application. However, for each form to respond to the keycode hook, the form's *KeyPreview* property must be set to true and each form's *KeyDown* event must be coded to react to the capture.

Table 2-3 lists the keycodes for all the device buttons.

Table 2-3. Device keycodes

Device component	Hex	Decimal
Menu button (silkscreen)	&H105	261
Command bar (via Graffiti stroke)	&H106	262
Launch button (silkscreen)	&H108	264
Keyboard button (silkscreen)	&H109	265
Find button (silkscreen)	&H10A	266
Calculator button (silkscreen)	&H10B	267
Alphabet keyboard (silkscreen)	&H110	272
Numeric keypad (silkscreen)	&H111	273
Leftmost device button (hard)	&H204	516
Center-left device button (hard)	&H205	517
Center-right device button (hard)	&H206	518
Rightmost device button (hard)	&H207	519
Power button (hard)	&H208	520
Cradle button (hard)	&H209	521
Contrast button (hard)	&H20B	523
Antenna switch (when raised)	&H20C	524

Once your application registers a keycode, it no longer responds to its default behavior (unless you pass the request on to the Palm OS; we'll discuss how to do this shortly). If you want to regain the keycode's original functionality, run the *ReleaseKeyCode* method to release it back to the OS. Of course, it's recommended that you release all the keycodes your application has registered when it unloads.

The last method in the System library, *GetDeviceUserName*, returns the current HotSync username (if this is important to your application).

Extended Functions library

The Extended Functions library contains a wide variety of methods that expose native Palm functions critical to making your application truly an enterprise-worthy application. Almost all the methods fall into groups that perform or assist in performing a certain task. Let's review this library by grouping:

Text editing and sizing. There are four methods to aid you in capturing and displaying text. The *ClipBoardGetString* and *ClipBoardSetString* methods copy and paste strings between your application and the native Palm clipboard.

The other two methods, *StringWidth* and *FontHeight*, help you determine the height and width of a string in pixels. You can then use this information to resize a text box, caption, grid cell, or any other text-oriented control in order to maximize screen space. When calling these methods, you provide them with the font name, size, and type. *StringWidth* also requires the actual string to size.

Capturing user and device actions. As we have previously seen with the *RegisterKeyCode* method from the System library, we can hook our application to receive many different Palm device actions, such as hard and silkscreen button captures. But what if you want to trigger these actions programmatically? Enter the *EnqueueKey* method. This method takes a *KeyAscii* value and a modifier flag (see Table 2-4) as parameters and places the simulated hardware action (e.g., a key press) on the Palm message queue for processing just as if a user did it. So, if you were to take a *keycode* that was previously shown in Table 2-3, such as the Launch button (264), and set the modifier flag to afExtLibCommandKeyMask (8), as follows:

```
EnqueueKey 264, afExtLibCommandKeyMask
```

then your application will close and the device will return to the application launcher view. Table 2-4 shows the full listing of the available modifiers.

Table 2-4. Enqueue modifiers

Value	Constant	Description
1	afExtLibShiftKeyMask	Simulates Graffiti as being in case-shift mode when sending the KeyAscii character
2	afExtLibCapsLockMask	Simulates Graffiti as being in caps-lock mode when sending the KeyAscii character
4	afExtLibNumLockMask	Simulates Graffiti as being in numeric-shift mode when sending the KeyAscii character
8	afExtLibCommandKeyMask	Signifies that KeyAscii is a virtual keycode or simulates a Graffiti menu command preceding the KeyAscii character
16	afExtLibOptionKeyMask	Not implemented
32	afExtLibControlKeyMask	Not implemented
64	afExtLibAutoRepeatKeyMask	Indicates that the event was generated by an auto-repeat
128	afExtLibDoubleTapKeyMask	Not implemented
256	afExtLibPoweredOnKeyMask	Indicates that the key press caused the device to be powered on
512	afExtLibAppEvtHookKeyMask	System use only
1024	afExtLibLibEvtHookKeyMask	System use only

The other set of methods deal specifically with the Graffiti shift mechanism. The Graffiti shift states include several possible modes:

Uppercase mode
> The shift stroke was entered and the next character will be a capitalized letter. The shift indicator shows an up arrow, usually in the lower right of the screen (or wherever the Graffiti shift indicator is positioned).

Lowercase mode
> Not used.

Caps-lock mode
> A double shift stroke was entered, and all characters entered will be capitalized. The shift indicator shows a segmented up arrow in the lower right of the screen.

Number-lock mode
> Not used.

Punctuation mode
> A dot (.) was tapped and the shift indicator will show a filled dot in the lower right of the screen. The next character typed will be a punctuation character.

Extended mode
> A backslash (\) was entered and provides access to the extended character set, such as copyright and trademark characters. The shift indicator shows a backslash in the lower right of the screen.

None
> The Graffiti shift is not activated (normal mode).

All of these states can be captured by using the *GetGraffitiShiftState* method, but only Upper, Caps-lock, and None can be set programmatically using the *SetGraffitiShiftState* method.

To access and use the Graffiti shift mechanism in your code, call the following three methods, in order, in the *Form_Activate* event:

```
GraffitiShiftIndicatorInitialize
GraffitiShiftIndicatorEnable True
GraffitiShiftIndicatorSetLocation 135, 150
```

The *GraffitiShiftIndicatorInitialize* method will return the shift state to normal. The *GraffitiShiftIndicatorEnable* will enable the shift indicator to display when activated. The *GraffitiShiftIndicatorSetLocation* allows you to move it from its default position at 135,150, which is the lower right corner of the display. If you do decide to move the shift indicator, remember the icon is 8 pixels wide × 10 pixels high, so make sure your coordinates keep it on the screen.

 There are several events that could cause the shift indicator to become hidden or disabled. This includes message box activation and ingots overlapping the shift indicator. If you plan to use the shift indicator in a form, call *GraffitiShiftIndicatorEnable* every time the desired form is activated (and after a message box has been displayed) to ensure the indicator will be displayed correctly.

One final method, *GraffitiShiftIndicatorIsEnable*, will simply return true if the shift indicator is currently enabled. This method can be useful as a programmatic check to ensure that your shift indicator is enabled per the note above, despite what is seen (or not seen) on the display.

Data transfer. There are three methods to help you find and locate databases on the device and then send them via beaming to another device. You'll need to provide the Type ID and Creator ID of the database you are looking for to the *GetFirstDatabaseName* method, which will search for and return the first database that matches these parameters. (Database Type and Creator ID values are discussed in detail in Chapter 3.) You will notice that the Type and Creator ID parameters are actually long values. What *GetFirstDatabaseName* expects is the conversion of the ASCII values of the letters in the parameter's decimal number. To get this number, you first convert the individual letters to hexadecimal and place them side by side to create a number that then is converted to a decimal. For example, if you created a database and gave it a type of DATA, then the value is calculated as follows:

(D=44,A=41,T=54,A=41) = 44415441, then converted to decimal = 1145132097

Below is a function from the AppForge web site that performs the conversion for you.

```
Public Function PalmIDtoLong(PalmID As String) As Long
    Dim myLng As Long, Counter As Integer
    If Len(PalmID) = 4 Then
        For Counter = 1 To Len(PalmID)
            myLng = myLng * 256 + Asc(Mid(PalmID, Counter, 1))
        Next Counter
        PalmIDtoLong = myLng
    End If
End Function
```

The *GetFirstDatabaseName* method will also allow you to set a boolean flag that will narrow the search down even further. When the flag is set to true, the method returns only the latest version of the database for the device (in the event that multiple versions of the database exist). *GetNextDatabaseName* will return the next database meeting the criteria. Finally, you can pass a zero in for either the *Type* or Creator ID parameter as a wildcard that will return everything.

Once you have the database name, you can beam it via the infrared port to another device using the *SendDatabase* method. This method simply needs the database name on the device (as returned from the get methods previously described) and the PC style name to include the extension (usually *.pdb*). You can also provide a description to display on the receiving device as the last method parameter, if desired. For example, to send the database called MyAppDB to another device, the code would look like the following (we'll use the *GetFirstDatabaseName* method, just for kicks):

```
Dim strDBName As String

strDBName = GetFirstDatabaseName(PalmIDtoLong("DATA"), _
    PalmIDtoLong("MyAppDB"), True)
SendDatabase(strDBName, strDBName & ".pdb", "Transferring" & strDBName)
```

Preferences management. This is functionality that many Palm applications leverage for storing state information that is similar to how desktop applications save their state in the windows registry or in INI files. The Palm OS way is to store them in the application preferences database. The Extended Functions library provides you with the methods necessary to interact with that database.

There are four methods to access the application preferences database, and another two to access the system preferences database. First, you must declare a UDT to hold your preferences.

```
Public Type tPrefs
    A as integer
    B as integer
End Type

Dim MyPrefs as tPrefs
```

Then, when opening the application, retrieve the settings by first getting the size of the preferences structure using *GetApplicationPreferencesSize*.

```
iPrefsSize = GetApplicationPreferencesSize({your creatorID}, 0, True)
```

Remember, the method requires your application's Creator ID to be converted to a long. Next, get the application preferences, if available. If the return from *GetApplicationPreferences* is not –1, then the preferences were retrieved successfully and are stored in the UDT. If no preferences were found, let's set new ones immediately using some default values.

```
iPrefsVer = GetApplicationPreferences({your creatorID}, 0, True, iPrefsSize,
VarPtr(MyPrefs))

    If iPrefsVer <> -1 Then
        'UDT now contains the retreived application prefs for you to use
    Else
        ' no prefs found, save new set by setting UDT values
         ' manually and setting the preferences now
        iPrefsSize = 4
        MyPrefs.A = 1 : MyPrefs.B = 2
        SetApplicationPreferences {your creatorID}, 0, True, iPrefsSize,
VarPtr(MyPrefs), iPrefsVer + 1
    End If
```

One thing to note is how *iPrefsSize* gets its value. This represents the size of our structure tPrefs. Every data type takes up a certain number of bytes. To calculate the size of the structure manually, total the number of bytes per data type for each variable in the structure. (We'll discuss the various data types and their physical sizes in Chapter 3.) To dynamically calculate the size correctly, the tPrefs structure must be altered by adding a delimiter variable, sized as a byte, to the end of the structure. So the structure becomes:

```
Public Type tPrefs
    A as integer
    B as integer
    EOStruct as byte
End Type

Dim MyPrefs as tPrefs
```

Then calculate *iPrefsSize* as follows:

```
iPrefsSize = VarPtr(MyPrefs.EOStruct) - VarPtr(MyPrefs)
```

GetApplicationPreferencesVersion can be called to get the version number of the preferences stored for the specified application, but the same value is returned when the preferences are retrieved successfully. Use this function when you want to get the version without physically retrieving the preferences.

AppForge has one major limitation to the application preferences functionality: it does not support strings (either variable or fixed-length). This is due to a problem internally mapping strings to the fixed-size byte blocks required by the Palm OS.

Limited access to system preferences is available via two methods: *GetSystemPreference* and *SetSystemPreference*. First, you must provide a constant that indicates the desired setting you want to retrieve. The return is always a long value. In cases when a string would be passed, such as a Creator ID, you must reverse the procedure described above to convert from a long to the string representation. Setting a preference is straightforward: simply provide the setting constant and new value (again, always a long). There are over 50 possible constants, which are listed in Appendix A. Not all of these settings is available for all devices; they are based on the version of the Palm OS. To determine what version is available, call the *GetSystemPreference* method with the afExtLibSysPrefVersion constant. Table 2-5 shows the relationship between the Preference and OS versions.

Table 2-5. System preference versions

Preference version	Palm OS version
-1	N/A
2	2.0
3	3.0
4	3.1
5	3.2
6	3.3
8	3.5
9	4.0

The table in the appendix indicates, where applicable, what preferences have version limitations.

Device status. These functions will return values about the current status of a part of the device. *GetHeapFree*, *GetHeapLargestFree*, and *GetHeapSize* provide information about a device's memory. There are two methods to *GetRomSerialNumber*, if a serial number exists, and one method to get the booster *RuntimeVersion* number. Finally, *GetBatteryRemaining* returns the status of the onboard battery, and *KeepAwake* will reset the automatic power-off timer that forces the device to stay powered up for long periods of user inactivity while your application is performing some task such as reading or writing data to a serial port. This last command is used in the alarm clock example later in the chapter.

Palm OS Extensibility library

This library appears unwittingly simple. It contains only two functions: *LaunchApp* and *CallApp*. These two functions are the starting point to gaining access to other Palm applications. The *LaunchApp* method takes only the name of a Palm aApplication (a PRC file) without the *.PRC* file extension. This method's purpose is to launch another application, as if the user clicked on its icon in the launcher, and to close down the calling application. So if you had a PRC called MyApp installed, then:

```
AfPalmOS.LaunchApp "MyApp"
```

would close the calling application and start MyApp. (Remember, we are passing the actual name of the PRC and not the name displayed in the application launcher.) You can use *CallApp* to make calls into another PRC and to have it perform functions without closing the calling application. You still pass it the PRC name, but you must also pass it a *Launch Code* and the pointer to a defined structure (in VB, this is accomplished by using the *VarPtr* function). Here's how this works. Every native Palm application written in C has a PilotMain() that is the entry point to the application. It accepts a launch code that is evaluated in a C Switch statement that determines what action to take.

For example, if a Palm application called CalcMe took two numbers and returned their sum, you would first declare a UDT.

```
Private Type CalcMeData
    A As Integer
    B As Integer
    Result As Integer
End Type
```

Then you would define the Const for the application's available launch codes.

```
Const cmdAdd = 32768
Const cmdSub = 32769
```

Now, making the call will perform the desired operation on the two numbers.

```
Dim X as CalcMeData
X.A = 3 : X.B = 6
Call AfPalmOS.CallApp("CalcMe",cmdAdd,VarPtr(X))
```

The result of 9 is stored in X.Result. Currently, AppForge does not provide a way to define application input parameters, so this must be accomplished by writing a fuser application. A fuser application provides a "bridge" between your AppForge application and other native Palm applications.

PDB library

This is a specialized library that provides a host of methods to accomplish all your Palm database management requirements. Chapter 3 will cover this library in detail, so we will defer further discussion until then.

So far, we've seen some example code on how to use these libraries. Now let's get started by using the libraries, the provided ingots, and a little ingenuity to get around some tasks that are not directly supported by AppForge.

Friction Loss Calculator Example

Our first example is quite simple, but covers a lot of functionality we've discussed to this point. Specifically, this example:

- Implements the UI design concepts that we previously discussed to include implementation of a dialog and tip window
- Introduces the CheckBox and ComboBox ingots
- Implements a complete menu system
- Demonstrates how to persist application state

Our basic friction loss calculator's purpose is to calculate the friction loss of water in pounds-per-square inch (PSI), as it travels the distance of a section of hose line. You might wonder who would use such a calculator. Well, a pump operator of a fire engine, for one. It's his responsibility to ensure that the correct PSI is being pumped at the nozzle so that the firefighter is discharging water at the correct gallons per minute (GPM). So, calculating the friction of all the hose sections from the pump to the nozzle (plus some other stuff we're not going into) can be added to the starting pump PSI to achieve the desired result.

Let's start with the interface, which is shown in Figure 2-13.

As we can see from the main screen, the calculation takes three parameters. Tapping the Compute button updates the label at the bottom. Checking Round Results will round the value off to the nearest whole number. (For a pump operator, the dial is usually calibrated in 10-PSI increments, so fractions are kind of meaningless.) As expected, the code for this example was derived from the previous example. Using this code as a starting point, the application was quickly completed. Since the base code for the menu already existed, it simply needed to be modified for our specific needs.

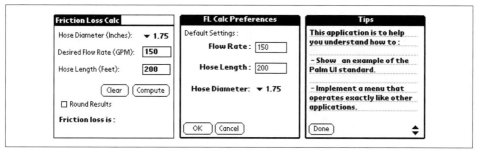

Figure 2-13. FlCalc application windows

The menu items were changed to meaningful labels (as seen in Figure 2-14) and the code for each Click event was modified to either open the tip or dialog window, respectively.

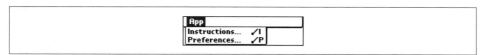

Figure 2-14. FlCalc Menu

The final addition to the application is storing application state. We've already seen, earlier in this chapter, the framework required to access and store values to the application preferences database. To recap, we will attempt to access the preferences database for any stored values. Our preferences structure looks like the following:

```
Public Type tPrefs
    Flow As Integer
    Length As Integer
    Diameter As Integer
End Type

Dim mudtPrefs As tPrefs
```

When the application opens, we attempt to retrieve the values from the preferences database. If we find them, they're retrieved into the UDT and made available for consumption by the application. If they're not found, we immediately set the database with a default set of values as a baseline for the next time we access it.

```
Private Sub GetAppPrefs()
  giPrefsSize=afExtLib.GetApplicationPreferencesSize(PalmIDtoLong("OR33"),0,
True)

    ' Initialize the state of the app, using saved preferences when possible
    giPrefsVer = afExtLib.GetApplicationPreferences(PalmIDtoLong("OR33"), 0, True,
giPrefsSize, VarPtr(mudtPrefs))

    If giPrefsVer <> -1 Then
        txtFlow.Text = mudtPrefs.Flow
        txtLength.Text = mudtPrefs.Length
        cboDiameter.ListIndex = mudtPrefs.Diameter
```

```
        Else
            ' no prefs, save new set
            giPrefsSize = 6 'Calced manually, 2 + 2 + 2 = 6
            mudtPrefs.Flow = 150
            mudtPrefs.Length = 200
            mudtPrefs.Diameter = 1
            afExtLib.SetApplicationPreferences PalmIDtoLong("OR33"), 0, True,
    giPrefsSize, VarPtr(mudtPrefs), giPrefsVer + 1
            txtFlow.Text = mudtPrefs.Flow
            txtLength.Text = mudtPrefs.Length
            cboDiameter.ListIndex = mudtPrefs.Diameter
        End If
        giDefFlow = mudtPrefs.Flow
        giDefLength = mudtPrefs.Length
        giDefDiameter = mudtPrefs.Diameter

    End Sub
```

Of course, you want the user to be able to store changes to the preferences from the preference dialog window. Once the user makes changes to the preferences in the window, update the UDT and save to the preference database. This is done using the *SetApplicationPreferences* function.

```
        afExtLib.SetApplicationPreferences PalmIDtoLong("OR33"), 0, True, giPrefsSize,
    VarPtr(mudtPrefs), giPrefsVer + 1
```

The next time the user taps the Clear button on the main form, the fields are replaced with the current values. Exiting and reopening the application will retrieve and display the new values.

Let's briefly look at the ingots introduced by this example, CheckBox and ComboBox.

CheckBox ingot

The CheckBox ingot allows users to make one or more selections that do not depend on the selection of other controls. The checkbox is used primarily to determine a true or false condition.

The checkbox differs from its Windows counterpart in several checkbox-specific attributes.

- The ingot's *AllowGreyState* property must be explicitly set in order to set the *Value* property to two (grayed). Windows checkboxes provide no such restriction.

- The ingot does not support the graphical button style that Windows checkboxes do.

Stylistically, controls and menu items are removed instead of being disabled or "grayed out" on the Palm. However, this usage emulates the third state of a Windows checkbox, in which the gray state usually signifies a subcollection of controls, such as a group of checkboxes, which have a mix of true and false states.

ComboBox ingot

The ComboBox ingot allows the user to enter data via a text box or to select from a list of options. The same three styles from the Windows combo box are available: simple combination, drop-down combination, or drop-down list. The major combo box-specific differences are:

- The ingot supports an *Alignment* property for the text in the text box portion of the control.
- The ingot does not support the *NewIndex*, *TopIndex*, *Integral Height* (auto-height resizing, ensuring no partial item displays), or *Sorted* properties.

Cut, Copy, Paste Example

This example details how to implement the cut, copy, and paste functionality using a command bar graffiti entry, which demonstrates the use of the Graffiti shift display mechanisms. As an added feature, we examine the use of the text sizing functions available from the Extended Functions library. The application provides for button and menu invocation of the cut, copy, and paste commands. The example also captures two keycodes during execution: the Menu and Find silkscreen buttons. The Menu button was captured in order to disable the display of the menu, since we have only one menu title. This is rather unorthodox, but it could have value if you did not want the menu displayed during operation, as with a game, but you still want your application to respond to menu shortcut commands. We intercept the Find button and use it to demonstrate how to implement context-sensitive help on the two text boxes, but this could be expanded for any controls you like.

The form is also configured to display the Graffiti shift state, as necessary. The Graffiti shift state is displayed as special symbols that visually indicate the mode in which you are operating. Figure 2-15 shows a symbol (.) in the lower right corner of the screen, indicating that the punctuation mode is active. For more information about the various shift states, refer to Palm's Graffiti help application on the device.

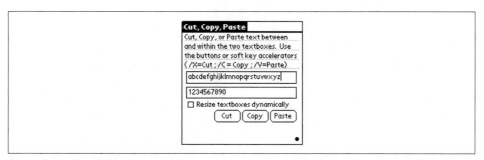

Figure 2-15. Cut, Copy, Paste example

Let's look at the additional code to support this. First we need to register the *keycode* for the `Find` and `Menu` silkscreen buttons in the *Form_Load* event. We must also remember to set the *KeyPreview* property of the form to True.

```
RegisterKeyCode vchrFind
RegisterKeyCode vchrMenu
```

A module-level variable, `mFocusBox`, is dimensioned as an `AFTextbox` that will be used to store a reference to the current text box to keep track of which control to get or put the copied text to. There are also other variables defined to store the *SelStart*, *SelLength*, and *SelText* values of the text box with focus. When a user taps focus to a text box, the following line is executed:

```
Set mFocusBox = txtSource1
```

The Graffiti shift mechanism is set up in the *Form_Activate* event.

```
GraffitiShiftIndicatorInitialize
GraffitiShiftIndicatorEnable True
GraffitiShiftIndicatorSetLocation 148, 148
GraffitiSetShiftState afExtLibShiftNone
```

The bulk of the code to handle the cut, copy, and paste in simple procedures is called by the button or menu activation.

```
Private Sub CopyOp( )
    afExtLib.ClipboardSetString mFocusBox.SelText
End Sub
Private Sub CutOp( )
    afExtLib.ClipboardSetString mFocusBox.SelText
    mFocusBox.SelText = ""
End Sub
Private Sub PasteOp( )
    If mFocusBox.SelLength = 0 Then
        mFocusBox.Text = Left(mFocusBox.Text, mFocusBox.SelStart) & _
                         afExtLib.ClipboardGetString & _
                         Mid(mFocusBox.Text, mFocusBox.SelStart + 1)
    Else
        mFocusBox.SelText = afExtLib.ClipboardGetString( )
    End If
End Sub
```

As you can see, selecting `Cut` or `Copy` will call *ClipBoardSetString*, passing it the selected text from the control. You'll note that the cut operation has the following line:

```
mFocusBox.SelText = ""
```

Setting the *SelText* will replace the string fragment cut with an empty string. Otherwise, the copied text is left in place. The paste operation will either insert the text from the *ClipBoardGetString* method at the current insertion point or replace the highlighted text if some text is selected.

When we capture the menu silkscreen key, we just ignore it; this will prevent our menu from displaying. Each text box's *Tag* property was set to a simple help text string. So when the user has focus in one of the text boxes and the Find silkscreen button is clicked, the form intercepts the request in the *Form_KeyDown* event as follows:

```
Private Sub Form_KeyDown(KeyCode As Integer, Shift As Integer)
    'intercept find silkscreen button
    If KeyCode = vchrFind Then MsgBox mFocusBox.Tag
End Sub
```

A message box with the appropriate help string is displayed. You can expand and enhance this context help concept as much as you desire.

Finally, if you elect to have the text boxes dynamically resized, the text box with focus will resize to fit the string size:

```
mFocusBox.Width = StringWidth("AFPalm", 12, 0, mFocusBox.Text)
mFocusBox.Height = FontHeight("AFPalm", 12, 0)
```

Alarm Clock Example

This example focuses on interacting with the device's hardware by implementing a simple alarm clock. Specifically, this example:

- Demonstrates how to use push-style buttons and custom fonts
- Demonstrates how to access the Palm date or time picker.
- Introduces the Timer and Tone ingots
- Captures the device's hard buttons

One of the first things you'll notice is the use of custom fonts. The font used is Times New Roman bold, 18- and 36-pixel size (the point weights are 13 and 26, respectively). The clock continually displays the time as long as the program is loaded. Tapping the Time button to set the alarm brings up the built-in Palm time picker. The returned time is displayed in the text box, as shown in Figure 2-16.

Figure 2-16. Alarm clock interface

Taping the On push button will enable the alarm to go off at the specified time. The Snooze button stops the alarm, but will sound the alarm every five minutes until the alarm is turned off. Simple, right? Let's take a look.

First and foremost, this is a clock, and therefore it displays the current time when the application loads. The clock face needs to be visible at a distance and therefore requires a larger font than provided. You can use the AppForge Font Conversion Tool to convert any subset of characters in any font.

The converter tool, which is shown in Figure 2-17, lets you select the desired True Type font, as well as the pixel size and style (bold, italic, etc.). You pick the upper and lower range of characters set to convert. This is very important, since the size and number of characters will determine the size of the resulting AppForge font file (*.CMF* extension). For example, the Times New Roman, 10-pixel conversion resulted in a 3K file, while the Clock face font, Times New Roman 36-pixel, converted to a 10K file. That's a big difference, so be wary of the increased size of your finished application.

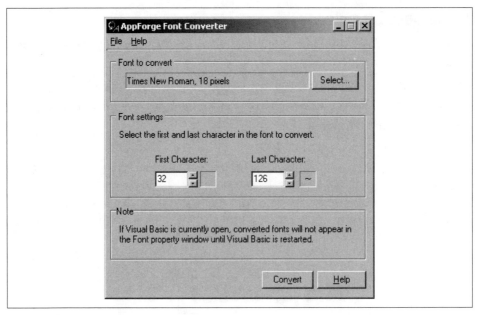

Figure 2-17. Font converter

 If you have Microsoft Plus!® installed, you must disable the "font smoothing" option for the Font Converter to work correctly.

AppForge also provides a font viewer tool that allows you to view the converted font character set and provides some useful information, especially the corresponding point weight of the font's pixel size.

The timer is turned on or off by tapping the Alarm On and Off buttons. Notice that these are push-type buttons and are larger than normal to allow for easier finger activation by the user. The application will also capture the rightmost hard button as another means of turning off the alarm and clearing the alarm time.

A label control array was used for the push buttons and, based on the state of which one was last clicked, will determine how to set both ingots' fore and background colors. Labels were used, but other ingot types, like a button, graphic button, or graphic, could have also been used.

The application operates around two Timer ingots:

Clock Timer (1-second cycle)
> The clock timer is used to continually set the time.

Snooze Timer (5-minute cycle)
> When the timer expires, the snooze timer sets the clock back to alarm-sounding mode.

For the clock to work, the device must never automatically power off. If it does power off, the clock stops, and when you finally reactivate the unit, you are back to square one. To avoid this, call the *KeepAwake* method, which suspends the auto-shutoff timer. It is important to periodically call this method to avoid potential problems in your application, since processing may nullify the effect of the call. In the clock example, you will see from the code that it is called at the end of every clock timer cycle.

Timer ingot

The Timer ingot operates exactly like the Windows timers, with one major exception: the ingot is not limited to a 65,535-millisecond interval, as is the Windows Timer control. The limit on the *Interval* property is due to its internal definition as an unsigned 2 byte integer.

Tone ingot

This unique ingot allows you to play tones via the handheld device's audio channel. The Tone ingot is very simple to use. Set the *Pitch* property to the desired tone in hertz (cycles per second). Then set the *Duration* of the tone (in milliseconds). Calling the *Play* method plays the tone for the specified duration. AppForge was nice enough to provide a list of approximate values for the notes in five octaves, as shown in Table 2-6. The "s" in the Note column of the table indicates a sharp note.

Table 2-6. Pitch values for musical notes

Note	1st octave	2nd octave	3rd octave	4th octave	5th octave
C	262	523	1047	2093	4186
Cs	277	554	1108	2218	-
D	295	587	1175	2349	-
Ds	311	622	1245	2489	-
E	330	659	1319	2637	-
F	349	699	1397	2794	-
Fs	370	740	1480	2960	-
G	392	784	1568	3136	-
Gs	415	831	1661	3322	-
A	440	880	1760	3520	-
As	466	932	1864	3729	-
B	494	988	1976	3951	-

When we enter the alarm state, we get an audible tone, and the time display flashes for every cycle of the clock timer.

```
Private Sub SoundAlarm( )
    'Sounds the alarm and flashes the time display
    Alarm.Pitch = 1760
    Alarm.Duration = 1000
    Alarm.Play
    If lblTime.BackColor = afLabelBackground Then
        lblTime.ForeColor = afLabelBackground
        lblTime.BackColor = afLabelBlack
    Else
        lblTime.ForeColor = afLabelBlack
        lblTime.BackColor = afLabelBackground
    End If
End Sub
```

Virtual Menu Example

Now let's look at expanding our capabilities to accessing wireless resources via the INetHTTP ingot. This ingot has a variety of methods and events that give you the means to connect to the Web by using the Palm Internet Library (InetLib) on the device, if it's installed. The library is part of the Palm OS 4.0 or later versions. If you don't have the library, you will need to install it *and* have a wireless modem attached to the target handheld device. This example application:

- Introduces the INetHTTP, Filmstrip, and Graphic button ingots
- Demonstrates how to access the World Wide Web and interact with an ASP page
- Demonstrates how to perform rudimentary parsing on an XML document

Our example application's purpose is to allow users to view a "virtual menu" of what to eat and drink at the fictitious Sterling Brewing Company's brewpub. It opens to an entry screen with the look-and-feel of a web page. Clicking on the Beers On Tap or Pub Grub buttons will cause the application to attempt to connect to the Sterling Brewing Company web site and download an XML file containing the desired data. Clicking the Contact Us button will open a form to collect the user's email address and will interact with an ASP page that would store the email and respond with a return string that is displayed in a message box to confirm the addition to the company's newsletter mailing list, as shown in Figure 2-18.

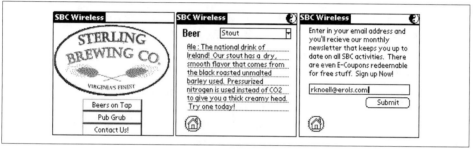

Figure 2-18. The Sterling Brewing Company wireless interface

In the upper righthand corner, we'll display a spinner (like a browser) that rotates while the request and responses to the Web occur. There is also the familiar Home button in the lower left corner, which returns you to the main page if tapped.

The application's detail window, frmDetail, is host to all three options from the main page. The buttons on the main page are actually a control index, so tapping a button hides the main form and shows the detail form calling a form initialization procedure, FormSet, and passing it the button index. The detail window then changes the UI appropriately for the option selected by the user and makes the HTTP request via the INtetHTTP ingot. Let's review what this ingot has to offer.

INetHTTP ingot

This ingot is very simple to use. What's important is to ensure that you have your device's wireless connection ready to go. Palm devices can connect to the Internet using an infrared-enabled mobile phone, a modem, or the built-in wireless support in the Palm VII.

Internet content is accessible to Palm devices via web clipping technology. This technology extracts only a subset of a web site's content, keeping undesirable or unusable information to a minimum. Chapter 6 provides detailed coverage of this topic.

The basic operation for using the ingot involves first setting the *URL* and *Document* properties. Table 2-7 shows the relationship between the two properties.

Table 2-7. Properties versus request type

Request type	URL property	Document property
Get	The fully qualified URL for which to search. Only *http://* or *https://* are valid protocol prefixes.	None, leave empty (*""*).
Post	The fully qualified base URL for which to search. Only *http://* or *https://* are valid protocol prefixes.	The parameters of the search to the right of the question mark in the URL. This usually represents the form data submitted by the user.

For example, the fully qualified URL for a Microsoft stock quote from Bloomberg.com, *http://quote.bloomberg.com/analytics/quote.cgi?ticker=MSFT,* would be coded as:

```
Inet1.URL = "http://quote.bloomberg.com/analytics/quote.cgi"
Inet1.Document = "ticker=MSFT"
```

In our example, we set the *URL* property to request the return of an XML document that contains the data for the beers currently on tap at the pub or the current menu items. The *Execute* method is called and the request is made. The ingot then monitors the connection and may trigger any of its three events:

StateChanged event
> This event receives notification about the state of the connection. There are 13 different states to capture and respond to.

ReceivedData event
> This event is triggered for every new block of data (or a "chunk") that is successfully received by the ingot. The event reports the total number of bytes received for this request.

Error event
> This event is triggered when an error is encountered on the connection. The error number is reported to the *SystemError* property. The AppForge documentation lists what these codes mean.

Sometimes the AppForge documentation lists the error numbers incorrectly. The actual error number is 5120 plus the listed number. For example, if the Palm Internet Library is missing from the device, the INetHTTP ingot will report 5129, which corresponds to error 9, no connection available.

When the *StateChanged* event reports a Response Received state, it's time to begin collecting the data from the HTTP inbound stream.

```
Dim strData As String
Dim strChunk As String
Dim bSuccess As Boolean

Select Case newState
    .
    .
    .
    Case afINetHTTPStatusResponseReceived
    lblStatus.Caption = "Response Rcved"
        lblStatus.Refresh
        Ying.Stop
        strData = ""
        strChunk = INet.GetChunk(100)
        Do While strChunk <> ""
            strData = strData + strChunk
            strChunk = INet.GetChunk(100)
        Loop
        'Parse the data and if valid display it
        If ParseData(strData) Then
            Displaydata
        Else
            lblStatus.Caption = "Retrieve Error"
            ClearData
        End If
        lblStatus.Caption = ""
End Select
```

We accomplish this by using the *GetChunk* method. This method takes a *long* as a parameter, indicating how many bytes to read at a time from the server. The method returns a string of data with a maximum length based on the size parameter. If no more data is available to be read, an empty string is returned.

Once you have the string, it is your responsibility to format the data for presentation to the user. In our example, the string is passed to the *ParseData* function, where applicable data is parsed out. The parsed data is temporarily stored in an array of UDTs before displaying the data in the appropriate ingots.

The final operation that our example application performs is interacting with an ASP page on the server. Our example collects an email address from the user and transmits it to the server via a POST operation:*

```
INet.URL = "http://{your server}/processReq.asp"
INet.Document = "email=" & txtEmail.Text
Ying.Play
INet.Execute
```

---

* The "Ying" object referenced in the code is a rotating yin-yang (implemented using the Filmstrip ingot) that is located in the top right corner of the application's forms (see Figure 2-18).

On the server, our ASP page receives the request, gets the value from the Form collection, and then responds with a custom message. In reality, we would potentially store the email in a database for future use.

```
<%@ Language=VBScript %>
<% Option Explicit %>
<% Response.Buffer = true%>
<html>
<head>
</head>
    <%
        dim strEmail
        strEmail = Request.Form("email")
    %>
<body>

    <% select case strEmail
        case "" %>
            <p ID="SBCreply">Sorry, your request was not processed
            correctly, please try again!</p>
        <% case else %>
            <p ID="SBCreply">Thanks for Joining SBC On-line.  Our
            newsletter will be send to <%=strEmail%></p>
    <%end select%>
</body>
</html>
```

That's about it. There are other methods and properties from the ingot that you'll want to use for your own applications. If you want to cancel a transaction in progress, you can check the *StillExecuting* method to ensure that there is still activity and then call the *Cancel* method to close the connection. Another useful property is *ConnectionAvailable*. This property can be checked at the start of an application to ensure that the device has the Palm Internet Library installed. If this returns false, the device is not configured to make a connection.

Some additional things you can do are set the *RequestTimeout* property so that your connection doesn't hang or so that you can provide additional information to the user via the *ResponseCode* and *ResponseInfo* properties. Finally, you can get and access POST header variables using the *GetHeader* method. If you need to send non-alphanumeric data, use the *URLEncodestring* method to make the data HTTP-compliant.

 If you want to use the INetHTTP ingot in an application over a LAN, you must ensure that it can access and communicate with the Palm. Net proxy server located at *http://oasis.palm.com/dev/proxy*. This is a requirement for the Palm Internet Library, since all HTTP transactions must go through this proxy server.

A maximum of four INetHTTP ingots can operate simultaneously on a form.

Filmstrip ingot

In our code samples, we used the Filmstrip ingot via the spinner control in the upper right of the screen. This control rotates as the HTTP transaction is in process. It is relatively simple to use after you configure it. First, convert all the graphics that will be used in the animation to AppForge RGX format (you can use bitmap files, if desired). Then insert each picture into a frame. A series of frames constitutes the animation. The frames can be added at design time by selecting and ordering the list of image files into the *Frames* property. A frame can also be added or removed at runtime using the *AddFrame* and *RemoveFrame* methods, respectively (all frames can be removed by calling the *ClearFrames* method). Each frame in an animation has a *FrameIndex* associated with it, ranging from 0 to − 1. To determine how the animation is to be played, the *AnimationStyle* can be set to play in:

Single play mode
> The animation is played to the end. When the last frame is displayed, the *LastFrame* event is triggered. The ingot leaves the last frame displayed.

Loop play mode
> The animation is played continuously, looping from the last to the first frame, until the animation is stopped. The *LastFrame* event is triggered each time the end frame is displayed.

Bounce mode
> The animation plays to the end and then plays in reverse to the beginning frame. The animation continues to play until it's stopped. The *LastFrame* event is triggered each time the end frame is displayed.

Finally, the time lag between displaying frames can be set using the *Interval* property. Its default value is set to 400 milliseconds, but you can change the value to whatever you like, although the actual hardware will determine how fast the animation can truly be displayed.

To control the animation, call the *Play* and *Stop* methods. Stopping an animation leaves it at the last frame displayed. It can be restarted from the current frame with another call to *Play*. An animation will also continue to play even if the form that it's on is hidden.

Graphic Button ingot

This ingot operates exactly as a command button does. Its only difference is that the button face itself can be a bitmap (for color) or a bitmap graphic converted to the AppForge RGX format. To configure this ingot, simply select an image file or files for each of the following properties: *FocusPicture*, *NoFocusPicture*, *DownPicture*, and *DisabledPicture*.

Signature Collector Example

This application is also rather unique in that its purpose is to collect a signature on the handheld device and to store it in a Palm database. After the user performs a HotSync to the desktop, the database is then available for access by a standard Windows desktop application. Our example takes a selected signature, converts it to a bitmap, and displays it in a fictitious sales receipt. The example uses the PDB library, which is covered in detail in Chapter 3, so we will not spend time here reviewing the database management code.

As you can see in Figure 2-19, the Signature Capture ingot takes up most of the screen. The application simply allows you to add, update, or delete the database records consisting of a name and signature.

Figure 2-19. Signature collector

The Signature ingot

This is another ingot that is very simple to use. Most of its properties simply adjust its appearance before and during operation. You can set a background picture via the *BackPicture* property or change the background color via the *BackColor* property. To contrast your background choices, you can also change the *PenWidth* and *PenColor* properties.

The most important property, *SignatureData*, is where your signature is stored. The property holds the data as a string, where each character is the x or y coordinate for each point in the signature. A flag character is used whenever the user lifts the pen.

The ingot also supports a *Clear* method, which clears the data from the display, and the *SignatureData* property.

The collector is the trivial part of this example, compared to the desktop application, which will convert the string data into a Picturebox control that will then allow us to save the signature to a bitmap file. The desktop application uses the PDB library to open and access the signature database. The signature is then rendered into the Picturebox control using a *RenderSignature* function, provided by AppForge.

```
Private Type SigPoint
    X As Long
    Y As Long
End Type
Const PENUP As Long = &HFFFF

Public Sub RenderSignature(ByVal SigData As String)
'This is the recommended way to render on
'picture control by AppForge
    Dim I As Long
    Dim lLength As Long
    Dim udtPoint As SigPoint
    Dim udtOldPoint As SigPoint

    lLength = Len(SigData)
    picSig.Cls

    'set point to start values
    udtOldPoint.X = -1
    udtOldPoint.Y = -1

    For I = 1 To lLength
        udtPoint.X = AscW(Mid(SigData, I, 1))
        'if pen is down then render point
        If udtPoint.X <> PENUP Then
            I = I + 1
            udtPoint.Y = AscW(Mid(SigData, I, 1))
            If udtOldPoint.X <> -1 Then
                picSig.Line (udtOldPoint.X, udtOldPoint.Y)-(udtPoint.X,
                            udtPoint.Y)
            End If
            udtOldPoint = udtPoint
        Else 'catch next pen down point
            If udtOldPoint.X <> -1 Then
                picSig.PSet (udtOldPoint.X, udtOldPoint.Y)
            End If
            udtOldPoint.X = -1
            udtOldPoint.Y = -1
        End If
    Next I
End Sub
```

To then save the contents of the Picturebox control, you can employ the services of a seldom-used VB method, *SavePicture*. The method requires the contents of the Picturebox's *Image* property and the name of the file to which it should save.

```
SavePicture picSig.Image, "c:\temp\sig.bmp"
```

From there, you can open it into any form of report generator. In our example, it is placed as part of a browser-based receipt (*receipt.html*) from our fictitious brewpub. (This example assumes you have the correct paths to both the Internet Explorer and *receipt.html* files.)

```
'open example reciept into browser
Shell "c:\program files\internet explorer\iexplore.exe
        c:\book\chap3\code\ex6\receipt.html", vbNormalFocus
```

The receipt with the bitmap is shown in Figure 2-20.

Figure 2-20. SBC receipt with signature

Specialized Ingots

There are a few ingots that have specialized purposes. This book will not cover them in detail, as we have covered the other ingots. However, it is important to know some general information about them. These ingots are Movie, Serial, ClientSocket, and Scanner.

Movie ingot

The Movie ingot is not difficult to use; it's just that its utility is limited for the average application. Predominantly, this ingot is used to "spice up" an application, but at a price. This ingot, like the Filmstrip and other graphical ingots, requires an external file for the graphic source that ultimately increases the size of the deployed application.

The Movie ingot requires that an AVI-formatted movie be converted to an AppForge movie (*.rmv*) file. This is generated using the AppForge Movie converter utility. Like the Graphic converter utility, the only requirement is to select the desired AVI file and click the Convert button. You do have some say in how it's converted by changing the *Lossiness* and *PreQuantize* settings on the Settings tab. Changes to these setting will impact the size of the resulting converted movie. This is important, because if the converted file is larger than 64K, it is not readable by the device.

Serial ingot

The Serial ingot's purpose is to provide you with the ability to send and receive data through the device's cradle connection, infrared port, or modem. The ingot operates similarly to its Windows counterpart, the MS Comm control, but only supports one serial port on the handheld device.

The model for communicating using the Serial ingot can be either a polling model (where you make direct requests to send or receive data) or an event-driven model (where incoming data triggers the ingot's DataComm event, at which point you react). Setting the serial ingot's *CommPort* property determines the physical means of transmission: RS-232 Serial via the cradle, IrDA raw data via the infrared port, or an IrCOMM "virtual serial cable" via the infrared port or modem.

There are some limitations to successfully communicating using the Serial ingot. First, unless you're running Palm OS version 3.3 or higher, you may be missing some of the required components, so check your documentation and the Palm web site for details. Also, if you're using the *IrCOMM* protocol, the receiving device must also support that protocol.

ClientSocket ingot

This is a great ingot that provides two-way socket communications between a client and a server. It can be set to any port you desire and supports TCP and UDP protocols. It's named ClientSocket for good reason—it can only participate in a socket session as a client, which means that the application must open the port and initiate communication. It cannot listen on a port, as a socket server can.

Its operation is quite simple; first, set the *RemoteHostIP* property with the server's IP address. (The ingot also provides a *ResolveHostName* method that returns the resolved IP address for the provided dotted-quad address.) Next, set the *RemotePort* and *Protocol* (TCP default) properties as desired. Finally, call the *Connect* method to connect the socket to the server.

Once the connection is established, you can send data via any of the following methods: *SendByte*, *SendInteger*, *SendLong*, or *SendString*.

When data arrives on the port from the server, a `DataWaiting` event is triggered, allowing you to retrieve the data via the following methods, as appropriate: *GetByte*, *GetInteger*, *GetLong*, or *GetString*.

When you are done communicating, call the *Close* method to close the socket.

Scanner ingot

The Scanner ingot is the most specialized ingot provided by AppForge. It has a wide variety of properties, methods, and events to provide support for the following scanners:

- Symbol Technologies® Model SPT1500
- Symbol Technologies® Model SPT1700
- Symbol Technologies® Model CSM-150 (Springboard module for Handspring Visor)

Appendix A provides the listings for all ingots.

Palm application development is a challenging task that can provide many benefits to end users—if applications are designed properly. AppForge provides a foundation on which to build Palm applications to meet almost any requirement. By following some basic Palm UI style guidelines, the AppForge developer can create dynamic and stimulating applications in the rapid development cycle demanded by today's software development firms.

CHAPTER 3

Palm Database Programming

Palm programs, like other programs, typically use some form of persistent data storage. In Chapter 2, we examined how to access the application preferences database to store and retrieve state information, but this form of storage is best suited for small amounts of data. The Palm database manager is the tool of choice for an application's working data.

In this chapter, we first explain what the Palm OS database manager is and how it works. We'll look at the different types of databases the Palm supports, and explain the physical layout and characteristics of the most common database—the Palm data file (PDB).

Then we show you how to access the Palm database features via the AppForge PDB library, which provides all the functionality needed to create and manipulate databases and records. We introduce many of the database features with snippets of code showing how the library is used. We also explain the AppForge database schema extensions, which free you from many bookkeeping chores normally associated with Palm database programming.

Next, we cover a very useful AppForge database tool: the Database Converter. This Windows program converts Microsoft Access databases into Palm PDB files for use in your applications.

Finally, we provide an example application that reinforces the material introduced both in Chapter 2 and in this chapter. We have migrated parts of the North Wind Traders Inventory application—a standard example program distributed by Microsoft—to the Palm device to show how to support some business functions on the Palm device.

The North Wind application also introduces the AppForge Grid ingot, which is a powerful method for displaying record data.

The Palm Database

There are two main types of databases in the Palm OS:

Palm Record Database (PDB)
    This is a record-oriented database that is used to store application data.

Palm Resource Database (PRC)
    This database is similar to the PDB, but stores application code and Palm OS resources. Palm applications themselves are PRC files.

This chapter focuses on the Palm Record databases, which are the main data repositories on the Palm device.* It is important to recognize that Palm databases have different physical implementations, depending if they are on the desktop or on the Palm device. The PDB is stored on the desktop as a normal disk file, with a well-defined format. Once uploaded to the Palm device, the PDB has a proprietary in-memory format, since the Palm OS does not support a filesystem. Instead, the database is organized as blocks of memory under the control of the Palm database and resource manager, which prevents direct programmer access to these structures. Most databases are slightly larger than their file size when stored on the Palm device due to the addition of control information by the memory manager.

Let's look at the logical structure of the Palm database (see Figure 3-1). The database consists of a fixed header block, a variable-length list of record location entries, and optional application and sort information blocks, followed by the physical data pages. The structure is essentially an Indexed Sequential Access Method (ISAM) database, where the record entry section contains indexes (pointers) to the actual record data blocks. The SortInfo block can also contain a pointer to the records to maintain a logical sorting, distinct from the physical record order.

If you are used to thinking about databases in relational terms, you should think of each Palm database as a *single* table. Because there is no defined structure to a Palm database, the application developer must provide code that implements any desired relationships. As you might imagine, this is a challenge when programming data-driven applications in the Palm environment. For now, consider the Palm database to be a flat-file database. We cover the conversion, use, and synchronization of SQL databases later in Chapter 4 and Chapter 5.

Database Header Block

The database header contains the administrative information for the PDB file, as shown in Table 3-1.

---

* There is a third type of Palm database, the Palm Query Application (PQA). This is just a PRC database that is handled specially by the Palm OS for wireless data access. We discuss building and using PQA files at length in Chapter 6, *Web Clipping Applications*.

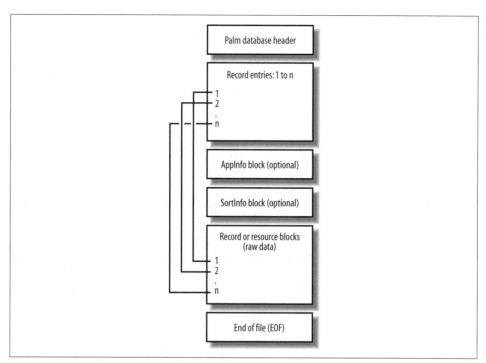

Figure 3-1. Palm database logical format

Table 3-1. PDB header fields

Field	Type/size (bytes)	Meaning
Name	String (32)	Internal name used by the Palm OS to reference the PDB
Attributes	Integer (2)	Flags, such as copy protected or read-only
Version	Integer (2)	Application-specific entry
CreationDate	Long (4)	Time database was created, specified in Palm date format[a]
ModificationDate	Long (4)	Time database was last changed
BackupDate	Long (4)	Time of most recent backup via the HotSync manager
ModificationNumber	Long (4)	Application-specific entry
AppInfoID	Long (4)	Offset from database header to application info block[b]
SortInfoID	Long (4)	Offset from database header to sort info block
Type	Long (4)	Application-specific field, governed by convention
Creator ID	Long (4)	The identifier of the application creator (registered with Palm)
UniqueIDSeed	Long (4)	Sequence number used for new records

[a] Palm dates are stored as the number of seconds since 12:00 AM, January 1, 1904.
[b] These offsets are only meaningful in the file representation of a Palm database.

None of these fields are directly accessible to the Palm VB programmer; we discuss how they are accessed using the AppForge PDB library later in this chapter. Of particular interest, however, are the Creator ID, Type, and Attributes fields.

The Palm OS uses the Creator ID to differentiate the applications and databases on the Palm device. In general, it is good practice to assign the same identifier to all the databases that your application creates and accesses. This is because the database manager uses the Creator ID to aggregate resource and record databases. For example, this is how the Palm OS application launcher calculates the "size" of an application. And, by assigning the same Creator ID to an application and its database, you ensure that all these entities will be removed if the application itself is deleted.

If you specify a Creator ID for a PRC file that is not unique among the applications loaded on a Palm device, then the Palm OS will not know which application to execute—or even which application to load or display.*

The Type field has many uses, most governed by undocumented convention. For resource databases, this field indicates the type of resource contained in the file: appl for a program; pqa for a wireless application, and so on. For record databases, the field may have any value, although DATA is common for many Palm programs.

 Since version 3.0, the Palm OS sorts databases by Type, Creator ID, and version number. If your application accesses multiple databases, then you can increase its efficiency by changing the type identifier of the most heavily used database to place it higher in the sort order. Your application must make frequent use of many databases for this to pay off.

The Type field can be used in conjunction with the Creator ID to locate a database, instead of finding it by name. This is very useful if you want to use the database name for other purposes, but still be able to access the database easily from within your code.

The Attributes field consists of bitmapped flags that describe the database and its properties to the operating system. The flags include such information as the database type (record or resource), or if the database should be hidden from the user. Other flags control whether a database is read-only, or if it can be beamed via the infrared port. We'll cover all the available attributes later in the chapter (see Table 3-5).

Next in the logical database layout is the record entries section. In the disk file representation, there can be zero entries or one set of entries. Each record entry consists of the unique record identifier, the record attributes flag, and an offset to the actual record data located elsewhere in the file.

---

* This is why you should always register your application's Creator ID with Palm. We covered registration of Creator IDs in Chapter 1.

Application and Sort Info Blocks

Next there is the `AppInfo` block. This block of memory, which is optional, may be used by the application to store any desired data, such as custom settings.

Applications that support standard Palm categories must have the initial bytes of the `AppInfo` block arranged in a predefined format. The application-defined data then follows this category data. The Palm categories allow you to group records into standard and user-defined categories.

The AppForge PDB library fully supports categories, which we cover later in the chapter. AppForge does not, however, support any other access to the `AppInfo` block, which means that you cannot use this space for other purposes.

The `SortInfo` block is another optional section of the database, which may also be used by the application as it sees fit. This section is usually used to store sort order information for a particular view or queries of data. AppForge provides no direct access for this section.

AppForge PDB Library

The Palm database provides a straightforward and efficient mechanism to store application data. In fact, it is the only way to store large amounts of data on the device because the Palm OS lacks a true filesystem.

AppForge provides the PDB library to encapsulate and extend the Palm database manager. Because the PDB library is implemented as a Microsoft COM component, you use it by adding a reference to *afPDBLib.dll* to your VB project. The PDB library is simple to use. Its methods can be broken into the following groups, which we will explain in turn:

Database management
>   Performs functions such as creating new databases dynamically, with or without schemas, opening and closing existing databases, and deleting databases

Record management
>   Handles most record operations, such as creating, editing, and deleting, as well as record categories

Navigation
>   Covers moving between records in the database, as well as finding and sorting functions

Other functions
>   Handles reporting or changing the state of a database or record via specified attributes, as well as record counts and database error information

Database Management

It is easy to create a database, either programmatically, with code, or by converting from an existing database into a Palm database, with the following techniques:

- Use the AppForge PDB library in a Palm VB application to create an empty database directly on the Palm device
- Use the AppForge PDB converter utility that converts Microsoft Access databases to PDB files on the Windows desktop
- Develop a conduit to synchronize data between a Windows desktop data source and a PDB file on the Palm device
- Develop a VB application that uses the PDB library to create and populate a Palm database on the Windows desktop

In this chapter, we focus on the first two techniques: using the AppForge PDB library and converter utilities to create and manipulate Palm databases. We cover the later techniques in Chapter 4 and Chapter 5.

In Figure 3-2, we show the various database management functions provided by the AppForge PDB library.

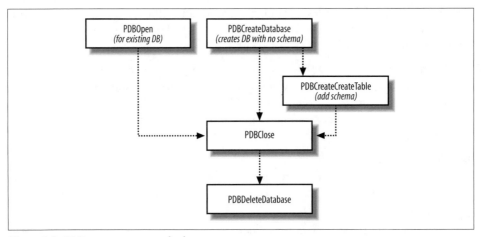

Figure 3-2. PDB management methods

To utilize the PDB library, you need to use *PDBCreateDatabase* to open a new database or *PDBOpen* to access an existing one. These methods return handles—long integers—to the just-opened database. Since these handles are used by almost every other method in the library, they must be carefully preserved.

Use the following code to create a database:

```
Const Creator ID As Long = &H4F523431 ' translates as "OR41"
Const TypeID As Long = &H44415441     ' translates as "DATA"

Dim lDB as Long
```

```
#If APPFORGE Then
    lDB = PDBCreateDatabase("MyDB", TypeID, Creator ID)
#Else
    lDB = PDBCreateDatabase(App.Path & "\MyDB", TypeID, Creator ID)
#End If
```

The *PDBCreateDatabase* method (along with others) requires the Creator ID and Type ID parameters to be long integer values, such as &H44415441. By convention, however, these identifiers are often expressed in code as string constants, such as DATA.[*]

Of course, this method also requires a name for the database of 31 characters or less. You do not specify an extension such as *.pdb*.

 Normally, you assign the PDB the same Creator ID as the PRC *app*lication. You *cannot* use the same name for both the PDB and PRC, since all database names must be unique. By convention, Palm developers append DB to get a unique PDB name. To ensure uniqueness, you might also add the creator to the name: MyDB-OR41.

We provide a simple function in Chapter 5 that converts from the string representation to a long integer. We convert each letter of the identifier to its ASCII hexadecimal value, and then place them side by side to create a number. For the type identifier DATA, this is:

(D=44,A=41,T=54,A=41) = 44415441 (Hex)

Note the use of the conditional compiler directive. The value APPFORGE is automatically defined; the AppForge VB add-in is compiling the code. This allows us to control the behavior of an application depending on the target runtime platform. In this case, we use this feature to control where the database is created when we are running on a Windows system. If a full path is not specified, then the AppForge library creates the file in the default working directory—often not where you expect it!

We cover the very complicated *PDBOpen* function, which is used to open existing databases, in detail later in this chapter.

Schemas

Once you have created a database on the Palm, you must consider what sort of data it will hold and how you will access it. There are two basic approaches:

1. Treat the record as an unstructured sequence of characters
2. Treat the record like a row in a SQL database

---

[*] Although we have never seen this proven, we suspect that this convention has its origins with the Apple operating system and compilers for the Macintosh. The Macintosh used a similar nomenclature for its system resources.

Database records appear to the Palm OS as unstructured regions of memory; they have no inherent structure other than what your program imposes. For some rare applications where the data varies extensively from record to record, this lack of structure is useful.

 The Palm Database Manager supports arbitrary 8-bit character data in records. The AppForge PDB library, however, does not—it uses a special character encoding sequence that more easily maps from Windows Unicode to Palm UTF-8. If you need to store binary data, you will have to code around this.

It is much more likely, however, that you will create records that have a structure similar to the columns in an SQL table. The AppForge PDB library provides direct support for this in database *schemas*.

To create a schema for a database, call the *PDBCreateTable* method on an open database. The method requires you to provide the database handle, the new schema name, and the schema definition. For example, to create a database with two columns to hold a string and an integer, use the code shown in Example 3-1.

Example 3-1. Creating a schema

```
PDBCreateTable 1DB, "MySchema," "Name string, Age integer"

PDBCreateTable 1DB, "MySchema", "Name string, Age integer"
```

If the schema creation is successful (that is, it returns non-zero), you can now use several schema-related functions to read and write whole records or individual columns. We'll provide some concrete examples later.

A schema is simply a string that contains the record definition, in the form of fieldname and data type for each column in the database. You can use any of the VB built-in data types, such as integer, string, or date. Recall our simple schema above:

```
"Name string, Age integer"
```

The format of the schema definition, such as the supported field types, is clearly spelled out in the AppForge documentation.

If you don't use the AppForge schema, you will have to access all data in the record by computing its offset in the record and then reading raw data from that location. Storing information is just as cumbersome. We don't provide tremendous coverage of direct reads and writes in this book; there are plenty of examples of this in the AppForge Knowledge Base.

 Use the AppForge schema if at all possible—it provides an interface to the database that is powerful, easily comprehensible and maintainable.

One caveat—databases with these schemas are most easily accessed by AppForge applications. This is because non-AppForge applications cannot understand the schema definition stored in the AppInfo block. For the same reason, AppForge applications that are reading and writing records in other Palm databases typically cannot use the schemas either.

Now let's look how to access databases that do not have a schema—those that were not created by the AppForge PDB library or using the PDB Converter tool, such as the native Palm databases for the Address, Date Book, and To-Do applications.

The easiest way to access databases like these is to create a temporary database schema that matches the PDB record structure. A temporary schema is one that is *not* written into the AppInfo block of the PDB. This is critical, since you probably don't own this database and cannot risk corrupting its data. AppForge provides for the construction of a temporary schema using the *PDBSetNumFields* and *PDBSetFieldType* methods.

Of course, you will have to do some upfront work to determine the record structure by poking around in the documentation or by examining the PDB file with a hex editor. We'll illustrate this technique by creating a temporary schema for the To-Do database.

AppForge ships an example application to read and write the To-Do database. The application declares a data structure like this:

```
Public Type tToDoRecord
   DueDate As Date
   Complete As Boolean
   Priority As Byte
   Description As String
   Note As String
End Type
```

There are five fields, each of a different data type, so creating a temporary schema will involve six function calls: one to specify the size of the schema itself, and five more to define the fields.

Example 3-2 shows how to create a schema for the To-Do database, assuming that the database is open and that the handle is stored in dbToDo:

Example 3-2. Declaring a temporary schema

```
PDBSetNumFields dbToDo, 5

PDBSetFieldType dbToDo, 0, eDateField, 4
PDBSetFieldType dbToDo, 1, eBooleanField, 1
PDBSetFieldType dbToDo, 2, eByteField, 1
PDBSetFieldType dbToDo, 3, eStringField, 0
PDBSetFieldType dbToDo, 4, eStringField, 0
```

Let's look more closely at *PDBSetFieldType*. Each call specifies a field number, an associated data type, and the size of the field. Table 3-2 lists the available field types. String data fields require special handling. In Example 3-2, we specified zero for the size of the two string fields—this indicates a variable-length field. If the field width is fixed, then we need to supply the correct width.

Table 3-2. Field type constants

Constant	Type	Description
eBooleanField	Boolean	True/False expression
eByteField	Byte	Unsigned numbers from 0 to 255
eDateField	Date	Date/Time expression
eFloatField	Single	Single-precision IEEE floating-point number
eIntegerField	Integer	VB Integer
eLongField	Long	VB Long
eStringField	String	String data

Closing and deleting databases

The other side of database management involves the closing and, occasionally, the deletion of the database. When you are done working with a database, you should call the *PDBClose* method in order to allow the AppForge Booster to clean up resources. This is as simple as:

```
PDBClose lDB
```

Open databases are automatically closed when your application exits. Due to the limited resources of the Palm device, however, you should try to close databases when you are done using them, not when your application exits.

If you want to permanently remove a database—and release the memory taken up by it—you should call the *PDBDeleteDatabase* method. A database *must* be closed before it can be deleted; of course, once a database is closed, its handle is no longer valid. For this reason, *PDBDeleteDatabase* requires the name of the database:

```
PDBDeleteDatabase "MyDB", 0, 0
```

The method returns a Boolean indicating success or failure of the delete operation.

 The AppForge documentation states that the Creator ID and Type ID fields can be used as wildcards to support deleting multiple databases. In practice, this is impossible, because no Palm databases can have the same name.

The PDBOpen method

Use the *PDBOpen* method to access existing databases. Here's the method signature:

```
PDBOpen(Style As tOpenStyle, Filename As String, CardNo As Long, dbID As Long, Type
    As Long, Creator As Long, mode As tOpenMode)
```

Whew—that's a lot of parameters! Let's look at them one by one.

The *Style* parameter governs how the method finds the Palm database to open, as shown in Table 3-3. It also dictates which of the other parameters are used and which are ignored.

Table 3-3. Database open styles

Style	Meaning
ByFileName	Open the database named in the Filename parameter.
ByID	Open the database referenced by the dbID parameter. This is rarely used by applications.
ByTypeCreator	Open the database that matches the supplied Type and Creator parameters. This is the most common way to open a database.

The *Filename* parameter is used when the *Style* parameter is set to ByFilename. On the Palm device, this name is case-sensitive. Note that this is the only way to open a Palm database on the Windows desktop.

The *CardNo* parameter is always zero, as the AppForge libraries do not support databases on expansion cards.

The *dbID* parameter is used when the *Style* parameter is set to ByID. The *dbID* parameter is almost never used for AppForge applications, because although each Palm database has a permanent identifier, the PDB library doesn't provide a way to access it.

The *Type* and the *Creator* parameters are used when the *Style* parameter is set to ByTypeCreator. Occasionally, you will find that you have these values available to you when the database name is not easily found.

The *Mode* parameter determines how the database is opened. Possible modes are shown in Table 3-4.

Table 3-4. Database open modes

Mode	Description
AfModeAsciiStrings	Treat strings as 8-bit ASCII strings rather than UTF8 strings. This is useful if you need to access native Palm databases.
AfModeExclusive	Database will only be accessible to current application.
AfModeLeaveOpen	Database will be left open when the application exits.
AfModeReadOnly	Database is read-only for this application.
AfModeReadWrite	Database is read-write for this application.
AfModeShowSecret	Application can see any records that are marked as private.
AfModeWrite	Database is write-only for this application.

You can combine these constants if necessary. For example, to open the native Palm Address database, the *PDBOpen* call should look like this:

```
lDB = PDBOpen(Byfilename, "AddressDB", 0, 0, 0, 0, _
    afModeAsciiStrings Or afModeReadWrite)
```

To open an AppForge database in read-only mode with access to private records, the *PDBOpen* call looks like:

```
lDB = PDBOpen(Byfilename, "MyDB", 0, 0, 0, 0, afModeShowSecret Or afModeReadOnly)
```

Database attributes

Like a file on the Windows desktop, the Palm PDB has a set of attributes that indicate its current state and that control how the operating system interacts with it. The database has a two-byte attribute field that stores different states as a set of flags. This field is maintained by the Palm database manager, and is returned by calling the *PDBGetDatabaseAttributes* method. There are a lot of flags, as shown in Table 3-5.

Table 3-5. Database attributes

Attribute	Meaning
AfHdrAttrResDB	Database is a resource database (PRC).
AfHdrAttrReadOnly	Database cannot be modified.
AfHdrAttrAppInfoDirty	AppInfo block has been changed since the last HotSync operation.
AfHdrAttrBackup	HotSync should use default backup conduit if no custom conduit available.
afHdrAttrOKToInstallNewer	The installation conduit should install a newer version of this database with a different name if the current database is open[a].
afHdrAttrResetAfterInstall	Palm device should be reset when database is installed; often used with shared libraries.
AfHdrAttrCopyPrevention	Disable Exchange Manager operations, such as IR beaming.
AfHdrAttrStream	Database is emulating a FAT file.
AfHdrAttrHidden	Database should not be displayed although it is still accessible; usually for PRC and PQA databases.
AfHdrAttrLaunchableData	Database can be "launched"; usually a PQA database.
AfHdrAttrOpen	Database is open.

[a] This description is from the AppForge PDB Library User's Guide.

Once you have retrieved the attribute field using *PDBGetDatabaseAttributes*, you can access the individual flags using the AND operator to determine what states are currently set in the PDB. The attribute flags are members of the enumeration tDatabaseAttributes.

For example, to see if a database is marked read-only by the Palm, you can use the following code:

```
If PDBGetDatabaseAttributes(lDB) And afHdrReadOnly Then
    ' Do something here
End If
```

The flags can be combined using the OR operator. For example, to see if the copy pre-vention and backup bit are both set, use the following code:

```
Dim Mask As Long
Mask = afHdrAttrCopyPrevention Or afHdrAttrBackup

If PDBGetDatabaseAttributes(lDB) And Mask Then
    ' Do something here
End If
```

You can change attributes using the *PDBSetDatabaseAttributes* method. Be fore-warned: this method is capable of making potentially catastrophic changes to data-bases on your Palm device. If you simply call *PDBSetDatabaseAttributes* with a single flag, you will accidentally turn off any other database flags that were enabled. For this reason, it is usually best to *first* retrieve the current database attributes, and *then* toggle the flags you need on or off. Only after this should you call *PDBSetDatabaseAttributes* with the new set of attributes.

To turn on an attribute, use the OR operator. For example, to make a database read-only while leaving all the other flags undisturbed, use the following code:

```
' Get all the current attributes
Dim lCurrent As Long
lCurrent = PDBGetDatabaseAttributes(lDB)

' Toggle ON just the read-only bit
PDBSetDatabaseAttributes lDB, lCurrent Or afHdrAttrReadOnly
```

To turn off an attribute, use the AND and NOT operators. To remove the copy protec-tion from a database, use this code:

```
' Get all the current attributes
Dim lCurrent As Long
lCurrent = PDBGetDatabaseAttributes(lDB)

' Toggle OFF just the copy bit
PDBSetDatabaseAttributes lDB, lCurrent And (Not afHdrAttrCopyPrevention)
```

Of course, you can also change more than one database attribute at a time. It is easy to combine all the flags to be changed by building a mask using the Or operator:

```
Dim lMask As Long
LMask = AfHdrAttrBackup Or AfHdrAttrHidden Or afHdrAttrResetAfterInstall
```

You can use this mask exactly like the single attributes discussed previously.

Record Management

Record management supports creating, reading, writing, and deleting database records. We consider an update operation to be a special case of the write operation.

Figure 3-3 shows the required relationship between the methods that create and update records when using the AppForge PDB library. Note that reading and deleting records are simple actions that do not have any prerequisite operations.

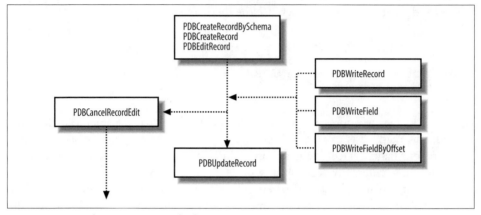

Figure 3-3. Record management methods

Creating records

There are several ways to create a database record, depending upon whether the database has an AppForge schema. If the database has a schema, then you should use the *PDBCreateRecordBySchema* method. Otherwise, use the *PDBCreateRecord* method, which also requires the initial size of the record to be created.

Table 3-6 shows the supported field data types and their respective sizes; you can use this information to calculate a PDB record size by adding up the sizes of all the fields in the record. Note that for this to work, string fields must have a fixed length.

Table 3-6. AppForge PDB record fields

PDB data type	Field size (bytes)
Boolean	1
Byte	1
Date	4
Integer	2
Long	4
String	Characters in string + 1
Single	4 [a]

[a] When specifying the field list parameter for the *PDBCreateTable* method, the call will fail if you use the word "single" to define a single data type column. Use the word "float" to correctly define the single data type column.

As we mentioned earlier, it is significantly easier to use databases with schemas than databases without them, since the AppForge PDB library takes care of calculating records sizes dynamically.

Regardless of how you create the PDB record, the *PDBUpdateRecord* method must be executed to actually save the record data to the database. Until this method is called, the library buffers the changes for your application; they may be lost if you create or manipulate another record.

Reading and editing records

The PDB library provides four methods to retrieve record data from an open database. The first three methods operate on databases that use an AppForge schema; they differ in the amount of data returned. The simplest is to retrieve the data from a single field using the *PDBGetField* method. This method accepts field numbers that are *zero-based*. Assuming 1DB is a handle to the database created earlier in this chapter in Example 3-1, use this code to retrieve the *second* column in the record:

```
Dim iAge As Integer
PDBGetField 1DB, 1, iAge
```

Of course, you also must supply a variable of the correct data type to hold the results. Remember—no variants. You can also use this method to retrieve either the field's name or type:

```
Dim strVal As String

'gets the field name - returns "Age"
PDBGetField ldbState, 1 OR afPDBFieldName, strVal

'gets the field type - returns "integer"
PDBGetField ldbState, 1 OR afPDBFieldType, strVal
```

When utilizing this technique, you use the numeric OR operator to combine the field number (in this case, 1) with the appropriate enumeration constant—either afPDBFieldType or afPDBFieldName.

The *PDBReadRecord* method will read the entire *current* record into a user-defined type (UDT) that matches the database schema.* Here is how to dimension and read a record for the database described earlier in Example 3-1:

```
Public Type MyRecord
    strName As String
    iAge As Integer
End Type

Dim tRec as MyRecord
PDBReadRecord 1DB, VarPtr(tRec)
```

---

* This record type is created automatically if you use either the AppForge Database Converter or the Universal Conduit to create PDB files from Microsoft Access or SQL data sources. We cover these tools later in this chapter and in Chapter 5.

AppForge does not support the variant data type, so *PDBReadRecord* must be capable of stashing data into records of all types. Calling the method with the *address* of the UDT record, obtained using the VB *VarPtr* function, does this. The method then fills the structure with the field values from the record, according to the schema. Exercise care to ensure that the schema and the field layout of the UDT record are properly aligned—this method does no error checking, and it is easy to crash your application.

The *PDBBulkRead* method is similar, except that it reads several records into a VB array. To use this method, first dimension an array of records of the appropriate type, and then pass the address of the first element of the array:

```
Dim tRec(10) As MyRecord
Dim NumRecs As Long

NumRecs = PDBBulkRead(lDB, 10, VarPtr(tRec(0)))
```

The method returns the actual number of records read. This method is faster than reading records in a loop, but should only be used when you really need the entire record, not simply one field. Otherwise you are wasting processing time and memory.

At this point, you might wonder how the AppForge PDB library knows where to start reading or writing data in the database? Until now, we have not mentioned the fact that every open AppForge PDB has a current record indicator, which is similar to the cursor in a relational database. *PDBReadRecord* and *PDBBulkRead* move the current record indicator as they process database records. Record navigation—which involves moving the indicator—is covered in detail later in this chapter.

To edit a record, first ensure that the PDB is in a state to accept changes. This is accomplished using the *PDBEditRecord* method. Once the record is conditioned for change, use the *PDBWriteField* method for single field changes and *PDBWriteRecord* to change an entire record. Here is what the method calls look like for the database defined earlier in Example 3-1:

```
PDBWriteField lDB, 1, iAge
PDBWriteRecord lDB, VarPtr(tRec)
```

Of course, these methods only work with AppForge schema databases.

Let's look at writing data to a database without an AppForge schema of either the permanent or temporary kind. After calling *PDBEditRecord* to enable changes, you have to use the *PDBWriteFieldByOffset* method to write data into the record.

The *PDBWriteFieldByOffset* method is a low-level routine that writes raw data bytes into a physical offset specified from the start of the record. This means that you must know where the fields are located in the record, and you must be sure the record is large enough to store the data. You can use the values in Table 3-2 (shown previously), along with the functions *PDBRecordSize* and *PDBResizeRecord,* to help determine this information. Consider the record shown in Figure 3-4.

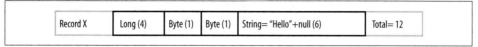

Figure 3-4. Sample record layout

From Table 3-2, shown earlier in this chapter, you know that the first field, a Long, occupies the initial four bytes of the record. And you can use the same reasoning for the next two fields, which are also data fields with fixed lengths.

The mapping gets trickier when the record contains string data, which is the only schema field that can vary in length.* The record shown above in Figure 3-4 is the simplest case—the sole string field is at the end of the record. More complex databases might have string fields embedded throughout the record. To handle those cases, you need to figure out the size of each string field or fields, and adjust the offset of any other fields accordingly. As you might imagine, this is very difficult to do dynamically.

> Stick with an AppForge schema if at all possible, even if you have to define temporary schemas on the fly. Your application will be much more maintainable with a minimal loss of performance.

Calling *PDBRecordSize* on the record shown in Figure 3-4 will return 12: four bytes for the Long field, one each for the two Byte fields, and six for the String. Because we are dealing with raw data fields here, the string length includes an extra byte for the C/C++ null terminator. You must account for this extra byte when sizing non-schema databases.

To update this record so that the string contains "Hello World", the record needs to increase in size by six bytes, as shown in Figure 3-5.

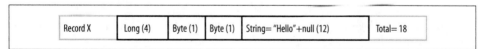

Figure 3-5. Resized sample record

---

* Many Palm applications pack and unpack PDB record data, often using some type of run-length encoding, where a byte or integer indicates how much data is in the rest of the record. These schemes are very complex and are hard to implement in VB.

Before you can write the expanded string into the record, you must first use the PDB library to resize the record to 18 bytes, and then write the new string data to the record at the proper offset:

```
Dim strVal As String

StrVal = "Hello World"
PDBResizeRecord lDB, 18
PDBWriteFieldByOffset lDB, 6, strVal
```

To commit the changes to the record, execute the *PDBUpdateRecord* method. If your application exits without calling the update routine, your changes will not be stored in the database. You can call the *PDBCancelRecordEdit* method at any time while editing a record; this rolls back any changes made to the record data. It also resets the record attributes to their previous state.

If there is not enough heap storage available, the *PDBResizeRecord* call will fail. This is not uncommon on the Palm device, and your application should be able to handle this condition.

Deleting records

There are several different ways to delete records from Palm databases; these exist primarily to support Palm's HotSync technology for synchronizing data between the Palm and the desktop. Table 3-7 summarizes the different ways to delete records.

Table 3-7. Record deletion modes

Deletion mode	Resulting action
AfDeleteModeArchive	Sets the record delete flag, but leaves the data intact
AfDeleteModeDelete	Same as afDeleteModeArchive; also sets the record's category to 15[a]
AfDeleteModePalmDelete	Sets the record delete flag and removes the data from the record
AfDeleteModeRemove	Immediately removes record from the database

[a] The AppForge documentation says that setting the category to 15 supports the Universal Conduit's ability to delete records from the Windows desktop during synchronization.

We cover the effect of the various delete modes on the synchronization process in Chapters 4 and 5.

The AppForge *PDBDeleteRecord* method deletes the database current record using the afDeleteModePalmDelete mode, which is the normal Palm way to delete. The AppForge PDB library also provides a *PDBRemoveAllRecords* method that will delete all the records in the database; it also uses afDeleteModePalmDelete.

Deleting the last record from the database will automatically set the current record indicator to be the first record in the database, if one exists.

If you need to specify one of the other delete modes on the current record, use the *PDBDeleteRecordEx* method and supply the desired mode from Table 3-4 (shown earlier in this chapter) as a parameter. For example, if you do not intend to synchronize your data with the desktop, use afDeleteModeRemove to minimize the resources used by your application.

Categories

By convention, most Palm applications provide some kind of support for categories, which offer a way to organize records in a database into manageable groupings.

Although the Palm Application Launcher also uses categories when grouping applications (such as All, Games, Main, and so on), those are not the categories we discuss in this chapter.

Usually there is a default Unfiled category, as well any other predefined categories that make sense for the application. See Figure 3-6 for a list of default categories supplied with the native Palm applications.

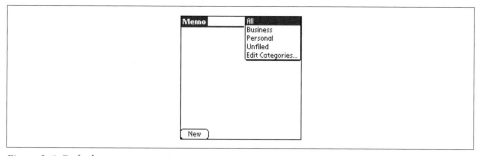

Figure 3-6. Default memo categories

The Palm OS Category manager supports up to 15 categories, indexed from zero, that are stored in the AppInfo block of a PDB. The AppForge PDB library provides methods to change these names. The *PDBGetCategoryName* method retrieves the category name for a specific category index from the AppInfo block. *PDBSetCategoryName* assigns a category name, overwriting any previous name. The category name may be up to 15 characters in length.

A common task that an application performs when starting up is to populate a List-Box or ComboBox ingot with the current categories stored in the PDB. Here is the code to do that:

```
Dim iIndex As Integer
Dim strCatName As String

'Loop through all valid category index values
For iIndex = 0 To 14
    PDBGetCategoryName lDB, iIndex, strCatName
```

```
            If strCatName <> "" Then Exit For
            AFListBox1.AddItem strCatName
            AFListBox1.ItemData(AFListBox1.NewIndex) = iIndex
     Next
```

Make sure to use a variable like strCatName for the *Name* parameter, as shown in the preceding code. Setting or retrieving the category name directly to an ingot property—such as *Text*—fails silently.

Each record in a PDB has a Category ID ranging from 0 to 15, although AppForge reserves the value 15.[*] This means that a record can be in only one category at a time. The Category ID is not part of the record field layout, but is maintained by the Palm database manager in an internal structure. The Category ID is an index into the category name table (which saves space).

Use the *PDBRecordCategoryID* method to retrieve the Category ID for the current record in a PDB. The *PDBSetRecordCategoryID* method assigns the current record to a category.

A common use for categories within an application is to filter records, such as on a form that should only display records in a Business category. We show how to filter records in the North Wind Traders Inventory application later in this chapter.

One final note: the AppForge Universal Conduit (UC) does not support categories when synchronizing data to the Windows desktop. If your application design calls for using the UC to HotSync, then you should probably not use categories.

Attributes

Like databases, Palm PDB records have attributes as well—just not as many. Each record has a one-byte attribute field that stores the flags. You can use the *PDBRecordAttributes* or *PDBRecordAttributesEx* methods to return the attribute field for the current database record. The individual flags are shown in Table 3-8.

Table 3-8. Record attributes

Attribute	Meaning
AfRecAttrBusy	Record is marked as busy and cannot be read (it can be written to, however).
AfRecAttrDelete	Record has been marked for deletion at the next HotSync operation.
AfRecAttrDirty	Record has been changed since the last HotSync operation.
AfRecAttrSecret	Record is secret and should be hidden if privacy is supported.

The only difference between the methods is that the "extended" method lets you specify a particular index, instead of using the current record index.

---

[*] The AppForge Universal Conduit uses a category index of 15 to indicate that the record has been deleted from the Palm and must also be removed from the Windows desktop. Note that the Palm OS also reserves the value 15 to indicate "all categories".

Once you have retrieved the attribute field, you can access the individual flags using the AND operator and the flags listed in Table 3-8. The attribute flags are members of the tAttributes enumeration.

 If you expect to process records with the secret attribute, be certain that you have opened the database using the afModeShowSecret flag. Otherwise, methods like *PDBMoveNext* will silently skip these records.

For example, to see if a record has been changed, but not yet synchronized with the Windows desktop, you can use the following code:

```
If (PDBRecordAttributes(lDB) And afRecAttrDiry) Then
    ' Do something here
End If
```

You can change attributes using the *PDBSetRecordAttributes* method. Again, exercise caution when setting the attribute flags, to avoid losing data. You should retrieve all the attributes first, and turn individual flags on or off. Then call *PDBSetRecordAttributes* with the new values. Unfortunately there is no *extended* method for setting attributes, so you must make the desired record current before updating the flags.

For historical reasons, the attribute field returned by *PDBRecordAttributes* (and its extended version) has the four attribute flags in the high bits of the field, and the four-bit record category in the low bits. The *PDBSetRecordAttributes* method ignores the category bits when updating the record.

Navigation

Effective database programming on the Palm, as on any platform, requires the ability to process a particular record or set of records. The AppForge PDB library provides a variety of methods that support moving, searching, or jumping through the database records. These methods are diagrammed in Figure 3-7.

The AppForge PDB library maintains beginning of file (BOF) and end of file (EOF) markers. The *PDBBOF* and *PDBEOF* methods return a Boolean value if the current record is at either BOF or EOF respectively.

To perform the most basic database operation—processing all the records—use the following code:

```
PDBMoveFirst dbHandle

Do While Not PDBEOF(dbHandle)
    ' do something here
    PDBMoveNext dbHandle
Loop
```

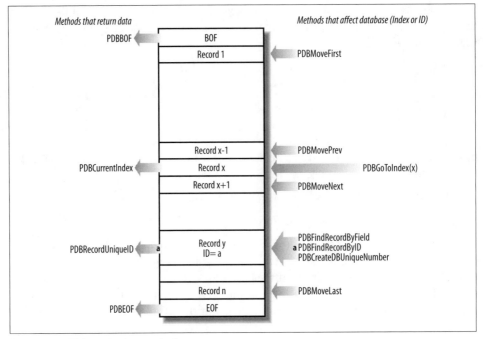

Figure 3-7. *PDB navigation methods*

Note that having the current record indicator at the first or last record does not set the BOF or EOF flag to TRUE. These flags are only set if an attempt is made to move beyond the first or last record in the database.

Figure 3-7 shows that the majority of the navigation methods act upon the database by moving the current record indicator around in the database. These methods are self-explanatory: *PDBMoveFirst*, *PDBMovePrev*, *PDBMoveNext*, and *PDBMoveLast*. We won't discuss these methods further in this chapter.

You may use the *PDBCurrentIndex* method, which returns the current record indicator, to determine your application's location in the database. And you can use *PDBGoToIndex* to seek directly to a specific record.

Searching

The simplest way to find a record in a database is to use *PDBGotoIndex*, which positions the PDB current record index to the value you supply as a parameter. This method returns TRUE if the desired index and the record exist, and FALSE otherwise. Since you need the index of the desired record before you access it, the *PDBGotoIndex* is only useful if you cache these index numbers someplace in your application. Frequently you may use the *ItemData* property of an ingot, and look up the record data when an item in the ingot is selected:

```
Private Sub AFComboBox1_Click( )
    Dim dbIndex As Long

    dbIndex = AFComboBox1.ItemData(AFComboBox1.ListIndex)
    If PDBGotoIndex(lDB, dbIndex) Then
        ' Process record data here...
    End If
End Sub
```

Of course, this example assumes that you stored the record index in the *ItemData* property when populating the combo box.

Every record in a PDB database has a unique identifier (UID). This UID is not part of the record field layout, but is maintained by the Palm database manager in an internal structure. Unlike the record location within the database, which will change if the database is sorted or if records are added or deleted, the record UID is constant.* Use *PDBRecordUniqueID* to retrieve the UID for the current record. Later, when you want to move directly to that record, call the *PDBFindRecordByID* method, passing it the UID.

Finally, you can find a record by searching within a field for a particular value, using the *PDBFindRecordByField* method. Like all field-oriented methods in the AppForge PDB library, this method only works if the database has a defined schema (permanent or temporary). Call this method with the column index (field) to search and the value for which to search.

```
PDBFindRecordByField lDB, Age_Field, Cint(21)
```

If successful, the method will set the current index to point to the first matching record. Be sure to pass an expression of the correct type for the value, as *PDBFindRecordByField* does no error checking.

> *PDBFindRecordByField* always searches from the beginning of the database, not the current index. This means that you cannot use this method to find the *next* matching record. To do that, you need to sort the database, which we address later.

Since *PDBFindRecordByField* can perform crude string matches, the method can be used to implement search-as-you-scribe functionality. We show you how to do this in the North Wind Traders Inventory example later in the chapter.

---

* The UID doesn't usually change, but it is only guaranteed to be the same from the time you open the PDB until the time you close it. During a HotSync operation, the Palm OS will close any open databases and turn control over to a conduit. This conduit is free to change the UID as needed.

Sorting

AppForge provides a built-in sort capability for databases. *PDBSetSortFields* sorts a database on a single record field, and *PDBSetSort* provides a multi-field sort. As before, these field-oriented functions only work on schema databases. We'll look at each function in turn, as there are some important differences between them.

Let's look at *PDBSetSortFields* first. This method is poorly named—it only sorts the database on a single record field. That field is specified by offset within the record layout, with the first or leftmost record field having offset 0, the next field having offset 1, and so on:

```
PDBSetSortFields 1DB, Age_Field
```

The method returns TRUE if the sort succeeded, and FALSE otherwise.

Once you have performed the sort operation, you can skip to the beginning of the database and process all the records in the new order.

These methods always sort in *ascending* order: A, then B, and so on. You will need to process records backward—from the end of the file to the first record—to simulate a descending sort.

You can use *PDBFindRecordByField*—specifying the same field used for the sort—to find the first record in a sequence of matching records, which you then cycle through using *PDBMoveNext*. Note that *PDBFindRecordByField* uses a binary search algorithm when searching a sorted database; this is much faster than its normal linear search of the database.

Now, let's look at the *PDBSetSort* method. This method sorts the database on multiple fields, which are specified in a specially formatted string. This string actually has two formats, one used with databases that have permanent schemas, and the other with temporary schemas.* Like the single-field sort, *PDBSetSort* sorts the database records in ascending order.

For databases with permanent schemas, the sort field string is a comma-separated list of the *field names* in the desired order. Here's how to sort the database created previously in Example 3-1, first by age, and then by name:

```
PDBSetSort 1DB, "age,name"
```

For databases with temporary schemas, the sort field string is a comma-separated list of the field offsets. Here's how to sort the To-Do database shown previously in Example 3-2, by priority, and then by due date:

```
PDBSetSort 1DB, "2,0"
```

---

* Remember, a permanent schema is created with a call to *PDBCreateTable*, or by using the Database Converter. A temporary schema is defined with calls to *PDBSetNumFields* and *PDBSetFieldType*.

These are the third and first fields in the record, but, like all the field-oriented methods, the offsets are specified from zero.

Although sorting a database will dramatically improve the speed of your application, the sort itself is a very time-consuming operation; you should sort only when absolutely needed. When designing your application and its database structure, AppForge recommends that you consider the following factors:[*]

- Make the sort field the first field in the record layout. If you are sorting on multiple fields, move them all to the start of the record. This helps speed up record data reads during the sort.

- Avoid sorting on string fields; convert them to another data type if possible. When sorting on multiple fields, place numeric fields first in the sort order and string fields later.

- Use *PDBSetSortFields* instead of *PDBSetSort*. Sorting on a single field is faster than sorting on multiple fields.

Other Database Topics

We've now covered the most common methods your application is likely to use while manipulating databases and records. In this section, we look at several other functions that you will need to complete your applications or to handle some special chores.

Errors

Palm database programming is not like Windows file system programming. The PDB exists only as fragments of memory in a low-powered device. Errors do occur, and it is critical that your application check for them. Only a few of the methods in the AppForge PDB library return error codes directly. Instead, error information is found by calling the *PDBGetLastError* method, which returns the last reported database error.

Like the VB error handler, error information for the PDB is reset with every method call, so you will need to think carefully about when and how often to check for errors. Certainly it is not unreasonable to check after *every* PDB library call, at least until you become comfortable programming on the Palm device.

PDBGetLastError returns a value that is a member of the tPDBError enumeration type. A zero return indicates no error, while a negative number indicates an error. Unfortunately, there is no function in the PDB library that returns a string equivalent, so you will have to look up each error in the AppForge PDB Library User Guide.

---

[*] See article 010515-000024 in the AppForge Knowledge Base for more detailed information.

Counting

It is often useful to determine the number of records in a database. You can use the *PDBNumRecords* method to get a count of all the records in the database. This method does not distinguish between current records, records marked for deletion but not yet erased, or records in other states. It simply returns the total number of records in the PDB (including private ones, regardless of how you opened the database).

Sometimes it is more useful to be able to determine the number of records in the database with a given state. For example, you might need to how many undeleted records are in the database. We wrote a function, *NumRecs,* that uses *PDBNumRecords* as well as *PDBRecordAttributesEx* to do just that, as shown in Example 3-3.

Example 3-3. Counting non-deleted records

```
Public Function NumRecs(ByVal lDB As Long) As Long
    Dim iIndex As Long
    Dim lRecCnt As Long

    lRecCnt = 0
    For iIndex = 0 To PDBNumRecords(lDB) - 1
        If Not PDBRecordAttributesEx(lDB, iIndex) And afRecAttrDelete Then
            lRecCnt = lRecCnt + 1
        End If
    Next iIndex

    NumRecs = lRecCnt
End Function
```

The critical test is:

```
    Not PDBRecordAttributesEx(lDB, iIndex) And afRecAttrDelete
```

This filters out those records that have been deleted, so lRecCnt is only incremented for active records.

Unique numbers

Although the Palm database manager automatically generates a UID when you create a new record, this UID is not guaranteed to be unique forever. There are times when you need some unique identifier that will never, ever change—for example, to provide a bookmark function that will work even if you beam the database to another Palm device.

The AppForge PDB library has the *PDBCreateDBUniqueNumber* method for just such purposes. This method uses the same algorithm as the underlying Palm database manager, but does not assign the new UID to a record. Instead, it returns the UID directly to the caller. You can then use this UID as the value for any field in the record layout.

The AppForge Database Converter

In this chapter, we've looked at how to create and manipulate a database programmatically, but we've ignored the issue of content—how do you get desktop data into the PDB? Typically, you accomplish this by using the HotSync process, with a custom conduit for your database, or with a conversion program developed specifically for your application.

There is an easier way: the AppForge Database Converter. This is a simple tool that moves existing data from the Windows desktop into Palm databases. This tool will create the PDB, populate its records, and generate VB source code that contains the Creator ID and Type ID, the record schema, and functions to read and write records.

The Database Converter requires its input to be in Microsoft Access format; it translates the internal tables into individual Palm PDB files. This is not as restrictive as it sounds, for it is possible to convert almost any data source into an Access MDB file or link table.[*]

The conversion is an excellent time to think about what information really needs to be transferred. If your Windows desktop database has information that will not be relevant to the user, filter it out *before* it gets to the Palm device. The more data on the handheld, the slower the handheld will run.

Once the information is in a Microsoft Access database, you must ensure that the tables to be converted to the Palm have supported data types. Table 3-9 shows how each MS Access data type is converted.

Table 3-9. Supported MS Access data type conversions

MS Access types	PDB field type	Manual alternate
Text	String	N/A
Memo	String	N/A
Number, Byte	Byte	N/A
Number, Integer	Integer	N/A
Number, Long Integer	Long	N/A
Number, Single	Single	N/A
Number, Double	Double	N/A
Number, Decimal	Not Supported	Double, Long
Number, Replication ID	Not Supported	Double
Date/Time	Date	N/A

---

[*] Microsoft Data Transformation Services, available with SQL Server, provide a tremendous number of automatic conversion utilities. And Access itself is capable of importing data from almost any SQL database, as well as Dbase, Excel, and formatted text.

Table 3-9. Supported MS Access data type conversions (continued)

MS Access types	PDB field type	Manual alternate
Currency	Currency	N/A
AutoNumber	Long	N/A
Yes/No	Boolean	N/A
OLE Object (long binary)	Not Supported	None
Hyperlink	Not Supported	Text

For unsupported data types, we suggest an alternate manual conversion in Table 3-9. You must change or eliminate all unsupported data fields in the Access file before running the Database Converter.

The converter program is quite simple to use. First, you select the Access database to convert; if the database has multiple tables, you must select one to convert. The new PDB takes its name from the converted Access table. At this time, you also supply creator and type identifiers for the database.

When you press the Convert button, you are prompted with the standard Windows file dialog to save the PDB. Remember, the Windows filename is not the internal PDB name. Figure 3-8 shows the Database Converter in action.

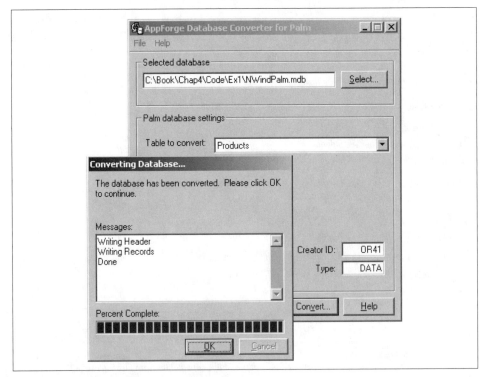

Figure 3-8. AppForge PDB Converter screen

If you didn't change a column into a supported data type, the Database Converter warns you that the column will be skipped (i.e., it will not be in the PDB record layout). The warning is shown in Figure 3-9.

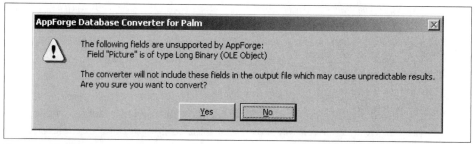

Figure 3-9. *Unsupported data type warning*

After the table is converted, you have the option to create a VB module of useful routines to access the new PDB. The module provides the following:

- Public constants for the creator and type identifiers, and a global variable for the database handle.
- Public enumeration with named offsets for all the fields in the record layout.
- A public record type with properly aligned members for all the fields in the record layout. The member names correspond to the Access column names.
- Public functions to open and close the database, using the global database handle mentioned above.
- Public functions to read and write records in the database. These functions use the record type mentioned above.

The code is straightforward, and will satisfy most basic data access needs. There are two pitfalls to avoid if you use the AppForge generated code:

1. If you regenerate the PDB file, be sure to use the new VB module in your application. Many subtle errors arise if the code (IDs, fields, and so on) doesn't agree with the new PDB file.

2. If your application uses many converted tables, your application can become bloated with duplicative functions. Consider writing generic database access functions instead of using the AppForge modules.

From here, you may wish to enhance the module for custom business logic or to consolidate this functionality into a data access class or module. Its real benefit is to get you running quickly if all you need is basic data access.

> The physical order of records in the generated PDB file will match the order in the Access table. Order the Access table properly before conversion to avoid expensive sorts on the Palm device.

Inventory Tracking Application

In this section, we'll put what we've learned to work building a mobile inventory application based on the Microsoft North Wind Traders Inventory sample.* This application models a small company that resells products via a regional sales force. Our Palm implementation offers several interesting features:

- A master-detail relationship view of the inventory
- Search-as-you-scribe (type-ahead) functionality
- PDB sorting by clicking/selecting Grid columns

We have rehosted a small portion of the application on the Palm device to allow the user to browse existing inventory, review suppliers, and update stock levels. The main user interface is shown in Figure 3-10.

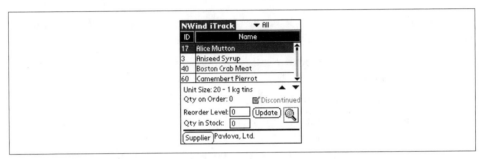

Figure 3-10. North Wind main screen

To support the on-device inventory, we'll use the Database Converter to process the North Wind Supplier, Product and Category tables. Prior to conversion, we had to convert the Homepage field in the Suppliers table from Hypertext—which is not a supported data type—to String. We also removed the Picture field from the Categories table entirely.

We used OR31 as the creator identifier and DATA as the type identifier for all three databases; the Creator ID matches the one we're going to use for the PRC. This will cause all three databases to be removed if the user deletes the application from the Palm device. We had the converter create VB modules for each table, which we will use in the application. Figure 3-11 shows how these three tables relate to each other.

Grid ingot

The North Wind application makes heavy use of the Grid ingot to display record data. There are many other ways to display record data, such as filling ListBox or ComboBox ingots, but the Grid ingot was ideal for this application because of its inherent support for rows and columns—perfect for tabular data.

---

* Microsoft distributes the North Wind Traders sample application with its Access and SQL Server products.

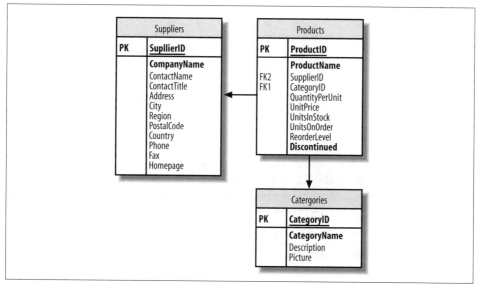

Figure 3-11. Inventory database relationships

Since we didn't cover the Grid ingot in Chapter 2, let's take a quick tour of its features. The Grid ingot displays data in cells that are organized into rows and columns. Cells occur at the intersection of a row and a column, which are referenced using a zero-based index; for example, the top left cell in a grid is (0, 0). The indexes increase as you move right and down through the grid.

Of course, to include the Grid icon in your project, you must add a reference from the VB Project → References menu. Remember, the Grid ingot requires that the Advanced Ingots Booster PRC is installed on the Palm device.

The Grid ingot supports most of the same display attributes as the ingots we covered in Chapter 2, such as Border, Foreground, and Background Color, and font characteristics. Unlike the other ingots, you can only set the text alignment at runtime, using the *ColAlignment* property. And the Grid ingot has some specialized properties, such as grid-line style and horizontal or vertical scrollbars.

Obviously, on a device like the Palm, with its tiny screen, the ability to page or scroll data is critical. The scrollbars are present for user navigation. You can drive the visible region programmatically by using the *LeftCol* and *TopRow* properties. Setting these properties to an index value that is offscreen causes the ingot to make the indicated region visible.

In order to minimize the amount of empty space in the Grid ingot, you can change the *RowHeight* and *ColWidth* properties to set the size of an individual cell. Since these properties are only accessible at runtime, you should set these properties while the form is initializing or when loading data into the Grid ingot.

The *ColWidth* is only specified once; it immediately affects all columns in the Grid ingot. The *RowHeight* property, however, has to be set for each new row if you change it from the default.

The Grid ingot supports the standard *AddItem* method to add data. Because the Grid ingot supports rows and columns, it is nice that *AddItem* allows you to load an entire row with one call:

```
gridUserInfo.AddItem "Roger Knoell" & Chr(9) & "Visa", -1
```

From this example, you can see that separate columns are indicated with the tab character—Chr(9). Note the last parameter—this is the index at which to insert the row. The -1 indicates that the new row should be appended to the Grid data. This is similar to how the list box and combo box control work in VB.

You can use the *NewRow* property to return the index of the most recent row added. You often use this when setting the *ItemData* property, as shown in this simple example:

```
gridUserInfo.ItemData(gridUserInfo.NewRow, 1) = 1234
```

The Grid ingot supports the notion of a current cell, which is usually selected by the user with the stylus. To set the current cell from code, use the *Row* and *Col* properties. Note that when the user taps the cell, the ingot fires the *SelectCell* event; this doesn't happen if you select the cell programmatically.

To change the contents of a cell, use the *Text* or *TextMatrix* properties. The *Text* property works on the current cell, while *TextMatrix* lets you specify a specific cell either on or off the screen.

The Grid ingot doesn't have the normal *Clear* method, so you will need to remove data rows manually, as shown here:

```
Do While Not (gridInv.Rows = 0)
    gridInv.RemoveItem 0
Loop
gridInv.Refresh
```

One last note: it is our experience that the Grid ingot loads considerably faster when its *Visible* property is FALSE.[*]

Application structure

The North Wind application is in the *NwindInv.vbp* project file; it consists of two forms—*frmInv.frm* for the inventory and *frmSupplier.frm* for the supplier information. The inventory form is the VB project startup object, which means that it will receive initial control when the application is started.

---

[*] The Grid ingot, like most controls of its kind, is very complicated. There are quite a few articles in the AppForge Knowledge Base and the user forums that discuss optimization tips for this Ingot.

In addition, there are the three VB modules generated by the Database Converter: *Products.bas*, *Suppliers.bas*, and *Categories.bas*. And because this is a database application, we must include a reference to the AppForge PDB library as well.

The source code for our version of the North Wind application is available on this book's web site. If you don't have Access or the North Wind Traders database from Microsoft, don't worry—we've placed the converted PDB files with the code.

When the user launches the application, control is passed to the inventory's *Form_ Load* method. This simple routine (which is not shown here) opens the three databases, initializes the category combo box using *InitCategories*, and reads in the Grid data using *InitProducts*. We'll discuss how the category values are loaded into the combo-box later in this section.

The *InitProducts* method is too large to show all at once, so we'll examine it in pieces. First, let's declare variables needed throughout the routine:

```
Public Sub InitProducts( )

    Dim iRow As Integer
    Dim bSuccess As Boolean
    Dim CurProd As tProductsRecord
```

Next, let's prepare the Grid ingot to receive data, clearing any old data and setting the width of each column to an optimum size (determined by trial and error):

```
gridInv.Visible = False

Do While Not (gridInv.Rows = 0)
    gridInv.RemoveItem (0)
Loop
gridInv.Refresh

gridInv.ColWidth(ProductID_Field) = 20
gridInv.ColWidth(ProductName_Field) = 150
```

Next, let's position the database index to the beginning of the PDB, and read in each record:

```
PDBMoveFirst dbProducts
iRow = 0

Do While Not PDBEOF(dbProducts)
    bSuccess = ReadProductsRecord(CurProd)
    If bSuccess Then
```

The user might have selected a particular category of record, so before we process the record, let's make sure that the category values match (category values are stored in the cboCats combo box) before we add the record data to the Grid ingot, and skip to the next record:

```
If CurProd.CategoryID = cboCats.ItemData(cboCats.ListIndex) Or _
        cboCats.ItemData(cboCats.ListIndex) = -1 Then
```

```
        gridInv.AddItem CStr(CurProd.ProductID)
        gridInv.Row = iRow
        gridInv.RowHeight(iRow) = 13
        gridInv.Col = ProductName_Field
        gridInv.Text = CurProd.ProductName
        iRow = iRow + 1
    End If
Loop
```

Because the category value is invariant during this loop, it would be more efficient to store it in a variable just one time outside the loop. We'd like to do the same with the Grid *RowHeight* property, but the ingot doesn't work that way—each row must have this property set individually.

Once all the records are in the grid, we highlight the first row, update the product details, and make the grid visible:

```
'select the first grid item
If gridInv.Rows > 0 Then
    gridInv.Row = 0
    gridInv.Col = 0
    ShowProdDetails CLng(gridInv.Text)
End If

'show the grid
gridInv.Visible = True

End Sub
```

In this example, we have loaded all of the PDB data into the grid. This is not a viable technique if your database has hundreds or thousands of records. In that case, you should implement a paging technique, perhaps reading in only as many records as would fit onto the screen.

Categories

We have implemented a non-standard method of handling categories in this application, because the North Wind sample already supported categories directly in the database. Sometimes you cannot limit your application to the maximum 15 categories that are supported by the Palm device; in that case, you can use this technique.

To the user, the combo box with the category names appears quite normal. We load the categories in the *InitCategories* routine shown in Example 3-4. We hardcode All as a special category; this pseudo-category displays all the product records in the grid. This category goes into the combo box first, followed by the rest of the data read from the PDB.

Example 3-4. Listing of InitCategories

```
Public Sub InitCategories()
    Dim tRec As tCategoriesRecord

    cboCats.AddItem "All"
    cboCats.ItemData(cboCats.NewIndex) = -1

    Do While Not PDBEOF(dbCategories)
        If ReadCategoriesRecord(tRec) Then
            cboCats.AddItem tRec.CategoryName
            cboCats.ItemData(cboCats.NewIndex) = tRec.CategoryID
        End If
        PDBMoveNext dbCategories
    Loop

    cboCats.ListIndex = 0
End Sub
```

The tCategoriesRecord UDT and *ReadCategoriesRecord* function are declared in the AppForge-generated VB module for the categories PDB, which was created when the database was converted. There are similar declarations for the other two databases as well.

Type-ahead search

Clicking the search button displays an edit field for the user query, which is a lookup of the product name. If the grid contains a lot of records, we'd like to implement some sort of *search-as-you scribe* functionality to let the user zero in on her data with each Graffiti stroke. Unfortunately, the *PDBFindRecordByField* method doesn't provide a partial string match. It matches the *first* character of a field if the search criterion is a single character, or the *entire* field if the criterion is longer, but it doesn't match anything in between. Here we use a little ingenuity to provide a partial text lookup function, by searching the grid first and then looking up the record in the database. This is shown in Example 3-5.

Example 3-5. Listing for txtSearch_Change

```
Private Sub txtSearch_Change()
    Dim I As Integer
    Dim lID As Long

    gridInv.Col = 1
    For I = 0 To gridInv.Rows - 1
        gridInv.Row = I
        If LCase(txtSearch.Text) = LCase(Left(gridInv.Text, Len(txtSearch.Text))) Then
            gridInv.TopRow = I
            Exit For
        End If
    Next I
```

Example 3-5. Listing for txtSearch_Change (continued)

```
    PDBFindRecordByField dbProducts, ProductName_Field, gridInv.Text
    If PDBCurrentIndex(dbProducts) >= 0 Then
        PDBGetField dbProducts, tProductsDatabaseFields.ProductID_Field, lID
        ShowProdDetails lID
    End If

    gridInv.Col = 0

End Sub
```

This is a complicated routine, so let's look at it in small pieces. The first thing we do is set up the Grid ingot for our search. We make the second column in the grid active—the product name column—and then we search all the rows:

```
    gridInv.Col = 1
    For I = 0 To gridInv.Rows - 1
```

Remember, virtually every property in the grid uses a zero-based index. Setting the active column once saves a little time during the scan of the text. Here's the partial match from the left:

```
    LCase(txtSearch.Text) = LCase(Left(gridInv.Text, Len(txtSearch.Text)))
```

If this matches, then we update the Grid *TopRow* property to make the matched record visible. If there is no match, then we redraw the current record. This is simple but clumsy code; a production Palm application would not do this extra work.

Now that we know there is a match, let's find the corresponding record in the database using the full product name from the Text of the found Grid cell:

```
    PDBFindRecordByField dbProducts, ProductName_Field, gridInv.Text
```

We won't discuss the details of the *ShowProdDetails* method, which reads values from the current database record and updates the text boxes on the main screen.

After you have completed the search, click the search button again to hide the text window.

Suppliers

Most of the user interface is contained on the main form, which was shown previously in Figure 3-10. There is a lot of detail in the database about the supplier of any product. To access this information, the user taps on the Supplier button to display the form shown in Figure 3-12.

This completes our discussion of the North Wind sample example. If you play with the application, you will discover other minor features, such as the horizontal scrollbar on the grid, the use of the Graffiti shift indicator to page through the data, or the option of sorting the data by tapping a column header.

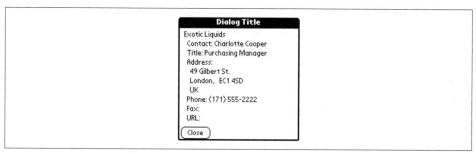

Figure 3-12. The Supplier form

Resources

The primary resource is the AppForge PDB library reference, which is part of the product. The reference is also available on the AppForge web site at *http://www.appforge.com/dev/usersguide.html*. The Palm File Format Specification, which describes the layout of databases in great detail, is available from Palm at *http://www.palmos.com/dev/tech/docs/*.

AppForge also provides sample applications that read and write the main Palm native application databases, such as Address Book and To-Do. These are distributed with the product.

There are also some excellent third-party tools that are invaluable for debugging; these provide the ability to explore and modify the attributes and contents of databases and records on the Palm device. Popular examples are *Z'Catalog* and *Insider*. Both are shareware products that are readily available on the Internet.

PART II

Data Connectivity

CHAPTER 4

Conduit Development

The original concept of the Palm was of a device tethered to data on the desktop. The PDA is an extension of the desktop, not its replacement. 3Com (the Palm PDA manufacturer) has expanded this design concept; it now calls the Palm device the "connected organizer." Palm wants you to build applications that function in today's mobile and connected world.

In this chapter, we look at building *conduits* using Microsoft Visual Basic (VB). Conceptually, a conduit is the tether that moves data back and forth, connecting your Palm application and its data store. A conduit is a piece of software that runs on the desktop when the PDA is synchronizing, under the control of the Palm HotSync manager.* In this book, we are going to build conduits using VB and ActiveX.

By design, a conduit is dedicated to a single Palm application, which will have one or more associated Palm databases. Keep in mind that, even though the conduit is a piece of desktop software, the application data may be located anywhere—on the desktop, in a relational database, or even on the Internet. Once you have decided where your application's data resides, it is then your responsibility to build a conduit capable of delivering that data to the Palm device. The Palm Conduit Development Kit provides a framework for ActiveX conduit development, which we'll explain in detail later in this chapter.

Note that conduits developed in VB can be used with any application and database on the PDA, not only those created with AppForge. The high-level HotSync architecture is shown in Figure 4-1.

The Palm HotSync manager is in control of the synchronization process. It maintains a list of configured conduits in the system registry, and it handles the interface with the Palm PDA. The HotSync manager uses a set of COM objects—the Sync Suite API—to communicate with ActiveX conduits. The conduit manages application-specific data and supplies a userinterface if appropriate.

---

* There are other HotSync managers for enterprise use that allow remote connections. Conduits can also be built using C/C++ or Java, but we won't discuss either of those languages in this book.

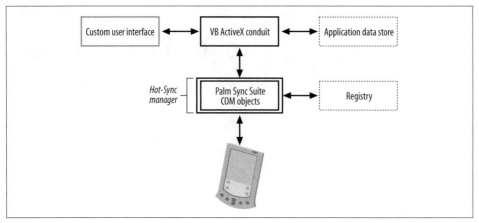

Figure 4-1. Overview of HotSync COM architecture

This chapter covers how to compile and register an ActiveX conduit with the HotSync manager, how to use the Sync Suite API to synchronize Palm PDA data with the desktop, and how to handle the user interface.

Applications and Conduits

Before we get to the mechanics of conduit development, let's review the concept of data synchronization as it applies to Palm applications and databases. If the handheld is an extension of the desktop, then it is natural to ask: How should the data flow between the handheld and the desktop? This is going to depend in great deal on the design and purpose of your application and its databases.

Entertainment or utility programs rarely have a conduit—they don't have data worth moving to the desktop. These applications usually save any data in the system Preferences database, which is automatically backed up and restored by the HotSync manager. We covered application preferences in Chapter 3.

More typical is the unidirectional conduit, in which the data flows from the Palm device to the desktop, or the other way around. This type of conduit is useful in applications like questionnaires, where the Palm is used primarily as a remote data collection tool.

The Palm PDA's native applications, like Address and To-Do, use a mirror-image conduit, where changes on the desktop and the device are replicated in both directions. This type of synchronization is so important that Palm has documented exactly how a mirror-image conduit should behave. We will cover mirror-image synchronization in detail later in this chapter.

A transactional conduit processes data to produce intermediate results, which are written back to the Palm device. The data flow in a transactional conduit can be in one or both directions. You could implement this sort of conduit for an application that uploads orders to a SQL database for fulfillment processing and then downloads invoices to the Palm. We discuss this type of conduit in Chapter 5.

Finally, there are system functions such as installation and backup that use special-purpose conduits to perform their functions. The default backup conduit synchronizes databases whose applications don't have a custom conduit, or databases that have a conduit but whose type is not DATA. The backup conduit, which is supplied by the Palm desktop installation, simply makes an exact copy of your application's database or databases on the desktop. (Technically, to be backed up by the default conduit, a Palm database must have the backup bit set.)

Conduit Types

Palm had to design the HotSync manager and conduit interface to support a wide variety of data synchronization and replication needs. Each conduit registers its unique creator identifier and synchronization type with the HotSync manager. Note that your conduit might support more than one type of synchronization; in that case, you should provide a user interface to allow the user to customize the behavior of your conduit. We'll show you how to do this later in the chapter.

Here are the types of conduits supported by the Palm Conduit Development Kit, as documented in the Conduit Reference manual:

Fast
:   Performs a fast synchronization

Slow
:   Performs a slow synchronization

HHtoPC
:   Copies handheld database to the desktop and overwrites all old records

PCtoHH
:   Copies desktop database to the handheld and overwrites all old records

Install
:   Installs new application to the handheld (system function)

Backup
:   Backs up handheld database to the desktop (system function)

DoNothing
:   Doesn't perform any synchronization

ProfileInstall
:   Performs a profile download (system function)

The HotSync manager on the desktop keeps track of when the user last synchronized his or her Palm device with this desktop. It uses this information to determine which conduits to call, and the type of synchronization each conduit is to perform.

The HotSync manager supports multiple users on the desktop. It also supports a single user with multiple Palm devices. The HotSync API provides identifiers during a HotSync session to enable a conduit to determine which user and/or device is synchronizing. We don't discuss this capability further in this book, but it is covered in the Palm Windows Conduit Companion and Reference.

Of course, the user may set the type of synchronization manually, as illustrated in Figure 4-2.

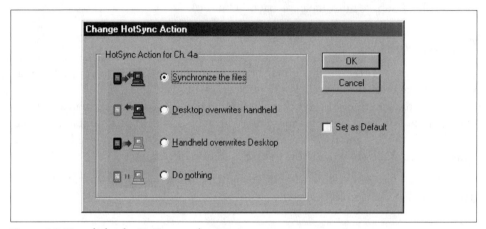

Figure 4-2. User dialog for HotSync preferences

If a conduit does not support a user interface, the HotSync manager uses the conduit's default synchronization type. We show how to implement a custom user interface for your conduit later in this chapter.

Conduits should always have a UI. Otherwise, your user will click the Change button in the Custom dialog and nothing will happen. Not only is this rude, it will leave your user wondering if something is broken.

Mirror Synchronization

As we mentioned earlier, mirror-image synchronization requires that a conduit replicate changes between the desktop and the Palm device. Mirror-image conduits should support both fast and slow synchronization. When your conduit is called to do a *FastSync*, it only needs to look for new or dirty records in your application's Palm database and on the desktop. If your conduit is called for a slow sync, it must look at every record on the PDA and the desktop. The HotSync manager requests a slow sync whenever it determines that the last sync was not with this desktop. Otherwise, it requests a *FastSync*.

The Palm database manager supports per-record flags that track any changes to records in the database. These flags are listed in Table 4-1. In order to successfully implement a mirror-image conduit, your desktop database must support some or all of these flags on a per-record basis.

Table 4-1. Palm database record flags

Flag	Meaning
Changed	Either create a new record or edit an existing record
Deleted	Delete the record
Archived	Make an archive copy, then delete the record
Secret	Mark record as private

The Windows CDK Companion has a section on design decisions and tradeoffs that you can use to evaluate the kind of conduit your application can support. We'll summarize a few key questions here:

- Do you have unique record identifiers that can be mapped into Palm record identifiers?
- Do you support per-record attributes, such as dirty, deleted, and archived?
- Is it easy to detect changes to desktop records?
- Are the desktop records categorized?
- Is it simple to map database records to desktop records or entities?
- Is it possible to partition the application and conduit to minimize synchronization times?

Unfortunately, there are no generic answers to these design questions. We will address these questions as they apply to a sample application and conduit that we will present later in this chapter. You'll have to consider them from the context of your own application.

If your user has experience with any of the Palm native applications, then he'll expect your conduit to replicate changes in the same manner. Palm has gone to great lengths to document this behavior, as it pertains to the native applications. (The synchronization logic is spelled out in the Palm Conduit Programmer's Companion for Windows, which is part of the CDK.) Your conduit should emulate as much of this behavior as makes sense for your application.

Table 4-2 shows the possible states for each record in an application. The desktop record states run along the top of the table and the Palm record states run down the left side.

Table 4-2. *Mirror conduit record states*

	No record	No change	Change	New	Delete
No record				D → P	
No change			D → P		Remove DP
Change		P → D	Conflict		P → D
New	P → D				
Delete		Remove DP	D → P		

The action that your conduit should take is found in the intersection of each of the possible states, and is spelled out in the following list:

D → P
Desktop record replaces Palm record

P → D
Palm record replaces desktop record

Remove (DP)
Delete the record from the desktop and/or the Palm

Conflict
Follow application rule to resolve synchronization conflict

After the conduit takes the indicated action, the record on the desktop is in the same state as the record on the Palm.

A conflict arises when a record is changed simultaneously on the Palm device and on the desktop. Palm recommends that this conflict be resolved by migrating the change in both directions. The user can then edit or delete the data on either the Palm or the desktop. At the next synchronization, the conduit will clean up all the changes.

Note that the blank cells in Table 4-2 correspond to conditions that Palm considers logically impossible or irrelevant to conduit design. Palm derived these conditions from the behavior of its native applications. Your conduit and application might not need to support all these conditions, or they might need to support different possibilities.

The situation is slightly more complicated if your application supports archive records. A Palm application such as Address offers to archive a record when it is deleted. This is an offer to preserve the data somewhere on the desktop; presumably, the desktop provides the corresponding restore operation.

The ability to archive older records, instead of deleting them forever, was crucial to the early Palm devices, which sported 128 KB of memory. Users were forever shuffling data between the device and the desktop. While it is less critical now, memory is still a scarce resource. So if you can support the archive option in your application, you certainly should.

In general, when a Palm record is marked for archival, the conduit archives the record in an application-specific fashion, and then deletes the record from both the Palm and the desktop.

Table 4-3 shows how to handle Palm database records that are marked for archiving. In this table, the desktop record states appear along the top of the table and the Palm record archive states appear on the left side.

Table 4-3. Mirror sync actions with Palm archive request

	Delete	No change	No record	Change
Archive	Archive, Remove DP	Archive, Remove DP	Archive, Remove DP	
Archive, Change				Conflict
Archive, No Change				D → P

A conflict arises if a record has changed in both databases as the same time. In such a case, the conflict is deepened because the user has also requested that the record be archived—this means that she doesn't want to see it again any time soon. Here's how the Palm CDK Companion says you should handle the conflict:

> If the changes are identical, archive both the device record and the desktop record. If the changes are not identical, do not archive the device record; instead, add the desktop record to the device database, and add the device record to the desktop database.

Table 4-4 shows what to do when a desktop record has been marked for archival. The most common case, in which the Palm device record has not changed, is handled by archiving the record and then removing it from both the device and the desktop.

Table 4-4. Mirror sync actions with desktop archive request

	Archive	Archive, change	Archive, no change
Delete			
No change	Archive, Remove DP		
No record			
Change		Conflict	P → D

Not surprisingly, a conflict occurs when the record to be archived has been changed in both databases. According to the Palm CDK Companion:

> If the changes are identical, archive the device record and then delete the records from both the device and desktop databases. If the changes are not identical, do not archive the desktop record; instead, add the desktop record to the device database and add the device record to the desktop database.

A mirror-image conduit should also support the HHtoPC and PCtoHH synchronization types. Recall that these sync types cause the handheld data to overwrite the desktop or vice versa. At first it might seem counter-intuitive that your conduit could be called to blindly overwrite user data, on either the desktop or the Palm device. But keep in mind that your conduit is almost always called this way as a result of user intervention.

For example, your user might accidentally delete an entire category of data records on the Palm device. Instead of then synchronizing these changes, and thereby deleting the data from the desktop as well, the user can direct the conduit to overwrite all the Palm data, effectively restoring the deleted records.

Categories

A conduit must synchronize changes in category data as well as record data. Because a category is actually a compound data type—it has both a name and a numeric ID—the synchronization logic is a little harder. Palm addresses the default logic for the native conduits in the CDK documentation. We summarize it here:

1. If the category ID has changed on either the desktop or the PDA, but the name is the same, update all desktop records to use the PDA category ID.

2. If the desktop category name has changed, but the category ID is the same, then update the PDA category name. Note that this only holds true if the new desktop category name is not already in use on the PDA.

3. If there is a category with a new name and ID on the desktop, and neither is in use on the PDA, then create a new category on the PDA. If the index is already in use, then assign a new index from the PDA, and update all the desktop records with it.

If your application supports categories, give careful consideration to the mapping between category names and identifiers on the Palm PDA and the desktop. And be aware that there is native support in the Palm operating system for only 15 active categories.

Other Types of Conduits

Your conduit will never be called for Install, Backup, or ProfileInstall synchronization. These are reserved to the HotSync manager to perform special system functions. Your conduit can be called for DoNothing synchronization, always at the user's request.

If you have a transactional conduit, you will have to masquerade as a mirror-image conduit. We don't discuss transactional conduits in this book. These conduits have the same structure and logic as the conduits we have already described, but they must handle distributed transactions and error rollback and recovery as well. We do cover the use of conduits to manage SQL data in Chapter 7.

Conduit Design

There are several major design principles for a conduit. The first, and most important, is that the conduit runs as quickly as possible. No one wants to wait while synchronization grinds on and on. Honoring the fast and slow sync flags will help you to optimize performance. A fast conduit also minimizes the use of the Palm device's serial port. This is important, because serial port use can drain the PDA's batteries very quickly.

The second principle is that a conduit must always move application data in a natural way between the Palm device and the desktop. Your user relies completely on this behavior. She also relies on the conduit to restore all data in case of a disaster. If your conduit is not correctly implemented, or has bugs, user acceptance of your application will suffer greatly.

A third principle is that your conduit must be able to run without attention from the user. While this is a good design principle for software in general, it is especially important for a conduit. This is because the user might be synchronizing from a remote location, communicating with the HotSync manager over a modem or network connection. The user will not be able to respond to any prompts or dialog boxes that a conduit might display on the desktop. This will cause the entire HotSync session to hang.

Palm provides some more design guidelines in the C/C++ Conduit Companion; you should certainly study those before implementing your own conduit.

If you are building a mirror-image conduit, then follow the logic diagrammed earlier in Tables 4-2, 4-3, and 4-4, as they apply to your application. If you don't allow desktop editing of data in your application, for example, then your conduit doesn't have to support it, either.

Having a user interface and allowing the user to override the conduit's default behavior will help you achieve acceptance. If at all possible, support uploading or downloading all records from your user interface.

Note that if your Palm database design maps into a relational database, and you used the AppForge database tools described in Chapter 4, then you can likely use the Universal Conduit. We discuss the pros and cons of the Universal Conduit in Chapter 5, and show you how to use it to integrate SQL Server data into your applications.

When Not to Use a Conduit

Not all synchronization situations require you to implement a conduit. It is perfectly appropriate to make a new database from scratch and download it to the device, if you know that all or most of your application's data has changed.

Simply generate your database from the new data, and put it in the HotSync installation directory.* The database will be automatically deployed to the device with the next synchronization, overwriting any existing PDA data in the process. If your application has a database that is read-only, and that is periodically refreshed, you can use this technique. If your sales department produces a list of prices that changes monthly, then you don't need to execute a conduit every day.

Not having a conduit can greatly simplify the distribution of your application. You don't have to worry about developing an installation script for your conduit and its associated runtime objects.

If the Palm Desktop is configured properly, the Windows default shell action for PRC and PDB files is to call the Palm *Instapp.exe* program, which will copy the file into the Palm desktop installation directory.

This means that you can post your database files on the Web or in ZIP archives. When your user downloads or extracts your file and double-clicks it, it is queued for installation at the next HotSync.

Installing the CDK

The Conduit Development Kit (CDK) is freely downloadable from the Palm web site.[†] The CDK contains libraries and runtime bindings for VB and COM, as well as the C/C++ language. The *InstallShield* wizard puts everything into the directory you select (see Figure 4-3).

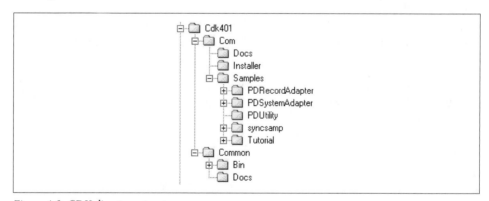

Figure 4-3. CDK directory structure

---

* You can use the *InstallAide* functions to do this, which are part of the Palm Desktop. These functions are described in the CDK documentation; we don't discuss them in this book.

† You want CDK release 4.01 DR1, which was the latest release available as of this writing. This release is the first that exposes a COM interface specifically for VB development.

You can choose to install only the COM libraries, samples, and documentation by using the custom installation procedure and deselecting the C/API. We recommend performing a full installation, because the C/API contains some additional documentation you will find useful.

The *Com* folder contains the VB tutorial and sample projects, an installation tool, and another directory that simply contains links to the documents mentioned above. Most of the sample projects in the CDK are primers that focus on explaining at most one or two parts of the CDK. There is also a longer example, *SyncSamp*, which replaces the default Memo conduit and illustrates a complete conduit.

The *Common* folder contains the CDK programs and libraries used when developing conduits. This folder also contains the documentation, in both Adobe PDF and Microsoft Help formats. Earlier releases of the CDK runtime are supplied for backward compatibility; these won't help you, because only the most recent release supports VB development.

If you have the Palm desktop software installed on your development machine, as is required to run AppForge, there are some issues you should be aware of when you install the CDK. By default, your system uses the HotSync manager that was installed with the Palm desktop software. Unfortunately, the ActiveX objects needed to develop and debug conduits are not installed with earlier releases of the Palm desktop.

If you have the luxury of developing your applications and software on separate computers, the following step is unnecessary. Otherwise, you will have to alter the desktop configuration so that the new HotSync manager runs during the synchronization process. Use the Microsoft *RegEdit.exe* tool, and alter the two registry keys as shown in Example 4-1. Note that the location of the updated HotSync manager depends on where you installed the CDK on your filesystem.

Example 4-1. Registry settings for HotSync manager

```
HKEY_CURRENT_USER\Software\U.S. Robotics\Pilot Desktop\Core
    HotSyncPath = C:\CDK401\Common\Bin\C4.01\Hotsync.exe
    Path = C:\CDK401\Common\Bin\C4.01
```

This is a good time to run the CDK tutorial *SimpleDB*, which shows how to run and debug a program under the control of the HotSync manager. This is how all conduits are executed, and it is important that you get comfortable with this environment. Running the tutorial also ensures that all of the CDK components are properly installed, and that the new HotSync manager is running correctly.

To run the tutorial, use the *CondCfg.exe* program to register the VB development environment as a conduit. Once the HotSync manager calls the VB IDE, you are in control and can test and debug your conduits with all the powerful VB features to which you are accustomed.

Let's walk through the steps required to configure the tutorial. Start the *CondCfg.exe* tool to show all the currently registered conduits, and to add, edit, and delete conduits. If you are developing on your own Palm desktop, be careful not to disturb the settings for the native Palm applications! We disable all conduits except those actually under development; this both increases the speed of the synchronization process and provides some security from data corruption. Press the Add button to bring up the Conduit Information dialog, into which you enter the settings for your conduit (see Figure 4-4). First, you must enter ComConduit.dll in the name field. The HotSync manager uses this DLL to locate and instantiate COM conduits.

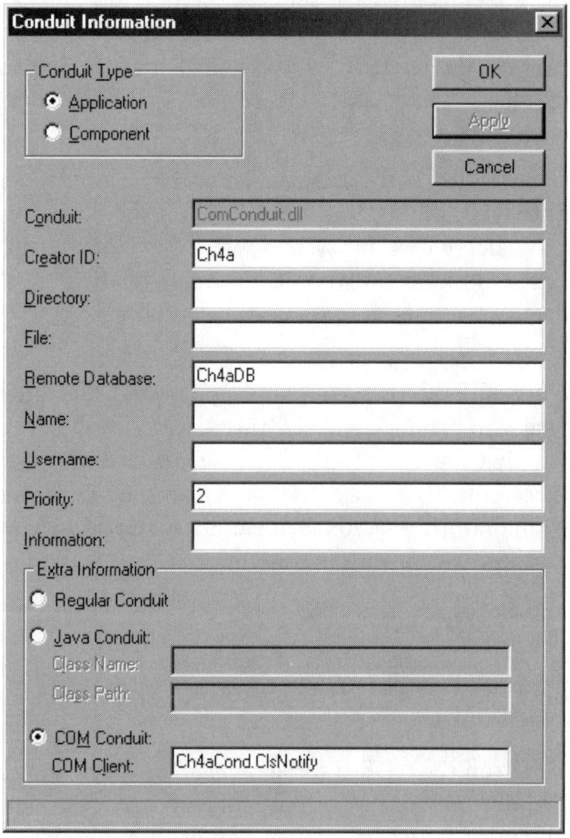

Figure 4-4. CondCfg.exe registration screen

Because each conduit handles exactly one application on the Palm device, you must enter the unique Creator ID of your application. (There must be only one conduit registered for any Palm application. *CondCfig.exe* will not allow you to register a second conduit for the same application, or, more precisely, an application with the same Creator ID).

If there is no application on the Palm device with this ID, then the conduit will not run. You must install your Palm application first.

For our sample conduit, we entered Ch4a as the Creator ID. In addition, we entered Ch4aDB in the optional remote database field. As we'll see later, the HotSync manager provides the conduit with a more accurate list of databases during an actual synchronization session.

In the extra information group box at the bottom of the dialog, select the COM Conduit radio option button. Enter the full path to the VB IDE in the COM client field.

Leave all the other fields blank or with the default values. These settings were shown earlier in Figure 4-4. Press the OK button to register the new settings, and restart the HotSync manager. Then exit the configuration tool.

Now put the Palm device into the cradle and press the HotSync button. Although the synchronization process runs normally, the VB IDE doesn't activate. That is because the HotSync manager could not find an application on the Palm device with a Creator ID of Ch4a.

You will need to download our sample application for this chapter and install the application file *Ch4a.prc*. After the application is installed, perform a HotSync one more time. This time, the HotSync manager on the desktop displays the message Status: Synchronizing COMConduit, and the VB IDE pops up.

Now you can test your environment by opening *SimpleDB.vbp* in the CDK *Tutorial* folder. This VB project opens the native Memo application, and reads all the records that match a search term. Set a breakpoint in the button click event, and press F8 to step through the program. Note that Palm device displays Synchronizing Memo Pad, because the Memo database has been opened during a HotSync session. You are now communicating as a conduit with the Palm device from VB!

If the VB IDE doesn't appear, put the HotSync manager into its verbose mode. First, stop the HotSync manager by right-clicking on its icon in the Windows system tray, and select Exit. Next, restart the HotSync manager with the -v option from the command line. After synchronizing, you can review the diagnostic log for errors. To do this, right-click on the icon and select View Log.

If the *SimpleDB* project doesn't connect to the Palm, or exhibits other errors, check that the Palm conduit references are set correctly (these are shown later in this chapter in Figure 4-7). You do this from the VB IDE by choosing the References option from the Project menu. If these references are missing, try registering those ActiveX libraries by hand and restarting VB.

Nuts and Bolts

If you stepped through the *SimpleDB* CDK sample project, you saw that the VB code manipulated the Palm device's databases and records using COM objects. Let's dig a little deeper into the HotSync architecture to see how a conduit communicates with the Palm device.

Recall from Figure 4-1 that the COM Sync Suite provides the interface to the HotSync manager and the Palm device.

The Sync Suite itself has several layers to isolate its interface from the underlying details of the HotSync application and to support both VB/COM and C/C++ conduits. This layered approach frees the VB programmer from worrying about messy details such as which serial port the HotSync manager is using to communicate with the Palm device.

To simplify conduit development, the Sync Suite provides COM objects and classes that encapsulate the HotSync manager, the user, and databases on the Palm device. A utility class is provided to handle things like Motorola byte ordering and unique record identifiers.* These classes and their relationships are shown in Figure 4-5.

There are VB projects in the CDK that cover these objects and interfaces. Rather than enumerate all of them here, we will discuss the major ones we encounter as we develop our simple conduit. Once you understand the framework, you can use the VB Object Browser and the Conduit Reference manual to find the special properties you need for your conduit.

The HotSync manager expects your ActiveX conduit to implement the *IPDClientNotify* interface, which it calls when it needs your services, either to synchronize or to access configuration settings and preferences.

Sample Application and Conduit

The sample code for this chapter includes an AppForge application project, *Ch4a.vbp*, and an ActiveX conduit project, *Ch4aCond.vbp*.

You can use the application to create, edit and delete records on the Palm device. This application creates a database that consists of text records with a single field. Figure 4-6 shows the application's user interface on the Palm PDA. The application has a Creator ID of Ch4a, and the database is named Ch4aDB.

---

* The Palm device currently uses the Motorola 68000 series processor. This CPU represents numbers in little-Endian order, which is different from the Intel 80x86 processors. Your conduit must handle the conversion if your application stores numeric data.

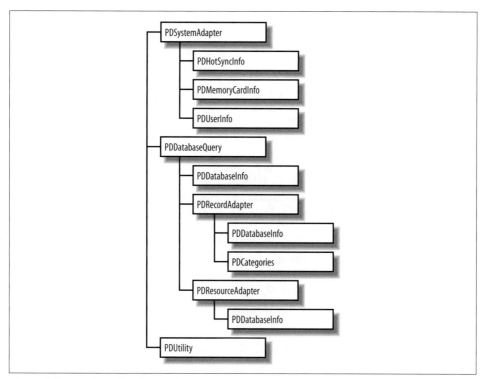

Figure 4-5. Sync Suite class hierarchy

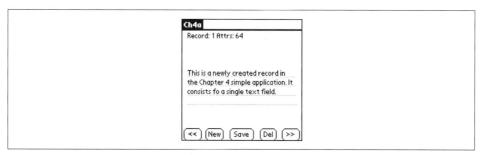

Figure 4-6. Main screen for sample application Ch4a

There is no corresponding Windows application for this example. Instead, we represent desktop records using text files in a desktop folder. We will use the record identifier from the Palm database as the filename—this will guarantee uniqueness in our naming system. Synchronized desktop records have the extension *.REC*. Newly added desktop records will have the extension *.NEW*, deleted records will have the extension *.DEL*, and changed desktop records will have the extension *.CHG*.

By following this scheme, we can implement all the synchronization possibilities shown previuosly in Table 4-2. Note that to simplify this example, we aren't going to support archived records or database categories.

Let's outline what this conduit example is going to demonstrate:

- How to implement all required COM interfaces
- How to support user customization
- How to read and write data on the Palm device (*FastSync* and *HHtoPC sync*)
- Log activity and errors
- Ways to demonstrate interactive debugging

Configure the VB Conduit Project

We start building the conduit by creating a new VB project. Using the New Project Wizard, choose ActiveX EXE. This will create the conduit as an out-of-process COM server. Normally, this is inefficient due to the marshaling of data between processes during method calls. But it gives us the ability to debug by running the conduit as a standalone process, and intercepting HotSync manager calls.

After creating the project, add in the references to two Palm COM Sync Suite type libraries used by all conduits: *ComStandard.dll* and *ComDirect.dll* (see Figure 4-7). As usual, you do this from the VB IDE by choosing the References option from the Project menu.

Save your project after renaming the default Class1 component and file to something more appropriate; we use SyncNotify and *Ch4aNotify.cls* in the example. We set the project name as Ch4aCond; note that you should use the default Thread Pool threading model.

Support IPDClientNotify

The HotSync manager expects COM conduits to support the *IPDClientNotify* public interface. It calls this interface to get information about your conduit, to allow the user to change settings for your conduit, and to synchronize your Palm application with its desktop data.

IPDClientNotify has four member routines that must be supported; these are summarized in Table 4-5.

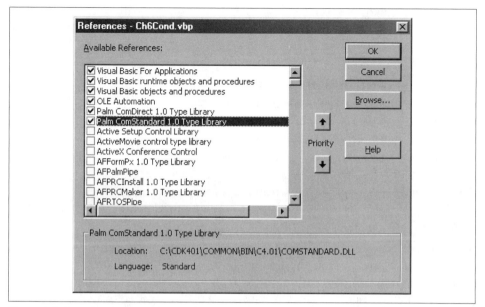

Figure 4-7. Sync Suite COM references

Table 4-5. IPDNotifyClient public interface

Interface method	Functionality
GetConduitInfo	Return conduit name, version, and default synchronization type to HotSync manager
CfgConduit	Allow user customization of sync type and return new settings to HotSync manager
ConfigureConduit	Same as *CfgConduit*, but called by earlier versions of HotSync manager
BeginProcess	Perform synchronization

To support a COM interface in VB, use the `Implements` keyword. We put this right at the top of our class module:

```
Implements IPDClientNotify
```

Any conduits registered with the HotSync manager as ActiveX or COM clients that do not respond to these calls are dropped from the list of active conduits. This happens if you don't implement some part of the interface, or if you throw a runtime error during processing.

You should review the VB documentation if you have never implemented multiple COM interfaces in your class objects before.

GetConduitInfo

When the HotSync manager is initialized, it looks at all the conduits that have been installed on the desktop. The HotSync manager calls the function *GetConduitInfo* for all registered conduits several times, each time requesting different information. Table 4-6 details the parameters to *GetConduitInfo*.

Table 4-6. Parameters to GetConduitInfo

Parameter	Direction/Type	Purpose
InfoType	[IN] EgetConduitInfo	Type of HotSync request
CreatorId	[IN] Long	Creator ID of current application
UserId	[IN] Long	Numeric ID of current user
UserName	[IN] String	String ID of current user

The HotSync manager passes the Creator ID of the application your conduit is registered to handle. This is not redundant, as nothing prevents the registration of your conduit for more than one application.

The HotSync manager also passes the identity of the current desktop user in UserId and UserName. Again, your application might be required to support more than one user. Note that the username is not the Windows login name; instead, it is whatever name the Palm device user chose when installing the HotSync software.

The HotSync manager passes a request for information in the *infoType* parameter. The request is one of the constants in the public enumeration EGetConduitInfo; *GetConduitInfo* returns a variant appropriate to the type of request made by the HotSync manager, as shown in Table 4-7.

Table 4-7. Return data types for GetConduitInfo

Request type	Function return value
EgetConduitName	String
EgetConduitVersion	Double
EgetDefaultAction	Value from enumeration ESyncType
EgetMfcVersion	Value from enumeration EMfcVersion

We have coded *GetConduitInfo* using a simple Select Case ... End Case statement, with a case for each possible request type. The code for *GetConduitInfo* is shown in Example 4-2.

Example 4-2. Listing for SyncNotify.GetConduitInfo

```
Private Function _
IPDClientNotify_GetConduitInfo(ByVal infoType As EGetConduitInfo, _
                               ByVal dwCreatorId As Long, _
                               ByVal dwUserId As Long, _
                               ByVal bstrUserName As String) As Variant

    Select Case infoType
    Case eGetConduitName
        IPDClientNotify_GetConduitInfo = "Ch4a Conduit"
```

Example 4-2. Listing for SyncNotify.GetConduitInfo (continued)

```
Case eGetConduitVersion
    IPDClientNotify_GetConduitInfo = 3#
Case eGetDefaultAction
    IPDClientNotify_GetConduitInfo = ESyncTypes.eFast
Case eGetMfcVersion
    IPDClientNotify_GetConduitInfo = EMfcVersion.ePDMFC_NOT_USED
End Select
```

```
End Function
```

The conduit name is displayed when the user selects the Custom option from the HotSync icon in the system tray, so this should be a string that is meaningful to your users. Palm does not document how the HotSync manager uses your conduit version, so it appears that a conduit can supply any double value.

The HotSync manager uses your conduit's default action when synchronizing, unless the user sets a new default type (see the following section). As with most conduits, we specify fast synchronization as the default:

```
Case eGetDefaultAction
    IPDClientNotify_GetConduitInfo = PDDirectlib.eFast
```

The HotSync manager supports multiple conduit architectures, among them conduits implemented using the Microsoft Foundation Class framework. ActiveX conduits should return ePDMFC_NOT_USED when asked for the MFC version, to avoid confusing the HotSync manager.

CfgConduit

When the user needs to change your conduit's behavior, the HotSync manager calls the interface function *CfgConduit*. This call is always in response to user interaction with a dialog similar to that shown in Figure 4-2. Table 4-8 details the parameters to *CfgConduit*.

Table 4-8. Parameters to CfgConduit

Parameter	Type/direction	Purpose
CreatorId	[IN] Long	Creator ID of current application
UserId	[IN] Long	Numeric ID of current user
UserId	[IN] String	String ID of current user
PathName	[IN] String	User folder in HotSync directory
SyncPerm	[IN/OUT] EsyncTypes	See text
SyncTemp	[IN/OUT] EsyncTypes	See text
SyncNew	[IN/OUT] EsyncTypes	See text
SyncPref	[OUT] ESyncPref	Tell HotSync manager that changes are permanent or temporary

Just like *GetConduitInfo*, the HotSync manager passes *CfgConduit* the application's Creator ID and the identity of the current desktop user. In addition, the HotSync manager passes the location of a folder on the desktop for this user. The folder location is usually relative to the HotSync manager; with our configuration, this looks something like:

C:\CDK401\Common\Bin\C4.01\HolmesM

Here's what the Palm Windows Conduit Reference says about the three sync-type parameters:

SyncNew
> The type of synchronization to perform for a new device

SyncTemp
> The type of synchronization to perform on a onetime (temporary) basis

SyncPerm
> The type of synchronization to perform on an ongoing (permanent) basis

The implication is that you set these variables to tell the HotSync manager how to run your conduit under different circumstances. Unfortunately, reading and setting these variables from a COM conduit does not work exactly as documented.

 On entry, you will find that all the variables have the same value, usually the default synchronization type for your conduit. On exit, you must set all three variables to the same value.

The HotSync manager uses the SyncPref variable to determine if the synchronization choice is to be made permanent, or if it is for the next synchronization session only. Set this value to either ePermanentPreference or eTemporaryPreference as appropriate.

Let's look at our implementation of this interface function; it is really quite simple. Example 4-3 shows the code for *CfgConduit*.

Example 4-3. Listing for SyncNotify.CfgConduit

```
Private Sub IPDClientNotify_CfgConduit(ByVal nCreatorId As Long, _
                            ByVal nUserId As Long, _
                            ByVal bstrUserName As String, _
                            ByVal bstrPathName As String, _
                            ByVal nSyncPerm As ESyncTypes, _
                            ByRef nSyncTemp As ESyncTypes, _
                            ByRef nSyncNew As ESyncTypes, _
                            ByRef nSyncPref As ESyncPref)

    ' Set up the form: type of sync to perform, user directory
    SyncForm.SetFields nSyncNew

    ' Let the user make choices, then retrieve them from the form. The
    ' form must be modal, this is required by COM.
```

Example 4-3. Listing for SyncNotify.CfgConduit (continued)

```
SyncForm.Show vbModal
SyncForm.GetFields nSyncNew, nSyncTemp, nSyncPerm, nSyncPref
```

```
End Sub
```

The project includes a form called SyncForm, through which the user makes changes. The first thing we do is to call *SetFields*, a public function in the form module. It sets private form variables that are used in the *Load* event to initialize the controls. Without it, we'd have to interact with the form elements directly. This is risky because accessing a form element usually causes the form to be shown before you are ready.

Next, we show the form and let the user interact with the dialog. Note that the form must be shown *modally*: a COM object cannot display a non-modal form without a lot of extra steps. The form will fail to load if you do not supply the *VBModal* parameter:

```
SyncForm.Show vbModal
```

SyncForm

Since this is a mirror-image conduit, our custom user interface is designed to look just like the Palm native applications.

The form is simple, consisting of a group of radio buttons for the sync types, a checkbox for making the selected sync preference the default, and OK and Cancel buttons. We added an image control, to depict graphically what each type of synchronization does. The control's bitmap is taken from a screen shot of the Palm Address conduit.

The form user interface was shown earlier, in Figure 4-2. In our example, the form name is SyncForm, and it is saved as *Ch4aForm.frm*.

Your conduit might not need to support all these synchronization types, so feel free to remove choices. For example, we have disabled the PCtoHH option in our sample conduit (see Figure 4-2). But you should always include an option for your conduit to do nothing. We guarantee that this option will be used more often than you think!

And if your conduit has special requirements or extra configuration options, this is the place to expose them.

Here is the implementation of *SetFields*, which was discussed earlier:

```
Public Sub SetFields(ByVal nSyncPerm As Long)
    m_nSyncType = nSyncPerm
End Sub
```

The code for the form *Load* event is shown in Example 4-4. *Load* assumes that the private form variables have already been set to appropriate values—so be sure to call *SetFields* before loading the form. In *Load,* we set the radio buttons and checkbox to the states indicated by the public form variable values.

Example 4-4. Listing for SyncForm.Load

```
Private Sub Form_Load( )

    ' Set the radio buttons based on the HotSync information
    optSync.Value = False
    optHHToPC.Value = False
    optPCToHH.Value = False
    optDoNothing.Value = False

    Select Case m_nSyncType
    Case eHHtoPC
        optHHToPC.Value = True
    Case ePCtoHH
        optPCToHH.Value = True
    Case eDoNothing
        optDoNothing.Value = True
    Case Else
        optSync.Value = True
    End Select

    ' Set the preference check box - default to temporary by convention
    m_nSyncPref = eTemporaryPreference
    chkDefault.Value = Unchecked

    ' Assume the user will cancel
    m_bCancel = True

End Sub
```

The only remarkable thing about *Load* is that it assumes any user changes will be temporary, unless explicitly made permanent. This is the conventional behavior for the Palm native conduits, and it is a good idea for your user interface to follow suit:

```
m_nSyncPref = eTemporaryPreference
chkDefault.Value = Unchecked
```

The user can exit the form a variety of ways. For this reason, the values in the form controls are only transferred to the form variables in the OK button's *Click* event (see Example 4-5). At this time, the cancellation flag is set to false, the form is unloaded, and control returns to *CfgConduit*.

Example 4-5. Listing for SyncForm.btn_OK.Click

```
Private Sub btnOk_Click( )

    ' Transfer form variables to
    If optSync.Value Then
        m_nSyncType = ESyncTypes.eFast
    ElseIf optPCToHH.Value Then
        m_nSyncType = ESyncTypes.ePCtoHH
    ElseIf optHHToPC.Value Then
        m_nSyncType = ESyncTypes.eHHtoPC
    ElseIf optDoNothing.Value Then
```

Example 4-5. Listing for SyncForm.btn_OK.Click (continued)

```
      m_nSyncType = ESyncTypes.eDoNothing
    End If

    If chkDefault.Value = Checked Then m_nSyncPref = ePermanentPreference

    ' Flag used in GetFields() to see if the variables are valid
    m_bCancel = False
    Unload Me

End Sub
```

If the user exits the form, either by pushing the Cancel button directly or pressing the ESC key, control is transferred to the Cancel button's *Click* event. We don't show that routine here, but in it, the cancellation flag is set to true, the form is unloaded, and control is returned to *CfgConduit*.

At this point, the user has dismissed the form. Now we retrieve the new variable settings using the *GetFields* routine (which is smart enough not to overwrite any values if the user canceled rather than applied the changes). The code for *GetFields* is shown in Example 4-6.

Example 4-6. Listing for SyncForm.GetFields

```
Public Sub GetFields(ByRef nSyncNew As Long, _
                     ByRef nSyncTemp As Long, _
                     ByRef nSyncPerm As Long, _
                     ByRef nSyncPref As Long)

    If m_bCancel Then Exit Sub

    ' Retrieve the "default" setting from the check box
    nSyncPref = m_nSyncPref

    ' Retrieve the action setting from the radio buttons
    nSyncNew = m_nSyncType
    nSyncTemp = m_nSyncType
    nSyncPerm = m_nSyncType

End Sub
```

If the user has canceled, then none of the form variables are transferred in *GetFields*. And note that all three sync-type parameters are set to the same user-configured value, despite the Conduit Reference documentation, for the reasons discussed earlier.

ConfigureConduit

This interface function is used by versions of the HotSync manager prior to release 3.0.1. For later releases of the HotSync manager, this function is only called if your conduit doesn't implement the *CfgConduit* interface. Table 4-9 lists the parameters for *SyncNotify.ConfigureConduit*.

Table 4-9. Parameters for SyncNotify.ConfigureConduit

Parameter	Type/direction	Purpose
PathName	[IN] String	User folder in HotSync directory
Registry	[IN] String	Numeric ID of current user
SyncPref	[IN/OUT] EsyncPref	Tell HotSync manager that changes are permanent or temporary
SyncType	[IN/OUT] EsyncTypes	The kind of synchronization to perform

The code for *ConfigureConduit* simply returns default values for the two output parameters:

```
Private Sub IPDClientNotify_ConfigureConduit(ByVal bstrPathName As String, _
                              ByVal bstrRegistry As String, _
                              ByRef nSyncPref As ESyncPref, _
                              ByRef nSyncType As ESyncTypes)

    nSyncType = PDdirectlib.eFast
    nSyncPref = PDdirectlib.ePermanentPreference

End Sub
```

BeginProcess

The HotSync manager calls the interface function *BeginProcess* when an actual synchronization should occur. At this point, you can assume that the Palm device is in the cradle and the user has pressed the HotSync button.

Our implementation of *BeginProcess* is intentionally minimal; we delegate all the real work of synchronization to a private class. The code for *BeginProcess* is shown in Example 4-7.

Example 4-7. Listing for SyncNotify.BeginProcess

```
Private Function IPDClientNotify_BeginProcess() As Boolean

    ' Create our sync object and do the work
    Dim Worker As New SyncLogic
    Worker.Synchronize

    ' Return false to signal completion!
    IPDClientNotify_BeginProcess = False

End Function
```

BeginProcess should return False when it has completed. That signals the HotSync manager that it can skip to the next conduit. Returning False doesn't indicate that your conduit was successful; instead, it means that it is finished executing. Later, we will see how to return status information to the user in the HotSync log.

The real work of synchronization occurs in these lines:

```
Dim Worker As New SyncLogic
Worker.Synchronize
```

Right away, you should notice that the *Worker.Synchronize* method doesn't take any arguments. It gets all the information it needs to synchronize from publicly creatable COM objects supplied by the Sync Suite API.

We have finished implementing the *IPDClientNotify* interface, including the user interface required to support configuring the conduit. The conduit is complete from the perspective of the HotSync manager: the conduit can identify itself and its properties, it can be configured, and it responds to synchronization requests.

Synchronization Logic

The SyncLogic object created in the *BeginProcess* routine encapsulates all of our synchronization logic. In our example, the class instancing property is set to *Private,* and the class file is saved as *Ch4aLogic.cls.* By partitioning a conduit in this fashion, between the public interface and the internal synchronization logic, we ensure that the interface code can be reused in other conduits.

Let's look at the *Synchronize* method, which is called to handle all of the synchronization requests made of this conduit. The code for *Synchronize* is shown in Example 4-8.

Example 4-8. Listing for SyncLogic.Synchronize

```
Public Sub Synchronize( )

    ' Get the HotSync information object for this conduit
    Dim pdSys As New PDSystemAdapter
    Dim pdHSInfo As PDHotsyncInfo
    Set pdHSInfo = pdSys.PDHotsyncInfo

    ' Route the requested synchronization to the local handler
    Select Case pdHSInfo.SyncType
        Case eFast
            FastSync pdSys, pdHSInfo
        Case eSlow
            SlowSync pdSys, pdHSInfo
        Case eHHtoPC
            HHtoPC pdSys, pdHSInfo
        Case Else
            LogSync pdSys, pdHSInfo.SyncType
    End Select

End Sub
```

The first thing the method does is to declare and initialize a Palm Sync Suite COM object:

```
Dim pdSys As New PDSystemAdapter
```

The PDSystemAdapter class represents the Palm device. This powerful class provides access to most features of the device (except databases, which are handled by a separate class). The PDSystemAdapter class has the methods and properties shown in Table 4-10.

Table 4-10. Properties and methods of PDSystemAdapter

Property or method name	Description
AddLogEntry	Makes a local or device HotSync log entry
CallRemoteModule	Runs a program on the device
DateTime	Retrieves the date/time on the device
HHOsVersion	Retrieves the device operating system version
LocalizationID	Retrieves the device localization setting
PDHotSyncInfo	Object representing current HotSync
PDMemoryCardInfo	Object representing device memory
PDUserInfo	Object representing current user
ProductId	Retrieves the device product ID
ReadAppPreference	Retrieves a device application setting
ReadFeature	Retrieves device feature memory
RebootSystem	Performs a device soft-reset
RomSoftwareVersion	Retrieves the device ROM version
SyncManagerAPIVersion	Retrieves HotSync API Version
WriteAppPreference	Stores an application setting on device

The PDSystemAdapter and its subobjects exist only when synchronization is actually occurring. You cannot create this object, or its subobjects, outside the scope of *BeginProcess*. Our example conduit uses only a fraction of PDSystemAdapter's features; you can explore the CDK samples to see how to use the other features.

If you look at the Sync Suite class hierarchy shown earlier in Figure 4-5, you see that one of the subobjects of the system adapter is PDHSInfo. This object represents the current HotSync session. From it, we can get the synchronization type that the HotSync manager wants our conduit to run:

```
Dim pdHSInfo As PDHotsyncInfo
Set pdHSInfo = pdSys.PDHotsyncInfo
```

Note that the PDHSInfo class is not a publicly creatable object. You must use the system adapter to get one, as shown. The PDHSInfo class has the methods and properties shown in Table 4-11.

Table 4-11. Properties and methods of PDHSInfo

Property or method name	Description
CardNum	Memory card on device for this application
ConnectionType	Indicator of local, modem, or network connection
Creator	Application Creator ID for this conduit
DbType	Database type for this conduit
FirstSync	Indicator of first synchronization for device or desktop
LocalName	Application name on device
NameList	Database(s) for this Creator ID on device
PathName	Path for user area in HotSync directory
RegistryKey	Registry key for this conduit
RegistryPath	Registry path for this conduit
RemoteNameCount	Number of databases for this Creator ID on device
SyncType	Type of synchronization to perform
UserName	Username on device for this conduit

As with `PDSystemAdapter`, we use only a couple of features from the `PDHSInfo` object. While our sample conduit only has one database, the HotSync manager provides your conduit with a list of all remote databases that belong to your application. (Even though a conduit might be responsible for synchronizing more than one database, it can only have one open at a time. This complicates the design if the conduit needs to enforce relationships between the databases (tables)).

We use the *SyncType* object property to route program flow to the function that handles the requested synchronization type, supplying the newly created COM objects as reference parameters:

```
Select Case pdHSInfo.SyncType
    Case eFast
        FastSync pdSys, pdHSInfo
    Case eSlow
        SlowSync pdSys, pdHSInfo
    Case eHHtoPC
        HHtoPC pdSys, pdHSInfo
    Case ePCtoHH
        PCtoHH pdSys, pdHSInfo
```

Because this conduit only supports `Fast`, `Slow`, `HHtoPC` and `PCtoHH` synchronization, we direct all other synchronization types to a function that simply logs the request:

```
    Case Else
        LogSync pdSys, pdHSInfo.SyncType
End Select
```

We won't spend any time looking at the code for *LogSync*; it consists of a large select statement that builds a string identifying the conduit and synchronization type, and then uses the *pdSystemAdapater.AddLogEntry* method to write the entry to the HotSync log:

```
pdSys.AddLogEntry "Ch4a - " + strType, eText, False, False
```

Calling *AddLogEntry* with an option other than eText, such as eWarning, causes the HotSync manager to alert the user after all conduits have finished executing, as shown in Figure 4-8. See the enumeration type ElogActivitity for the supported log types.

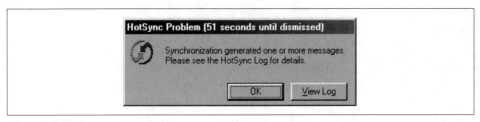

Figure 4-8. HotSync warning dialog

The *AddLogEntry* method supports writing to either the desktop or the device HotSync log. Set the optional fourth parameter to True to write to the device. Take care when writing to the device log to keep the amount of information to a minimum.

That wraps up the high-level presentation of the Synchronize object: we've seen how it is created, how it routes HotSync commands to the correct internal functions, and how it logs information to the HotSync log. Next, we are going to look at the low-level synchronization functions *HHtoPC* and *FastSync*.

HHtoPC

In our simple conduit, the *HHtoPC* routine is called only at the user's request. The purpose of this routine couldn't be simpler: it deletes all records from the desktop and then copies any records from the Palm device. The code for *HHtoPC* is shown in Example 4-9.

Example 4-9. Listing for SyncLogic.HHtoPC

```
Private Sub HHtoPC(ByRef pdSys As PDSystemAdapter, _
                ByRef pdHSInfo As PDHotsyncInfo)

    ' Data is under user's directory in HotSync area.
    Dim DBPath As String
    DBPath = pdHSInfo.PathName + "Ch4a"

    ' Purge the PC data - force a new directory if necessary.
    Dim FSO As New FileSystemObject
    On Error Resume Next
    FSO.DeleteFile DBPath + "\*.*", True
```

Example 4-9. Listing for SyncLogic.HHtoPC (continued)

```
    FSO.CreateFolder DBPath
    On Error GoTo 0

    ' Get the Palm database from the HotSync manager
    Dim DBName As String
    DBName = pdHSInfo.NameList(0)

    Dim pdQuery As New PDDatabaseQuery
    Dim pdRecords As PDRecordAdapter
    Set pdRecords = pdQuery.OpenRecordDatabase(DBName, "PDDirect.PDRecordAdapter")

    ' Open the handheld database, and iterate over the records
    Dim Index As Long
    Dim RecordId As Variant
    Dim Category As Long
    Dim Attributes As ERecordAttributes
    Dim Data As Variant

    pdRecords.IterationIndex = 0
    Data = pdRecords.ReadNext(Index, RecordId, Category, Attributes)
    Do While Not pdRecords.EOF

        ' In a HHtoPC sync, process all but deleted records
        If Not CBool(CByte(Attributes) And CByte(eDelete)) Then
            WriteRecContents DBPath, RecordId, Data
        End If

        ' Read the next record and skip to the top of the loop
        Data = pdRecords.ReadNext(Index, RecordId, Category, Attributes)
    Loop

    '  Remove any deleted records, clear  flags in Palm database
    pdRecords.RemoveSet eRemoveAllDeletedRecords
    pdRecords.ResetAllModifiedFlags

    LogSync pdSys, pdHSInfo.SyncType

End Sub
```

Let's examine the *HHtoPC* routine a little bit at a time. First, the routine locates the desktop data store, which is located under the user's Palm desktop directory. It is customary for Palm conduits to keep their information in this directory. The directory is available as the *PathName* method of the PDHSInfo object; the routine tacks on a folder name to create a subdirectory.

```
    Dim DBPath As String
    DBPath = pdHSInfo.PathName + "Ch4a"
```

The routine then deletes any files in that folder. Wrapping the delete operation in an error handler is necessary, because the FileSystemObject throws an error if the folder doesn't exist or if it is empty.

```
Dim FSO As New FileSystemObject
On Error Resume Next
FSO.DeleteFile DBPath + "\*.*", True
FSO.CreateFolder DBPath
```

Next, *HHtoPC* creates an instance of the Sync Suite PDDatabaseQuery class:

```
Dim pdQuery As New PDDatabaseQuery
```

This class provides programmatic access to the Palm database manager on the device. Remember, instances of this class are only available when the user is synchronizing the device, not during conduit configuration. This class has methods and properties, as shown in Table 4-12, that allow us to manage Palm databases.

Table 4-12. Properties and methods of PDDatabaseQuery

Property or method name	Description
AddLogEntry	Makes an entry in either the desktop or device HotSync log.
CreateRecordDatabase	Creates a data type database. Records are unstructured.
CreateResourceDatabase	Creates a resource-type database. Each record has a structure, such as an icon or form.
MaxAllowedRecordSize	Retrieves maximum supported record size on the device.
OpenRecordDatabase	Opens an existing data type database.
OpenResourceDatabase	Opens an existing resource-type database.
RamDbCount	Retrieves number of databases in device RAM.
ReadDbInfoByCreatorType	Retrieves statistics and settings for a database.
ReadDbInfoByName	Retrieves statistics and settings for a database.
ReadDbNameList	Retrieves list of databases in RAM or ROM.
RemoveDatabase	Deletes a RAM or ROM database.
RomDbCount	Retrieves number of databases in device ROM.

Again, look at the class hierarchy shown earlier in Figure 4-5. PDDatabaseQuery is a publicly created object. Our main interest in this class is its ability to return objects representing actual databases on the Palm device. We get the name of our database from the PDHSInfo object:

```
' Get the Palm database from the HotSync manager
Dim DBName As String
DBName = pdHSInfo.NameList(0)
```

Note that NameList is an array. If your application has more than one database on the Palm PDA, each is listed in the array. The total number of databases is available in the *RemoteNameCount* property.

The Sync Suite API provides the PDRecordAdapter to access the contents of any one database on the Palm device. This object is created in an unusual way, by passing the programmatic identifier of a class factory into the database query object.

The class factory is responsible for producing an object that satisfies all the interface requirements for an instance of PDRecordAdapter. The CDK provides this unusual construction technique so developers can subclass the record adapter, and supply extra capabilities tailored for a specific application. In our conduit, we use the default record adapter supplied by Palm:

```
Dim pdRecords As PDRecordAdapter
Set pdRecords = pdQuery.OpenRecordDatabase(DBName, "PDDirect.PDRecordAdapter")
```

Table 4-13 shows the many methods and properties of PDRecordAdapter. This large class is heavily used in our sample conduit. In the table, two sets of functions have been grouped together: direct record access, denoted in the table by *ReadBy**, and iterator access, denoted in the table by *ReadNext**. The direct access functions allow the retrieval of a single record, either by index or record identifier. The iterator access functions allow the sequential retrieval of many records, either by index or by category or other attribute.

Table 4-13. Properties and methods of PDRecordAdapter

Property or method name	Description
AccessMode	Retrieves mode(s) used to open database
AddLogEntry	Makes an entry in either the desktop or device HotSync log
ChangeCategory	Changes the Category ID for a group of records
CloseOptions	Sets modification date/time on database prior to close
DbName	Retrieves the database name
EOF	Indicates end-of-file when using an iterator
InputBufferSize	Sets the maximum size for read/write buffers
IterationIndex	Sets the start offset in the database for an iterator
PDCategories	Represents category data for this database
PDDatabaseInfo	Represents database for this record adapter
ReadAppInfoBlock	Reads application-specific data, including categories
ReadBy*	Gets record information by index or identifier
ReadNext*	Gets record information from an iterator
ReadSortInfoBlock	Retrieves application-specific data, notionally used for sorting
ReadUniqueIdList	Retrieves list of record identifiers in database
RecordCount	Retrieves count of records in database
Remove	Permanently erases a record from database
RemoveSet	Permanently erases a group of records from database
ResetAllModifiedFlags	Clears the dirty bit for all records in database
Write	Creates or updates a database record and attributes
WriteAppInfoBlock	Writes application-specific data, including categories
WriteSortInfoBlock	Writes application-specific data, notionally used for sorting

All the iterator functions support a starting index position. In *HHtoPC*, we use the simple iterator to process all the records in the database, starting at index zero, and reading both the actual data and other record attributes:

```
pdRecords.IterationIndex = 0
Data = pdRecords.ReadNext(Index, RecordId, Category, Attributes)
Do While Not pdRecords.EOF
```

All of the `PDRecordAdapter` read functions return a VB variant, with the record data actually stored in a byte array. The read functions also set an attribute byte indicating the status of the current record. If the record is not marked for deletion, we copy it to the desktop by calling *WriteRecContents*.

```
If Not CBool(CByte(Attributes) And CByte(eDelete)) Then
    WriteRecContents DBPath, RecordId, Data
End
```

If your conduit supports record archival, then you should test for that condition as well, with the *eArchive* attribute. After we have processed the record, we read the next record, and skip to the top of the loop:

```
    Data = pdRecords.ReadNext(Index, RecordId, Category, Attributes)
Loop
```

Eventually, the read function will cause the record adapter to reach the end-of-file condition and we will exit the loop after all of the database records have been processed. *HHtoPC* then purges the Palm database of any logically deleted records, and clears the modification flag for all dirty records:

```
pdRecords.RemoveSet eRemoveAllDeletedRecords
pdRecords.ResetAllModifiedFlags
```

Now let's look at how the *WriteRecContents* routine stores the Palm device record data to a desktop file. We aren't going to show all the code in *WriteRecContents*, but just the highlights. This routine uses a new Sync Suite object, `PDUtility`, to transform the Palm Record ID into a string:

```
Dim pdUtil As New PDUtility
Filename = DBPath + "\" + pdUtil.RecordIdToString(RecordId) + ".REC"
```

The Palm CDK documentation strongly encourages developers to use this function, rather than dissecting the variant data type holding a Record ID. This is because the Record ID format, currently a long integer, may change in the future. The `PDUtility` class has other methods to convert data between the Palm and desktop formats. We will see some of these as we pack and unpack string data for our records.

This completes the presentation of the *HHtoPC* synchronization logic for our simple conduit. Although this section presented a great deal of information quickly, you should now have an appreciation of how to use the Sync Suite COM objects to access features and data on the Palm device.

FastSync

The *HHtoPC sync* didn't require much of a design—just take the Palm records and write them to the desktop, removing any existing desktop records in the process. Mirror synchronization is much harder.

Before we start into coding the *FastSync*, let's reexamine what mirror synchronization means for the *Ch4a* application. In Table 4-14, we've recast our table of possibilities to include the desktop file extensions instead of attribute flags. The code for our conduit has to identify all these possibilities, and then take the action indicated in the table. Preparing a table or state diagram like this when designing your conduit will prove helpful.

Table 4-14. Ch4a conduit actions

	No record	No change	.CHG	.NEW	.DEL
No record				D → P	
No change			D → P		Remove DP
Change		P → D	Conflict		P → D
New	P → D				
Delete		Remove DP	D → P		

In this simple conduit, the change conflict is handled in a straightforward manner: changes to a record on the Palm device take precedence over changes to the same desktop record. This is different from the Palm CDK recommendation of creating two new records, one on each platform that mirrors the changes. Of course, you will have to decide how to resolve any conflict in a fashion that is appropriate for your application.

Now let's look at *FastSync*, the low-level function that actually moves the data between the Palm device and the Windows desktop. It is shown in Example 4-10.

Example 4-10. Listing for SyncLogic.HHtoPC

```
Private Sub FastSync(ByRef pdSys As PDSystemAdapter, _
               ByRef pdHSInfo As PDHotsyncInfo)

    Dim Index As Long
    Dim Category As Long
    Dim Data As Variant
    Dim RecordId As Variant
    Dim Attributes As ERecordAttributes

    ' Data is under user's directory in HotSync area.
    Dim DBPath As String
    DBPath = pdHSInfo.PathName + "Ch4a"

    ' Get Palm database name from HotSync manager
```

Example 4-10. Listing for SyncLogic.HHtoPC (continued)

```
    Dim DBName As String
    DBName = pdHSInfo.NameList(0)

    ' Open the handheld database, and get the record interface.
    Dim pdQuery As New PDDatabaseQuery
    Dim pdRecords As PDRecordAdapter
    Set pdRecords = pdQuery.OpenRecordDatabase(DBName, "PDDirect.PDRecordAdapter")

    ' Iterate over the *modified* records
    pdRecords.IterationIndex = 0
    Data = pdRecords.ReadNextModified(Index, RecordId, Category, Attributes)
    Do While Not pdRecords.EOF

        Dim strID As String
        Dim pdUtil As New PDUtility
        strID = pdUtil.RecordIdToString(RecordId)

         If CBool(CByte(Attributes) And CByte(eDelete)) Then
            DeletedRec DBPath, strID, Data
        Else
            DirtyRec DBPath, strID, Data
        End If

        ' Get the next record
        Data = pdRecords.ReadNext(Index, RecordId, Category, Attributes)
    Loop

    Dim File As File
    Dim Folder As Folder
    Dim FSO As New FileSystemObject

    Set Folder = FSO.GetFolder(DBPath)
    For Each File In Folder.Files
        Select Case UCase(FSO.GetExtensionName(File.Name))
        Case "NEW"
            NewFile DBPath, File, pdRecords, pdUtil
        Case "DEL"
            DeletedFile File, pdRecords, pdUtil
        Case "CHG"
            DirtyFile DBPath, File, pdRecords, pdUtil
        End Select
    Next

    pdRecords.RemoveSet eRemoveAllDeletedRecords
    pdRecords.ResetAllModifiedFlags

    LogSync pdSys, pdHSInfo.SyncType

End Sub
```

We won't go over every line, as we have seen a lot of this code already in *HHtoPC*. The routine consists of some setup code, and then two main loops. The first loop pulls changes from the Palm device, and the second loop writes changes to the Palm device.

One large difference between *FastSync* and *HHtoPC* is that with *FastSync*, we only want to process records that have changed since the last synchronization. Remember, this is the definition of a *FastSync*. The PDRecordAdapter provides the *ReadNextModified* iterator that is specially designed for this circumstance. Each call to this iterator skips through the Palm database, returning only the changed records. As a side effect, the index variable will be incremented, not by one, but by however many records the iterator skipped over to find the next changed record.

```
Data = pdRecords.ReadNextModified(Index, RecordId, Category, Attributes)
```

In a Palm database, it is possible for a record to be both deleted and dirty at the same time. Actually, it can be archived as well, but remember that we don't support the Palm archive attribute.

A Palm application usually asks the user if the deleted record should be archived or simply removed from the database. Deleted records have no data, but they are still present in the physical database; you test for them using the *eDelete* attribute.

```
If CBool(CByte(Attributes) And CByte(eDelete)) Then
    DeletedRec DBPath, strID, Data
Else
    DirtyRec DBPath, strID, Data
End If
```

Archived records have data in order to support the archive operation; typically, the archived record is also marked for deletion.

> If your application uses the AppForge database library, call the extended delete function *PDBDeleteRecordEx* to mark a record as both archived and deleted. You do this by passing afDeleteModeArchive to the function.

For our conduit, there is no difference between a new record and a changed record; both are dirty relative to the desktop. Note that the CDK doesn't provide a method to distinguish the two cases (there is no *eNew* attribute). You can tell, of course, because a new Palm database record won't have a corresponding desktop file.

At this point, all the changed records from the Palm device are safely written to the desktop folder. As we'll see later, *DirtyRec* and *DeletedRec* take care of any conflicts between desktop and Palm device records. Now *FastSync* needs to write any changed data from the desktop to the Palm database.

FastSync loops through the files on the desktop, looking for those with extensions that require some processing. For each file found, it calls a routine to do the actual work, supplying the file object, the record adapter, and the utility object as reference parameters:

```
Select Case UCase(FSO.GetExtensionName(File.Name))
Case "NEW"
    NewFile DBPath, File, pdRecords, pdUtil
Case "DEL"
    DeletedFile File, pdRecords, pdUtil
Case "CHG"
    DirtyFile DBPath, File, pdRecords, pdUtil
End Select
```

The last thing the *FastSync* routine has to do is to clean up deleted records on the Palm device, and clear the change bit(s). The data is now synchronized, so nothing is dirty! *FastSync* uses the same calls we saw in *HHtoPC* to do this cleanup work.

Now that the top-level structure of *FastSync* is clear, let's look at the auxiliary functions that move the bits and bytes. The implementation of *DirtyRec* is shown in Example 4-11. To understand its logic, recall that in our conduit, a change to a Palm record has precedence over a change to the corresponding desktop record.

Example 4-11. Listing for SyncLogic.DirtyRec

```
Private Sub DirtyRec(ByVal DBPath As String, _
                     ByVal strID As String, _
                     ByRef Data As Variant)

    Dim Filenum As Integer
    Dim Filename As String
    Dim FSO As New FileSystemObject

    ' Remove any changed or deleted desktop record
    On Error Resume Next
    FSO.DeleteFile DBPath + "\" + strID + ".DEL", True
    FSO.DeleteFile DBPath + "\" + strID + ".CHG", True
    On Error GoTo 0

    ' Write device data to desktop record
    Filenum = FreeFile
    Filename = DBPath + "\" + strID + ".REC"
    Open Filename For Output As #Filenum
    Write #Filenum, StrConv(Data, vbUnicode)
    Close #Filenum

End Sub
```

Because changes to desktop records are stored in files with the extension *.DEL* or *.CHG*, *DirtyRec* simply removes those files. Then the contents of the Palm record are written into the desktop file. This process overwrites the old desktop record, if it existed, or creates a new record file with the correct name and extension.

This is in accordance with our design decision that changes to the Palm record have precedence over the desktop. A conduit that implemented Palm's recommended mirroring strategy would have to reconcile the contents of the files with the Palm record data.

The implementation of *DeletedRec* is very similar.

```
Private Sub DeletedRec(ByVal DBPath As String, _
                       ByVal strID As String, _
                       ByRef Data As Variant)

    Dim FSO As New FileSystemObject

    On Error Resume Next
    FSO.DeleteFile DBPath + "\" + strID + ".REC", True
    On Error GoTo 0

End Sub
```

However, note that *DeletedRec* does not remove the *.CHG* record, which gets processed later. This is because a change on the desktop has precedence over deletions on the Palm device. If this seems unclear, look over Table 4-14 again.

The *NewFile* function creates a new record in the Palm database when the user has created one on the desktop:

```
Private Sub NewFile(ByVal DBPath As String, _
                    ByRef File As File, _
                    ByRef pdRecords As PDRecordAdapter, _
                    ByRef pdUtil As PDUtility)

    Dim Data As Variant
    Dim RecordId As Variant

    GetFileContents File, Data, pdUtil

    ' Create a new Palm device record
    RecordId = vbEmpty
    pdRecords.Write RecordId, 0, 0, Data

    File.Move DBPath + "\" + pdUtil.RecordIdToString(RecordId) + ".REC"

End Sub
```

Despite its simplicity, there is a lot going on in *NewFile*. First, the routine calls *GetFileContents* to read the file data into a variant byte array for uploading to the Palm database record. We'll see how this is done later.

Next, we create a new record in the Palm database. The PDRecordAdapter class doesn't have an explicit record creation method; instead, you call its *Write* function with a special record identifier. Passing a variant set to vbEmpty does the trick. When the *Write* function returns, it has replaced vbEmpty with the new Record ID.

It is not always possible to create a record on the device—for example the storage heap could be exhausted. We don't handle that error in our simple conduit, but your conduit should.

The last thing *NewFile* does is to rename the *.NEW* desktop file so we don't process it again later. We generate a filename using the new Record ID and an extension of *.REC*. The records are now synchronized on the desktop and the device. If the user later changes this record on the Palm, our conduit will be able to locate the corresponding desktop file using the Record ID as filename.

Now let's look at *GetFileContents*, shown in Example 4-12. Reading in the file contents is simple enough; the routine assumes all the text is a single input field delimited by quotation marks, and reads it into the string variable sBuf.

Example 4-12. Listing for SyncLogic.GetFileContents

```
Private Sub GetFileContents(ByRef File As File, _
                            ByRef Data As Variant, _
                            ByRef pdUtil As PDUtility)

    Dim Filenum As Integer
    Dim sBuf As Variant
    Dim RecordId As Variant
    Dim bArray() As Byte

    Filenum = FreeFile
    Open File.Path For Input As #Filenum
    Input #Filenum, sBuf
    Close #Filenum

    ' Convert to a byte array
    Data = bArray
    ReDim Data(0 To Len(sBuf))
    pdUtil.BSTRToByteArray Data, 0, sBuf

End Sub
```

Next, we convert the input string, sBuf (which may or may not be Unicode, depending on your operating system), into a byte array. To do this, declare an empty byte array and assign the reference parameter *Data* to it:

```
Dim bArray() As Byte
...
Data = bArray
```

This effectively converts *Data*, which is a type-less variant, into a byte array. Redimension *Data* to hold the input string, and use the utility function *BSTRToByteArray* to pack the string data into the array:

```
ReDim Data(0 To Len(sBuf))
pdUtil.BSTRToByteArray Data, 0, sBuf
```

We resort to this trickery because you cannot pass a VB byte array directly into a COM function call. If your conduit's data is more complicated, you should look at the other conversion functions in PDUtility.

The conduit calls *DeletedFile* to handle desktop files that the user has marked for deletion. This function is very straightforward: convert the desktop filename into a Palm Record ID using the *StringToRecordId* utility function, and then call the PDRecordAdapter *Remove* function to erase the database record. Here's the code for *DeletedFile*:

```
Private Sub DeletedFile(ByRef File As File, _
                        ByRef pdRecords As PDRecordAdapter, _
                        ByRef pdUtil As PDUtility)

    Dim RecordId As Variant
    Dim FSO As New FileSystemObject

    RecordId = pdUtil.StringToRecordId(FSO.GetBaseName(File.Name))
    On Error Resume Next
    pdRecords.Remove RecordId
    File.Delete True
    On Error GoTo 0

End Sub
```

We wrap the actual *Remove* call in an error handler, because it raises a runtime error if the requested record does not exist. This is an unlikely condition in a well-designed application, but it happens frequently during development. A simple On Error Resume Next ensures that we handle that possibility.

The conduit calls *DirtyFile* to handle desktop files that the user has changed. The code for *DirtyFile* is shown in Example 4-13. This routine repackages some functionality we have seen earlier. It calls *GetFileContents* to read in the changed desktop data, and builds a Palm Record ID using the *StringToRecordId* utility function.

Example 4-13. Listing for SyncLogic.DirtyFile

```
Private Sub DirtyFile(ByVal DBPath As String, _
                      ByRef File As File, _
                      ByRef pdRecords As PDRecordAdapter, _
                      ByRef pdUtil As PDUtility)

    Dim Data As Variant
    Dim RecordId As Variant
    Dim FSO As New FileSystemObject

    GetFileContents File, Data, pdUtil

    ' Find correct Palm device record based on file name
    RecordId = pdUtil.StringToRecordId(FSO.GetBaseName(File.Name))

    On Error Resume Next
```

Example 4-13. Listing for SyncLogic.DirtyFile (continued)

```
    pdRecords.Write RecordId, 0, eDirty, Data
    If Err.Number <> 0 Then
        ' Record deleted on device without warning.
        RecordId = vbEmpty
        pdRecords.Write RecordId, 0, eDirty, Data
    End If
    On Error GoTo 0

    ' Rename from .CHG to .REC
    File.Move DBPath + "\" + pdUtil.RecordIdToString(RecordId) + ".REC"

End Sub
```

If *DirtyFile* encounters an error when updating the Palm database, it assumes that the record no longer exists. In this case, *DirtyFile* creates a new record by writing the data using a Record ID of vbEmpty. As we mentioned before, this is an unlikely condition, but you should take great care to make your conduit very robust. Note that the original Record ID is lost.

As usual, we rename the desktop file to have the *.REC* extension. Note the use of the *eDirty* attribute when writing the record. Assigning this attribute overwrites any other Palm record attributes, including *eDelete*. When *FastSync* cleans up the Palm database by purging deleted records, these dirty records won't be among them.

Other Sync Types

In contrast to fast synchronization, slow synchronization requires looking at all records, not just those that are marked as dirty or new. In our simple application, we just had to change the PDRecordAdapter iterator function—for example, *ReadNext* instead of *ReadNextModified*. This causes *SlowSync* to look at every record in the Palm database, not simply the changed ones.

Particular care must be taken if you expect your users to synchronize their application data with different desktops or devices. When that happens, it is easy to lose track of data—usually with very bad results for your users.* Design carefully to avoid this.

For the sake of completeness, we support the *PCtoHH* sync type in the sample application. There is nothing noteworthy in the code that we haven't already covered, so we won't detail it here.

---

* The slow sync logic given here fails to handle this important case. If the user syncs with his desktop, then does a delete on the handheld, and then syncs with another desktop, the deleted record on the handheld is gone. Now, if the user syncs with his desktop, the conduit doesn't see the deleted record on the handheld, and so it shouldn't delete it on the desktop. Whew. You'll need to iterate through the records on the desktop. Any that aren't on the handheld (and aren't new) have been deleted, and must be deleted from the desktop (unless, of course, they've been modified on the desktop).

Running the Conduit

At this point, you have seen all the code in the sample conduit. You can compile it as an ActiveX EXE, and register it with the HotSync manager using the *CondCfg.exe* tool covered earlier in this chapter (see Figure 4-4). Instead of the VB IDE, enter the programmatic identifier of the conduit as the COM client. In the case of our sample, this is Ch4aCond.SyncNotify.

To debug, stop the HotSync manager, and then run the conduit from the VB IDE. Make sure you have enabled the default debug setting: Wait for components to be created. You do this from the VB IDE by choosing the Properties option from the Project menu, and then selecting the Debugging tab.

Next, set a breakpoint in each of the routines for IPDClientNotify, and then press F5 to run the project. This generates a new temporary GUID for your public class, but the programmatic id stays the same. Once the project is running, restart the HotSync manager.

The debugger should launch into the breakpoint in *GetConduitInfo* first, because the HotSync manager checks every registered conduit as it initializes. The HotSync manager will call this function several times, once for each information request type.

You can trigger the other breakpoints by choosing the Custom option for our conduit from the HotSync manager user interface (in the Windows system tray), or by actually performing a HotSync with the device in the cradle.

Test the conduit by using the Palm application *Ch4a.prc* to manipulate records on the Palm device, and a text editor to edit files on the desktop. Then synchronize with the HotSync manager.

Data Formats

Until now, our focus has been on how to interface with the HotSync manager, and how to use the Sync Suite API to synchronize databases and records. It was easy to read and write the actual record data, because we only supported ASCII strings. A real Palm program is going to have a much more complicated record structure, with a mixture of string and binary data.

The sample code for this section includes a new AppForge project, *Ch4b.vbp.*, and a new conduit project, *Ch4bCond.vbp*. Together, these show how to handle the low-level chores associated with packing and unpacking record data, converting numbers between the Intel and Motorola formats, and handling differences between Palm and Windows date formats.

Note that if you use the AppForge database utilities and the Universal Conduit, you don't have to worry about packing and unpacking records and fields, or converting between Palm PDA and Windows data types. We covered the database utilities in Chapter 3, and will look at the Universal Conduit in Chapter 5.

Creating Packed Record Data

Our new application creates a database that consists of structured records with four fields: a Date value, a Time value, a Boolean value, an Integer value, a Long integer, and a String with 20 characters. Figure 4-9 shows the application's user interface on the Palm PDA.

Figure 4-9. Mains screen for sample application Ch4b

First, let's look at how to create a packed record on the Palm. You'll find this code in the form module *Ch4b.frm* in the new application.

The AppForge documentation provides the size of each of the built-in data types: four bytes for a Date or Time field, one byte for a Boolean, two bytes for an Integer, four bytes for a Long, and one byte for each character in a string variable.

When the user presses the WriteDB button in the application, we use *PDBCreateRecord* to allocate a record large enough to hold the six fields.

```
Dim Count As Long
Count = 4 + 4 + 1 + 2 + 4 + 20
PDBCreateRecord hPdb, Count
```

We pack the fields into our record in this order: Date, Time, Boolean, Integer, Long, and then String. Knowing the layout of the fields—their type, order and size—is critical when unpacking the data. AppForge lists the sizes of the basic data types in their documentation. As under Windows, both Date and Time values are stored in the Date data type.

The *PDBWriteFieldByOffset* stores the binary representation of a value into the record. Here's how to write a single Long integer field into the Palm record:

```
Dim lVar As Long
lVar = CLng(AFTextLong.Text)
PDBWriteFieldByOffset hPdb, 5, lVar
```

Note that this function requires that the field offset into the record be specified. In this example, we are writing a Long value at offset 5. The AppForge VB runtime engine already knows that the size of this variable is 4 bytes, so we don't have to pass that also.

After we have written all six fields, we call *PDBUpdateRecord* to flush the new record into the Palm database.

Reading Packed Record Data

Now let's look at how to unpack the field data in the conduit. There are two main issues we address when unpacking the record data: finding the start and end of fields, and converting formats between the Palm device and Windows. You'll find the code for this section in *Ch4bLogic.cls*—note the 'b'—in the new conduit. This conduit is structured just like the first one.

Locating the field data is just the reverse of how the record was created. First we get the record bytes into the variant array Data, using one of the `PDRecordAdapter` *Read* iterator functions. Because the array data is a byte-wise copy of the Palm record, the offsets used for writing are identical to those used for reading.

If the data is byte- or character-oriented, such as `String` or `Boolean` data, simply copy the needed bytes from the array:

```
Dim b As Boolean
b = Data(8)
```

For `String` data, you need to know the size ahead of time. In this example, we read from offset 15 until the end of the record data:

```
Dim s As String
pdUtil.ByteArrayToBSTR Data, 15, UBound(Data) - LBound(Data) + 1 - 15, s
```

It is probably overkill to use the *UBound* and *LBound* functions here. These are two of the rare VB functions that index from zero, not one, which is why there is an extra +1 in the *ByteArrayToBSTR* function call.

Numeric data, such as `Integer` or `Long` values, must be converted from Motorola to Intel byte ordering. The `PDUtility` object has methods that explicitly do this: *SwapWORD* and *SwapDWORD* take 16-bit and 32-bit quantities and reverse the high and low bytes as appropriate.

There is another issue when converting numbers: the data in the array is byte-oriented, while we want whole `Integer` or `Long` values. Here's how we convert both at once in the sample conduit:

```
Dim i As Integer
pdUtil.ByteArrayToWORD Data, 9, True, i
```

The *ByteArrayToWORD* function locates the two bytes at offset 9 in the data array and converts them to an `Integer` quantity, and it swaps the byte ordering as well. We request the swapping by passing `True` as the third parameter; if you don't want the implicit conversion, pass `False` instead. To convert a 32-bit quantity, use the *ByteArrayToDWORD* function.

Converting Dates and Times

Dates and times are the hardest values to convert, because they are a blend of application code and operating system convention. Dates and times on the Palm are represented in the Palm operating system as seconds since January 1, 1904. How these values are stored in database files, however, varies wildly from application to application.

The Palm native applications, for example, use a packed unsigned 16-bit quantity to represent the date: 7 bits for the year since 1904, 4 bits for the month, and 5 bits for the day. These applications use an unsigned 16-bit quantity to represent the time: 8 bits for the hour, and 8 bits for the minute.[*]

Our application stores dates and times exactly as returned by the AppForge VB runtime functions *Date* and *Time*. These values are the Palm operating system values: seconds since January 1, 1904. Depending on how the value is constructed, a Date value may or may not have the day or time component:

```
Dim d As Date
d = Date        ' No time component
d = Date + Time ' Has time component
```

Although it's not documented, AppForge Date values are 32-bit quantities.

First we extract the 32-bit date from the packed record data using *ByteArrayToDWORD* (not shown). Then we call *PalmLongToDate* to convert the Long value to a VB Date value. The code for *PalmLongToDate* is shown in Example 4-14.

Example 4-14. Listing for PalmLongToDate

```
Private Function PalmLongToDate(ByVal d As Long) As Date

    Dim SecsSince1904 As Double
    Dim DaysSince1904 As Double

    Const SecsPerDay As Long = 86400
    Const UnsignedLngMax As Double = 4294967296#

    ' Handle signed/unsigned issues and use a double to prevent overflow.
    If d < 0 Then
        SecsSince1904 = UnsignedLngMax + d
    Else
        SecsSince1904 = d
    End If

    ' Figure out how many days have passed since 1904. Then add to
```

---

[*] We don't cover the native Palm date and time formats here. The AppForge knowledge base has an article with a code sample on how to convert those formats.

Example 4-14. Listing for PalmLongToDate (continued)

```
' earliest possible date. Let VB adjust for leap year, etc!
DaysSince1904 = SecsSince1904 / SecsPerDay
PalmLongToDate = DateSerial(1904, 1, 1) + CLng(DaysSince1904)

End Function
```

First we convert the Long argument, which represents seconds since January 1, 1904, into a double. We also adjust the argument if it is negative. This is necessary because the Palm data type is unsigned, so a negative number indicates that we have lost a bit! Adding the huge UnsignedLngMax brings it back.*

Next, we can calculate how many days have passed since January 1, 1904.

```
DaysSince1904 = SecsSince1904 / SecsPerDay
```

That's the hard part. Finally, we create a VB Date with the initial magic value using the *DateSerial* function, and add the correct number of days to it to obtain the converted date:

```
PalmLongToDate = DateSerial(1904, 1, 1) + CLng(DaysSince1904)
```

By using VB date arithmetic, we avoid issues such as leap year, which are better handled by the operating system and runtime libraries.

> *PalmLongToDate* is only accurate if it is given a pure date—one that has no time component. During normal integer division, the remainder is silently discarded. But because the calculation to get DaysSince1904 is done in Double arithmetic, this truncation doesn't occur. This can cause the function to be inaccurate with some inputs.

Compared to getting the Date, the Time routine is almost trivial. It is shown in Example 4-15.

Example 4-15. Listing for PalmLongToTime

```
Private Function PalmLongToTime(ByVal T As Long) As Date

    Dim Hours As Integer
    Dim Minutes As Integer
    Dim Seconds As Integer

    ' Strip off any vestigal seconds, handle signed/unsigned issues.
    If T < 0 Then T = T + &H10000
    T = T And &H1FFFF

    ' Calculate hours, minutes and seconds based
```

---

* Additionally, this is why we convert to a double internally. The conversion to unsigned 32-bit data would cause a silent overflow and our dates would be incorrect.

Example 4-15. Listing for PalmLongToTime (continued)

```
    Hours = T \ 3600
    Minutes = (T \ 60) Mod 60
    Seconds = T Mod 60

    PalmLongToTime = TimeSerial(Hours, Minutes, Seconds)

End Function
```

The `Time` value is stored in the lower 17 bits of the 32-bit quantity. This means that we don't have to worry about overflow while converting between signed and unsigned formats:

```
    If T < 0 Then T = T + &H10000
    T = T And &H1FFFF
```

We can discard any high-order bits that belong to a `Date` component, which means that *PalmLongToTime* may be safely called with any valid `Date`.

At this point, the variable `T` holds the number of seconds since midnight; this is converted to hours, minutes, and seconds. Adding these together with the VB *TimeSerial* function gives us the correct time, which we return as the value of the function.

Resources

This chapter presented the fundamentals of conduit development using VB. At this point, you should understand what a conduit is and how it fits into Palm's HotSync architecture. You should be comfortable with building and running conduits under the Palm HotSync manager, and you should be able to address the issues encountered when designing a conduit.

There are many resources available from Palm to assist in the conduit development process. The Palm OS development web site has a page for conduit development at *http://www.palmos.com/dev/tech/conduits*. This web page has several resources, including an active mailing list, the Palm knowledge base, and links to documentation.

There are two sets of official Palm documents for the CDK. One set is based on the COM specification, and the other is based on the C/C++ language. Like all Palm documentation, the sets come in two parts: a Reference and a Companion. The companion document explains high-level concepts; the reference provides a description of every class, method, and property in the CDK. Other documentation on the web site includes presentations from the PalmSource developer conferences on conduit development.

Palm OS Programming (O'Reilly & Associates, Inc.), now in its second edition, provides a lot of detail and insight into conduit logic and the inner workings of the HotSync manager. Be aware, however, that the book is intended primarily for C/C++ developers.

CHAPTER 5

SQL Databases

In this chapter, we look at several techniques for distributing and manipulating enterprise SQL data on the Palm handheld device. In keeping with the "Zen of Palm," our aim is to present techniques that provide timely data for the user, not to burden him or her with the complexities of a desktop application.

Our first example shows how to use the AppForge libraries under Windows to prepare relational data for use on the road. We build a simple VB desktop application that uses Active Data Objects (ADO) to create a PDB file from a database query. The database holds thousands of Internet dial-up numbers; the PDB we create contains only those numbers the user wants.

Our second example shows how to use a powerful tool, the AppForge Universal Conduit, to synchronize data between a simple application on the Palm and an SQL database. Our application uses a small database; changes on the Palm device are uploaded to the SQL server, and vice versa. The Universal Conduit allows synchronization without any VB development—quite an accomplishment, considering that we devoted all of Chapter 4 to coding custom conduits.[*]

SQL Publishing

The Palm device is a very good tool for displaying information to the user, provided that the data display is quick and pertinent. The mobile user wants a fraction of the SQL database *published* to his or her Palm device—just the facts or figures that will be relevant today, not yesterday or next month. This push technology is perfect for the Palm world, where users are eager to have a relevant subset of data delivered into their hands.

---

[*] If your application requires a true data replication architecture, you should consider using a tool from a database vendor such as Sybase or Oracle.

In this section, we build a simple Windows application that migrates read-only data from an enterprise SQL database to a desktop Palm PDB file. The database stores dial-up access numbers for a global Internet service provider (ISP) in a simple database, hosted in Microsoft SQL Server. The Windows application uses the AppForge libraries to write the PDB file. We also build a simple Palm application that reads the PDB file and displays the data to the user.

This application is ideal for someone who travels frequently to different locations, and needs to have an up-to-date list of access numbers always available.

Internet Phone Database

Our sample database contains thousands of telephone numbers from more than 50 countries. Table 5-1 shows example entries for Hungary.

Table 5-1. ISP access numbers for Hungary

Region	Number	Attributes
Budapest	1-482-9300	(PPP/SLIP/V.90/ISDN)
Budapest	51-301335	(PPP/SLIP/V.90/ISDN)
GSM-direct-nationwide)	20-9000-899	(PPP/SLIP)
Szekesfehervar	22-536-700	(PPP/SLIP/V.90/ISDN)
Szekesfehervar	51-301335	(PPP/SLIP/V.90/ISDN)

The phone database schema is very simple, and is shown in Figure 5-1. The database is normalized and supports referential integrity through the use of primary and foreign keys. This stops us from mixing up phone numbers for Cordoba, Argentina with Cordoba, Spain—that could be a very expensive mistake.

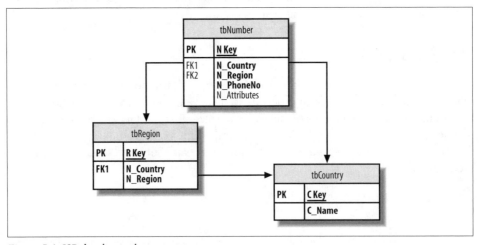

Figure 5-1. ISP database schema

The database has the following tables:

tbNumber
> Contains an entry for each of the dial-up access numbers, and other attributes such as country, region and connection type.

tbRegion
> Contains an entry for each region in a country. In the United States, the region data are city and state; for other countries, the data varies.

tbCountry
> Contains an entry for each country supported by the global ISP.

The database is fully scripted in the file *ISP.sql*, and we have included a physical database backup with the data in *ISPBackup.dat*. These files are included with the source code for this chapter on this book's web site.[*]

ISPQuery Program

The ISP database contains thousands of phone numbers. This amount of data is easily managed on the Windows desktop, but is more of a problem on the Palm. For example, it takes several seconds just to load a combo-box control with the country names on the Palm.

Instead of loading all the data on the Palm and requiring the user to navigate through it, the ISPQuery desktop program allows the user to query the database for records of interest. Once the relevant records are identified, a simple PDB file is generated, and the records are written into it. This PDB file can then be HotSynced onto the Palm device.

ISPQuery consists of a single form with input fields to limit the query to a single country and, optionally, to a region or state. The form also contains a large text box for displaying results (see Figure 5-2).

The Get Data button retrieves the record set using the supplied selection criteria, and the Make PDB button creates the physical PDB file.

The project file for this example program is *ISPQuery.vbp*. We start by adding references for several components to our project. We use the Microsoft ADO library, *msado15.dll*, to manage interaction with the SQL database, and the AppForge PDB library, *afPDBLib.dll*, to create and populate the PDB file.

All the code for this application is in *Query.frm*. We declare several form-level ADO object variables to manage our interaction with the SQL database:

---

[*] Our database is implemented with Microsoft SQL Server 7.0, running on Windows 2000 Advanced Server. The create script should be easily portable to almost any database server, but the physical backup will only work with Microsoft SQL Server.

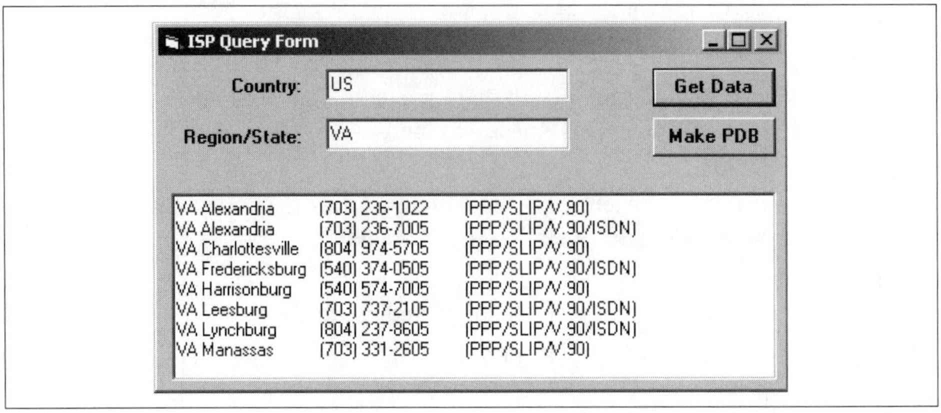

Figure 5-2. ISP Query Form

```
Option Explicit

Private ConnObj As ADODB.Connection
Private CmdObj As ADODB.Command
Private RecordObj As ADODB.Recordset
```

We initialize the connection to the SQL database in the *form load* event:

```
Private Sub Form_Load( )
    Set ConnObj = New ADODB.Connection
    ConnObj.Open "Provider=sqloledb;Data Source= ..."
End Sub
```

We have hard-coded the connection string for our Microsoft SQL Server database in the *Form_Load* routine. You will have to modify the connection string to a value suitable for your database provider. After entering the desired country and region parameters, press the Get Data button to trigger the click event handler shown in Example 5-1.

Example 5-1. Listing for cmdQuery_Click

```
Private Sub cmdQuery_Click( )

    Dim Data As String

    RunQuery

    If RecordObj.RecordCount > 0 Then
        Do While Not RecordObj.EOF
            Data = Data & Trim(RecordObj("R_Name")) & vbTab _
                    & Trim(RecordObj("N_PhoneNo")) & vbTab _
                    & Trim(RecordObj("N_Attributes")) & vbCrLf
            RecordObj.MoveNext
        Loop
    End If

    txtResults.Text = Data
End Sub
```

This event first calls *RunQuery*, which handles most of the work of interfacing to the relational database. The data rows returned from the query are in an ADO record-set object. This record set is processed in a loop, with each data row written into a separate line in the txtResults window.

The code for *RunQuery* is shown in Example 5-2.

Example 5-2. Listing for RunQuery

```
Private Sub RunQuery( )

    Set CmdObj = New ADODB.Command
    Set CmdObj.ActiveConnection = ConnObj
    CmdObj.CommandText = MakeSQL
    CmdObj.Execute

    Set RecordObj = New ADODB.Recordset
    RecordObj.CursorLocation = adUseClient
    RecordObj.CursorType = adOpenStatic
    RecordObj.Open CmdObj
End Sub
```

First, *RunQuery* connects a command object to the database server and executes an SQL query. Then it retrieves the query results and binds them into the form-level ADO record-set object.

Here is the function *MakeSQL*, which is called from *RunQuery* to build a SQL statement that reflects the user's input:

```
Private Function MakeSQL( ) As String

    Dim qStr As String
    qStr = "select C.C_Name, R.R_Name, N.N_PhoneNo, N.N_Attributes from tbCountry C,
        tbRegion R, tbNumber N where N.N_Country = C.C_Key and N.N_Region = R.R_Key"

    ' Append the [optional] country
    If txtCountry.Text <> "" Then
        qStr = qStr & " and C.C_Name = '" & Trim(txtCountry.Text) & "'"
    End If

    ' Append the [optional] region. Note the LIKE operator and wildcard
    If txtRegion.Text <> "" Then
        qStr = qStr & " and R.R_Name like '" & Trim(txtRegion.Text) & "%'"
    End If

    MakeSQL = qStr
End Function
```

The basic SQL query is a three-table join of the country, region, and number tables. If the user has filled in the form text boxes, the function modifies the SQL statement, building the WHERE clause according to how the user filled in the form. Handling the country condition is straightforward, but the region is a little trickier:

```
qStr = qStr & " and R.R_Name like '" & Trim(txtRegion.Text) & "%'"
```

We use the SQL LIKE operator to force a text search of the region table's name column. We append the wildcard character % to the query string to force a partial string match from the lefthand side. We do this mainly to simplify searching within the United States entries. For example, in the US entries, each region corresponds to a state. In the Belgian entries, however, most regions correspond to a city.

PDB Generation

So far, the code we have presented is vanilla Microsoft VB, using standard techniques to form SQL queries, retrieve data, and display data. The second half of *ISPQuery* is a little different: here, we use the AppForge PDB library under Windows to build Palm databases. These are exactly the same functions we saw in Chapter 3 when we discussed databases on the Palm device.

Creating the PDB file starts when the user selects the Make PDB button. This triggers the *cmdPDB_Click* event handler, which is shown in Example 5-3.

Example 5-3. Listing of cmdPDB_Click

```
Private Sub cmdPDB_Click( )

    Dim db As Long
    Dim rec As PhoneRecord

    If RecordObj.RecordCount = 0 Then Exit Sub

    db = CreatePDBFile

    RecordObj.MoveFirst
    Do While Not RecordObj.EOF

        rec.Region = Trim(RecordObj("R_Name"))
        rec.PhoneNo = Trim(RecordObj("N_PhoneNo"))
        rec.Attributes = Trim(RecordObj("N_Attributes"))

        PDBCreateRecordBySchema db
        PDBWriteRecord db, VarPtr(rec)
        PDBUpdateRecord db

        RecordObj.MoveNext
    Loop

    PDBClose db
End Sub
```

First, we declare variables for the database reference and a database record. Let's look at the definition of PhoneRecord, shown in Example 5-4.

Example 5-4. PhoneRecord data type

```
Private Type PhoneRecord
    Region As String
    PhoneNo As String
    Attributes As String
End Type
```

This data type contains all the fields from the ISP database that we want to store on the Palm. The data type forms the basis for an AppForge schema, which we covered in Chapter 3.

We ensure that the record set is not empty. If it is, we exit the subroutine, since there's no reason to create an empty database:

```
If RecordObj.RecordCount = 0 Then Exit Sub
```

Next. we call *CreatePDBFile* to make a PDB file on the Windows filesystem. This function returns a reference to an open Palm database, which we store in the db variable:

```
db = CreatePDBFile
```

We'll see the definition of this function and the AppForge PDB schema later in this section.

Now we process each of the data rows stored in the returned ADO record-set object. First, we populate each field in the record variable with the corresponding column from the row:

```
rec.Region = Trim(RecordObj("R_Name"))
rec.PhoneNo = Trim(RecordObj("N_PhoneNo"))
rec.Attributes = Trim(RecordObj("N_Attributes"))
```

Then we create a new record and write it to the AppForge database manager, which stores it in the PDB file:

```
PDBCreateRecordBySchema db
PDBWriteRecord db, VarPtr(rec)
PDBUpdateRecord db
```

Note that we create the new record using the AppForge schema; this makes it simple to write the entire database record variable in one function call. Don't forget to call *PDBUpdateRecord* to commit the new record data to the file. When the loop ends, we call *PDBClose* to release the database file and to return control to the user.

Let's return to *CreatePDBFile*, shown in Example 5-5.

Example 5-5. Listing of CreatePDBFile

```
Private Function CreatePDBFile() As Long

    Dim db As Long
    Dim schema As String
```

Example 5-5. Listing of CreatePDBFile (continued)

```
    On Error Resume Next
    Kill App.Path & "\PhoneDB.pdb"

    db = PDBCreateDatabase(App.Path & "\PhoneDB", Id2Long("DATA"), Id2Long("tISP"))

    schema = "region string, phoneno string, attributes string"
    PDBCreateTable db, "numbers", schema

    CreatePDBFile = db
End Function
```

First, we remove any existing PDB files using the VB *Kill* method. The error handler is necessary because VB throws a runtime error if the file to be removed doesn't exist.

Next, we create the database in the application's working directory, which we obtain from the global VB *App.Path* property:

```
    db = PDBCreateDatabase(App.Path & "\PhoneDB", Id2Long("DATA"), Id2Long("tISP"))
```

You never specify a file extension with *PDBCreateDatabase*, either on the Palm or under Windows. We use a Creator ID of tISP, and a database type of DATA. We will need these identifiers later, when we open *PhoneDB* on the Palm device.

Finally, we use the AppForge database function *PDBCreateTable* to create both the PDB file and the schema. Our schema simply defines the AppForge record format for PhoneDB to have three string fields named region, phoneno, and attributes:

```
    schema = "region string, phoneno string, attributes string"
    PDBCreateTable db, "numbers", schema
```

Of course, this is exactly the layout of our PhoneRecord data type (see Example 5-4, shown earlier in this section). A schema created with *PDBCreateTable* is permanent; it is stored in the application info block of the database. This is convenient for us, because it is one less thing to worry about in the Palm application.

The handy *Id2Long* function, shown in Example 5-6, is cribbed from an AppForge sample; it converts a four-character string into a long integer. We've removed all the error checking to make it simpler.

Example 5-6. Listing for Id2Long

```
Private Function Id2Long(Id As String) As Long

    Dim i As Integer
    Dim value As Long

    For i = 1 To Len(Id)
        value = value * 256 + Asc(Mid(Id, i, 1))
    Next i

    Id2Long = value
End Function
```

Palm Display Application

At this point, we have a working Windows application that queries a SQL database and uses the resulting record set to create and populate a PDB file suitable for installation on a Palm device.

In this section, we build a small AppForge application to read the database and display our Internet access numbers. Our application—PhoneNo—is shown in Figure 5-3. The VB project for the application is *PhoneNo.vbp*, and the single form is *Phone.frm*.

Figure 5-3. Phone number application

The form consists of a list box that displays all the regional entries in the database. The user scrolls through the list, looking for a nearby number. When an entry is selected in the list, the region, phone, and attributes fields are populated with the appropriate record details.

The list box is populated when the form is loaded, as shown in Example 5-7.

Example 5-7. Listing for Phone Form_Load

```
Private Sub Form_Load()

    Dim rec As PhoneRecord

    db = PDBOpen(ByTypeCreator, "PhoneDB", 0, 0, Id2Long("DATA"), Id2Long("tISP"),
        afModeReadOnly)
    If db = 0 Then MsgBox "Couldn't open PhoneDB database!"

    While Not PDBEOF(db)
        PDBReadRecord db, VarPtr(rec)
        lstRecords.AddItem rec.Region
        PDBMoveNext db
    Wend
End Sub
```

First, we declare a record variable of type PhoneRecord—the same data type that we used in the Windows program (see Example 5-4, earlier in this chapter). This is one of the strengths of the AppForge PDB libraries: the schema and database operations are completely portable between Windows and the Palm.

After opening the database, we loop through the database, reading records into the *rec* variable, and appending the region field to the list box. Note that we do not have to declare the schema for this database, since it was stored in the AppInfo block of the database when we created the PDB file on Windows.[*]

The only other code in the form is the *lstRecords_Click* routine, which is triggered when the user taps an entry in the list box with the stylus:

```
Private Sub lstRecords_Click()

    Dim rec As PhoneRecord

    PDBGotoIndex db, lstRecords.ListIndex
    PDBReadRecord db, VarPtr(rec)

    txtRegion.Text = rec.Region
    txtPhone.Text = rec.PhoneNo
    txtAttributes.Text = rec.Attributes
End Sub
```

Because we added the list elements in the same order as the records in our database, the list index equals the record's position in the database. We use *PDBGotoIndex* to skip to the selected item, and then read in the record data.[†] Finally, we update the text fields with the record data.

This completes our first example of getting SQL data onto the Palm device. We could extend the data publishing model, for example, by using HotSync technology to distribute the new PDB file straight to the Palm device. This sample could also be combined with an interactive web server that allows customers to build and download custom content on the fly.

Universal Conduit

The previous example covered static data, whereas in the following example, data can change on either the Palm or the SQL database. In Chapter 4 we showed how to build a custom conduit to move data between the Palm and the desktop. Here, we show how to configure the AppForge Universal Conduit (UC) to synchronize changes between the PDB files on Palm and a Microsoft SQL server, and how to design around some constraints imposed by the UC.

---

[*] AppForge documents the record schema, making it possible (but difficult) for non-AppForge applications to use it; they even provide sample code. See AppForge Knowledge Base articles #010427-0020 and #01028-007.

[†] If you use the sort capability of the PDB library after you have added records to the list, you will need to store the record's unique identifier in the *ItemData* property. This allows unambiguous retrieval even if the database sort order changes.

The UC works with Microsoft Object Database Connector (ODBC) data sources. It has a wizard-like utility for selecting SQL data tables to synchronize. The utility takes care of mapping SQL data fields to the appropriate Palm data types. Like the App-Forge Database Converter, which we covered in Chapter 3, the wizard can produce PDB files as well as a VB module with record layouts. We'll look at how to configure the UC in detail later in this section.

 The UC is only available as a feature of the AppForge Professional edition. You must have the Professional edition to synchronize SQL data using the techniques we cover in this section.

Our example program supports a simple sales application, which is loaded onto a Palm device issued to each member of a sales force. This type of application might be used to sign up customers and take orders. During synchronization, any new data entered in the field is uploaded to the SQL server. At the same time, new product or pricing information is downloaded from the SQL server to the Palm device.

Sales Database

The SQL database contains tables of employees, customers, products, and orders. The schema for the Sales database is shown in Figure 5-4.

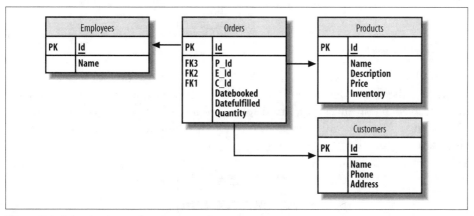

Figure 5-4. Sales database schema

The Sales database has the following tables:

Employees
    Contains an entry for each member of the sales team.

Products
    Contains each product in the catalog, including description, price, and quantity in stock.

Customers

Contains the customer list for the sales team.

Orders

Contains pending and completed sales. The table is completely normalized, with a foreign key for the Employees, Customers, and Products tables.

We have provided a database build script and a physical backup file (*Sales.sql* and *SalesBack.dat*, respectively) with the sample code for this chapter. The backup file contains the sample data we use in the examples in this section.

Palm Sales Application

The Sales application has two main forms: a products form that displays the current product inventory, and an orders form that records sales orders. The products form is shown in Figure 5-5.

Figure 5-5. Products form

The Products table is read-only in the application, because the product line is not created in the field. Details for each product, such as the current price and the amount available in inventory, are displayed when an entry is selected in the list. This form has a menu with a single choice for switching to the order form, which is shown in Figure 5-6.

Figure 5-6. Orders form

The orders form draws its data from the Customers, Products, and Orders tables. Selecting a customer from a drop-down combo box in the title line populates the central list box of orders.* Details and action buttons for an individual order are displayed at the bottom of the screen—we'll explain what these do later. This form also has a menu with a single entry that transfers control back to the products form.

Configuring the UC

Before we look at the code in the Sales application, we need to set up a UC descriptor, which tells the UC how to synchronize the Palm device with the SQL database. You use the AppForge UC Configuration program to do this. (Normally, the configuration program is installed only on the development machine. AppForge provides components that can be used in a set-up program to install the UC settings.) The configuration program has a wizard for new descriptors, with the following steps:

1. Naming UC configuration. In this step, you name the configuration and assign a 4-character Creator ID.
2. Select ODBC data source. In this step, you select the ODBC data source that is used with this configuration.
3. Table selection. In this step, you pick the SQL tables to be synchronized.
4. Synchronization type. In this step, you tell the UC how each selected SQL table is to be synchronized (see Table 5-2 for details).
5. ID field. The UC needs a field or set of fields that uniquely identify a table row. In a normalized database, this is the table's primary key.
6. Support file creation. In this optional step, you can create a VB database module and an empty PDB file.

We aren't going to describe all these steps because the AppForge documentation covers them. Instead, we look at some of the more interesting options.

Initially, we configure a single conduit to synchronize just the Products table. We register the conduit with a Creator ID of SALE, and select the ID field as the App-Forge Table Sync Key. The Sales database on our development computer has an ODBC data source named Sales, which we use.

Synchronization type

The UC supports a slightly different set of synchronization options from those we presented in Chapter 4. The UC options are shown in Table 5-2. The *replace* and *two-way* options are the same as the similarly named Palm standard conduit actions.

---

* Putting controls or other interface gadgets in the title line is common on the Palm, where every pixel counts. This combo box has its top property set to -1 to exactly fit the title bar on a Palm.

Table 5-2. UC synchronization types

Synch type	Description
Nothing	Conduit is present but doesn't run.
Two-way	Full synchronization—the same as the Palm CDK mirror-sync option.
PC appends to Palm	New SQL table rows are added to the PDB file.
Palm appends to PC	New records on the Palm are inserted in the SQL table.
PC replaces Palm	All records on the Palm are deleted and replaced with the current contents of the SQL table.
Palm replaces PC	All SQL table rows are deleted and are replaced with the current contents of the PDB file.

AppForge has added a new type of synchronization: *append*. With this option, new records are appended to the existing data set, and all other records are ignored. This results in efficient transfers of new records, but does not remove deleted records, nor does it update changed records. Be sure this is the effect you desire before using the append option.

Even though the Products table is going to be read-only on the Palm, we choose Two-way sync because the price and inventory can change in the SQL database. Only this synchronization type will result in an update of existing but changed records in the Palm PDB file.

> If a record is changed simultaneously in both the SQL database and the Palm PDB, the PDB record takes priority, even with two-way synchronization. This is different from the guidelines in the Palm CDK, but makes sense for relational data. How could one duplicate a primary key without an integrity constraint violation?

As we saw in Chapter 4, it is difficult to describe all possible interactions of synchronization type, updates to the SQL database, and changes to the Palm PDB. You should model the behavior of the UC as you design and prototype your application to make sure it suits all your needs.

PDB and VB module

The configuration wizard has an optional, but useful, step that generates a PDB file and a VB database module for each configured SQL table. The PDB file is created with an AppForge schema that matches the table column types from the SQL database. The PDB file is created without any records.

The VB module contains a record type definition that corresponds to the schema in the PDB file (see Example 5-8). We discuss how the UC maps SQL data types into VB data types later in this chapter.

Example 5-8. tProductRecord definition

```
Public Type tProductsRecord
    Id As Long
    Name As String
    Description As String
    Price As Single
    Inventory As Long
End Type
```

The VB module contains some other code to open and close the database, and to read in records. We chose not to use that code, preferring to write our own generic database routines instead. This keeps the final application as small as possible—we don't need the duplicated code for each table in the application.

It is easy for the generated VB record type to get out of sync with the database when the SQL table definition changes, as often happens during development. This is also true of the database Creator ID and the type identifiers.

HotSync manager

After the UC wizard finishes, a new entry is made in the HotSync manager's list of conduits, and the configuration settings are stored in the system registry, just as for any other conduit (see Figure 5-7).

Figure 5-7. Product table UC registry settings

In addition, the configuration wizard stores per-table synchronization settings in subkeys in the registry; the subkey name is the same as the table name. For example, in Figure 5-8, one subkey is named `Products`. This subkey contains settings for UC-specific settings for each table, such as the primary key.

After configuring the conduit, you must perform one more step before synchronization can occur. You must install an application with a Creator ID of `SALE` onto the Palm device, and optionally upload a PDB file to the Palm device. (Instead of uploading a PDB file, you could create one on the Palm the first time the `Sales` application runs. This requires that you create the appropriate AppForge schema, however).

The AppForge UC configuration program does not function under the normal HotSync manager user interface. You must run the program again to reconfigure a universal conduit setting (see Figure 5-8), or to access advanced settings not available from the wizard. This means that the end user will not usually be able to configure the conduit herself.

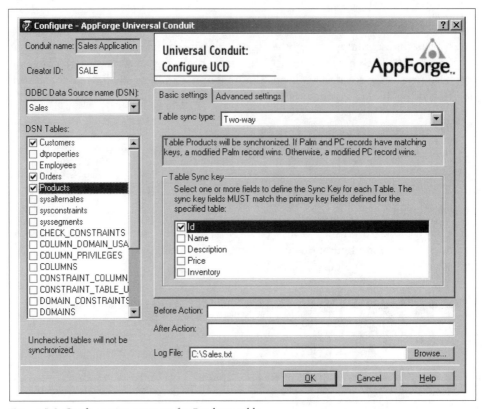

Figure 5-8. Configuration program for Products table

These configuration steps were taken on our development machine. AppForge provides two ways to create or change these settings in a production environment: the *UCmdConfig.exe* command-line program or automation components in the *UCConfig.dll* COM server. See the "Resources" section at the end of this chapter for articles and sample programs from AppForge documenting the use of these tools, and instructions on how to install them onto an end user's computer.

Sales Application: Products

Returning to the Sales application, we have a global VB module—*Startup.bas*—with a *Main* function for loading the product form (see Figure 5-5, shown earlier):

```
Sub Main( )

    Load Products
    Products.Show
End Sub
```

The module also contains the record definition for the Products table from Example 5-8, and the *Id2Long* routine from Example 5-6. (Both examples appeared earlier in this chapter).

The product form consists of a list box for the records; there is one list box entry for each product (see Figure 5-5, which appeared previously in this chapter). The list box is populated during the *Form_Load* event.

```
Private Sub Form_Load( )

    Dim rec As tProductsRecord

    db = PDBOpen(ByTypeCreator, "Products", 0, 0, Id2Long("DATA"), Id2Long("SALE"),
        afModeReadOnly)
    If db = 0 Then MsgBox "Couldn't open Products database!"

    While Not PDBEOF(db)
        PDBReadRecord db, VarPtr(rec)
        lstRecords.AddItem rec.Id & vbTab & rec.Name
        PDBMoveNext db
    Wend
End Sub
```

We open the Products database using the `afModeReadOnly` flag; we don't allow the sales force to modify product data in the field. When the user selects an entry in the list box, code in *lstRecords_Click* populates the text fields for price, inventory, and description.

Finally, to switch to the Orders form, the user clicks on the View → Orders menu choice.

```
Private Sub mnuOrders_Click(Index As Integer)
    Me.Hide
    Orders.Show
End Sub
```

As we pointed out in Chapter 2, form handling must be carefully managed in VB on the Palm. Hide the current form first, and then show the next one.

Products table synchronization

At this point, we can compile the application and install *Sales.prc* and *Product.pdb* onto a Palm device. The next HotSync operation activates the UC, which connects to the specified data source and downloads the Products table data. Opening the Sales application again displays the newly synchronized data.

Two Ways to Simulate A HotSync

It is often necessary to test an application or conduit with more than one type of hand-held. Few developers are lucky enough to have every combination of device and operating system, however. Here are two ways to test a conduit without any actual device hardware.

First, it is possible to HotSync with the Palm Emulator by using a development computer with two serial ports. First, connect the two COM ports with a null-modem cable. Then, after configuring the HotSync manager and the Emulator to use these ports, tap the HotSync button on the Emulator. See Palm KB articles 1674 and 2069 for more specific details.

However, it's even easier to test with the Palm Emulator using Network HotSync. You need to configure both the Palm Emulator and the desktop HotSync Manager to use the Local Area Network. See pages 490–491 of *Palm OS Programming* (O'Reilly & Associates, Inc.) for specifics.

As a simple test of the UC, we sell two laptops by updating our database, using this SQL statement:

```
update products set inventory=inventory-2 where id = 2
```

From Figure 5-8, shown previously in this chapter, you can see that we direct the UC to create a synchronization log in the file *C:\Sales.txt*. Our simple update test produces the log file shown in Example 5-9. Note the boldface entry for Record ID 2.

Example 5-9. Listing of Sales.txt log file

```
********************************************************************************
* Synchronizing: Sales
* Creator:       SALE
* Time:          01-09-2001 14:29:52
*

Driver for DSN 'Sales' not mentioned in configuration file.
Using config file 'C:\Program Files\AppForge\Universal Conduit\UCTypes.ini'
------------------------------------------------------------------------
----- Begin sync of database Products
------------------------------------------------------------------------
Synchronizing Products
Using synchronization type "Two-way"
Opened host table Products
Opened handheld database Products
Handheld Key  Host Key
------------  ---------
[1]           [1]        => Records match -- do nothing
[2]           [2]        => Overwrote handheld record with PC record
[3]           [3]        => Records match -- do nothing
```

Design Issues

AppForge developed the UC as a simple tool to manage a common synchronization chore—moving data from the Palm device to or from an ODBC data source. As the previous example shows, the UC manages this task nicely.

In this section, we extend the Sales application by adding functionality to track, create, change, and delete sales orders, and to organize the orders by customer. To do this, we need to consider more complicated SQL topics, such as data integrity, primary key management, foreign key relationships, and replication (synchronization) problems.

Minimize on-device data

An order in our Sales application joins three tables: the Employees, Customers, and Products tables. In a production application, these tables are going to be very large—which makes it prohibitively expensive to store and access them on the Palm. We decided not to use the Employees table, since all we really need is the ID of the employee who is using the handheld. We keep the Employee ID as a manifest constant in the source code, but in a real application, it would be an application preference.

Similar logic can be applied to the Customers and Orders tables. In many sales applications, the customer base can be divided, either by individual or by territory or some other value. A shortcoming of the UC is that you cannot access its internal SQL statements to accommodate these criteria, perhaps by adding a WHERE clause. One workaround is to use SQL views, with the filter based on the user login credentials. (We tested the UC using SQL views; the view statement had a WHERE clause based on the user login ID. If you take this approach, make sure your database views can be updated.)

We keep the entire Products table on the Palm device. This is important data to have locally, because in most real-world applications, prices and inventory are constantly changing.

The method you use to simplify the data sources for your application is up to you. But it is very important to make good design decisions about which data are truly important. Minimizing the data in the PDB increases the speed of the application and reduces the time spent synchronizing.

Primary key generation

In general, we prefer to use primary key columns with the *IDENTITY* attribute in our SQL tables. Using the *IDENTITY* attribute in Microsoft SQL Server causes the database engine to generate a primary key by incrementing an internal seed integer.

The primary key column is not specified when inserting rows into the database. For example, to create a new employee, use the following SQL statement:

```
insert Employees values ('New Employee')
```

When the UC detects a new record in a PDB file, it generates a SQL statement based on all the fields (columns) in the schema. The UC generates this statement when it adds a row to the Orders table:

```
INSERT INTO Orders  VALUES (?, ?, ?, ?, { ts '2001-09-05 00:00:00' }, { ts '1904-01-
    01 00:00:00' }, ?)\ 0"
```

The query looks a little unusual because the UC hasn't bound parameters to the SQL statement values yet, but there is one entry (the ?) for each table column—including the primary key column.*

This means that we cannot use identity columns for primary keys. As an alternative, we use an algorithm based on the employee identifier. Although this works for our simple application, you must design your key routine carefully. It is difficult to write a function that guarantees a unique number in all circumstances.

It is tempting to try and work around this with an INSERT trigger. That won't work, because the UC will no longer be able to associate the PDB record with the SQL table row. This is because the table row has a new primary key that no longer matches the record field on the Palm.

Database foreign key relationships

The Palm database manager does not support or enforce referential integrity between PDB files. An application that works with SQL data on the Palm device must handle the table relationships by itself. We can't present a general solution in this section, since that would involve writing a good portion of a relational database manager. But the PDB library does have sorting functions that speed up record access. We covered these functions in Chapter 3.

In our Sales application, the Orders table has three foreign keys: the Product ID, the Customer ID, and the Employee ID. If the user selects a customer, we need to display only the orders for that customer. We use *PDBSetSort* to sort the PDB file on the Customer IDcustomer ID field, and *PDBFindRecord* to seek to the first order for that particular customer. Now we can read off all the orders sequentially. This is very fast.

One problem with this approach, however, is that a table can only be sorted on one field (or set of fields) at a time, and resorting the table is very expensive. Later, if we want to access customer orders by date, we must resort the PDB file. Alternatively,

---

* You can see the SQL statements created by the UC by turning on ODBC tracing. This is done from the Tracing tab of the ODBC Data Source applet in the Windows Control Panel.

you could have a separate index for each sort order, perhaps stored in a separate database. Of course, then you have to maintain these indexes as the data changes—which is the function of a relational database manager! Part of your design should include analyzing the access paths your application takes in order to serve up data quickly.

The UC itself is only designed to support single table operations; it has no knowledge of database constraints such as foreign keys. This can make it an unsuitable choice if you need to create a lot of interdependent data on the Palm device.

Consider the relationship between the Customers table and the Orders table in the Sales database. New customers must be inserted before new orders can be taken for that customer, because of the foreign-key constraint on the Orders table. Unless the UC synchronizes the tables in the correct order, the SQL server will reject the Palm data, because the customer key doesn't yet exist in the database.* Of course, there is a similar problem with delete operations.

If your application data has dependencies that are enforced in your database, you should consider alternatives to the UC, such as writing a custom conduit. If you don't need to create large amounts of data, you can preallocate a few table rows and store the new database keys on the Palm. Then when the Palm user needs to sign up a new customer, they can use one of these reserved entries. This addresses the issue of table dependencies, which you can now manage using the techniques described in this chapter.

UC data types

When we ran the UC configuration wizard for Version 2.0 for the first time, we were surprised by how it handled a wide range of data types—almost every native MS SQL data type. There are a few data types that are not supported by the UC, such as the huge `Bigint`, and fields that contain arbitrary data like `Binary`, `Sqlvariant`, and `Image`.

The UC has an INI file—*UCTypes.ini*—that contains mappings for data types based on ODBC driver provider. In the version of the file we used, there are mappings for most of the Microsoft data-oriented products, including:

- Visual Fox Pro
- SQL Server
- Access
- Excel

---

* The UC appears to synchronize tables in alphabetical order. This is fortunate for the Sales application, because the Customers table precedes the Orders table, but you cannot rely on this behavior.

In addition, there is a common section that contains default values used for other ODBC driver providers. It is possible to customize these settings for any ODBC driver. For example, the AppForge Knowledge Base article #010628-0009 shows how to modify the INI file to support Lotus Notes.

Table 5-3 shows how the Universal Conduit maps data values for MS SQL Server.

Table 5-3. Universal Conduit data mappings for SQL Server

SQL data type	AppForge data type	Remarks
Char, Varchar, Text	String	The UC handles Unicode strings.
Datetime, Smalldatetime	Date	There is no support for timestamp fields.
Int	Long	
Smallint	Integer	
Tinyint	Byte	
Bit	Boolean	
Decimal, Numeric	Currency	All precisions are mapped to currency.
Money, Smallmoney	Currency	
Float	Double	
Real	Single	

You may need to study the *UCTypes.ini* file entries for your ODBC provider before relying on the UC to correctly synchronize your application's data. AppForge provides *UCQueryDriver.exe*, a command-line tool, to help with this process; see the "Resources" section, at the end of this chapter, for details.

If your application has a legacy database that relies on data types not supported by the UC, you should consider developing a custom conduit, as shown in Chapter 4.

Replication conflicts

The UC is a general-purpose tool, capable of synchronizing many different data sources. There are two types of problems it expects to encounter routinely:

SQL conflict
    A row couldn't be inserted into the database.

Archival
    A PDB record has the archive bit set.

AppForge has a strategy for handling these problems: the UC saves the offending record(s) in a special sync table in the SQL database. This new table must have the same structure—field types and order—as the base table, with three additional columns, as shown in Table 5-4.

Table 5-4. Sync table structure

Column name	MS SQL type	Remarks
AfsyncDate	datetime	When HotSync occurred
AfsyncRecordId	integer	Contains PDB unique Record ID
afsyncDisposition	tinyint	Flag—Conflict=1, Archive=2

These columns must be the last three columns in the table. In addition, the sync table name must consist of the original table name with _hh appended.

Let's look at an example using the Orders table in the Sales database (see Figure 5-4, shown earlier in this chapter). Each row in the Orders table must contain a valid Product ID. Suppose we create a record on the Palm that contains good information for each column except for P_Id—the foreign key into the Product table, which we set to the illegal value of 8888.

When the UC attempts to insert the new record into the SQL database, an integrity constraint error such as the following will occur:

```
DIAG [23000] [Microsoft][ODBC SQL Server Driver][SQL Server]INSERT statement
conflicted with COLUMN FOREIGN KEY constraint 'FK_OrdersProducts'. The conflict
occurred in database 'Sales', table 'Products', column 'Id'. (547)
```

A query of the Orders_hh table shows the following data (we've removed some columns for clarity):

```
Id     P_Id   AfsyncDate                  afSyncRecordId  afSyncDisposition
------ ------ --------------------------- --------------- ------------------
889910 8888   2001-09-08 00:40:00.000     335906          1
```

Notice that the UC has preserved the PDB record values, such as the invalid P_Id value of 8888. In addition, the date of the synchronization is recorded, and the disposition column indicates that the cause of failure was a conflict.* Nothing automatic happens after the replication conflict is logged: it is up to you to determine the appropriate resolution.

You can configure the UC to simply discard conflicting records, avoiding the need for a sync table. This is done using the UC configuration utility. Select a UC descriptor and table to configure, go to the Advanced tab, and check the Discard Conflict records box. If you choose this option, you don't need a sync table in your database at all.

---

* As of this writing, there were some bugs involving two-way sync. In this case, the Palm record is deleted during the *next* HotSync: since the record is no longer marked dirty in the PDB, and there is no corresponding table row, the UC concludes that it has been intentionally deleted from the SQL database, and then synchronizes that deletion.

NULL fields

AppForge does not support NULL columns. Most attempts to write records to a Palm PDB using *PDBWriteRecord* fail spectacularly with uninitialized or NULL data. This is particularly true of string and date fields.

If your data requires NULL columns, you must write each field to the PDB record by hand using the *PDBWriteFieldByOffset* routine. You are responsible for writing a bit-pattern of the correct length, with the correct value, and to the correct offset in the record.

In general, we do not design SQL databases that use NULL columns. One rare exception is dates. If a date is unknown, it is best to leave it NULL in the database. When the UC synchronizes an AppForge record with an empty date, it inserts a value of 1904-01-01 00:00:00:00.000 into the SQL database. You can then have an INSERT or UPDATE trigger that replaces this pattern with a true NULL.

Deleted records

There are three ways to delete records from a Palm PDB, using the AppForge *PDBDeleteRecordEx* function:

Normal delete
>   The record is marked as deleted. Only a placeholder—including the Palm unique identifier—remains in the database. Use the AppForge constant afDeleteModePalmDelete in the *PDBDeleteRecordEx* call.

Archival delete
>   The record is marked as deleted and archived. The record data remains in the database, and is accessible during HotSync. Use the AppForge constant afDeleteModeArchive.

Physical delete
>   The record is removed from the database. There is no remaining trace of the record, including its unique identifier. Use the AppForge constant afDeleteModeRemove.

If you are using two-way synchronization, you should use the archival delete option. This is the only option that preserves the SQL table primary key in the record data. The other delete operations destroy this data, making it impossible to locate and remove the appropriate row in the database table. In fact, with two-way synchronization, the deleted record is recreated on the Palm device during HotSync. This is because the UC has no way of knowing that the record ever existed on the Palm device, but it does see one in the SQL database.

If you aren't using a sync table, as shown earlier in the chapter, you should instruct the AppForge conduit to discard archived records. You can do this in the UC configuration program, on the table's Advanced tab.

Sales Application: Orders

We put all these design decisions to the test in the Orders form for the Sales application. The code for this section is in *Order.frm*, with the exception of definitions for the Customer and Order records, which are in *Startup.bas*.

 Although functional, the Sales application is not very user-friendly. We omit some important features, such as refreshing the display after submitting an order, so we can focus on design issues for the UC.

The *Form_Load* event is shown in Example 5-10.

Example 5-10. Listing for Order Form_Load

```
Private Sub Form_Load( )

    Dim rec As tCustomersRecord

    dbC = PDBOpen(ByTypeCreator, "Customers", 0, 0, Id2Long("DATA"), Id2Long("SALE"),
        afModeReadOnly)

    dbO = PDBOpen(ByTypeCreator, "Orders", 0, 0, Id2Long("DATA"), Id2Long("SALE"),
        afModeReadWrite)

    PDBSetSortFields dbO, C_Id_Field

    While Not PDBEOF(dbC)
        PDBReadRecord dbC, VarPtr(rec)
        cboCustomer.AddItem rec.Name
        cboCustomer.ItemData(PDBCurrentIndex(dbC)) = rec.Id
        PDBMoveNext dbC
    Wend
End Sub
```

First, we open the Customer and Order PDBs. Like the Products table, the Customers table on the Palm is read-only. The Orders table is opened in read-write mode because we will be changing it. We sort the Orders table on the Customer ID field:

```
PDBSetSortFields dbO, C_Id_Field
```

This is important because we want to filter our orders by customer, and it would be too slow to scan the PDB file from beginning to end for each customer.

Next, we read in all the customers, and store each customer name in the combo box. We also keep track of the Customer ID:

```
cboCustomer.ItemData(PDBCurrentIndex(dbC)) = rec.Id
```

When the user selects a customer, we have the ID readily available. This saves us an expensive table lookup to retrieve the ID. There is a cost of four bytes per customer lookup, but it seems like a reasonable tradeoff if we keep the number of customers small. This is another reason to seek a design that minimizes the number of records in a PDB file.

Here is the code for *cboCustomer_Click*, the event handler triggered when an entry in the customer combo box is selected:

```
Private Sub cboCustomer_Click()

    Dim cid As Long
    Dim str As String
    Dim idx As Integer
    Dim rec As tOrdersRecord

    lstRecords.Clear
    ClearFormData

    cid = cboCustomer.ItemData(cboCustomer.ListIndex)
    PDBFindRecordByField dbO, C_Id_Field, cid

    While Not PDBEOF(dbO)
        PDBReadRecord dbO, VarPtr(rec)
        If cid <> rec.C_Id Then Exit Sub

        str = Trim(Products.GetProductName(rec.P_Id)) & _
            " : " & CStr(rec.DateBooked) & " : " & CStr(rec.Quantity)
        lstRecords.AddItem str
        lstRecords.ItemData(idx) = PDBCurrentIndex(dbO)

        idx = idx + 1
        PDBMoveNext dbO
    Wend
End Sub
```

First, we clear the screen of data from the previous customer. The *ClearFormData* subroutine (not listed) simply erases the four text fields on the form. Then we retrieve the Customer ID from the combo box *ItemData* property, and use *PDBFindRecordByField* to look up the relevant sales orders.

Unfortunately, there is no way to know if the lookup succeeded or failed. We read in the current record, and check if it matches the search criteria. If the IDs do not match, we exit the routine, since there are no orders for this customer:

```
PDBReadRecord dbO, VarPtr(rec)
If cid <> rec.C_Id Then Exit Sub
```

Otherwise, we concatenate the product name, the order date, and the number of items ordered, and add them to the list box. We also store the record index in the list entry *ItemData* property:

```
lstRecords.AddItem str
lstRecords.ItemData(idx) = PDBCurrentIndex(dbO)
```

Remembering the index allows us to access the record directly when the user wants to update or delete it.

We also need a function that looks up the Product ID from the Orders PDB and returns the corresponding name. Rather than opening another database, we modify the Products form code, adding the public function *GetProductName*:

```
Public Function GetProductName(ByVal pid As Long) As String

    Dim rec As tProductsRecord

    PDBFindRecordByField db, 0, pid
    PDBReadRecord db, VarPtr(rec)
    If rec.Id = pid Then
        GetProductName = rec.Name
    Else
        GetProductName = ""
    End If
End Function
```

Remember, the Products form is hidden, not unloaded, so it is perfectly legal to access its public methods. For this to work, the Products PDB must be sorted, so we added the following line to the Product *Form_Load* procedure:

```
PDBSetSortFields db, P_Id_Field
```

The constant P_Id_Field is zero, which means to sort on the first field in the PDB schema.

Selecting an item in the list box triggers *lstRecords_Click*, which populates the four text fields with details from the corresponding order record:

```
Private Sub lstRecords_Click()

    Dim rec As tOrdersRecord

    PDBGotoIndex db0, lstRecords.ItemData(lstRecords.ListIndex)
    PDBReadRecord db0, VarPtr(rec)

    txtProduct.Text = CStr(rec.P_Id)
    txtQuantity.Text = CStr(rec.Quantity)
    txtDtOrdered.Text = CStr(rec.DateBooked)
    txtDtDelivered.Text = CStr(rec.DateFulfilled)

    g_OrderId = rec.Id
End Sub
```

First, the correct record is located, using the index stored in the *ItemData* property, and read into a record variable. Then the form text fields are populated with data from the record. Finally, we save the Record ID—the primary key—in a global variable:

```
g_OrderId = rec.Id
```

We'll explain why we do this later in this chapter.

Now we turn to the action buttons at the bottom of the form. Pressing the New button transfers the values on the screen into an order record, and adds that record to the database. Here is the code for the *btnNew_Click* event:

```
Private Sub btnNew_Click()

    Dim rec As tOrdersRecord

    rec.Id = NewOrderId
    LoadFormData rec

    PDBCreateRecordBySchema dbO
    PDBWriteRecord dbO, VarPtr(rec)
    PDBUpdateRecord dbO
End Sub
```

Remember, record creation can and will fail if the storage heap is full. Unlike the code shown above, your application must check for errors and take some appropriate action.

In order to successfully synchronize a new record with the SQL database, the UC must have a unique Record ID for the new order. The *NewOrderId* function handles that chore:

```
Private Function NewOrderId() As Long
    NewOrderId = TimerMS
End Function
```

TimerMS is an AppForge function that returns the number of milliseconds since the Palm device was last reset. While this is unique enough for our example Sales application, you will want a more reliable function for a production application.

The *LoadFormData* routine is a little more complex:

```
Private Sub LoadFormData(ByRef rec As tOrdersRecord)

    rec.C_Id = CLng(cboCustomer.ItemData(cboCustomer.ListIndex))
    rec.E_Id = E_Id_Key

    rec.P_Id = CLng(txtProduct.Text)
    rec.Quantity = CLng(txtQuantity.Text)
    rec.DateBooked = CDate(txtDtOrdered.Text)
    If txtDtDelivered.Text <> "" Then
        rec.DateFulfilled = CDate(txtDtDelivered.Text)
    End If
End Sub
```

First, we retrieve the Customer ID from the combo box *ItemData* property. This was assigned in the *Form_Load* event (see Example 5-10, shown earlier in this chapter). We have a constant for the Employee ID:

```
    rec.E_Id = E_Id_Key
```

Normally, this important value wouldn't be a constant, but might be stored in a configuration PDB file or as an application preference. This latter technique might be used in conjunction with a sign-in screen. The rest of the field values are read in from the text controls on the form.

Pressing the Update button triggers the *btnUpdate_Click* event:

```
Private Sub btnUpdate_Click()

    Dim rec As tOrdersRecord

    rec.Id = g_OrderId
    LoadFormData rec

    PDBEditRecord dbO
    PDBWriteRecord dbO, VarPtr(rec)
    PDBUpdateRecord dbO
End Sub
```

The code is very similar to *btnNew_Click*. This is where we use the previously stored order key—g_OrderId—instead of generating a new primary key. *btnUpdate_Click* also uses *LoadFormData* to populate the other record fields. Of course, we update the PDB record instead of creating a new one.

Here is the code for the *mnuProducts_Click* event to switch from the Order form to the Product form.

```
Private Sub mnuProducts_Click(Index As Integer)
    Me.Hide
    Products.Show
End Sub
```

We clear the form fields, as a reminder to the user that the record no longer exists, and then delete the record from the PDB. As we discussed earlier in the chapter, it is important to set the archive bit by using afDeleteModeArchive when deleting the record. If you don't do this, the UC simply replaces the deleted record with a new copy from the SQL database.

Resources

Information about the AppForge PDB library and the UC is available as part of the Professional Edition. This documentation is also available from the AppForge web site.

Installation of the runtime components for the UC is covered generally in the App-Forge documentation. See Knowledge Base article #010419-0023 for more detailed information. Note that the UC assumes that all the Microsoft data access components, or their equivalents from your database vendor, are already installed on the machine.

Article #010827-0039 explains how to download and use the *UCQueryDriver.exe* program as an aid to configure the UC for non-Microsoft ODBC data sources.

The AppForge Knowledge Base also has several good articles that cover how the UC interacts with the Palm HotSync manager. See articles #010629-0023 and #010801-0030.

CHAPTER 6

Web Clipping Applications

When the Palm VII was released in 1999, it was a device that took Palm's message of *the connected organizer* to the next level. By supplying a device with an integrated cellular radio capable of connecting to digital wireless networks in the United States and Canada, the ability to attach to data anywhere, anytime became a reality.

In addition, the Palm VII is poised to revolutionize mobile electronic commerce, by supplying a secure means of coordinating field automation with customer needs. For example, a company that equips its sales staff with appropriate web software can enable real-time processing of purchases on the customer premises—wherever they are.[*]

In this chapter, we will look at how to build a distributed application using Palm's *Web Clipping* technology. A Web Clipping Application (WCA) is a special type of Palm database that consists of HTML documents and graphics. Unlike a typical Internet web site, which resides entirely on a web server, the WCA is precompiled and stored on the Palm PDA. The operating system knows how to display the data and graphics in a WCA to the device user. And a special library in the Palm—called INetLib—uses the Palm radio network to access the Internet and retrieve remote data when necessary.

The HTML code that is retrieved over the Internet from the remote web server is called the Web Clipping, or sometimes simply the clipping.

Occasionally, you will see the Web Clipping Application referred to as a Palm Query Application (PQA). This is a legacy term, which is still present in the online litera-ture and tools. In their latest documentation, however, Palm makes it clear that Web Clipping Application is the preferred term.

---

[*] Currently, the Palm VII uses wireless service from BellSouth. Radio attachments for the Palm III and V use different wireless networks. Palm also has a Mobile Internet Kit, which works with both cellular telephones and normal modems.

It is important to note that there is no separate web browser used to display a WCA—rather, an internal viewer displays the text and graphics in a WCA when the user launches the application.* In this sense, a WCA is just like any other Palm application—the user's attention is entirely devoted to the application's content, and not to the operation of a software program.

Because the user doesn't have a browser, there is no navigation on the Palm VII to a home page on a web site. Instead, WCA applications are partitioned into two parts: a preinstalled component on the Palm PDA and a dynamic component on the web server. The preinstalled part contains links to remote web servers that return static or dynamic HTML pages—web clippings, in Palm's terms. Any web server that supports the Common Gateway Interface (CGI) can be used for a clipping application.

We will use a variety of tools to build clipping applications. For the client-side application construction, there is the WCA Builder tool developed by Palm. This application converts HTML documents and graphical images into the WCA format suitable for upload to the Palm VII. For the server-side components, we use Microsoft Internet Information Server (IIS), Active Server Pages (ASP), and VB Script. We construct VB COM objects and SQL queries to handle back-end automation.

Before examining the implementation of a clipping application, we need to look at some features of Palm's radio network. Several important things happen when the user extends the antenna of a Palm VII and connects to a remote web server. To build a responsive and secure WCA, you will need to understand these events.

Palm.Net Wireless Architecture

The wireless industry in North America consists of competing and still emerging standards, radio frequencies and types, hardware, and, of course, different wireless network operators. Palm decided to equip its Palm VII with one type of radio and to operate on one network, neatly sidestepping a host of compatibility and interoperability issues.

As mentioned earlier, the Palm's wireless service—called Palm.Net—uses the Bell-South wireless network. Palm also maintains a gateway service that connects the wireless network to the Internet. Specialized proxy servers translate the Palm VII radio packets to the Internet packet format, and forward the packets to the appropriate web server.† Figure 6-1 presents an overview of this network.

---

* Palm calls its pseudo-browser the Web Clipping Application Viewer. There are several third party web browsers available for the Palm, but they are not used with WCAs.

† Currently, the Palm proxy servers only support Hyper-Text Transfer Protocol (HTTP), in both normal and secure mode.

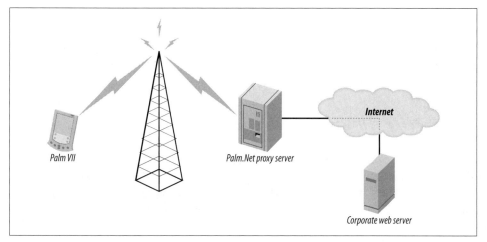

Internet

Palm VII

Palm.Net proxy server

Corporate web server

Figure 6-1. Palm.Net infrastructure

The Palm Web Clipping Developer's Guide spells out exactly what happens when the user selects a hypertext link in a clipping application:

1. If the linked page or graphic is installed on the Palm VII organizer, the page or graphic is displayed.

2. Otherwise, the Palm VII organizer compresses the query into a small file in Palm Query Format and sends this packet over the air to the local base station.

3. The local base station relays the compressed packet to the Web Clipping proxy servers at a Palm.Net data center.

4. The Web Clipping proxy server translates the query packet into a standard HTTP packet and then sends the decompressed query to the appropriate Internet address.

5. The HTTP server returns an HTML page to the Web Clipping proxy server.

6. The Web Clipping proxy server compresses the HTML page into a Palm Proxy Format file and sends it back to the local base station.

7. The local base station relays the clipping to the Palm VII organizer, where the Web Clipping Application Viewer renders the page.

As you can see, the data passes through a lot of communication links on its way back and forth between the Palm VII user and a remote web site. Fortunately, the INetLib library on the Palm, the wireless network, and the proxy server handle almost all the details. The developer of a WCA is only responsible for the two end-points: the HTML in the WCA resident in the Palm PDA and the ASP code on the remote web server.

Palm Proxy Server

The Palm network operations center houses the proxy servers that connect the Palm. Net wireless network to the Internet. All wireless data from a Palm VII passes through the proxy server on its way to and from a web server. The Palm proxy server has several key functions: it maintains network connections, it provides data transformation and caching services, and it handles Internet security.

The Palm VII wireless network is completely separate from the Internet. When the proxy server transforms wireless data into Internet packets, it tracks the origin of the wireless data. When the response data is received from the web server, the proxy server knows how to send it back to the correct Palm VII radio. The proxy server must also be able to redirect Internet data to another web server.[*]

Clipping applications and INetLib don't deal with HTML data directly; instead, the data sent between the Palm VII and the proxy server is in Compressed Markup Language (CML). Palm recognized that HTTP data is easily compressed and very regular in expression, and invented CML as a way to minimize the amount of data transmitted on the slow wireless networks. The proxy server does most of the computationally intensive transformation between HTML and CML. The viewer application decodes the CML for display, which is a much simpler operation.

The proxy server provides more than a simple compression service. Because the proxy server is aware of the underlying data formats (CML and HTML), Palm enabled certain data transformations and mappings as well. These are chiefly aimed at conserving wireless bandwidth or modifying the data to display properly on the Palm's 160×160-pixel screen.

Truncation
   HTML pages returned from Internet web servers are truncated after 1 KB, unless special Palm metatags are used.

Clipping
   Images are clipped to a maximum size of 153×144 pixels, the largest size available in the WCA viewer. HTML tables are also clipped at 153 pixels wide, although they have unlimited depth.

Hashing
   Hypertext links and other form elements are compressed by computing a simple checksum. In order to save bandwidth, the much smaller checksum and an index are sent to the WCA viewer, instead of the more verbose link or form element.

Caching
   Web clippings are cached at the proxy server. If the clipping is static, this caching dramatically improves application response time. The proxy server can be told not to cache a page.

The proxy server transformation and caching services can sometimes interfere with an application's proper or desired behavior. For example, if two form elements have

---

[*] The current proxy servers support up to three HTTP redirect operations per connection. After that, they abort the transaction.

the same checksum value, then the proxy server might be unable to determine which element the user intended to use. For this reason, Palm advises that all form elements and names be at least two characters in length.

Use of the Palm.Net proxy servers is not optional when developing or deploying Palm OS web applications, because the Palm InetLib software only understands CML. This means that your development environment must support a reliable connection to the Internet, so that your web server is accessible by the Palm proxy server. This is also true if you are using the Palm Emulator to perform testing—which we discuss later in this chapter.

The Palm proxy servers are configured to use a small range of available ports for normal and secure HTTP data. This can pose issues for software developers behind corporate firewalls, since those ports might be blocked.*

Palm.Net supports both production and development proxy servers. There are two main development proxy servers. One server runs the same software version as the production servers, and the other server runs updated software with bug fixes and new features. Which of the two development servers you use depends on your development and testing needs. The production servers, however, should only be used for deployed applications.

Palm provides an online web page that contains information for all the proxy servers at *http://oasis.palm.com/dev/proxy/*. This information includes the current IP address of the proxy servers, their operational status and software revision level, and any notes or planned changes.

Wireless Security on Palm.Net

Palm designed its wireless security architecture to support electronic transactions. Its security architecture has three components: encryption of sensitive data transmitted on the airwaves; secure proxy servers to bridge the wireless and wired networks; and full support for the Internet Secure Socket Layer (SSL) protocol.

Data transmitted from the Palm PDA is encrypted before transmission and decrypted only after reception. The Palm VII uses Elliptic Curve Cryptography (ECC), which forms the basis for a public key cryptosystem. ECC is significantly smaller and faster than the more traditional public key techniques based on factoring large prime numbers, and is often used in cellphones and other wireless applications with limited computing power.

The actual data packets are encrypted using an extension of the DES algorithm. This encryption prevents eavesdroppers from listening to private data conversations. In

---

* We won't discuss firewalls or network addressing issues further in this book. Palm documents which ports can be used with the proxy server and the Emulator in the knowledge base; see articles 1409, 1810, and 1818.

addition, each message contains a digital signature that prevents tampering with data packets, or reusing them. A different encryption key is generated for each transmission; this session key is then encrypted with the Palm.Net public key and sent along with the data.

The data packets remain encrypted throughout the wireless carrier's network until they reach the Palm.Net proxy server. There, they are decrypted, reencrypted using one of the algorithms specified by the SSL protocol, and sent over the Internet to the specified web server.

 Wireless data encryption only occurs when exchanging data using Secure HTTP (also called HTTPS). Regular HTTP data is sent over the airwaves scrambled, but it is not encrypted.

There are some procedural issues you should consider before deploying a very sensitive application on Palm.Net. Foremost, all data passes through the Palm.Net proxy servers. You must trust Palm to preserve the integrity of ECC public/private key pairs and to not examine your data. Also important is the level of service that Palm.Net will provide—is the proxy server online when your application needs it? Palm has set up procedures and policies to provide a high level of security, availability, and redundancy in Palm.Net data centers. These policies are documented in several white papers, listed at the end of this chapter.

There are also some technical issues to consider, primarily concerning encryption key and certificate management. The data security in Palm.Net depends on the integrity of the ECC keys—if the private key is compromised, then many session keys are potentially compromised as well. Palm does not document how often it replaces the ECC public/private keys or how those keys are distributed. And Palm does not document how it generates the DES session key used to encrypt each individual transmission. If the key generation algorithm is even partially predictable, then it is possible for an eavesdropper to guess at the key and decode the transmitted data.

Internet data security—in particular, HTTPS and SSL—depends upon the exchange of certificates that vouch for the authenticity of a web site or a user. Encryption occurs only after the web server presents a valid and trusted certificate to the client that requested secure communications. The user has the prerogative to review the certificate—to make sure that the server is really hosted by its owner, for example. Although rarely used, the popular web browsers all provide a means to inspect and reject certificates.

Unfortunately, the Palm VII user can never directly view the certificate used by the secure web server, because the proxy server is acting on the user's behalf. This means that the user must trust Palm.Net to route the HTTPS request to the proper server, and to ensure that the certificate the web server presents is valid and in fact corresponds to the resource originally requested.

For the same reason, the Palm proxy server automatically handles redirection of a secure request to an insecure web server. And it is impossible to send client certificates from the Palm PDA through the proxy server to authenticate the user and his right to access the web server.

Palm has tried hard to provide a secure data center and wireless network useful for the majority of electronic commerce applications. You need to examine the security requirements of your application before hosting it on Palm.Net—or any wireless network, for that matter. This is no different from outsourcing any other aspect of your application's infrastructure.

Simple WCA Tour

In this section, we build a simple but complete WCA application. The application contains both local HTML pages and graphical images. In addition, it has a standard HTML form that posts to an ASP on Microsoft's IIS. The ASP simply reverses the text and writes the data back to the WCA.

We are not going to discuss creating or debugging Microsoft IIS applications in this chapter. We assume that you know how to build an ASP application, and are reasonably familiar with VB script and object construction techniques.

The standard tool for building WCA applications is the WCA Builder for Windows: *WCABuild.exe.*[*] This application compiles HTML pages and linked graphics into the proprietary PQA format used on the Palm PDA. The WCA Builder expects your application to be organized in a strict hierarchy with one HTML document at the top level. Of course, this document may have multiple links to other local (and remote) pages and images.

During compilation, the WCA Builder scans the index page for references to other local HTML pages or images. It pulls any pages found into the WCA, and then recursively scans those pages looking for more links. As it compiles, the tool compresses the files to save space on the Palm PDA. If there are no errors, the WCA Builder creates a PQA file that is ready to run.

Our application consists of a WCA top-level—or index—page, *Ch6a.html*. In our case, the index page has a link to another local page, *Ch6aAbout.html*. The home page also has a standard HTML form that posts to a remote script, *Reverse.asp*, which resides on an IIS server and is only available over the Internet. Figure 6-2 shows the relationship between the PQA, the web server, and the data pages.

---

[*] Earlier releases of this tool were named *QAB.exe*. We are using the current release—version 1.5—in this chapter, because it supports extensions previously available only from the command line.

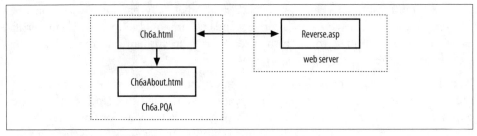

Figure 6-2. Structure of Ch6a.pqa

Let's look at the code for *Ch6a.html*, which is shown in Example 6-1. Note that this is a plain, simple HTML document. The WCA compiler and viewer are based on a subset of HTML version 3.2.

Example 6-1. Listing of Ch6a.html

```
<html>
<head>
<meta name="PalmLauncherRevision" content="1.1">
<meta name="PalmComputingPlatform" content="true">
<title>Ch6a Home</title>
</head>
<body>
<br>
This is the home page. A <a href="Ch6aAbout.html">local page</A>
provides help.
<hr>
<form method="post" action="http://website/Ch6a/Reverse.asp">
Enter a string to reverse on the server:
<input type="text" name="data" size="10">
<br>
<input type="submit" value="Reverse">
</form>
</body>
</html>
```

Next, look at the two metatags in the HTML document header. You use `PalmLauncherRevision` to set the version of the application, which is helpful for maintenance. The very important `PalmComputingPlatform` indicates that the content in this web page has been optimized for the Palm PDA. In general, the proxy server and the local viewer do not alter HTML pages with this tag.

The link a `href="Ch6aAbout.html"` in this context refers to a local page within the PQA itself (see Figure 6-2 above). If the WCA Builder application cannot find the HTML page in the current directory when compiling, it silently generates a remote link instead. You can detect this error manually, because the local HTML file will not be present in the list of files scanned by the WCA Builder.

Now let's look at the very simple *Ch6aAbout.html*.

```
<html>
<head>
<meta name="PalmComputingPlatform" content="true">
<title>Ch6a About</title>
</head>
<body>
This is the about page. This is where you might put static
or reference information.
</body>
</html>
```

This HTML document has no links at all, not even a back button—that's supplied by the WCA viewer. This minimalist format is typical in a WCA application, which is focused on content delivery.

Note that *Ch6aAbout.html* also has the metatag indicating Palm-specific content. Palm recommends that this tag be placed in all pages of a WCA—both local and remote.

The server-side *Reverse.asp* is the last piece of our application. It is a very simple script that uses the VB StrReverse function to reverse the form input:

```
<%@ Language=VBScript %>
<html>
<head>
<title>Ch6a</title>
<meta name="PalmComputingPlatform" content="true">
<meta name="HistoryListText" content="Reverse-&time">
</head>
<body>
Server says "<%=StrReverse(Request.Form("data"))%>".<p>
<a href="file:Ch6a.pqa">Go back</a> to the main page.
</body>
</html>
```

There is a new metatag in this listing, HistoryListText. Using this metatag causes the string Reverse- to be added to the viewer's history list. Palm recommends that the history metatag be used in every dynamic web page.* The &time pseudo-variable expands to the current time on the Palm PDA; of course, there is a corresponding &date as well.

Look at the link back to the index page—*Ch6a.html*—of the WCA:

```
<a href="file:Ch6a.pqa">Go back</a> to the main page.
```

---

* Since the viewer doesn't maintain a history list of precompiled web pages stored in the WCA, you don't need to use this metatag for local pages. This is a reflection of Palm's minimalist approach: why waste precious cache space for an HTML page that's always available?

This is how to refer to the index page of a WCA. Static pages in the application can be addressed directly. For example, use a href="file:Ch6a.pqa/Ch6aAbout.html" in dynamically generated code to reference the help page of our WCA.* Unlike most hypertext links, references to on-device HTML pages are case-sensitive.

The Palm Web Clipping Guide and WCA Builder documentation discuss the various types of links supported in a PQA.

That's all the code in our simple WCA, which we will now compile into a PQA. To do this, start the WCA Builder, and use the File → Open Index option to select a top-level page; in our sample, this is *Ch6a.html*. The tool will automatically detect the link to the local page, as shown in Figure 6-3.

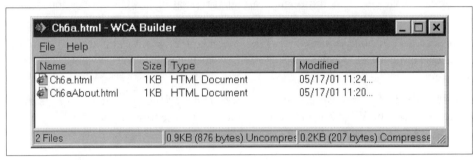

Figure 6-3. WCA Builder for Ch6a

Notice on the program status line that the two files have been compressed from 876 bytes down to 207 bytes. This is a typical ratio for text; images, however, don't compress nearly as well.

Once all the local files have been recognized, select File → Build PQA to bring up the build dialog. You use this dialog to set the output filename, icons and any special PQA features for your application. By default, the name of your application that is displayed on the Palm is the same as the output filename. We'll see how to change these properties later in this chapter.

The Emulator uses the network adapter in the desktop computer to connect to the Internet. By default, this feature is turned off. To enable it, use the Emulator context menu and select Settings → Properties. On the dialog shown in Figure 6-4, make certain that the check box labeled Redirect NetLib calls to host TCP/IP is selected.

Recall that all network traffic for a WCA goes through a Palm.Net proxy server. If you are using the Emulator with a downloaded ROM, your proxy server address is

---

* There is a bug in the newest WCA Builder tool that prevents you from referring to the index page by name if you are not running Palm OS 4.0. For example, a href="file:Ch6a.pqa/Ch6a.html" will not work. If this addressing is necessary for your application, you should use *Qab.exe*.

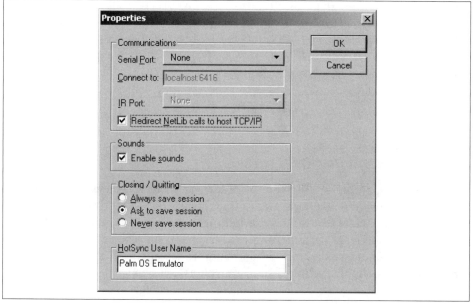

Figure 6-4. Emulator Properties dialog

most likely out of date.* You can use the `Wireless Preferences` dialog on the real or emulated Palm VII to update the proxy server's Internet address, as shown in Figure 6-5. (The dialog for Palm OS 4.0 is slightly different; it accepts the proxy server address using the symbolic machine name, such as *proxy.palm.net*.)

Figure 6-5. Proxy server preference dialog

Load the *Ch6a.pqa* into either an actual Palm VII or the Emulator.

---

* As previously discussed, there are two types of proxy server at Palm.Net—production servers and development servers. Use the development server until your application is in production. Palm maintains up-to-date information on the address and status of the Palm.Net proxy servers at *http://www.oasis.palm.com/dev/proxy/*.

The WCA Builder provides default icons for WCA applications, as shown in Figure 6-6. The clipping toolkit contains template bitmap files that can be customized with any graphical editor. The large bitmap, used in icon mode, measures 32 × 22 pixels; the small bitmap, used in list view mode, is 15 × 9. These bitmaps have a color depth of 1 bit—they are monochrome.

Figure 6-6. Application launcher icon for Ch6a.pqa

Launching the application brings up the index page, which is shown in Figure 6-7. The viewer has rendered the local link to *Ch6aAbout.html* as underlined text, as any browser might do. Note that the Reverse button, which posts to a remote web site, is adorned with a special glyph indicating a radio connection. The WCA Builder generates this glyph automatically for links and buttons. An application that uses images for a remote link should include a similar glyph as a cue to the user that following the link will take some time and possibly incur airtime charges.

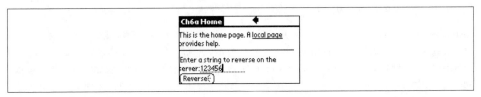

Figure 6-7. Ch6a.html

Pressing the Reverse button causes the viewer to post any form data on the remote web server. The data is transmitted by the Palm VII radio to a local base station in the BellSouth wireless network. From there, the data is routed to one of the Palm. Net proxy servers. The proxy server connects to the Internet, and generates the HTTP Post request to *Reverse.asp* on the web server.

After the ASP script has finished processing the request, the data is sent back to the proxy server, which compresses it and transmits it over the wireless network. Finally it is received on the Palm VII, where it is decompressed and displayed, as shown Figure 6-8. This involved sequence, which occurs with every remote data access, highlights the need to keep your wireless applications as small and simple as possible.

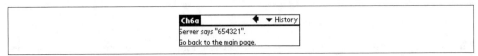

Figure 6-8. HTML output of Reverse.asp

In Figure 6-8, you can see that the link to the WCA index page generated by the ASP script does not have the radio glyph—the link was *generated* remotely, but it references a *local* page. And notice that the History—in the top right corner of the screen—is now active. This is a result of using the PalmHistoryList metatag in the clipping.

Building a Large Application

Our simple example glossed over many design and implementation issues encountered when building large or complex applications. In this section, we build a more complete example that covers these issues. In particular, we look at HTML 3.2 limitations and extensions in the Palm WCA viewer, application partitioning, security, and access control, as well as some basic user interface techniques that work well on the Palm.

As we discuss these design topics and present the details of a larger application, we will work in other important details of Clipping application development using VB. Our focus is how to develop the HTML and ASP code necessary to produce good distributed applications. When necessary, we will go into the details of COM objects and the SQL database to make a point.

 There are many other techniques, such as the use of XML data and XSL templates or Microsoft Transaction Server components, which aid the development of efficient ASP applications. However, we will not cover development using these tools here.

The large example project for this chapter, Ch6b, is an application designed for a hypothetical company that has field technicians performing jobs at client sites. The technicians of our hypothetical company can use Ch6b to check their daily job schedule, review customer information, and update work orders in real time. The managers use Ch6b to check on the progress of customer jobs throughout the day.

Obviously, such an application could do much more. We have purposefully simplified the functionality so that we can focus on design and implementation techniques. We have also designed Ch6b as an exclusively wireless application, although normally an application of this nature would have a blended interface accessible from both the radio and the desktop.

Ch6b uses an SQL database to manage the user, customer, and job data. User login and security data are stored in the SQL database in the session table, which is discussed in detail later in this chapter (see Figure 6-9).

The SQL database structure is considerably simpler than a production database, so we can focus on functionality here. We won't provide any further discussion of the table attributes or SQL queries.

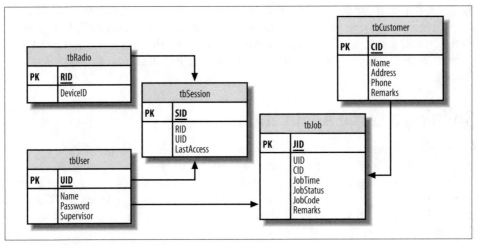

Figure 6-9. SQL table structure for Ch6b

User Interface Limitations and Extensions

The WCA viewer implemented by Palm supports a substantial subset of the features in HTML version 3.2. There are a few things missing, however:

- Client-side scripting of any sort. This means no JavaScript, no VBScript, no ActiveX, no Java applets, no cascading style sheets, no named typefaces. There are no cookies, either.

- There is no support for frames or image maps. Image support is limited to regular GIF and JPG formats. Of course, color is limited to four shades of gray.

- There is no horizontal scrolling. This means that tables, images, and other HTML elements are truncated at the right margin—153 pixels. In addition, tables do not nest. There are no tables within tables.

The Palm Web Clipping Guide and the *WCABuild* program help file cover these and other unsupported features of HTML 3.2 in detail. Some of these restrictions were lifted with the release of Palm OS 4.0, which we cover later in this chapter.

 The Palm proxy server and the WCA Viewer program are very sensitive to even minor errors in an HTML page. A malformed document can hang a session or display in unexpected ways. You should validate all static and dynamic HTML before shipping an application. See the Palm Knowledge Base—article 2049—for how to validate an HTML file for use in Web Clipping.

The Palm screen is very small, and the WCA viewer is quite slow when rendering even simple HTML. Taken together, these factors demand that a PQA limit user data to just what is most important. For example, our main schedule page for field technicians is limited to just the current day's jobs.

Not all data can be limited this way, so it is also important to implement a paging strategy for lengthy query results. And, as we mentioned earlier, there are no client-side techniques we can use for this, which means that paging must be implemented on the server. We show a simple paging scheme in our managerial reports.

Table 6-1 describes the Palm metatags recognized by the WCA Builder or the WCA viewer program. We show how to use all these metatags later in this chapter.

Table 6-1. Palm-specific metatags

Metatag	Meaning
PalmLauncherName	Lists the display name for PQA file on the Palm device
PalmComputingPlatform	Causes the proxy server to pass HTML content through largely unaltered
PalmLauncherRevision	Provides version information for display on the Palm device
LocalIcon	Causes the *WCABuild* program to include the indicated resource even if it is not referenced directly
HistoryListText	Places the page in the WCA viewer history list

There are also several Palm-specific keywords that you can use in ASP scripts, as shown in Table 6-2. When used in an HTML request, the Palm proxy server expands these keywords before relaying the request to the Web server. We show how the %DeviceId keyword can provide authentication later in this chapter.

Table 6-2. Palm.Net keywords

Keyword	Meaning
%DeviceId	Unique ID of radio. This keyword is 0.0.0 in the Emulator. The keyword may have a different format on radio networks other than Palm.Net.
%ZipCode	Approximate location of radio. This keyword will be 00000 in the Emulator or for unknown base stations.

The WCA viewer uses the standard Palm user interface controls for the password, date, and time input fields in forms. We show how to use these input types on HTML forms in the next section.

In place of client-side scripting, the WCA viewer provides two additional types of links that can be used to access local applications. These links use the palm and palmcall protocol keywords. For example, the following link exits the WCA viewer and calls the built-in memo pad application:

```
<a href="palm:memo.appl">Memo Pad</a>
```

It is possible to pass arguments to the application as query parameters. The palmcall keyword is similar, but functions as a subroutine call to the desired application. These keywords are described in detail in the Web Clipping Guide documentation.

Application Partitioning

Our application, like all Web Clipping applications, is partitioned: one part is the static HTML and images on the Palm PDA, and the other is the dynamic HTML pages generated on the web server. The goal of application partitioning is to minimize the amount of data transmitted over the network, while maximizing the user experience—presenting up-to-date information, and streamlining navigation through the application.

In our application, we store the query screens, application help pages, and other reference materials in the PQA file. This information does not change frequently enough to warrant downloading it over the wireless network. All volatile information, such as appointment times and job descriptions, is generated dynamically in response to a user query. We decided to make the customer information, such as address and phone number, dynamic as well. There is no static HTML content on the web server in our application. This is typical of Web Clipping applications; if the HTML doesn't change, then is should be stored in the PQA file on the Palm handheld.

Figure 6-10 shows the high-level application structure. All the HTML pages are stored on the Palm VII, and all the ASP scripts are executed on the web server.

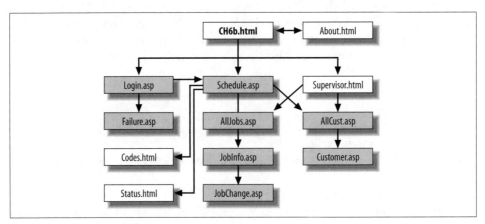

Figure 6-10. Structure of Ch6b.pqa

If Ch6b were a real application, you might analyze how frequently the customer information changes before making it dynamic. Another design question: how often do the users HotSync their Palm devices? If the customers HotSync every day, then it would be appropriate to place the customer list into the PQA. We might automate a build of the application daily, with up-do-date customer information, and download it to the Palm VII with each HotSync.

If you do not expect the user to HotSync frequently, or you cannot deliver the PQA file to the desktop for installation, then the dynamic approach is more appropriate.

Security and Access Control

Security is a critical component in a wireless application. We covered some security aspects of the wireless network and Palm.Net infrastructure earlier in this chapter. In this section, we discuss methods for implementing security features in a WCA: data encryption, strong authentication, and session management.

An application should always encrypt sensitive data before sending it over a wireless network or the Internet using SSL encryption. To do this, you install a recognized certificate in the IIS application, and use the https protocol identifier in the relevant hypertext links.[*] The WCA viewer automatically adds a special secure glyph to the link; see Figure 6-11.

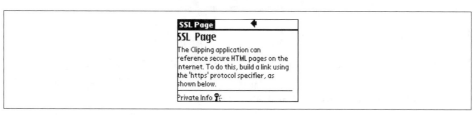

Figure 6-11. Secure HTTP link

Encrypting the data is not always sufficient, however. It is also important that sensitive data be restricted to those with permission to access it. This requires that users be authenticated, so that an application can reject those without the proper credentials. We support strong user authentication in the Ch6b sample application, using a combination of a token—the unique Palm VII radio device ID—and a shared secret—the user password.

Our application maintains a list of radios that are authorized to access the Ch6b web site in a SQL database table. The username and password are also stored in a database table. Whenever a user logs into the application, the login information—radio device ID, username, and password—is validated against the database. This approach works well when you know your users in advance.

We track authenticated users by creating sessions. Normally, the IIS server and the ASP application handle this through the default ASP Session object. This approach doesn't work with Web Clipping applications, because it requires the use of cookies, which are not supported unless you use Palm OS 4.0.

---

[*] We do not cover the process of generating a certificate and configuring the IIS server to use that certificate. Consult the IIS documentation for details. Palm supports most major signature authorities for certificates; see *http://www.palmos.com/security*.

Instead, we maintain session information in a SQL database table, and provide a VB COM object to supply some of the functionality of the ASP Session object. The logical session in the database joins a single user with a single radio, as shown in Figure 6-12.

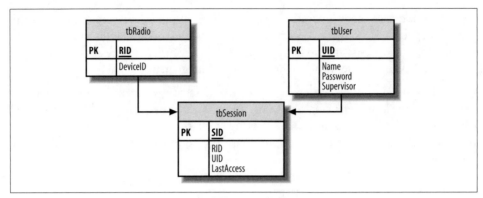

Figure 6-12. Radio, user, and session SQL tables

We don't support the same interfaces as the Microsoft ASP object; for example, we don't provide a method for the ASP scripts to store information in the session object.* Table 6-3 lists the authentication and security methods of our object.

Table 6-3. Ch6b session security-oriented methods

Method	Description
Create	Creates new session in database based on user ID, password, and radio. Fails if session already exists or if the password is bad.
Attach	Retrieves existing session information from database based on radio ID. Fails if the session doesn't exist or is expired.
Manager	Returns true if the current user is a manager.
Drop	Deletes a session in the database.

Our object implements several business rules for user sessions and logins. The first is that a user may only participate in a single session—no multiple logins. Likewise, a radio may only participate in a single session. Finally, the Session object has a life of four hours, and any attempts to access an expired session will fail. These rules provide additional security to prevent unauthorized users from breaking into the application.

---

* There are articles in the Microsoft Developer Studio Network and Knowledge Base that discuss the pros and cons of using ASP sessions. And there are several replacements for the Session object on the Internet that do not depend on cookies.

Once the user has logged in, a new entry and time stamp are placed in the session table. On each new connection attempt, our application consults the session table to make sure the user has a valid login. If so, the timestamp is updated to prevent the session from expiring.

Ch6b Details

The user's first experience with the schedule application is at the index page, *Ch6b. html* (see Figure 6-13). This HTML page prompts the user to resume an existing login session, or to establish a new session. In addition, online help and the manager's module are provided at the bottom of the page.

Figure 6-13. Ch6b.html

We provide both the login form and a link to a preexisting session as a convenience. A Palm user will launch and shut down a Clipping application many times during the day—and each time, the WCA viewer places them on *Ch6b.html*. By providing links to both the login form and preexisting sessions, we save the user many additional keystrokes and slow page redraws.

The HTML source code for *Ch6b.html* is shown in Example 6-2.

Example 6-2. Listing of Ch6b.html

```
<html>
<head>
<meta name="PalmLauncherName" content="Ch. 6b">
<meta name="PalmLauncherRevision" content="1.03">
<meta name="PalmComputingPlatform" content="true">
<meta name="LocalIcon" content="Codes.html">
<meta name="LocalIcon" content="Status.html">
<title>Ch. 6b Home</title>
</head>
<body>
<h1>Remote Schedule</h1>
If you have already logged in, here are
<a href="http://website/Ch6b/Schedule.asp?did=%deviceid">
today's jobs</a>. Otherwise please log in below:
```

Example 6-2. Listing of Ch6b.html (continued)

```
<br>
<form method="post" action="http://website/Ch6b/Login.asp">
<center>
<table>
<tr><td>Username: <input name="uid"></td>
<tr><td>Password: <input name="pwd" type="password"></td>
</table>
<br>
<input type="submit" value="Login">
<input type="hidden" name="did" value="%deviceid">
</center>
</form>
<hr>
<a href="About.html">About</a>  <a href="Manager.html">For Managers</a>
</body>
</html>
```

As usual, the familiar `PalmComputingPlatform` metatag indicates that this HTML code is formatted for the Palm PDA. Note the new metatags for the application name and version information.

```
<meta name="PalmLauncherName" content="Ch. 6b">
<meta name="PalmLauncherRevision" content="1.03">
```

Also note the metatag "`Local Icon`"— this tag is used to include resources in the PQA file that are not directly referenced by the HTML, but rather, are later used by dynamic Clipping pages. Despite its name, the `Local Icons` tag can be used to include HTML pages, as well as icons and other graphical images.

The link to the schedule must be a fully qualified hypertext link, complete with the web server name and a path to the ASP script, because this is a reference to an off-device page. The same is true of the form action parameter.

Placing the manager's page link at the end of the main screen means that we don't have two separate PQA files, one for managers and one for employees.

We use the special Palm keyword %deviceid both as a query parameter:

```
<a href="http://website/Ch6b/Schedule.asp?did=%deviceid">
```

and later as a hidden form variable:

```
<input type="hidden" name="did" value="%deviceid">
```

The Palm.Net proxy server then will expand this keyword into a text string, such as `1.16465337.185111781`, that uniquely identifies the Palm VII radio. This keyword plays an important role in our security architecture, because it allows us to associate a particular radio with a particular user connection request.

If you are using the Emulator, then this keyword expands to `0.0.0`—effectively limiting your application to one distinct emulated user.

Let's see what happens when the form is used to sign into the schedule application. Pressing the Login button posts the form data—including the radio ID—to the web server, where a simple script, *Login.asp*, handles it.

```
<%@ Language=VBScript %>
<!-- #include file="_ScriptLibrary\Security.asp" -->
<%
    dim username, password, deviceid
    username = Request.Form("uid")
    password = Request.Form("pwd")
    deviceid = Request.Form("did")

    ' Create a new session.
    NewSession username, password, deviceid
    Server.Transfer("Schedule.asp")
%>
```

This ASP script retrieves the form variables and calls a VBScript procedure called NewSession, which we'll examine next. Assuming we established a new session, we call an IIS 5.0-specific function, Server.Transfer. This function immediately transfers control from the current ASP script to the ASP script named as an argument. This function is performed entirely on the server side—there is no costly network redirection back to the client. For this reason, we use this feature heavily throughout Ch6b.

Now, let's see how NewSession authenticates the user and creates a login session. Here is the function, which is implemented in *Security.asp*:

```
function NewSession(uid, pwd, did)

    call CheckIP()

    dim obj
    set obj = Server.CreateObject("Ch6b.Session")
    if obj.Create(uid, pwd, did) <> 0 then Server.Transfer("Failure.asp")
    set NewSession = obj

end function
```

From NewSession, we call CheckIP, another VBScript function also in *Security.asp*, to ensure that the user is logging in from a valid IP address. CheckIP simply screens out requests not originating from the Palm proxy servers.

```
function CheckIP()

    ' Validate the source IP address. Must be from Palm.Net!
    select case Request.ServerVariables("REMOTE_ADDR")
    case "63.97.179.2"
    case "206.112.114.81"
    case else
        Server.Transfer("Failure.asp")
    end select

end function
```

Remember that the Emulator IP addresses will reflect one of the Palm.Net development proxy servers. For debugging purposes, you might also enter any local IP addresses you use when accessing the site with a traditional browser. (Of course, you can also restrict access using the ASP Application Properties dialog from the IIS server console.)

After the IP address is validated, NewSession allocates an instance of our custom session object. We call the *Create* method to log the user into the application. An unsuccessful login attempt results in the transfer to *Failure.asp*, which displays the screen shown in Figure 6-14. We use a generic error screen for simplicity, even though the Session object knows why the login attempt failed.

Figure 6-14. HTML output of Failure.asp

If the method completes successfully, a new row is inserted into the SQL database session table. At this point, the user is authenticated, and *Login.asp* transfers control to *Schedule.asp*, which displays the current day's jobs, as shown in Figure 6-15.

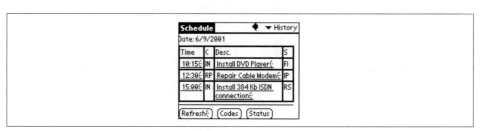

Figure 6-15. HTML output of Schedule.asp

This simple but important screen is designed to show the highest-priority data quickly to the user. The code for *Schedule.asp* is shown in Example 6-3.

Example 6-3. Listing for Schedule.asp

```
<%@ Language=VBScript %>
<!-- #include file="_ScriptLibrary\Security.asp" -->
<%
    dim deviceid, objsession, ADO
    deviceid = Request.QueryString("did")
    if deviceid = "" then
        deviceid = Request.Form("did")
```

Example 6-3. Listing for Schedule.asp (continued)

```
    end if

    set objsession = FindSession(deviceid)
    if objsession.GetJobList(ADO) <> 0 then
        Server.Transfer("Error.asp")
    end if
%>
<html>
<head>
<title>Schedule</title>
<meta name="palmcomputingplatform" content="true">
<meta name="historylisttext" content="Schedule-&time">
</head>
<body>
Date: <%=datevalue(date)%>
<br>
<%    if ADO.RecordCount = 0 then %>
No jobs scheduled for today.
<% else %>
<table border=1>
<tr><td>Time</td><td>C</td><td>Desc.</td><td>S</td></tr>
<% do while not ADO.EOF %>
<tr>
<td><a href="Customer.asp?did=%deviceid&cid=<%=ADO("CID")%>">
    <%=ADO("JobTime")%></a></td>
<td><%=ADO("JobCode")%></td>
<td><a href="JobInfo.asp?did=%deviceid&jid=<%=ADO("JID")%>">
    <%=ADO("Description")%></a></td>
<td><%=ADO("JobStatus")%></td>
</tr>
<%    ADO.MoveNext
    loop
%>
    </table>
<% end if %>
<hr>
<a href="Schedule.asp?did=%deviceid" button>Refresh</a>
<a href="file:Ch6b.pqa/Codes.html" button>Codes</a>
<a href="file:Ch6b.pqa/Status.html" button>Status</a>
</body>
</html>
```

Like all the ASP scripts in the application, we immediately retrieve the radio ID from the HTTP data. Because this script can be accessed in two ways (directly from *Ch6b. html*, or by transfer from *Login.asp*), we check for the device ID in the Form object first, and then in the Query object.

Once we get the device ID, we look up the user session, using the FindSession function in *Security.asp*. This function is similar to NewSession. If this method fails—usually indicating that a session doesn't exist—we transfer control to *Failure.asp*.

Now that the session is located, we use it to retrieve the user's jobs by calling the *GetJobList* method. This method is one of several data-oriented methods (see Table 6-4). A production application wouldn't have data methods in the session security object, but we have implemented it that way here for the sake of simplicity.

Table 6-4. Ch6b session data-oriented methods

Method	Description
GetJobList	Returns listing of jobs for current user
GetJobDetail	Returns detailed information about a job
ChangeJob	Updates details of a job
GetCustomerList	Returns listing of all customers; managers only
GetCustomerDetail	Returns detailed information about a customer

The *GetJobList* method returns a disconnected ADO record set, which contains the daily job list:

```
if objsession.GetJobList(ADO) <> 0 then Server.Transfer("Error.asp")
```

Now we are ready to write the HTML data back to the client. As always, we start with the Palm metatags in the HTML header to indicate proper formatting and to add this page to the WCA History list.

Most of the work in *Schedule.asp* is writing the job information out to a table, as we loop through the records in the ADO record set. For efficiency, we display only the most critical fields to the user; the details of each customer appointment and job are referenced by links such as the following:

```
<td><a href="Customer.asp?did=%deviceid&cid=<%=ADO("CID")%>">
    <%=ADO("JobTime")%></a></td>
```

This keeps the table small enough to display on the Palm screen and minimizes the amount of transmitted data. Note the use of relative referencing in the hypertext link—again, we try to keep the links as small as possible.

We write the job code field and the job status field as abbreviated codes, not as verbose text strings. We provide local HTML tables for the codes (see Figure 6-16), using the Palm-specific PQA addressing syntax:

```
<a href="file:Ch6b.pqa/Codes.html" button>Codes</a>
<a href="file:Ch6b.pqa/Status.html" button>Status</a>
```

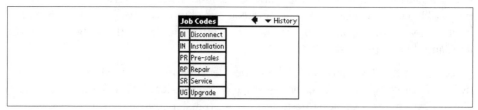

Figure 6-16. Codes.html

Had we used the full text string instead of the code, the table would have wrapped each row across two lines. There just isn't enough space on the screen for that. Partitioning the application like this reduces the amount of transmitted data, and increases the application response time. Accessing a local HTML page is very quick compared to the wireless network.

Our hypothetical field technician has now logged into the system and can review the jobs scheduled for the day. Selecting the job description shows details about the job, and allows the user to update key information (see Figure 6-17).

Figure 6-17. HTML output of JobInfo.asp

The code for *JobInfo.asp* is shown in Example 6-4.

Example 6-4. Listing for JobInfo.asp

```
<%@ Language=VBScript %>
<!-- #include file="_ScriptLibrary\Security.asp" -->
<%
    dim deviceid, objsession, jobid, ADO
    deviceid = Request.QueryString("did")
    set objsession = FindSession(deviceid)

    jobid = Request.QueryString("jid")
    if objsession.GetJobDetail(jobid, ADO) <> 0 then
        Server.Transfer("Error.asp")
    end if

    ' Format date, time information from ADO
    dim  datestr, timestr
    datestr = datevalue(ADO.Fields("JobTime").Value)
    timestr = timevalue(ADO.Fields("JobTime").Value)
%>

<html>
<head>
<title>Job <%=jobid%> Info</title>
<meta name="palmcomputingplatform" content="true">
<meta name="historylisttext" content="Job Info-&time">
</head>
<body>
<br>
<form method="post" action="JobChange.asp" id=form1 name=form1>
```

Example 6-4. Listing for JobInfo.asp (continued)

```
<table border=1>
<tr><td>Name</td>
    <td><a href=" "Customer.asp?did=deviceid&cid=<%=ADO("CID")%>"><%=ADO("Name")%></a></
td>
<tr><td><a href="file:Ch6b.pqa/Codes.html">Code</a></td><td><%=ADO("JobCode")%></td>
<tr><td>Desc</td><td><%=ADO("Description")%></td>
<tr><td><a href="file:Ch6b.pqa/Status.html">Status</a></td>
    <td><input maxlength=2 name="status" value="<%=ADO("JobStatus")%>"></td>
<tr><td>Date</td>
    <td><input type="datepicker" name="date1" value="<%=datestr%>"> 
        <input type="timepicker" name="time1" value="<%=timestr%>"></td>
<tr><td>Remarks</td>
    <td><textarea name="remarks" cols=17 rows="2"><%=ADO("Remarks")%></textarea></td>>
</table><br>
<center><input type="submit" value="Update" id=submit1 name=submit1></center>
<input type="hidden" name="did" value="%deviceid">
<input type="hidden" name="jid" value="<%=jobid%>">
</form>
</body>
</html>
```

This ASP script first validates the user by looking up the session in the database, and then uses the Session object to retrieve the details of the job. The unique job identifier and the radio device ID are passed in the query string.

Next, the date and time part of the appointment time are extracted, using the appropriate VBScript functions:

```
datestr = datevalue(ADO("JobTime"))
timestr = timevalue(ADO("JobTime"))
```

After writing the standard header information, we create a form and write out the input fields. The HTML layout routines in the WCA viewer are not as powerful as those on the desktop, so we prefer to place a form's fields within a table. This results in better alignment of input fields.

Palm's version of HTML 3.2 provides two special input types that are useful for editing dates and times: datepicker and timepicker. It is easy to use these types. Just set their values to the date and time strings retrieved from the database earlier:

```
<td><input type="datepicker" name="date1" value="<%=datestr%>"> 
    <input type="timepicker" name="time1" value="<%=timestr%>"></td>
```

These input types correspond to the Palm OS native date and time user interface elements, which will be very familiar to Palm users. These user interface elements also force the entry of valid data, so error handling in the ASP application is simplified.

We must store the device ID and job ID as hidden fields on the form, so that we can later validate the post request on the web server:

```
<input type="hidden" name="did" value="%deviceid">
<input type="hidden" name="jid" value="<%=jobid%>">
```

After the user has made any changes to the job details, such as changing the status from SC—scheduled—to FI—finished, pressing the submit button posts the form data to the IIS server.

On the server, the form data is passed to *JobChange.asp* (see Example 6-5), which is responsible for updating the database with the new information.

Example 6-5. Listing for JobChange.asp

```
<%@ Language=VBScript %>
<!-- #include file="_ScriptLibrary\Security.asp" -->
<%
    dim deviceid, objsession, jobid, dictionary
    deviceid = Request.Form("did")
    set objsession = FindSession(deviceid)

    jobid = Request.Form("jid")

    set dictionary = server.CreateObject("Scripting.Dictionary")
    dictionary.Add 0, Request.Form("status")
    dictionary.Add 1, Request.Form("date1")
    dictionary.Add 2, Request.Form("time1")
    dictionary.Add 3, Request.Form("remarks")

    if objsession.ChangeJob(jobid, dictionary) <> 0 then
        Server.Transfer("Error.asp")
    end if

    Server.Transfer("Schedule.asp")
%>
```

After validating the user session, the script collects the form parameters into a standard Dictionary object, and calls the *ChangeJob* method. This method updates the SQL database row with the information supplied by the user. If the method fails, then control is passed to *Error.asp*. If the method succeeds, then control is passed to *Schedule.asp*, where the user sees an updated job list.

Let's go back to our main job screen and see what happens when the field user selects the job time from the appointment list. This link calls *Customer.asp* to produce the customer detail screen shown in Figure 6-18.

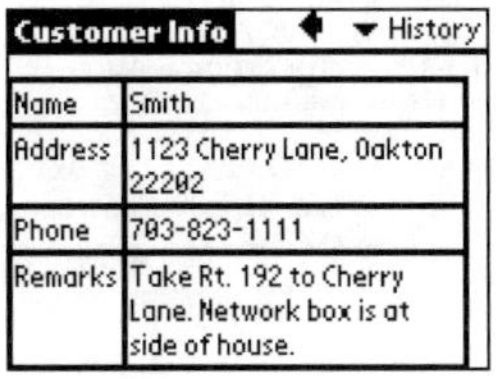

Customer Info	◀ ▼ History
Name	Smith
Address	1123 Cherry Lane, Oakton 22202
Phone	703-823-1111
Remarks	Take Rt. 192 to Cherry Lane. Network box is at side of house.

Figure 6-18. HTML output of Customer.asp

Customer.asp retrieves and displays information about the customer whose database record identifier is supplied in the query parameter. This includes the customer's name, address, phone number, and remarks. The code for *Customer.asp* is shown in Example 6-6.

Example 6-6. Listing for Customer.asp

```
<%@ Language=VBScript %>
<!-- #include file="_ScriptLibrary\Security.asp" -->
<%
    dim objsession, ADO
    set objsession = FindSession(Request.QueryString("did"))
    if objsession.GetCustomerDetails(Request.QueryString("cid"), ADO) <> 0 then
        Server.Transfer("Error.asp")
    end if
%>
<html>
<head>
<title>Customer Info</title>
<meta name="palmcomputingplatform" content="true">
<meta name="historylisttext" content="Customer-&time">
</head>
<body>
<br>
<table border=1>
<tr><td>Name</td><td><%=ADO("Name")%></td>
<tr><td>Address</td><td><%=ADO("Address")%></td>
<tr><td>Phone</td><td><%=ADO("Phone")%></td>
<tr><td>Remarks</td><td><%=ADO("Remarks")%></td>
</body>
</html>
```

This completes our presentation of the field technician portions of Ch6b.

We have one more area of the application to review—the manager's page. This page contains links to several reports not available to employees. *Manager.html* is shown in Figure 6-19. The page contains links to several ASP scripts, which return tabular report data to the Palm VII device.

Figure 6-19. Manager.html

It is very important to limit the size of each report, and therefore the amount of data transmitted to the device. We have implemented a very simple paging strategy to handle even short reports—the Palm will scroll after only a half dozen table entries.

The following code is attached to the customer report link in *Manager.html*:

```
<li><a href="http://website/Ch6b/AllCust.asp?did=%deviceid&pag=1">Customers</a>
```

Notice that this hypertext link contains a query parameter of *pag*, which is initially set to one. This will start our report at the first page; from then on, we will manage pagination within the ASP script.

Let's look at the customer report, which is shown in Figure 6-20. Notice the page count in the first line, and the Next button at the end of the report.

Figure 6-20. HTML output of AllCust.asp

Our strategy is based on simple properties of the ADO record object: the page size, count, and absolute position. In ADO, the page size can be set before a query is executed. After the data is returned, you position the record set to the desired page and print the report.

We will examine snippets of *AllCust.asp* to see exactly how we page through the data. After creating the Session object (not shown), we limit access to the report to managers.

```
if objsession.Manager( ) = 0 then
        Server.Transfer("Failure.asp")
end if
```

Next, we initialize the page from the query string, and call the Session object's *GetCustomerList* method:

```
size = 5
page = CInt(Request.QueryString("pag"))
if objsession.GetCustomerList(page, size, ADO) <> 0 then
    Server.Transfer("Error.asp")
end if
```

The method parameters ask that the report start at the supplied value, and the ADO page size is five records. When the method returns, the ADO record set is positioned to the requested page—page one for the first execution of this ASP script.

As we write the report, it's simple to use properties of the ADO record set to display the current page and size of the report.

```
Page <%=page%> of <%=ADO.PageCount%>
```

The body of the report is a simple loop that prints each record in the page.

```
<% record = 1
   do while not ADO.EOF and record <= ADO.PageSize%>
...
<%   ADO.MoveNext
   record = record + 1
   loop %>
```

After the report body, we display the `Prev` button if the current page is not the first page.

```
<% if page > 1 then %>
<a href="AllCust.asp?did=%deviceid&pag=<%=page-1%>" button>Prev</a>  
<% end if %>
```

Note the useful Palm HTML extension—the `button` keyword—that turns a hypertext link into a button. We display the `Next` button if the current page is not the last page.

```
<% if page < ADO.PageCount then %>
<a href="AllCust.asp?did=%deviceid&pag=<%=page+1%>" button>Next</a>
<% end if %>
```

This simple paging scheme is adequate for our sample project, but will not scale for a production application. You will need to investigate which paging solution works best with your database and display requirements.

Palm OS 4.0

Palm has recently made changes to its Web Clipping architecture that have been incorporated into the Palm OS version 4.0. Fortunately, none of the fundamentals have changed—everything we built in this chapter still works and the design principles are unaltered. Instead, Palm has added features that simplify developing an application, and that make the delivered application more powerful.

Many of the changes recognize that wireless applications are not hosted only on the Palm VII. In addition to the wireless attachments offered by other vendors, there is the Palm Mobile Internet Kit (MIK), which allows Palm OS devices to access Clipping applications using standard modems or cellular phones. The WCA viewer in Palm OS 4.0 supports color screens. In addition, there are changes that enable an application to determine other device capabilities, such as pixel depth of the Palm PDA screen in use.

One important change is that devices using the MIK do not necessarily have a unique radio ID like the Palm VII has. Instead, the Palm device forwards its serial number to the proxy server and then to your web site. Unfortunately, not all Palm devices have serial numbers! If you want the strong authentication we described earlier, and you have to support access via devices without serial numbers, you will have to encode something into the PQA itself.

The WCA viewer and Palm OS 4.0 now support cookies. Besides providing application state, cookies can often provide authentication. And the WCA viewer also scrolls images that are wider than the earlier limitation of 153 pixels.

Finally, the proxy server and the WCA viewer for Palm OS 4.0 support text compression using the LZ-77 algorithm. This is enabled automatically for WCA applications. This capability is available with earlier releases of the Palm OS, but the compression libraries have to be installed by hand.

Database Download

A new hypertext link type—PalmBinary—supports the binary download of applications and databases. The following HTML listing is a very simple WCA program to download an application:

```
<html>
<head>
<meta name="PalmComputingPlatform" content="true">
<title>Download</title>
</head>
<body>
<h1>Download PQA</h1>
This application downloads a PQA file from the web server to the Palm handheld.
This feature of Palm OS 4.0 is sure to be a winner!
<hr>
<a href="http://website/Ch6c/Ch7a.pqa" PalmBinary>Download PQA</a>
</body>
```

Compile this HTML code into a Clipping application and install it on the Palm device. Selecting the link causes *Ch6a.pqa* to be downloaded into the Palm device and registered as an application. This process is shown in Figure 6-21.

Figure 6-21. WCA viewer downloading Ch6a.pqa

This very powerful feature of the new Clipping application supports the distribution of applications over wireless and dial-up networks with a single link.

Additional Metatags and Keywords

Table 6-5 describes the additional metatags recognized by the WCABuild application or the WCA viewer program. The new tags provide more flexibility in detecting the device on which an application is running and the features that are available.

Table 6-5. Additional Palm-specific metatags in OS 4.0

Metatag	Meaning
PalmDoNotCache	Causes the WCA viewer not to cache the clipping; useful for sensitive data like credit card numbers
PalmHREFStyle	Causes the proxy server to send full links or indexes to the handheld
PalmPostEncoding	Causes the WCA viewer to format posted data in the specified format (code page)
PalmPQAVersion	Specifies the minimum version of the WCA viewer required to run an application
PalmPQABitDepth	Causes the WCABuild program to translate images to the indicated pixel depth
PalmLargeIconFilename	Causes the WCABuild program to use the specified file as the large icon, overriding the default
PalmSmallIconFilename	Causes the WCABuild program to use the specified file as the large icon, overriding the default

The Palm OS 4.0 version of the WCA viewer recognizes the PalmHREFStyle metatag, which instructs the proxy server not to hash the hypertext link. This tag is obsolete, however, since the newest releases of the proxy server no longer index links.

Table 6-6 describes the additional keywords expanded by the proxy server.

Table 6-6. Additional Palm.Net keywords in OS 4.0

Keyword	Meaning
%Location	International geographic location of radio, including locale and country. Palm OS 4.0 only.
%WCDevCaps	Device capabilities of Palm, such as color screen or operating system memory. Palm OS 4.0 only.

The Location keyword expands into country, state, city, and local province—positioning Palm for global use. Be aware that the location is only available when using radio devices that communicate with a cellular tower. This keyword is empty when using a normal modem on a Palm device.

The device capability string encodes all sorts of information about the connecting Palm handheld—the screen configuration, the version of Palm OS on the device, and even how much global and heap memory is available. The string format—a sequence of hexadecimal characters such as 87708400—is interpreted as a sequence of bits, as shown in Table 6-7.

Table 6-7. Bit encoding for the %WCDevCaps string

Bits	Meaning
0–4	Screen pixel depth
5–6	Reserved
7	LZ-77 compression available
8–11	Radio network
12–15	Free memory
16–20	Palm OS version
21–23	Heap size

Here is a very simple HTML page that passes the %WCDevCaps keyword to the web server:

```
<html>
<head>
<meta name="palmcomputingplatform" content="true">
<title>Ch6d Home</title>
</head>
<body>
Use <a href="http://website/Colors.asp?caps=%WCDevCaps">this feature</a> of
Palm OS 4.0 Web Clipping to see the capabilities of your Palm device.
</body>
</html>
```

This HTML page uses a simple query variable—named cap—to hold the device capabilities value. When the user presses the link, control is passed to an ASP script on the server. The code for *Colors.asp* is shown in Example 6-7.

Example 6-7. Listing of Colors.asp

```
<%@ Language=VBScript %>
<% Response.Expires = -1 %>
<%
    strCaps = Request.QueryString("caps")
    strTemp = Left(strCaps, 2)

    While Len(strTemp) > 0
        C = Mid(strTemp, 1, 1)
        If C <= "9" And C >= "0" Then
            D = Asc(C) - Asc("0")
        Else
            D = 10 + Asc(UCase(C)) - Asc("A")
        End If
        lngVal = (lngVal * 16) + D
        strTemp = Right(strTemp, Len(strTemp) - 1)
    Wend

    If (lngVal And &H1F) <= 7 Then
        isColor = False
    Else
```

Example 6-7. Listing of Colors.asp (continued)

```
        isColor = True
    End If
%>
<html>
<head>
<title>WCA OS 4.0</title>
<meta name="palmcomputingplatform" content="true">
</head>
<body>
The raw capabilities string is <%=strCaps%>.Only the first 6 hex
bytes are valid.<hr>
According to this string, this device
<% if isColor then %>
DOES support color!
<% else %>
does not support color.
<% end if %>
</body>
</html>
```

A fair amount of code is dedicated to converting the hexadecimal-formatted input string into a number. In this case, we are only interested in the 5 bits used to represent the capabilities of the screen, so we peel off the leftmost 2 characters (each hex character holds 4 bits).

```
    strTemp = Left(strCaps, 2)
```

Once these two characters are converted to an integer, we mask off the low 5 bits we are interested in, and test the value like this:

```
    If (lngVal And &H1F) <= 7 Then
```

Any value above 7 indicates color. Values of 7 and below indicate a monochrome display. You will have to change the code listed above to get at the other device properties, by indexing into different parts of the string and masking off different bits.

Bits 0–7 from Table 6-7 (shown previously in this section) are in the first two hex characters of the string. Bits 8–15 are in the second two characters, and bits 16–24 are in the third two characters. Currently, the final two characters of the string are unused.

Output is formatted according to the capabilities of the device, and displayed as shown in Figure 6-22. This example used a Palm m500 with Palm OS 4.0, connecting to a web server using the MIK.

You can now use the isColor variable in an ASP script to set the foreground and background colors for those HTML elements that accept color. According to the Palm documentation, you must use colors from the Netscape web-safe color palette.

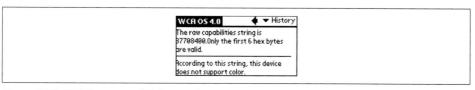

Figure 6-22. HTML output of Colors.asp

Resources

There are many resources available for the Web Clipping developer. The online resources are especially useful because this area of the Palm is evolving very quickly. We have mentioned the proxy server status page several times: *http://oasis.palm.com/dev/proxy/*. Palm posts fast-breaking news here first.

The two primary developer resources are the Web Clipping Guide and the help file distributed with the WCA Builder application, available from the Palm developer home page at *http://www.palmos.com*. These guides provide in-depth reference material for the developer of wireless applications.

The original white paper on the Palm VII and the Palm.Net wireless service and data centers is *http://www.palm.com/pr/palmvii/7whitepaper.pdf*.

Finally, there are two email forums available. One forum has announcements from Palm about the proxy server status; the other is a developer forum. Details on joining and using the email services are on the Palm developer home page.

Advanced Topics

Operating System Access

Some things are not easily done in Visual Basic, and this is especially true when using VB on the Palm. This chapter and the following chapters show how to program around the limits of the VB language, either by using the resources of the Palm operating system or by developing reusable components.

You will recall from our discussion in Chapter 3 that AppForge provides many Palm OS features as a library of functions. In this chapter, we'll look at how to call into the operating system to access features not exposed by the standard AppForge library. And we'll build an extended example that uses encryption features in the Palm operating system to secure application data or database records from prying eyes.

In VB for the Windows desktop, accessing OS functions is straightforward once you know a few simple facts about the subroutine or function you want to call. The information needed—the function name and result type, the DLL in which the function resides, and the number and type of any arguments—is easily obtained from the Microsoft Platform SDK.

For example, to retrieve the name of a logged-on Windows user, you might add the following declaration to any VB form or module:

```
Declare Function GetUserName Lib "advapi32.dll" (ByVal Buf as String,_
    ByRef Size as Long) as Long
```

Now, it is possible to call the function as if it were a built-in VB function. There are some issues, such as passing strings and memory between VB and C/C++, but these are generally well documented.

Unfortunately, things are not so simple when using the AppForge version of VB. Accessing a Palm OS function requires a lot more work than simply understanding the syntax of the Declare statement. This is because AppForge didn't build support into the Booster runtime engine to provide this access directly.

You have to understand the Palm inter-process communication (IPC) model to see why AppForge didn't provide this support. On Windows, the IPC mechanism is usually either the Component Object Model (COM) or function export from a dynamic library. In general, the VB runtime handles *marshaling*—copying and translating—the data between the different components.

On the Palm, IPC is handled by sending a special *launch code* to an application. The receipt of the launch code signals the target application to perform the required function. The caller might also pass an application-specific data structure to the target application. Any parameter copying or translation—especially for return values—must be handled directly by the programmer through this data structure.

Because the Palm operating system is single-threaded, this is a natural mechanism: stop the current application, and start the called application. When done, return to the original process.

The AppForge Extensibility library provides a way to send launch codes to a C/C++ application, and to pass parameters within VB data structures you define. AppForge calls such an application a *fuser*—and gives the application a special type (FUSR). The fuser application, in turn, can call any native operating system function or third-party application on the Palm.

> The Extensibility library is only available as a feature of the AppForge Professional edition. You must have the Professional edition to call the Palm operating system using the techniques we cover in this chapter.

When writing a fuser to access the operating system, as we do in this chapter, it is easy to define the launch codes and parameters needed to do the job. This can be more difficult if the fuser is to access functionality in another application.*

Although this seems inefficient, consider the Palm mantra to do only what is absolutely required. AppForge places this burden only on those applications that need this additional functionality—not on every Palm that has the Booster runtime. And because every application is resident in memory, calling an application with a launch code is not as expensive as it initially seems.

Fuser Mechanics

In this section, we build a simple AppForge application and a C/C++ fuser to set and retrieve *features*. A feature is a persistent 32-bit data value that the Palm operating system maintains.† Features are set, retrieved, or changed through calls to the operating system.

---

* Applications developed in C/C++ rarely publish their launch codes or parameters. You must have access to the source code to figure out how to call these applications. The Palm application source code is available as part of the Palm OS SDK.

† Other operating systems have similar mechanisms. The corresponding Windows system mechanisms are *global atoms* and shared memory. Palm also has feature memory, which we'll explore later in the chapter

Since Palm applications cannot access conventional global variables when processing launch codes, fusers cannot access them either. Using features is one possible solution to this problem.

Features provide a simple way to share small amounts of information between applications. C/C++ applications running on the Palm do not always have access to global variables, while a feature is always available. These applications can use feature memory as a cache to store global information. Features are not automatically removed when your application is deleted, so you should exercise caution when using them. They are, however, removed when the device is reset (hard or soft).

You can also use features to pass parameters between AppForge applications, which is normally hard to do because the Booster doesn't provide access to any command or launch parameters. Your applications just need to agree upon a name for the feature, and what each feature ID and value means. All your applications can share one fuser application to set and retrieve parameters.

CallApp Interface

Our VB application—FtrApp—has a simple interface that allows the user to set and retrieve feature values (see Figure 7-1). There are other feature functions in the Palm OS, but we don't use them in this introductory application.

Figure 7-1. Feature application user interface

While FtrApp handles the display chores, it relies on our C/C++ fuser—FtrFuser—to do the heavy work. You include a reference to the AppForge Extensibility library (*afPalmOS.dll*) in your VB project to access library functions in a fuser. A call to the fuser application has the following general form:

```
Function CallApp(AppName, LaunchCommand, [ParameterBlock]) As Boolean
```

Table 7-1 lists the parameters to this function.[*]

Table 7-1. CallApp Parameters

Name	Type	Purpose
AppName	String	Fuser application to invoke. This must be a PRC file with type FUSR.
LaunchCommand	Long	Constant that directs the fuser to take some specific action.
ParameterBlock	Long	Address of a user-defined data structure containing additional arguments. Optional parameter; 0 by default.

Note that the ParameterBlock variable's structure type is often different for each launch code. The address of this variable is obtained using the *VarPtr* function. The function returns True if the application is found; it returns False otherwise.

There is a very tight coupling between the application and the fuser—they share a binary interface that is fixed when the programs are compiled. This raises an important design question: how much functionality should be in the VB application and how much should be in the fuser? This is an open issue, but since this book is about VB, we code as much as possible in VB. Developing a fuser in C/C++ results in an additional component to be coded, tested, supported and deployed. You should be absolutely certain that your application needs this functionality before designing it into your application.

Data Access

Table 7-2 shows how the VB types map to native C/C++ types in a fuser. Except for the String and Date types, the C/C++ types correspond to Visual Basic's underlying representation.

Table 7-2. Visual Basic and C/C++ data type mappings

Visual Basic type	Size	C/C++ type
Byte	1 byte	unsigned char (1 byte)
Boolean	2 bytes	unsigned char (1 byte)
Integer	2 bytes	short (2 bytes)
Long (long integer)	4 bytes	long (4 bytes)
Single (single-precision floating-point)	4 bytes	float (4 bytes)
Double (double-precision floating-point)	8 bytes	double (8 bytes)
String	Variable	unsigned long (AFString pointer)
Currency (scaled 64-bit integer)	8 bytes	signed long long int (8 bytes)
Date	8 bytes	unsigned long (AFDate pointer)

[*] There is another function in *afPalmOS.dll*, called *LaunchApp*, which exits the current application and starts another one. You provide the application to launch as a parameter. *LaunchApp* is not discussed in this chapter.

Strings are mapped to an `AFString` pointer. AppForge uses the `AFString` type to store strings within its VM. Likewise, Dates are mapped to an `AFDate` pointer. Each pointer is stored as an `unsigned long` in the fuser.

You must use the *Fuser* SDK, which comes with AppForge, to convert between these types and native C/C++ types. The SDK is located in the *Platforms\PalmOS\FuserSDK* subdirectory of the AppForge installation directory. The *AFFuserGlue.h* header file contains functions for working with these types. There are also libraries for linking into your fuser using CodeWarrior or PRC-Tools.

You can convert strings using these two functions:

MemHandle AFStringToMemHandle(UInt32 AFString)
     Extracts an ANSI string from an `AFString`

Err MemHandleToAFString(MemHandle mhString, UInt32 pAFString)*
     Assigns the contents of a `MemHandle` to an `AFString`

Of course, you need to allocate and free memory as necessary when using these functions. For example, assume a VB application calls a fuser to retrieve the name of a database. You might declare VB and C/C++ types like these:

```
//VB type declaration
Public Type dbNameType
    dbName As String   ' IN parameter
End Type

//C/C++ type declaration
#define DB_NAME_LEN 256
typedef struct tag_DBName
{
    UInt32 dbName;  // OUT parameter
} DBName;
```

In the *PilotMain* routine for handling the `getDBName` command, we free the incoming string before allocating memory for, and assigning, the return value.

```
UInt32 PilotMain(UInt16 cmd, MemPtr cmdPBP, UInt16 launchFlags)
{
    Err errVal = 0;

    switch(cmd)
    {
       case getDBName:
       {
          DBName *ptr = (DBName *)cmdPBP;
          Char *pdbName;

          //Extract incoming string
          MemHandle hdbName = AFStringToMemHandle(ptr->dbName);

          //Free incoming string if allocated
          if(hdbName != NULL)
```

```
            MemHandleFree(hdbName);

            //Allocate memory for return string
            hdbName = MemHandleNew(DB_NAME_LEN);
            pdbName = (Char *)MemHandleLock(hdbName);
            StrCopy(pdbName, "db_name");

            //Assign return string
            errVal = MemHandleToAFString(hdbName, &(ptr->dbName));

            MemPtrUnlock(pdbName);
        }
        break;

        default:
            return 1;
    }

    return errVal;
}
```

You can convert dates using these four functions:

UInt32 AFDateToSeconds(UInt32 AFDate)
  Converts an AFDate to the number of seconds since 1/1/1904

Err AFDateToDateTime(UInt32 AFDate, DateTimePtr pDateTime)
  Converts an AFDate to a Palm DateTime structure

Err SecondsToAFDate(UInt32 seconds, UInt32 pAFDate)*
  Converts seconds since 1/1/1904 to an AFDate

Err DateTimeToAFDate(DateTimePtr pDateTime, UInt32 pAFDate)*
  Converts a Palm DateTime structure to an AFDate

You also need to be careful when using Boolean values within a fuser. In Visual Basic, a Boolean True is stored as −1, and False is stored as 0. Since a Boolean is stored as an unsigned char on the Palm, -1 is stored as decimal 255, or 0xFF, and 0 is stored as decimal 0, or 0x00. If your fuser requires a unique true or false value, you must first convert the value before using it:

```
Boolean bValue;

//... bValue passed into fuser from VB

//Convert bValue to true or false
if(bValue)
    bValue = true;
else
    bValue = false;

//Call some function requiring a uniquely true or false value
someVoidFunction(bValue);
```

Launch Codes and Parameters

In this section, we create our interface to the fuser application, and then call it from the VB form shown earlier in Figure 7-1. This project is contained in *Features.vbp*, and is available on this book's web site. The project consists of a single form, *Features.frm*, which contains all the source code in this section.

First, we create a constant for our fuser name:

```
Const FuserName As String = "FtrFuser"
```

Next, we define three launch codes to tell the fuser which function we wish to execute. The first launch code retrieves the value of a feature; the second sets its value; and the third allows us to remove the feature value from the Palm device memory.

```
Const GetFtrValue   = 32768 + 0
Const SetFtrValue   = 32768 + 1
Const ClearFtrValue = 32768 + 2
```

Palm has reserved launch codes in the range 0 to 32767, so our codes start at 32768.

Finally, we define a data structure with the information required to access feature memory: the application creator and the feature identifier. There is also a data field to hold the feature value itself.

```
Type FtrData
    CreatorId as Long
    FeatureId as Integer
    FeatureVal as Long
End Type
```

Of course, this data structure will be different for each kind of operating system call or function to be executed. We used the Palm OS Reference to find the function calls and parameters needed to access feature values, and to make certain our data type had fields for all the necessary information.

The code shown in Example 7-1 can retrieve an existing feature value. This code is executed when the user presses the Get button.

Example 7-1. Listing for BtnFtr_Get_Click

```
Private Sub BtnFtr_Get_Click()

    Dim Buffer As FtrData
    Buffer.CreatorId = Str2Long(txtCreator.Text)
    Buffer.FeatureId = CInt(txtFeature.Text)

    If afPalmOS.CallApp(FuserName, GetFtrValue, VarPtr(Buffer)) = False Then
        MsgBox "CallApp(" + FuserName + "-Get) Failed!"
    Else
        txtValue.Text = Buffer.FeatureVal
    End If
End Sub
```

First, we transfer values from the Creator ID and Feature ID text fields to the FtrData structure. These text fields were shown earlier in Figure 7-1. We coded a special function, *Str2Long*, which converts a string to a numeric Creator ID. We'll look at this function later.

The call to the fuser returns False if application is not found, or if the fuser application exits with a non-zero code; otherwise, it returns True. The driver program displays the message box shown in Figure 7-2 if an error occurs.

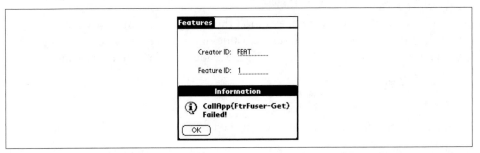

Figure 7-2. Error accessing fuser application

Let's look closely at the actual call through the AppForge *afPalmOS* extensibility library to the fuser application:

```
RC = AfPalmOS.CallApp(FuserName, GetFtrValue, VarPtr(Buffer))
```

Note the use of the *VarPtr* function to pass the data structure's *address*. It is very important to pass the data by reference to the fuser application—in C/C++, this means supplying a pointer to the data buffer's location. Because the fuser is passed the address of the buffer, instead of a copy, the fuser is able to return results by modifying fields in the variable.

If our call to the fuser application succeeds, we update the feature value text field with the result. Otherwise, we display a very simple error string using a message box.

As mentioned earlier, the *Str2Long* function is used to convert the string entered in the screen text field to a VB long integer. If the user keys in **DEMO**, then the function returns 1145392463. Let's look at *Str2Long*:

```
Private Function Str2Long(ByVal Str As String) As Long

    Dim total As Long

    total = Asc(Mid(Str, 4, 1))
    total = total + (Asc(Mid(Str, 3, 1)) * (2 ^ 8))
    total = total + (Asc(Mid(Str, 2, 1)) * (2 ^ 16))
    total = total + (Asc(Mid(Str, 1, 1)) * (2 ^ 24))
    Str2Long = total
End Function
```

The function converts each character in the string into its ASCII decimal equivalent—for example, 'A' is 65. Then the number is multiplied according to its position in the string, effectively shifting that number left by a specified power of two. The sum of these conversions is the numeric Creator ID.

The code for setting a feature value is very similar, and is run when the user clicks on the Set button (see Example 7-2).

Example 7-2. Listing for BtnFtr_Set_Click

```
Private Sub BtnFtr_Set_Click()

    Dim Buffer As FtrData
    Buffer.CreatorId = Str2Long(txtCreator.Text)
    Buffer.FeatureId = CInt(txtFeature.Text)
    Buffer.FeatureVal = CLng(txtValue.Text)

    If afPalmOS.CallApp(FuserName, SetFtrValue, VarPtr(Buffer)) = False Then
        MsgBox "CallApp(" + FuserName + "-Set) Failed!"
    End If
End Sub
```

Because we need to pass the user-supplied value into the fuser, we set the feature value field in the buffer to the value entered on the screen:

```
    Buffer.FeatureVal = CLng(TxtValue.Text)
```

Of course, we call the C/C++ fuser using the SetFtrValue launch code, which indicates we want to set a feature value.

Finally, here is the code for clearing a feature value:

```
    Private Sub BtnFtr_Clear_Click()

        Dim Buffer As FtrData
        Buffer.CreatorId = Str2Long(txtCreator.Text)
        Buffer.FeatureId = CInt(txtFeature.Text)

        If afPalmOS.CallApp(FuserName, ClearFtrValue, VarPtr(Buffer)) = False Then
            MsgBox "CallApp(" + FuserName + "-Clear) Failed!"
        End If
    End Sub
```

This completes our VB interface and driver. This project compiles to a sample driver, *Features.prc*. You don't need to install it yet, because it won't work without the C/C++ fuser application, which we develop in the next section.

A Simple Fuser

Now let's see how the C/C++ fuser application calls the operating system to manipulate features. We have implemented our fuser application using the Metrowerks

CodeWarrior compiler.* Projects in CodeWarrior consist of a project file (MCP) and the associated C/C++ source code files. Our fuser project file is *FtrFuser.mcp*.

 Almost all error handling has been removed from this example to make it easy for a VB programmer to follow the C/C++ code.

There is only one source code file in our project: *FtrFuser.c*. First, we include the necessary C/C++ header files for compiling on the Palm and accessing the feature manager:

```
#include <PalmOS.h>
#include <FeatureMgr.h>
```

Then we define an enumeration type with the possible launch codes:

```
typedef enum
{
    GetFtrValue    = 32768,
    SetFtrValue,
    ClearFtrValue
}
FeatureCodes;
```

We made the enumeration value names the same as those in the VB application, for clarity, even though this is not necessary. Next, we define a data structure to mirror the VB parameter data structure:

```
typedef struct
{
    UInt32 CreatorId;
    UInt16 FeatureId;
    UInt32 FeatureVal;
}
FtrData;
```

Again, we make the structure field names the same between C/C++ and VB for consistency. This is a good design practice whenever two or more applications are linked—even if it makes for boring code. It is critical that the size and layout of this data structure exactly match the one declared in VB. The AppForge knowledge base has an article that explains how to match up the data types. (The fuser application must be compiled with data structures aligned on four-byte boundaries as well. We discuss this later in this chapter.)

Every C/C++ application for the Palm must have a startup function called *PilotMain*. This function always takes the three parameters shown in Table 7-3. As indicated in

---

* Fuser applications can also be implemented using the GNU suite of C/C++ tools. Although the source code for our fuser application can be compiled under GNU, using these command-line tools is beyond the scope of this book.

---

the table, the first two parameters are supplied by the VB application to the *CallApp* function, and then passed to the fuser.

Table 7-3. PilotMain parameters

Name	Type	Purpose
Cmd	Integer	Command supplied by caller
CmdPBP	Pointer	Address of parameter structure supplied by caller
LaunchFlags	Integer	Flags supplied by Palm OS indicating startup mode; e.g., alarm triggered

Like all C/C++ applications, the main routine returns an integer to the caller. This return code is eventually passed back to the VB application as a Boolean value, where it indicates success or failure.

Because FtrFuser is so straightforward, we have put all the application functionality into the single main routine, as shown in Example 7-3.

Example 7-3. Listing for PilotMain

```
UInt32 PilotMain(UInt16 cmd, MemPtr cmdPBP, UInt16 launchFlags)
{
    Err RC;
    FtrData *ptr = (FtrData *)cmdPBP;

    switch(cmd) {
    case GetFtrValue:
        RC = FtrGet(ptr->CreatorId, ptr->FeatureId, &(ptr->FeatureVal));
        break;
    case SetFtrValue:
        RC = FtrSet(ptr->CreatorId, ptr->FeatureId, ptr->FeatureVal);
        break;
    case ClearFtrValue:
        RC = FtrUnregister(ptr->CreatorId, ptr->FeatureId);
        break;
    default:
        return 1; // Hmmm. Called incorrectly, so return failure.
    }

    return RC;
}
```

This function is quite simple. First, it retrieves the data structure, and then it calls the proper operating system feature function. If indicated, it stores the feature value in the structure. In all cases, the function returns a status code to the caller.

We retrieve the data structure by casting the memory address in cmdPBP to a pointer to our application-specific data structure:

```
FtrData *ptr = (FtrData *)cmdPBP;
```

The command code is evaluated using a case statement, which transfers control to the appropriate code label. For example, the fragment shown below is ultimately executed from the VB function *btnGetFeature_Click*:

```
switch(cmd) {
case GetFtrValue:
    RC = FtrGet(ptr->CreatorId, ptr->FeatureId, &(ptr->FeatureVal));
```

The Palm OS routine *FtrGet* uses the creator and feature identifiers to look up the feature value. If the OS routine finds the feature, it stores the value in our data structure FeatureVal field and returns zero. We pass the address of FeatureVal, since *FtrGet* expects a reference parameter.

We immediately return an error if the caller supplies an invalid command code:

```
default:
    return 1; // Hmmm. Called incorrectly, so return failure
}
```

Otherwise, we return the result code from the Palm OS feature function call:

```
    return RC;
}
```

Before building the fuser application, you must change the following compiler switches, which are located on the project settings dialog:

1. Change the structure alignment from the default to *68K 4-byte* alignment. Do this on the Code Generation → 68K Processor tab.

2. Change the database type from the default appl to FUSR. Do this on the Linker → PalmRez Post Linker tab.

After you have made these changes, compile the fuser application into a PRC file and install it onto the Palm.

This completes both the VB and C/C++ portions of our simple fuser demonstration. Remember that you must install both the application and the fuser on the Palm device to run this demonstration.

Test the application—use it to set, query, and remove integer feature values. Exit the application, and start it again. Any features from the last session should still be present. To erase features, do a soft reset on the device.

There is another Palm API call—*FtrGetByIndex*—that enumerates feature values on the Palm device. If you suspect that your Palm device memory is cluttered with features, or you are curious about what other features are present on the Palm device, you can extend this sample to display a list of all features, along with their Creator IDs.

A Data Encryption Program

In this section, we build a more practical example that uses the encryption routines in the Palm OS to safeguard both memory and database records. We expand on the previous simple example to show how to use feature memory to store larger data structures. And we package the VB code as a module—a BAS file—so other applications can use our encryption and decryption routines.

DES

Palm included the US government Data Encryption Standard (DES) as part of its operating system. Although DES is an older cryptographic standard, it is adequate for providing security in many situations.* Technically, we are using the DES electronic codebook mode (ECM); this means that each block of text can be encrypted or decrypted independently. We provide some cryptography references at the end of the chapter that discuss DES and other encryption algorithms in some detail.

DES is a block cipher—it encrypts and decrypts data in blocks of 8 bytes. It requires a key to operate; in fact, it uses the same key to encrypt and decrypt data. The DES key is 56 bits long and consists of eight 7-bit bytes (for historical reasons, the algorithm ignores one bit of each key byte). The DES key must be kept secret, because anyone who has it can decrypt the data. For this reason, we won't store the key in our code, but instead will require the user to enter it into a program when it is running.

Encryption and decryption of text blocks is simple under DES: merely provide the 56-bit key and 8 bytes of data on which to operate. Normal text is called the *plaintext*; text that has been encrypted is called the *ciphertext*. Note that DES requires fixed blocks of eight bytes—if the amount of data is not a multiple of eight, it must be padded. We'll show how to do this when we study the C/C++ fuser application.

Not all Palm devices have the DES routines; they are an optional feature of the operating system. As you will see, the Palm OS feature manager lets us query for the presence or absence of DES. We'll show how to do this in the fuser.

Driver Application

We have made a simple application that encrypts and decrypts database records with a password. The program, *DESDriver.prc*, works with any Palm database, and is shown in Figure 7-3.

---

* DES dates from the late 1960s, when it was developed by the IBM Corporation. Many experts consider original DES to be compromised by increases in computing power. The standard recognizes different modes of operation, which offer greater security.

Figure 7-3. DESDriver main screen

The program has fields for entering the target database, the record index, and the password. There are buttons for initialization, encryption, decryption, and to display a record using a simple message box.

The driver application is contained in the VB project *DESDriver.vbp*. We aren't going to present the driver code in any detail. The buttons for initialization, encryption, and decryption simply call code that is presented in detail later in this chapter. The button for showing a record uses the AppForge database API described in Chapter 3 to open a record; it displays the record data using a message box. We use it to quickly verify the record contents. For example, Figure 7-4 shows the second record in the Memo database after it has been encrypted.

Figure 7-4. Encrypted record data

VB Encryption Module

We have provided a small package of functions to encrypt and decrypt database records. The VB interface functions are in the module *VBEncrypt.bas*, while the actual work is performed in the C/C++ fuser. Both of these are described later in this chapter.

In general, we would prefer to implement as much of the code as possible in VB, and perform only operating system calls in the C/C++ fuser. Unfortunately, and unlike our previous example, most of the functionality for encrypting and decrypting records will reside in the fuser application.

There are two reasons for this. Foremost, AppForge strings don't directly support binary characters. This makes it hard to return an encrypted string from a fuser application. Efficiency is also a concern: because DES operates on small 8-byte blocks, many calls to the fuser would be needed to encrypt a single database record.

The VB encryption module is in *VBCrypt.bas*. This module must be included in an AppForge project that wants to encrypt or decrypt records. The AppForge Extensibility and PDB libraries are used in the module and must be referenced in the project prior to compilation.

Fuser interface

The interface to the fuser consists of the application name and constants for the supported cryptographic operations of initialization, encryption, and decryption:

```
Public Const DES_Fuser = "DESFuser"

Public Const InitDES = 32768 + 0
Public Const Encrypt = 32768 + 1
Public Const Decrypt = 32768 + 2
```

We'll look at each of these operations in turn later in the chapter. Next, we define the DESParam data structure that contains parameters we pass for cryptographic operations:

```
Public Type DESParam
    DbName As String
    DESKey As String
    Index As Integer
    Reserved As Integer
End Type
```

The DbName field holds the database name we are trying to open. This name must be unique on the device. The DESKey field holds the encryption key. Index is the physical position of the record within the database. Note the Reserved field—this is used by the C/C++ fuser application for internal processing. We don't need to access it in the VB code.

Initialization

The DES algorithm, as mentioned earlier, operates on blocks of eight bytes. To encrypt a chunk of data, you feed it to DES eight bytes at a time. Unfortunately, database records do not normally come sized in multiples of eight. This means that we will have to do three things while encrypting and decrypting records:

1. Preserve the original database record size
2. Resize the record to a multiple of eight before encryption
3. Restore the record to its original size after decryption

In order to do this, the fuser must know whether or not the record is encrypted. If it is encrypted, then the fuser also needs to know the original record size. In order to do this, the fuser allocates a data structure—feature memory, actually—with one element for each record.

The initialization function tells the fuser how many database records it needs to support. It does this by setting the parameter block field Index to the maximum number of records needed, and by calling the fuser with the *InitDES* parameter:

```
Public Sub StartDES(ByVal MaxRecs As Integer)

    Dim Block As DESParam

    Block.Index = MaxRecs
    afPalmOS.CallApp DES_Fuser, InitDES, VarPtr(Block)
End Sub
```

In our driver application, this limit is hard-coded to 500.

Key generation

All of the security in DES is in the *strength* of the secret key. This means that we want to select the 56 bits of the key at random. This makes it hard for a cryptographer to guess at the key. People, however, do not choose keys at random; instead, they use words, names, or phrases that they can remember

Our module has a simple function—*MakeKey*—that accepts a password and scrambles it to generate a more random string suitable for use as a DES key. The function is shown in Example 7-4. *MakeKey* should be called before using other functions in the module, to ensure that a good DES key is available.

Example 7-4. Listing for MakeKey

```
Public Sub MakeKey(ByVal Password As String, ByRef Key As String)

    Dim i As Integer
    Dim Hi As Single
    Dim Lo As Single

    Hi = 1
    For i = 1 To Len(Password)
        Lo = Lo + Asc(Mid(Password, i, 1)) ^ i
        Hi = Hi * Asc(Mid(Password, i, 1))
    Next i

    While Hi > (2 ^ 31): Hi = Hi / 2: Wend
    While Lo > (2 ^ 31): Lo = Lo / 2: Wend

    Key = Right(Hex(Hi), 4) + Left(Hex(Lo), 4)
End Sub
```

The initial loop in *MakeKey* blends different bits from each password character into the two variables Hi and Lo. Then the two variables are adjusted to fit into a Long. Finally, part of the hexadecimal string equivalent of each variable is used to make up the key. For example, a password of *bottle* produces a key string of *F6D07D4F* while *laptop* produces *788073E2*.

This function is not intended to be cryptographically strong. For example, it doesn't handle even the trivial case of an empty password. There are other, better techniques for obtaining good DES encryption keys; these can be found in the "Resources" section at the end of this chapter.

Encryption and decryption functions

The VB module provides functions to encrypt and decrypt individual database records. An application using the encryption service can call the decrypt routine, manipulate the record, and then encrypt it. These routines are simple wrappers that call on the C/C++ fuser, which handles all the details.

Most of the work in each routine is initializing the parameter block before calling the fuser. Here is the code for *EncryptRec*:

```
Public Sub EncryptRec(DbName As String, Index As Integer, Key As String)

    Dim Block As DESParam

    Block.DbName = DbName
    Block.Index = Index
    Block.DESKey = Key
    afPalmOS.CallApp DES_Fuser, Encrypt, VarPtr(Block)
End Sub
```

The caller provides the database name and record index to encrypt, and the DES key to use. Note that the record index is zero-based, just like the AppForge database functions.

This is what *DecryptRec* looks like:

```
Public Sub DecryptRec(DbName As String, Index As Integer, Key As String)

    Dim Block As DESParam

    Block.DbName = DbName
    Block.Index = Index
    Block.DESKey = Key
    afPalmOS.CallApp DES_Fuser, Decrypt, VarPtr(Block)
End Sub
```

The only difference between the two functions is the launch code supplied to the fuser application: Encrypt versus Decrypt.

C/C++ Encryption Fuser

The DESFuser fuser application is more complicated than the modest fuser we presented earlier in the chapter, but the techniques used to implement it are the same. The project file is *DESFuser.mcp*, and all the source code is in the C/C++ file *DESFuser.c*. The project compiles into *DESFuser.prc*—a PRC file with type FUSR, as required by AppForge.

We start with an enumeration for the launch codes that maps into the VB constants declared earlier:

```
typedef enum
{
    InitDES = 32768, // launch codes
    Encrypt,
    Decrypt,
    GetMem = 0,      // internal flags
    SetMem,
}
LaunchCodes;
```

We also include two additional enumeration constants, GetMem and SetMem, which we have given the values zero and one. This is outside the legal range for Palm launch codes, as a reminder that they are for internal use only.

We declare a structure, DESParam, that corresponds to the VB type of the same name. Here, it is translated as C/C++ structure:

```
typedef struct
{
    UInt32 DbName;
    UInt32 DESKey;
    UInt16 Index;
    Int16 Data;     // internal field
}
DESParam;
```

The main routine for the fuser application follows the format of the main routine of a C/C++ application, which we discussed earlier in Table 7-3. Example 7-5 shows the code for *PilotMain*.

Example 7-5. Listing for PilotMain

```
UInt32 PilotMain(UInt16 cmd, MemPtr cmdPBP, UInt16 launchFlags)
{
    Err RC = 1;

    switch(cmd) {
    case InitDES:
        RC = DoFeature(cmd, (DESParam *)cmdPBP);
        break;

    case Encrypt:
```

Example 7-5. Listing for PilotMain (continued)

```
    case Decrypt:
        RC = DoDES(cmd, (DESParam *)cmdPBP);
        break;
    }

    return RC;
}
```

Here, *PilotMain* is simply a large case statement, which routes the parameter data to the appropriate function. One function handles the encryption requests and one function handles initialization. Any other launch code results in an error code being returned to the caller.

Note the cast operation to convert cmdPBP into a DESParam structure. Remember that this pointer is really the address of a VB data structure passed from the driver application.

Feature memory

DES operates on data that is sized in multiples of eight. As we will show later, the fuser code that encrypts and decrypts records also expands and shrinks the physical record, so that its size is always a multiple of eight when encrypted.

Because of this change in the record size, the fuser needs a place to store two pieces of information for each record:

1. Is the record encrypted or not?
2. If the record is encrypted, how many bytes of padding were added?

When the DES library is initialized, feature memory that is large enough for a fixed number of records is allocated. Although the Palm OS considers feature memory simply a chunk of raw bytes, the C/C++ fuser can use this memory in any way desired.

In our case, we treat the feature memory as an array of small integers; each array element corresponds to a database record. Each element is initialized to –1, which indicates that the record at the same location in the database is not encrypted.

Just before a record is encrypted, its size is adjusted to be a multiple of eight bytes. This adjustment is always a number from zero to seven. Before encrypting a record, we store the adjustment in the feature memory slot that corresponds to the record's physical database index. After decrypting a record, we look up the adjustment, and shrink the record's size by that amount.

As a bonus, we can use the feature memory to see if a record is encrypted or not. A –1 means that the record is not encrypted, and any other number means that it is.

Of course, this approach is somewhat wasteful of space, especially for databases with a large number of records, but it suffices for our simple application.

Anything that alters the location of a record within the physical database will corrupt our tracking scheme. If you adapt this code, consider using the record's unique record identifier rather than its index.

Let's look at the code that implements the feature memory operations: *DoFeature*, shown in Example 7-6.

Example 7-6. Listing for DoFeature

```
static Err DoFeature(UInt16 cmd, DESParam *Ptr)
{
    Int8 byte;
    Int8 *chunk;

    #define CREATOR 'DESL'
    #define FEATURE 1

    switch(cmd) {
    case InitDES:
        byte = -1;
        if (FtrPtrNew(CREATOR, FEATURE, Ptr->Index, (void **)&chunk) == 0)
            DmSet(chunk, 0, Ptr->Index, byte);
        break;

    case SetMem:
        FtrGet(CREATOR, FEATURE, (UInt32 *)&chunk);
        byte = Ptr->Data;
        DmWrite(chunk, Ptr->Index, &byte, 1);
        break;

    case GetMem:
        FtrGet(CREATOR, FEATURE, (UInt32 *)&chunk);
        byte = *(chunk + Ptr->Index);
        Ptr->Data = byte;
        break;
    }
}
```

We process the three feature memory requests within a case statement. Feature memory, like feature values, is always associated with a particular Creator ID and feature number. We use a couple of local constants, CREATOR and FEATURE, to uniquely define our feature memory.

Let's start with the initialization launch code, InitDES:

```
    case InitDES:
        byte = -1;
        if (FtrPtrNew(CREATOR, FEATURE, Ptr->Index, (void **)&chunk) == 0)
            DmSet(chunk, 0, Ptr->Index, byte);
        break;
```

The Palm OS function *FtrPtrNew* is simple enough: feature memory has a fixed size. In this case, the caller has supplied the size in the parameter block Index field. We allocate one byte—an 8-bit integer— for each record. Because the database manager owns feature memory, an application cannot write it directly. We use *DmSet* to set each record flag to –1.

 Feature memory is allocated on the storage heap, which is protected against stray writes by the database manager. *DmSet* and *DmWrite* are the only ways to change the value of feature memory.

When we are asked to set the record flag—by receiving the command SetMem—we must first retrieve a pointer to the requested feature memory. Then we use the *DmWrite* database routine to write Ptr → Data at the appropriate offset into the feature memory:

```
case SetMem:
    FtrGet(CREATOR, FEATURE, (UInt32 *)&chunk);
    byte = Ptr->Data;
    DmWrite(chunk, Ptr->Index, &byte, 1);
```

The Ptr → Index value must be within range! A more robust approach would trap this value by storing the allocated feature memory size in another feature value, or by using the *MemPtrSize* function.

We process the command to retrieve the record flag—GetMem—in the same fashion, except we read from the feature memory instead of writing to it. There is no special function necessary for reading feature memory.

```
case GetMem:
    FtrGet(CREATOR, FEATURE, (UInt32 *)&chunk);
    byte = *(chunk + Ptr->Index);
    Ptr->Data = byte;
```

The DoDES function

Encryption and decryption of database records is much more complicated than simply encrypting blocks of text. There is a lot of code simply for database manipulation—opening a database and finding a record using the Palm database API. And there is the issue of record size; we do a lot of work to read, write and resize the record in the database.

Finally, we actually have to encrypt and decrypt the records. It's easy to see why so few applications actually implement meaningful security.

We have coded the *DoDES* function, shown in Example 7-7, to handle the database functions common to both encryption and decryption.

Example 7-7. Listing for DoDES

```
static Err DoDES(UInt16 cmd, DESParam *Ptr)
{
    Err Rc = 1;
    UInt32 value;
    LocalID hId;
    DmOpenRef dbRef;
    MemHandle hRec;
    MemHandle hDbName;

    FtrGet(sysFtrCreator, sysFtrNumEncryption, &value);
    if (!(value & sysFtrNumEncryptionMaskDES))
        return Rc;

    hDbName = AFStringToMemHandle(Ptr->DbName);
    hId = DmFindDatabase(0, MemHandleLock(hDbName));
    MemHandleUnlock(hDbName);
    if (!hId)
        return Rc;

    dbRef = DmOpenDatabase(0, hId, dmModeReadWrite | dmModeShowSecret);
    if (!dbRef)
        return Rc;

    hRec = DmQueryRecord(dbRef, Ptr->Index);
    if (hRec == NULL)
        goto close_db;

    value = MemHandleSize(hRec);
    if (value == 0)
        goto close_db;

    if (cmd == Encrypt)
        Rc = DES_Encrypt(dbRef, value, Ptr);
    else
        Rc = DES_Decrypt(dbRef, value, Ptr);

close_db:
    DmCloseDatabase(dbRef);

    return Rc;
}
```

First, we test for the presence of the DES encryption libraries—remember, they are optional and might not be present. The test uses feature manager calls with system constants defined by Palm in the header file *SystemMgr.h*:

```
FtrGet(sysFtrCreator, sysFtrNumEncryption, &value);
```

If the DES libraries are present, then this call sets a bit in the *value* parameter. We test for that bit using a system-defined mask and exit the routine with an error if it is not set.

```
if (!(value & sysFtrNumEncryptionMaskDES))
    return Rc;
```

Next, we find and open the database using the name passed in from the VB application. If we can't find the database, or if another application is using the database exclusively, then we exit with an error. AppForge strings are passed as UInt32 pointers to internally maintained string interfaces. We first call the fuser SDK *AFStringToMemHandle* function to convert the pointer to a memory handle. In the Palm OS, a handle must be locked before access, and it should be unlocked when no longer needed.

```
hDbName = AFStringToMemHandle(Ptr->DbName);
hId = DmFindDatabase(0, MemHandleLock(hDbName));
MemHandleUnlock(hDbName);
```

Note the use of the dmModeShowSecret flag when opening the database:

```
dbRef = DmOpenDatabase(0, hId, dmModeReadWrite | dmModeShowSecret);
```

This tells the Palm OS that all records, even those marked private or hidden, should be available. Next, we look up the requested record, and query the memory manager for its size. If the record doesn't exist, or has zero length, then we exit, again indicating an error.

If everything has been successful to this point, we are ready to encrypt or decrypt the record:

```
if (cmd == Encrypt)
    Rc = DES_Encrypt(dbRef, value, Ptr);
else
    Rc = DES_Decrypt(dbRef, value, Ptr);
```

After the encryption function, the database reference is released and a result code is returned to the caller.

The DES_Encrypt function

The *DES_Encrypt* function, shown in Example 7-8, encapsulates all operations specific to encrypting a record, such as expanding the record if necessary, doing the actual encryption, and handling error conditions.

Example 7-8. DES_Encrypt

```
static Err DES_Decrypt(DmOpenRef dbRef, UInt32 RecSize, DESParam *Ptr)
{
    UInt32 i;
    MemPtr pRec;
    MemPtr pKey;
    MemHandle hRec;
```

Example 7-8. DES_Encrypt (continued)

```
    MemHandle hDESKey;
    Int8 Delta ;

    // A feature setting of -1 indicates record is not encrypted!
    DoFeature(GetMem, Ptr);
    if (Ptr->Data == -1)
        return 1;

    Delta = Ptr->Data;

    hDESKey = AFStringToMemHandle(Ptr->DESKey);
    pKey = MemHandleLock(hDESKey);
    hRec = DmGetRecord(dbRef, Ptr->Index);
    pRec = MemHandleLock(hRec);

    for (i = 0; i < RecSize; i += 8)
    {
        UInt8 buffer[8];
        UInt8 amount = 8;

        MemMove(buffer, (unsigned char *)pRec + i, 8);
        EncDES(buffer, pKey, buffer, false);

        if ((i + 8) > (RecSize - Delta))
            amount -= Delta;
        DmWrite(pRec, i, buffer, amount);
    }

    MemHandleUnlock(hRec);
    DmReleaseRecord(dbRef, Ptr->Index, true);
    MemHandleUnlock(hDESKey);

    if (Delta)
        DmResizeRecord(dbRef, Ptr->Index, RecSize - Delta);

    Ptr->Data = -1;
    DoFeature(SetMem, Ptr);

    return 0;
}
```

First, we check that this record is not already encrypted. If it is, then we can safely return without doing anything:

```
    // A feature setting other than -1 indicates record already encrypted!
    DoFeature(GetMem, Ptr);
    if (Ptr->Data != -1)
        return 1;
```

Next, we calculate the amount of padding needed for this record, if the record size isn't already a multiple of eight. If necessary, the record size is adjusted, and the physical record is expanded using a database API call:

```
DmResizeRecord(dbRef, Ptr->Index, RecSize);
```

The DES key string is locked, and the database record is marked as busy using the *DmGetRecord* API call.

In the ensuing for loop, we get eight bytes of record data, call the DES routine to encrypt it with the secret key, and then write the data back into the record:

```
MemMove(buffer, (unsigned char *)pRec + i, 8);
EncDES(buffer, pKey, buffer, true);
DmWrite(pRec, i, buffer, 8);
```

The Palm operating system function *EncDES* handles both the encryption and decryption operations. This function is declared by Palm in the header file *Encrypt.h*, and has the parameters shown in Table 7-4.

Table 7-4. EncDES parameters

Name	Type	Purpose
SrcP	UInt8 *	Pointer to 8-byte input buffer
KeyP	UInt8 *	Pointer to 8-byte secret key
DstP	UInt8 *	Pointer to 8-byte output buffer
Encrypt	Boolean	Flag indicating mode; e.g., true means encrypt, false means decrypt

A nice feature of the DES routine is its ability to encrypt or decrypt data in place. This allows us to pass the same storage array as both the input and output buffers.

After encrypting the record, we release the encryption key, database record, and associated memory. Now that the record has been encrypted successfully, we update the feature memory at the appropriate index.

```
Ptr->Data = Delta;
DoFeature(SetMem, Ptr);
```

Remember that Delta ranges from zero to seven, and that any non-negative number in the feature memory indicates that the record is encrypted. We don't need to set the parameter block's Index field, since it already references the correct record.

The DES_Decrypt function

The *DES_Decrypt* function, shown in Example 7-9, is responsible for decrypting a database record. It is very similar to *DES_Encrypt*, which we discussed at length above, so we will only look at the differences between the two.

Example 7-9. Listing of DES_Decrypt.

```c
static Err DES_Decrypt(DmOpenRef dbRef, UInt32 RecSize, DESParam *Ptr)
{
    UInt32 i;
    MemPtr pRec;
    MemPtr pKey;
    MemHandle hRec;
    MemHandle hDESKey;
    Int8 Delta ;

    // A feature setting of -1 indicates record is not encrypted!
    DoFeature(GetMem, Ptr);
    if (Ptr->Data == -1)
        return 1;

    Delta = Ptr->Data;

    hDESKey = AFStringToMemHandle(Ptr->DESKey);
    pKey = MemHandleLock(hDESKey);
    hRec = DmGetRecord(dbRef, Ptr->Index);
    pRec = MemHandleLock(hRec);

    for (i = 0; i < RecSize; i += 8)
    {
        UInt8 buffer[8];
        UInt8 amount = 8;

        MemMove(buffer, (unsigned char *)pRec + i, 8);
        EncDES(buffer, pKey, buffer, false);

        if ((i + 8) > (RecSize - Delta))
            amount -= Delta;
        DmWrite(pRec, i, buffer, amount);
    }

    MemHandleUnlock(hRec);
    DmReleaseRecord(dbRef, Ptr->Index, true);
    MemHandleUnlock(hDESKey);

    if (Delta)
        DmResizeRecord(dbRef, Ptr->Index, RecSize - Delta);

    Ptr->Data = -1;
    DoFeature(SetMem, Ptr);

    return 0;
}
```

If the record is encrypted, then the record size is already a multiple of eight. We test this at the top of the function. To decrypt data, pass `false` as the final parameter to the *EncDES* operation.

```c
EncDES(buffer, pKey, buffer, false);
```

Because the record was resized, the final decrypted block will contain some padding characters. We test for this condition, and adjust amount downward before writing the block to the database:

```
if ((i + 8) > (RecSize - Delta))
    amount -= Delta;
```

After decryption, we use the Palm database API function *DmResizeRecord* to physically shrink the record in the database. And we reset the corresponding feature memory cell to −1, to indicate the record is no longer encrypted.

Resources

There are two primary resources for the Palm operating system: the OS Reference and the OS Companion. The Companion outlines the various operating system capabilities and subsystems. The Reference provides the details of API data structures and function call syntax.

AppForge provides a sample fuser application. It covers marshaling most data types, including structures and strings, and also shows how to safely access the device screen from a fuser. See the AppForge Knowledge Base (reference #010326-0012).

Those interested in the cryptographic ideas presented in this chapter should look at Bruce Schneier's *Applied Cryptography: Protocols, Algorithms and Source Code in C*. This book covers the details of DES encryption and key management, and many other things as well. It also has a very comprehensive bibliography.

Finally, the National Institute of Standards maintains federal information processing standards (FIPS) required by the US Government for sensitive data systems. Their web site includes the following useful references at *http://www.nist.gov*: FIPS-46.2 (DES), FIPS-81 (DES Modes of Operation), and FIPS 112 (Password Security).

CHAPTER 8
Shared Libraries

In this chapter, we look at extending an application's functionality through the use of shared libraries. A shared library is a unit of reusable code that typically contains a small, but often used, set of functionality. Instead of compiling the same code into every application, a shared library can be loaded and used by other programs as necessary.

We show you how to develop a shared library for the Palm that can be used by a conventional Palm application. Next, we integrate our shared library into an App-Forge *fuser*. A fuser is a Palm application with modifications to enable marshaling data between it and an AppForge application. The fuser provides a bridge between your AppForge application and Palm applications or libraries. Depending on the needs of your application, a fuser can contain substantial functionality of its own.

We assume you are familiar with writing conventional C/C++ applications for the Palm Pilot using the Metrowerks CodeWarrior development environment for Windows. We also assume you are familiar with writing AppForge applications and fusers. We covered fuser development in Chapter 7.

Memory Concepts

Before diving into the shared library model, it is important to understand how shared library memory differs from memory in a conventional Palm application. One significant difference between Palm applications and shared libraries is that libraries do not have global variables. Since global variables only make sense to the current application, a shared library cannot access them.

As an example, in order to implement an object reference counter in a standard Palm application, you might declare a global reference counter such as:

```
    int g_nRefCount = 0;
```

or:

```
    static int g_nRefCount = 0;
```

However, this method is not supported in a shared library. Instead, the general approach is to dynamically allocate a memory chunk for your globals, then assign the handle to the memory chunk to a globals pointer that the Palm OS provides when your library is loaded for the first time. Once you have a pointer to your global memory tucked away, your library can access any variables as needed through this pointer. In essence, this is equivalent to conventional global memory that is dynamically created and destroyed. (Although shared libraries do not support conventional global memory, we still use the g or g_ variable prefix for memory accessed this way, since the shared library can access it globally.)

When working with global or other memory in a shared library, you should use movable memory chunk-based routines for library globals and other variables to minimize dynamic heap fragmentation. Routines that use a MemHandle work with movable, or unlocked, chunks, and routines that use a MemPtr work with nonmovable, or locked, chunks. In addition to using handle-based routines, your library should only lock its memory each time it accesses the memory. The library unlocks the memory as soon as it is finished with it. This allows the Palm OS memory manager to reorganize memory chunks to avoid heap fragmentation.

In addition to carefully managing memory, your library must assign ownership of its memory to the operating system. Although this seems unusual at first, consider how your library is used. You will typically allocate global memory when the first application opens your library. Since your library is running in the first application's space, your global memory is owned by that application. Now assume a second application opens your library. Since you already created global memory, your library may perhaps update its reference count, and continue working. Now the first application exits and closes your library. Since it owns the global memory, Palm's memory manager will free that chunk of memory. Your library has just lost its global memory, and you can no longer access it!

The solution to this problem is to assign ownership of your memory to the Palm OS. The Palm's memory manager will not automatically reclaim your memory as applications close your library. Of course, it is important to follow good memory management practices and release all of your library's resources when no applications are using the library.

Memory Management Functions

Let's review some of the common Palm OS SDK functions for managing memory.

To allocate memory, use *MemHandleNew* as follows:

```
typedef struct GlobalVarsType
{
    Int16    nOpenCount;     // library open count
    Int16    nContextCount;  // number of contexts using this library
    //Other library global variables
```

```
}GlobalVarsType;

UInt32 nMemSize = sizeof(GlobalVarsType);
//Allocate global memory
MemHandle gHandle = MemHandleNew(nMemSize);
```

To lock a chunk of memory for read/write access, use the following sequence.

```
MemPtr gLockPtr;
gLockPtr = MemHandleLock(gHandle);
//read from or write to global memory
MemHandleUnlock(gHandle);
```

Alternatively, since *MemHandleLock* returns a `MemPtr`, you may use the following *MemHandleLock/MemPtrUnlock* pair:

```
MemPtr gLockPtr;
gLockPtr = MemHandleLock(gHandle);
//read from or write to global memory
MemPtrUnlock(gLockPtr);
```

To set the owner ID of memory so it belongs to the OS, you must first lock the memory chunk, set the owner ID, and then unlock the memory chunk. You typically set the owner ID immediately after creating the memory:

```
MemHandle gHandle = MemHandleNew(nMemSize);
MemPtr gLockPtr = MemHandleLock(gHandle);
//Set the owner to the OS, so it is not freed automatically.
MemPtrSetOwner(gLockPtr, 0);
MemPtrUnlock(gLockPtr);
```

When your library is done with its global memory—which is typically when the last application unloads it from memory—the library should free its memory using *MemHandleFree*, as follows:

```
//Our library is being closed by the last application,
//so free our globals
MemHandleFree (gHandle);
```

Alternatively, if you have locked memory, you can use *MemPtrFree* to unlock and free it in one step:

```
MemPtr gLockPtr = MemHandleLock(gHandle)
//Access our memory one last time
//Unlock and free our memory in one step
MemPtrFree(gLockPtr)
```

We will see these functions in use in the next section as we develop the *DBSLib* sample shared library.

DBSLib Shared Library

We illustrate shared library implementation with a library that creates databases and populates them with records. The database schema and record data come in the

---

form of an XML string.* DBSLib can be used by any conventional Palm application or integrated with an AppForge application using a fuser. We discuss both approaches later in this chapter.

DBSLib parses the XML string to determine the database schema, creates the database, and then adds records according to the schema with data from the XML string. An example of a schema and data in XML format is shown in Example 8-1.

Example 8-1. Database schema and record data in XML format

```
<Database Name=Employee Type=DATA Creator=AFLD>
  <Schema>
    <Field>
      <Num>0</Num>
      <Name>FirstName</Name>
      <Type>6</Type>
      <Length>0</Length>
    </Field>
    <Field>
      <Num>1</Num>
      <Name>LastName</Name>
      <Type>6<Type/>
      <Length>0</Length>
    </Field>
    <Field>
      <Num>2</Num>
      <Name>Phone</Name>
      <Type>6</Type>
      <Length>0</Length>
    </Field>
  </Schema>
  <Data>
    <Record>
      <FirstName>Bob H.</FirstName>
      <LastName>Smith</LastName>
      <Phone>(703) 555-1212</Phone>
    </Record>
    <Record>
      <FirstName>Lucy D.</FirstName>
      <LastName>Anderson</LastName>
      <Phone>(703) 555-2121</Phone>
    </Record>
  </Data>
</Database>
```

DBSLib packages its functionality in a reusable library that other applications can load and use as needed. Applications benefit from using DBSLib because it will work

---

* Although the DBSLib example shared library does not support formal XML constructs and syntax, we refer to the string as an XML string for the sake of simplicity. We want to focus on the steps required to develop and integrate a shared library, rather than the complex details of formal XML processing.

with different schemas and data without being modified. In addition, the XML schema string can come from anywhere. It can come from a Conduit that fetches the schema from the desktop, the Internet, or another remote source. Or the XML string can come from a custom application that loads the string from a web site to provide a field user with database updates.

CodeWarrior Setup

Before getting started, you will need to configure CodeWarrior for the DBSLib project. Appendix B outlines the steps for creating and configuring the DBSLib shared library project in CodeWarrior.

Global Memory Management

To manage memory in a shared library, you need to know when to create, destroy, and access the memory. As discussed previously, your library is responsible for managing its own global memory.

We take Jeff Ishaq's approach to global memory management, outlined in his article "Mastering Shared Libraries" (see Palm's Knowledge Base at *http://oasis.palm.com/ dev/kb*). We follow the implementation in the *SampleLib* project that comes with the Palm OS SDK.

In this approach, you create global memory the first time your library is loaded. Within your global memory, you maintain a reference count, incrementing it each time your library is loaded. When you need global memory, you query the Palm OS for your library's system library table entry (see Example 8-2) and obtain the pointer to memory. When your library is unloaded, you decrement the reference count, finally freeing global memory when the count goes to zero.

Example 8-2. Palm OS system library table entry

```
typedef struct SysLibTblEntryType
{
   MemPtr   *dispatchTblP; // pointer to library dispatch table
   void   *globalsP;       // pointer to library global memory
   //other fields...
}SysLibTblEntryType;

typedef SysLibTblEntryType*   SysLibTblEntryPtr;
```

Let's take a look at the global memory structure used in DBSLib.

```
   typedef struct DBSLibGlobalMemType
   {
       UInt16 refNum;       // our library's reference number
       Int16  libRefCount;  // library reference count; number of times it
                            // has been opened by client applications
```

```
    Int16  clntRefCount;  // number of client contexts we are servicing

    //Additional application specific globals

} DBSLibGlobalMemType;
typedef DBSLibGlobalMemType* DBSLibGlobalMemPtr;
```

refNum is the OS assigned reference number for our library. libRefCount serves as a reference counter for our library. We initialize it to zero upon creating our global memory, and increment each time a client application opens our library. Each time a client closes our library, we decrement this counter. Finally, when it goes back down to zero, we delete our global memory. clntRefCount is a reference counter for the number of client applications we are servicing.

The library's functions for managing global memory are summarized in Table 8-1.

Table 8-1. Global memory management functions

Function	Description
CreateGlobalMem	Creates the library's global memory and stores its handle in the globalsP pointer of the library's system library table entry
FreeGlobalMem	Frees global memory that was created by the *CreateGlobalMem* function
LockGlobalMem	Locks global memory for read/write access
UnlockGlobalMem	Unlocks global memory
IsDBSLibOpen	Determines if the library is open

Let's look at each function in detail. Later we will see how they are integrated to support the DBSLib shared library.

CreateGlobalMem

In this function, we verify that global memory has not already been allocated. We then create global memory if necessary.

```
DBSLibGlobalMemPtr CreateGlobalMem(UInt16 refNum)
{
    DBSLibGlobalMemPtr globalMemPtr = NULL;
    MemHandle globalMemHandle;
    SysLibTblEntryPtr libEntryPtr;

    libEntryPtr = SysLibTblEntry(refNum);
    ErrFatalDisplayIf(libEntryPtr == NULL, "DBSLib: Invalid refNum.");

    ErrFatalDisplayIf(libEntryPtr->globalsP != NULL,
                      "DBSLib: Globals already exist.");

    globalMemHandle = MemHandleNew(sizeof(DBSLibGlobalMemType));
    if (globalMemHandle == NULL)
        return NULL;
```

```
        libEntryPtr->globalsP = (void*)globalMemHandle;

        globalMemPtr = LockGlobalMem(refNum);
        ErrFatalDisplayIf(globalMemPtr == NULL, "DBSLib: Failed to lock globals.");

        MemPtrSetOwner(globalMemPtr, 0);

        MemSet(globalMemPtr, sizeof(DBSLibGlobalMemType), 0);
        globalMemPtr->refNum = refNum;
        globalMemPtr->libRefCount = 0;

        return globalMemPtr;
    }
```

We start by calling *SysLibTblEntry* to obtain a pointer to the library's system library table entry. You will become very familiar with the *SysLibTblEntry* function by the end of this chapter. It is almost always called first so we can access our library's global memory pointer.

After verifying that global memory is not already allocated, we create it with a call to *MemHandleNew*, and save the global memory handle in the globalsP pointer of the SysLibTableEntry structure. Note the call to *MemPtrSetOwner*, where we assign ownership of our memory to the operating system. We store the OS assigned reference number, and initialize the library's reference count to zero. We return the locked global memory pointer. The calling routine is responsible for unlocking the memory. We use the *ErrFatalDisplayIf* routine to report serious or unrecoverable errors.

FreeGlobalMem

In this function, we free the global memory that was created in *CreateGlobalMem*.

```
    void FreeGlobalMem(UInt16 refNum)
    {
        MemHandle globalMemHandle;
        SysLibTblEntryPtr libEntryPtr;

        libEntryPtr = SysLibTblEntry(refNum);
        ErrFatalDisplayIf(libEntryPtr == NULL, "DBSLib: Invalid refNum.");
        globalMemHandle = (MemHandle)(libEntryPtr->globalsP);

        if(globalMemHandle != NULL)
        {
            libEntryPtr->globalsP = NULL;
            MemHandleFree(globalMemHandle);
        }
    }
```

First, we obtain the pointer to the library's system library table entry with a call to *SysLibTblEntry*. Next, we assign the globalsP variable to NULL, and call *MemHandleFree* to release the memory.

LockGlobalMem

The library calls this function to lock global memory before modifying it. This function is important because it prevents the OS from reorganizing our memory on the heap while the library is accessing it.

```
DBSLibGlobalMemPtr LockGlobalMem(UInt16 refNum)
{
    DBSLibGlobalMemPtr globalMemPtr = NULL;
    MemHandle globalMemHandle;
    SysLibTblEntryPtr libEntryPtr;

    libEntryPtr = SysLibTblEntry(refNum);
    if (libEntryPtr != NULL)
        globalMemHandle = (MemHandle)(libEntryPtr->globalsP);

    if (globalMemHandle != NULL)
        globalMemPtr = (DBSLibGlobalMemPtr)MemHandleLock(globalMemHandle);

    return globalMemPtr;
}
```

We call *SysLibTblEntry* and get the handle to the global memory from the globalsP pointer. Then we call *MemHandleLock* to lock the memory.

UnlockGlobalMem

This function is the analog to *LockGlobalMem*. The library calls this function to unlock global memory after accessing it.

In *LockGlobalMem*, the call to *MemHandleLock* returns a MemPtr. To unlock the memory, use *MemPtrUnlock*, since it takes a MemPtr variable as its argument. To simplify things, we implement *UnlockGlobalMem* as a macro.

```
#define UnlockGlobalMem(gP)    MemPtrUnlock(gP)
```

IsDBSLibOpen

We use *IsDBSLibOpen* to determine if the library has been opened.

```
Boolean IsDBSLibOpen(UInt16 refNum)
{
    DBSLibGlobalMemPtr globalMemPtr;
    Boolean    isOpen = false;

    globalMemPtr = LockGlobalMem(refNum);

    if (globalMemPtr != NULL)
    {
        isOpen = true;
        UnlockGlobalMem(globalMemPtr);
    }

    return isOpen;
}
```

If locking the library's global memory succeeds, then the library has been opened. We will see how this function is used later in this chapter.

Client Memory Management

In addition to the global memory used by the library, we manage memory for each client application. Client memory is typically used to maintain persistence, or state, between library calls. (By client memory, we mean memory that the shared library owns and manages on behalf of a particular application. This memory is typically transparent to the client application.)

There is one important difference between global and client memory. We can store the handle to our global memory in the globalsP pointer of our library's SysLibTableEntry structure. For client memory, however, we require that the caller use a context variable to store a handle to their memory. The client maintains the context variable as long as it uses the library, and passes it as an argument to each of our library's functions that need to access client memory. The client context variable is just a pointer in which we store the handle to the client's memory after it is created.

Here is the client memory structure.

```
#define DB_NAME_LEN 64
#define DB_SCHEMA_LEN 128
typedef struct DBSLibClientMemType
{
    Int16   nState;                  //Keep track of where we are
    Char    szName[DB_NAME_LEN];     //Name of the database we are creating
    Char    szSchema[DB_SCHEMA_LEN]; //Database schema
    Int16   nNumFields;              //Number of fields in each record
    Int16   nNumRecords;             //Number of records in the database
} DBSLibClientMemType;

typedef DBSLibClientMemType* DBSLibClientMemPtr;
```

nState maintains state between library function calls. We will see how it is used later to prevent our library from being called incorrectly. szName and szSchema are the name and schema, respectively, of the database that the library creates. This information is determined from the <Schema></Schema> tag pair in the XML-formatted string (see Example 8-1, earlier in this chapter) that gets passed into our library. nNumFields is the number of fields per record, and nNumRecords is the number of records that were created, based on the <Data></Data> tags.

The functions for managing client memory (see Table 8-2) are analogous to those for managing global memory.

Table 8-2. Client memory management functions

Function	Description
CreateClientMem	Creates the client memory and initializes the client's context variable (pointer)
FreeClientMem	Frees the client memory that was created by the *CreateClientMem* function
LockClientMem	Locks a client's memory for read/write access
UnlockClientMem	Unlocks a client's memory

CreateClientMem

In this function, we verify that global memory has been created and proceed to create client memory.

```
Err CreateClientMem(DBSLibGlobalMemPtr globalMemPtr, UInt32 * clientContextPtr)
{
    Err retVal = errNone;
    MemHandle clientMemHandle;
    DBSLibClientMemPtr clientMemPtr;

    ErrFatalDisplayIf(globalMemPtr == NULL,
                    "DBSLib: NULL global memory pointer.");
    ErrFatalDisplayIf(clientContextPtr == NULL,
                    "DBSLib: NULL client context pointer.");


    *clientContextPtr = NULL;

    clientMemHandle = MemHandleNew(sizeof(DBSLibClientMemType));
    if(clientMemHandle == NULL)
        retVal = dbsLibErrMemory;
    else
    {
        *clientContextPtr = (UInt32)clientMemHandle;

        clientMemPtr = (DBSLibClientMemPtr)MemHandleLock(clientMemHandle);
        MemSet(clientMemPtr, sizeof(DBSLibClientMemType), 0);
        UnlockClientMem(clientMemPtr);

        globalMemPtr->clntRefCount++;

    }

    return retVal;
}
```

The client's context variable is declared as a UInt32 by the client application, and a pointer to this variable is passed in as the second argument. We verify the parameters passed in and initialize the client context to NULL. Then we create the client memory using *MemHandleNew* and store the handle in the client context variable. Finally we lock the client memory, initialize it, and then unlock it.

FreeClientMem

The library calls this function to free the client memory, which was created in *CreateClientMem*.

```
Err FreeClientMem(DBSLibGlobalMemPtr globalMemPtr, UInt32 clientContext)
{
    DBSLibClientMemPtr clientMemPtr;

    ErrFatalDisplayIf(globalMemPtr == NULL,
                    "DBSLib: NULL global memory pointer.");

    clientMemPtr = LockClientMem(clientContext);

    if(clientMemPtr != NULL)
    {
        MemPtrFree(clientMemPtr);
        globalMemPtr->clntRefCount--;

        ErrFatalDisplayIf(globalMemPtr->clntRefCount < 0,
                    "DBSLib: client ref count underflow.");
    }

    return errNone;
}
```

We lock the client's memory with a call to *LockClientMem*, and free it with a call to *MemPtrFree*.

LockClientMem

The library calls this function to lock client memory before modifying it. As with *LockGlobalMem*, this function prevents the OS from reorganizing client memory on the heap while the library is accessing it.

```
DBSLibClientMemPtr LockClientMem(UInt32 clientContext)
{
    DBSLibClientMemPtr clientMemPtr = NULL;

    ErrFatalDisplayIf(clientContext == NULL, "DBSLib: NULL client context.");
    clientMemPtr = (DBSLibClientMemPtr)MemHandleLock((MemHandle)clientContext);
    ErrFatalDisplayIf(clientMemPtr == NULL,
                    "DBSLib: Failed to lock client memory.");

    return clientMemPtr;
}
```

Here, we simply call *MemHandleLock* to lock the client memory based on the clientContext argument and return the memory pointer.

UnlockClientMem

This function is the analog to *LockClientMem*. The library calls this function to unlock client memory after accessing it.

In *LockClientMem*, the call to *MemHandleLock* returns a `MemPtr`. Thus, to unlock the memory, we use *MemPtrUnlock*, since it takes a `MemPtr` variable as its argument. As with *UnlockGlobalMem*, we have implemented *UnlockClientMem* as a macro.

```
#define UnlockClientMem(contextP) MemPtrUnlock(contextP)
```

Required Functions

A shared library must implement an installation entry point and four standard functions. Together, these five functions allow the library to be loaded, opened, closed, and notified when the PDA goes idle. Each function is described in Table 8-3.

Table 8-3. Required shared library functions

Function	Description
__Startup__	Installation entry point, called when an application loads the library for the first time. You must use this name, and the function must appear at the top of the code resource.
Open	Clients must call this function before calling any other functions. You will use it to perform initialization, including creating global and client memory.
Close	Clients call this function when they are finished using the library. Here, you decrement your library's open count and free client memory. If the library's open count is zero, you will also free global memory.
Sleep	The Palm OS calls this function automatically when the system is going to sleep.
Wake	The Palm OS calls this function automatically when the system is waking up.

Other than *__Startup__*, you may give these functions any name. *Open*, *Close*, *Sleep*, and *Wake* must be the first four functions in the library's dispatch table, and must appear in that order. We will discuss dispatch tables in detail later in this chapter. All of these functions must take the library reference number as their first argument.

Sleep and *Wake* are most useful for libraries that must provide device power management. Since our library does not service any hardware, we provide empty implementations for these functions. (If your library services hardware, Palm's Developer Knowledge Base article Mastering Shared Libraries (Article ID 1670) covers these functions in good detail.)

__Startup__ function

A shared library's installation entry point is called when an application loads the library for the first time. Your shared library's entry point must correspond to the following signature, and it must be the first function in your library's code resource.

(CodeWarrior takes care of this for you by automatically placing the *__Startup__* function at the beginning of the resource.)

```
Err __Startup__(UInt16 refNum, SysLibTblEntryPtr entryP)
```

refNum is an OS-assigned reference number for your library and is used by client applications when calling your library's functions. entryP is a pointer to a SysLibTableEntry structure shown earlier in Example 8-2 and repeated here:

```
typedef struct SysLibTblEntryType
{
    MemPtr   *dispatchTblP; // pointer to library dispatch table
    void   *globalsP;       // pointer to library global memory
    //other fields...
}SysLibTblEntryType;

typedef SysLibTblEntryType*    SysLibTblEntryPtr;
```

When your library is loaded, the Palm OS creates a corresponding SysLibTableEntry structure and maintains it in an internal array. As we have seen previously, you can obtain this structure with a call to *SysLibTblEntry*.

dispatchTblP is a pointer to the library's dispatch table, which is essentially a lookup table that tells the Palm OS where to find the library's functions. The dispatch table pointer is a critical piece of the library's initialization. We cover building the dispatch table in detail later in this chapter. globalsP contains the library's global memory handle.

We use a #define statement to give the *__Startup__* entry point the more intuitive name of *DBSLibInstall*.

```
#define DBSLibInstall __Startup__

Err DBSLibInstall(UInt16 refNum, SysLibTblEntryPtr entryP)
{
    entryP->dispatchTblP = (MemPtr*)DBSLibDispatchTable();
    entryP->globalsP = NULL;
    return errNone;
}
```

We assign the library's dispatch table and initialize the globalsP pointer to NULL.

DBSLibOpen (Open) function

As we will see later, however, DBSLib's *DBSLibGetAPIVersion* function can be safely called first, since it does not access global or client memory.

```
Err DBSLibOpen(UInt16 refNum, UInt32 * clientContextPtr)
{
    DBSLibGlobalMemPtr globalMemPtr;
```

```
        Err retVal = errNone;
        Int16 origRefCount = 0;

        ErrFatalDisplayIf(clientContextPtr == NULL,
                        "DBSLib: NULL client context pointer");

        *clientContextPtr = 0;
        globalMemPtr = LockGlobalMem(refNum);

        if (globalMemPtr == NULL)
        {
            globalMemPtr = CreateGlobalMem(refNum);
            if (globalMemPtr == NULL )
                retVal = dbsLibErrMemory;
        }

        if (globalMemPtr != NULL)
        {
            origRefCount = globalMemPtr->libRefCount;

            retVal = CreateClientMem(globalMemPtr, clientContextPtr);

            if (retVal == errNone)
                globalMemPtr->libRefCount++;

            UnlockGlobalMem(globalMemPtr);

            if ( retVal != errNone && (origRefCount == 0) )
                FreeGlobalMem(refNum);
        }

        return retVal;
    }
```

We first attempt to lock the library's global memory. If *LockGlobalMem* returns NULL, global memory has not been created, and our library is being opened for the very first time.

After creating global memory, we create the client's memory with a call to *CreateClientMem*. *CreateClientMem* stores the client's context in the value pointed to by the clientContextPtr argument. If the client's memory is created successfully, we increment the reference count.

If the client's memory cannot be created, and this is the first time the library is being loaded, we free global memory as follows.

```
    if ( retVal != errNone && (origRefCount == 0) )
        FreeGlobalMem(refNum);
```

DBSLibClose (Close) function

Clients call this function when they are done using the library. Here, you typically free client memory, and decrement the library's global open count.

```
Err DBSLibClose(UInt16 refNum, UInt32 clientContext)
{
    DBSLibGlobalMemPtr globalMemPtr;
    Int16 currLibCount;
    Int16 currCtxCount;
    Err retVal = errNone;

    globalMemPtr = LockGlobalMem(refNum);

    if(globalMemPtr == NULL)
        return retVal;

    FreeClientMem(globalMemPtr, clientContext);

    globalMemPtr->libRefCount--;

    ErrFatalDisplayIf(globalMemPtr->libRefCount < 0,
                    "DBSLib: Lib ref count underflow.");

    currLibCount = globalMemPtr->libRefCount;
    currCtxCount = globalMemPtr->clntRefCount;

    UnlockGlobalMem(globalMemPtr);

    if (currLibCount <= 0)
    {
        ErrFatalDisplayIf(currCtxCount != 0,
                        "DBSLib: Not all client memory was freed.");

        FreeGlobalMem(refNum);
    }
    else
    {
        retVal = dbsLibErrStillOpen;
    }

    return retVal;
}
```

As with *DBSLibOpen*, we call *LockGlobalMem* to determine if global memory exists. If global memory does not exist, the library has already been closed, and we return immediately.

If global memory exists, we free the client's memory by calling *FreeClientMem*. Recall that *FreeClientMem* decrements the client context count, so we don't need to do that here. After decrementing the library's reference counter and unlocking global memory, we check the reference counter to see if we can free global memory. If the library is still open, we return dbsLibErrStillOpen. This informs the client that others are still using our library and that it is not safe to unload it.

DBSLibSleep (Sleep) and DBSLibWake (Wake) functions

Since our library doesn't care when the system is sleeping, we provide empty implementations for these functions.

```
Err DBSLibSleep(UInt16 refNum)
{
    return errNone;
}

Err DBSLibWake(UInt16 refNum)
{
    return errNone;
}
```

Custom Library Functions

Here is where we get to the business at hand: creating databases from an XML schema. With the exception of a few special functions, a client calls these functions after opening the library and before closing it.

Data types and constants

As with any C application, there are a number of constants, declarations, and other housekeeping information that need to be declared. We provide declarations to support versioning, tracking internal state, and error values, among others.

To track the internal state of our library, we use the following definitions.

```
#define dbsLibDBCreatePending      0x00
#define dbsLibQuerySchemaPending   0x02
```

dbsLibDBCreatePending indicates that our library is waiting to receive a client's XML string to parse and process. Upon successfully processing the XML string, we have created a database. We then move to the dbsLibQuerySchemaPending state. In this state, a client may query our library for information about the database, which was created by parsing the XML string. The following defines and type declaration (see Example 8-3) match the definition for a field in the <Schema></Schema> tags of the XML string (shown in Example 8-1, earlier in this chapter).

Example 8-3. Field element data type

```
#define F_TYPE_BOOL    0
#define F_TYPE_BYTE    1
#define F_TYPE_DATE    2
#define F_TYPE_FLOAT   3
#define F_TYPE_INT     4
#define F_TYPE_LONG    5
#define F_TYPE_STR     6

#define MAX_DATA_LEN 128
typedef struct DBSLibFieldElemType
{
```

Example 8-3. Field element data type (continued)

```
    Int32 nNum;
    Char szName[DB_NAME_LEN];
    Int16 nType;
    UInt32 nDataLen;
    MemHandle hData;
    Int32 nLength;

} DBSLibFieldElemType;

typedef DBSLibFieldElemType* DBSLibFieldElemTypePtr;
```

Table 8-4 contains a description of each item in the DBSLibFieldElemType structure. The field type definitions F_TYPE_BOOL through F_TYPE_STR determine how to interpret each field's data. These definitions also map to Visual Basic types used by an AppForge application. MAX_DATA_LEN defines the maximum size of the XML data for a particular field.

Table 8-4. Schema field items

Item	Description
nNum	Unique field number; for use by AppForge in identifying this field
szName	Name of the field, as it will appear in the <Record></Record> tags of the XML string
nType	Field type; contains a number corresponding to one of the assignments F_TYPE_BOOL through F_TYPE_STR
nDataLen	Length of this field's data
hData	Handle to allocated memory for this field's data
nLength	Length of this field; used to support AppForge applications; hard-coded to zero (variable length)

For client applications that load our library, we provide the following definitions for Creator ID, type, and name:

```
    #define dbsLibCreatorID 'DBSL'
    #define dbsLibTypeID    'libr'
    #define dbsLibName      "DBSLib.lib"
```

Here are the error codes that our library returns.

```
    #define dbsLibErrParam     (appErrorClass | 1)
    #define dbsLibErrNotOpen   (appErrorClass | 2)
    #define dbsLibErrStillOpen (appErrorClass | 3)
    #define dbsLibErrMemory    (appErrorClass | 4)
    #define dbsLibErrParse     (appErrorClass | 5)
    #define dbsLibErrArg       (appErrorClass | 6)
    #define dbsLibErrDB        (appErrorClass | 7)
    #define dbsLibErrState     (appErrorClass | 8)
```

All of these errors start from appErrorClass, which is defined as 0x8000 in the header file *ErrorBase.h*, which is part of the Palm OS SDK.

Let's look at the functions that actually perform the work in the DBSLib shared library. DBSLib exposes the following custom functions to the client.

DBSLibGetAPIVersion
Retrieves the API version of the shared library

DBSLibParseSchema
Parses the XML string, creates the database, and populates it with records

DBSLibGetDBInfo
Retrieves database information from the newly created database, including database name, number of records, and database schema

DBSLibGetAPIVersion

DBSLibGetAPIVersion allows a client to determine the API version of the library, perhaps to ensure compatibility with the client's implementation.

```
#define dbsLibVersion sysMakeROMVersion(1,0,0,sysROMStageRelease,0)
Err DBSLibGetAPIVersion(UInt16 refNum, UInt32 *pVer)
{
    ErrFatalDisplayIf(pVer == NULL, "DBSLib: Null pointer argument.");
    *pVer = dbsLibVersion;
    return errNone;
}
```

We use the sysMakeROMVersion macro found in the *SystemMgr.h* file of the Palm OS SDK to establish the library's version. We declare version 1.0, sysROMStageRelease.

Here, we simply store the version in the pVer argument and return errNone. A standard Palm application that calls our library can subsequently use the sysGetROMVerMajor, sysGetROMVerMinor, or other similar macros to extract specific information from the version number. We will see how these macros are used in the DBSLib driver application.

DBSLibParseSchema

This function is the workhorse of the DBSLib library. This function parses the XML string to determine the database schema, creates the database, and populates the database with corresponding record data. We assume that the XML string is properly formatted. *DBSLibParseSchema* focuses on extracting the necessary elements from the string and manipulating the database—not handling XML schema errors.

DBSLibParseSchema is a large function, so we will present it in manageable pieces. Here are the function and variable declarations.

```
Err DBSLibParseSchema(UInt16 refNum, UInt32 clientContext,
                Char* pszXML, Boolean bDeleteDB)
{
```

```
Err retVal = errNone;
//Start and end pointers for string parsing
Char *pszStart, *pszEnd;
Int16 nFieldIndex = 0, nRecIndex = 0;
Int16 nNumFields = 0, nNumRecs = 0;
MemHandle hFieldElemArray = NULL;
DBSLibFieldElemTypePtr pFieldElemArray, pCurrFieldElem;
DBSLibClientMemPtr pClientMem;

//Database attributes, as contained in the
//XML string
Char szDBName[DB_NAME_LEN];
UInt32 nDBType = 0, nDBCreator = 0;

//Variables for PalmOS database functions
DmOpenRef dbOpenRef;         //A reference to the database we will open
Boolean bIsResDB = false;    //we are not creating a resource database
Boolean bIsDirty = true;
UInt16 nDBMode = dmModeReadWrite; //Open database for read/write access
UInt16 nCardNum = 0;
UInt16 nRecNum = 0;                  //Current record being added
UInt32 nRecLen = 0;
UInt32 nRecOffset = 0;  //Offset into record to begin writing
LocalID dbID;
MemHandle hRecord;
MemPtr pRecordLock;
Boolean bCreateDB = false;
```

In addition to the required *refNum* parameter, *DBSLibParseSchema* takes three parameters. *clientContext* contains the client's handle to their memory. *pszXML* contains the XML string we will parse. *bDeleteDB* indicates whether we should delete an existing database named in the XML string. If true, delete the database; if false; add records to the existing database.

The local variables for *DBSLibParseSchema* fall into three groups. The first group consists of handles and pointers for parsing the XML string and iterating through the field element array that is created from the schema. The second group consists of the database attributes: name, type, and creator. The third group contains variables for manipulating the database we will create.

Next, we initialize some variables and verify the existence of the database attributes.

```
if(IsDBSLibOpen(refNum) == false)
    return dbsLibErrNotOpen;
pClientMem = LockClientMem(clientContext);
MemSet(pClientMem, sizeof(DBSLibClientMemType), 0);
pClientMem->nState = dbsLibDBCreatePending;
MemPtrUnlock(pClientMem);

MemSet(szDBName, DB_NAME_LEN, 0);

retVal = ParseDBAttributes(pszXML, szDBName, &nDBType, &nDBCreator);
```

```
if(retVal != errNone)
{
    return retVal;
}
```

We verify that the library is open and initialize the state variable in client memory to dbsLibCreatePending. Next, we call *ParseDBAttributes*, which extracts szDBName, nDBType, and nDBCreator from the XML string.

We then initialize the database and create it if necessary.

```
dbID = DmFindDatabase(nCardNum, szDBName);

if(dbID == 0)
    bCreateDB = true;
else
{
    if(bDeleteDB == true)
    {
        retVal = DmDeleteDatabase(nCardNum, dbID);
        if(retVal != errNone)
            return dbsLibErrDB;
        bCreateDB = true;
    }
}

if(bCreateDB == true)
{
    retVal = DmCreateDatabase(nCardNum, (const Char*)szDBName, nDBCreator,
                              nDBType, bIsResDB);
    if(retVal != errNone)
        return retVal;
}
```

We call *DmFindDatabase* to see if the database already exists. If it exists, and the client asked that we delete it, we call *DmDeleteDatabase*. Then we create the database, if needed, by calling *DmCreateDatabase*.

Next, we parse the XML schema to obtain the field definitions for each record.

```
pszStart = StrStr(pszXML, "<Schema>");
pszEnd = StrStr(pszXML, "</Schema>");

if(pszStart == NULL || pszEnd == NULL)
    return dbsLibErrParse;

pszStart += StrLen("<Schema>");

retVal = ParseFields(pszStart, &nNumFields, &hFieldElemArray);

if(retVal != errNone)
    return retVal;
```

After verifying the existence of the <Schema></Schema> tags, we call *ParseFields*, which parses through the field definitions and creates an array of DBSLibFieldElemType structures (see Example 8-3, shown earlier in this chapter). On return, nNumFields contains the number of elements in the array, and hFieldElemArray contains the handle to the created array. Each element in the array corresponds to a particular tag pair. The entire array defines the format for each database record.

Once we know how many fields are in a record, we count the number of records in the database.

```
pszStart = StrStr(pszXML, "<Data>");
pszEnd = StrStr(pszXML, "</Data>");
if(pszStart == NULL || pszEnd == NULL)
{
    MemHandleFree(hFieldElemArray);
    return dbsLibErrParse;
}
pszStart += StrLen("<Data>");

nNumRecs = CountItems(pszStart, "<Record>", "</Record>");

if(nNumRecs == 0)
    return dbsLibErrParse;
```

We start by verifying the existence of the <Data></Data> tag pair. Then we call *CountItems*, an internal library function that returns the number of times a particular pair of XML tags appears within a string. We open the database by calling *DmOpenDatabaseByTypeCreator*.

```
dbOpenRef = DmOpenDatabaseByTypeCreator(nDBType, nDBCreator, nDBMode);
if(dbOpenRef == 0)
{
    FreeFieldElemArray(hFieldElemArray, nNumFields);
    return dbsLibErrDB;
}
```

If the database cannot be opened, we free the field element array and return dbsLibErrDB.

After the database is opened, we add each record to the database (see Example 8-4). For each record, we search for its data in the XML string, and then add the record to the database. Example 8-4 lists the pseudocode steps for doing this.

Example 8-4. Pseudocode for DBSLibParseSchema record creation

```
//For each record in the database, get its data from the XML string,
//and add it to the database
for(nRecIndex = 0; nRecIndex < nNumRecs; nRecIndex++)
{
```

Example 8-4. Pseudocode for DBSLibParseSchema record creation (continued)

```
    //Find the <Record></Record> tags for this record's data

    //Retreive field data for given record

    //Create a new database record for our data

    //Lock the record for editing

    //Lock the field element array, and add the elements
    //to the currently locked record

    // Unlock the record handle

    // Release the record

    //Free this record's field element array data
}
```

To find the <Record></Record> tags for a given record, we use the *StrStr* function to find each tag. We do not check for a NULL result here, since the previous call to *CountItems* takes this into account when counting the number of XML tag pairs in a string.

```
pszStart = StrStr(pszStart, "<Record>");
pszStart += StrLen("<Record>");
pszEnd = StrStr(pszStart, "</Record>");
```

We retrieve the record's data by calling *ParseRecData*.

```
retVal = ParseRecData(pszStart, hFieldElemArray, nNumFields, &nRecLen);

if(retVal != errNone)
{
    FreeFieldElemArray(hFieldElemArray, nNumFields);
    DmCloseDatabase(dbOpenRef);
    return retVal;
}
```

ParseRecData extracts the data between the <Record></Record> and stores it in the field element array. If *ParseRecData* fails, we free the field element array, close the database, and return.

Now we have all of the data to add a record to the database. We create the new record and lock it for editing with calls to *DmNewRecord* and *MemHandleLock*, respectively.

```
hRecord = DmNewRecord (dbOpenRef, &nRecNum, nRecLen);
pRecordLock = MemHandleLock(hRecord);
```

Adding the field data is simply a matter of appending each array element's data to the record.

```
pFieldElemArray = (DBSLibFieldElemTypePtr)MemHandleLock(hFieldElemArray);
pCurrFieldElem = pFieldElemArray;
nRecOffset = 0;
for(nFieldIndex = 0; nFieldIndex < nNumFields; nFieldIndex++)
{
    void *pData;

    pData = (void *)MemHandleLock(pCurrFieldElem->hData);
    retVal = DmWrite(pRecordLock, nRecOffset, pData,
                     pCurrFieldElem->nDataLen);
    MemPtrUnlock(pData);

    nRecOffset += pCurrFieldElem->nDataLen;
    pCurrFieldElem++;
}
MemPtrUnlock(pFieldElemArray);
```

For each element in the array, we write its data to the record with a call to *DmWrite*. Then we update nRecOffset and pCurrFieldElem in preparation for writing the next field's data.

We finish up the record creation loop by unlocking the record's handle, releasing the record, and freeing the record's data from the field element array.

```
MemPtrUnlock(pRecordLock);
DmReleaseRecord(dbOpenRef, nRecNum, bIsDirty);
FreeFieldElemArrayData(hFieldElemArray, nNumFields);
}
```

DmReleaseRecord clears the busy bit for the record, and sets the dirty bit. *FreeFieldElemArrayData* clears the data for each field element in the array.

After all the records have been added, we close the database.

```
retVal = DmCloseDatabase(dbOpenRef);
```

Before leaving the *DBSLibParseSchema* function, we update the client's memory with the database's information: name, number of fields, number of records, and schema.

```
pClientMem = LockClientMem(clientContext);
StrCopy(pClientMem->szName, szDBName);
CreateSchema(hFieldElemArray, nNumFields, pClientMem->szSchema);
pClientMem->nNumFields = nNumFields;
pClientMem->nNumRecords = nNumRecs;
pClientMem->nState = dbsLibQuerySchemaPending;
MemPtrUnlock(pClientMem);
```

CreateSchema prepares the schema in a format suitable for parsing by the client. We call *CreateSchema* here so that the schema is available when the client calls *DBSLibGetDBInfo*. We also assign the nState member of client memory to dbsLibQuerySchemaPending, which signals successful database creation.

Finally, we free the field element array and return.

```
    FreeFieldElemArray(hFieldElemArray, nNumFields);
    return retVal;
}
```

DBSLibGetDBInfo

This function allows a client to retrieve metadata for the database that was created in a previous call to *DBSLibParseSchema*.

```
Err DBSLibGetDBInfo(UInt16 refNum, UInt32 clientContext, Char* pszName,
                    Int16 *pnNumRecs, Int16 *pnNumFields, Char* pszSchema)
{
    DBSLibClientMemPtr pClientMem;

    if(IsDBSLibOpen(refNum) == false)
        return dbsLibErrNotOpen;

    pClientMem = LockClientMem(clientContext);
    if(pClientMem->nState != dbsLibQuerySchemaPending)
        return dbsLibErrState;

    StrCopy(pszName, pClientMem->szName);
    *pnNumRecs = pClientMem->nNumRecords;
    *pnNumFields = pClientMem->nNumFields;
    StrCopy(pszSchema, pClientMem->szSchema);

    MemPtrUnlock(pClientMem);

    return errNone;
}
```

After verifying that the library is open, we retrieve the requested information from client memory and assign the corresponding arguments.

Internal Library Functions

The custom library functions make use of the following internal helper functions:

ParseDBAttributes
Verifies existence of the database tags in the XML string and extracts the database attributes

ParseFields
Parses the schema section of the XML string, extracts the field definitions, and creates the field element array

ParseRecData
Extracts the field data from the XML string for a given record based on the elements in the field array

CreateSchema

Uses the field element array to format the database schema in a format suitable for parsing

FreeFieldElemArray

Frees the field element array that defines the database schema

FreeFieldElemArrayData

Frees the data associated with an individual field element

CountItems

Counts the number of occurrences of a given XML tag pair within a string

ExtractData

Extracts data between two string delimiters within a larger string

ParseDBAttributes

A database's attributes appear in the `<Database>` start tag and consist of *Name*, *Type*, and *Creator*.

```
<Database Name="Employee" Type="DATA" Creator="AFVM">
...
</Database>
```

ParseDBAttributes gets these attributes, as shown below.

```
Err ParseDBAttributes(Char *pszXML, Char *pszDBName, UInt32 *pnDBType,
                      UInt32 *pnDBCreator)
{
   Err retVal = errNone;
   Char *pszStart, *pszEnd;
   UInt16 nResult;
   Char szTemp[16];

   if(pszXML == NULL)
      return dbsLibErrArg;

   pszStart = StrStr(pszXML, "<Database");
   pszEnd = StrStr(pszXML, "</Database>");
   if(pszStart == NULL || pszEnd == NULL)
      return dbsLibErrParse;

   nResult = ExtractData(pszStart, "Name=", " ", DB_NAME_LEN, pszDBName);
   if(nResult != errNone)
      return nResult;

   MemSet(szTemp, sizeof(szTemp), 0);
   nResult = ExtractData(pszStart, "Type=", " ", sizeof(*pnDBType), szTemp);
   if(nResult != errNone)
      return nResult;

   *pnDBType = (*(UInt32*)szTemp);

   MemSet(szTemp, sizeof(szTemp), 0);
```

```
            nResult = ExtractData(pszStart, "Creator=", ">",
                                    sizeof(*pnDBCreator), szTemp);
            if(nResult != errNone)
                return nResult;

            *pnDBCreator = (*(UInt32*)szTemp);

            return retVal;
        }
```

We verify the XML string is not NULL, and then look for the database tags. If either tag is missing, we return an error. Then we use *ExtractData* to get each attribute.

ParseFields

As shown below, the <Num>, <Name>, <Type>, and <Length> tags define each field.

```
<Schema>
  <Field>
    <Num>0</Num>
    <Name>FirstName</Name>
    <Type>6</Type>
    <Length>0</Length>
  </Field>
</Schema>
```

Recall from Table 8-4 that AppForge uses Num to uniquely identify this field. Name is the field's name, as it appears in the <Record></Record> tags of the XML string. Type is a number corresponding to one of the assignments F_TYPE_BOOL through F_TYPE_STR. Length corresponds to an AppForge field type declaration. We hardcode this tag to 0, which indicates a variable length field in AppForge.

The declaration and initialization for *ParseFields* is shown below.

```
Err ParseFields(Char* pszSchemaStart, Int16* npNumFields,
                MemHandle *phFieldElemArray)
{
    Err retVal = errNone;
    Boolean bContinue = true;
    Char *pszStart, *pszEnd;
    Int16 nIndex;
    MemHandle hFieldElemArray;
    DBSLibFieldElemTypePtr pFieldElemArray, pCurrFieldElem;
    Int16 nFieldElemTypeSize;
    UInt32 nFieldArraySize;

    Char szTemp[32];

    *npNumFields = 0;
    *phFieldElemArray = NULL;

    *(npNumFields) = CountItems(pszSchemaStart, "<Field>", "</Field>");

    if(*(npNumFields) < 1)
        return dbsLibErrParse;
```

We assume pszSchemaStart points to a string containing tag pairs. We initialize the function arguments and call *CountItems* to determine how many fields are in the schema. There must be at least one field or we return an error.

We create and initialize a field array element of the proper size.

```
nFieldElemTypeSize = sizeof(DBSLibFieldElemType);
nFieldArraySize = (*npNumFields)*nFieldElemTypeSize;

hFieldElemArray = MemHandleNew(nFieldArraySize);
if(hFieldElemArray == 0)
    return dbsLibErrMemory;

pFieldElemArray = (DBSLibFieldElemTypePtr)MemHandleLock(hFieldElemArray);

MemSet(pFieldElemArray, (*npNumFields)*sizeof(DBSLibFieldElemType), 0);
```

Now we loop over each tag pair.

```
pszStart = pszSchemaStart;
pCurrFieldElem = pFieldElemArray;
for(nIndex = 0; nIndex < *(npNumFields); nIndex++)
{
    pszStart = StrStr(pszStart, "<Field>"); //Find beginning field tag
    if(pszStart == NULL)
    {
        MemPtrFree(pFieldElemArray);
        return dbsLibErrParse;
    }

    pszStart += StrLen("<Field>");

    pszEnd = StrStr(pszStart, "</Field>"); //Find end field tag
    if(pszEnd == NULL)
    {
        MemPtrFree(pFieldElemArray);
        return dbsLibErrParse;
    }

//Extract the data between the <Num></Num> tag pair
    MemSet(szTemp, 32, 0);
    nResult = ExtractData(pszStart, "<Num>", "</Num>", 31, szTemp);
    if(nResult != errNone)
    {
        MemPtrFree(pFieldElemArray);
        return nResult;
    }
    pCurrFieldElem->nNum = StrAToI(szTemp);

//Extract the data between the <Name></Name> tag pair
    MemSet(pCurrFieldElem->szName, DB_NAME_LEN, 0);
    nResult = ExtractData(pszStart, "<Name>", "</Name>",
                          DB_NAME_LEN-1, pCurrFieldElem->szName);
    if(nResult != errNone)
```

```
   {
      MemPtrFree(pFieldElemArray);
      return nResult;
   }

//Extract the data between the <Type></Type> tag pair
   MemSet(szTemp, 32, 0);
   nResult = ExtractData(pszStart, "<Type>", "</Type>", 31, szTemp);
   if(nResult != errNone)
   {
      MemPtrFree(pFieldElemArray);
      return nResult;
   }
   pCurrFieldElem->nType = StrAToI(szTemp);

//Extract  the data between the <Length></Length> tag pair
   MemSet(szTemp, 32, 0);
   nResult = ExtractData(pszStart, "<Length>", "</Length>", 31, szTemp);
   if(nResult != errNone)
   {
      MemPtrFree(pFieldElemArray);
      return nResult;
   }
   pCurrFieldElem->nLength = StrAToI(szTemp);

   pCurrFieldElem++;
}
```

For each of these fields, we extract the data between the <Num></Num>, <Name></Name>, <Type></Type>, and <Length></Length> tag pairs, and store it in the corresponding field element. For each tag pair, we call *ExtractData*. If this function fails, we free the field element array and return. At the end of the loop, we move pCurrFieldElem to the next element in the array.

Before returning from *ParseFields*, we assign the handle pointer argument to the array and unlock it.

```
   (*phFieldElemArray) = hFieldElemArray;
   MemPtrUnlock(pFieldElemArray);
   return retVal;
}
```

ParseRecData

Given a field element array defining the set of fields for a record, *ParseRecData* loops through the array looking for each field in an XML string, extracts the field's data, and stores it in the corresponding array element. For the example record below, the field element array would contain elements defining the <FirstName>, <LastName>, and <Phone> tags for the record.

```
<Data>
  <Record>
    <FirstName>Bob H.</FirstName>
```

```
      <LastName>Smith</LastName>
      <Phone>(703) 555-1212</Phone>
   </Record>
</Data>
```

The data and length of each field are stored in the hData and nDataLen members in
the corresponding array element.

We accomplish this parsing with a for loop, as shown below:

```
Err ParseRecData(Char *pszStartDelim, MemHandle hFieldElemArray,
                 Int16 nNumFields, UInt32 *pnRecLen)
{
   DBSLibFieldElemTypePtr pFieldElemArray, pCurrFieldElem;
   Int16 nFieldIndex;
   Char *pszTemp;
   Char szBeginTag[64];
   Char szEndTag[64];
   Char szData[MAX_DATA_LEN];
   UInt16 nResult;

   pFieldElemArray = pCurrFieldElem = NULL;
   *pnRecLen = 0;

   pFieldElemArray = (DBSLibFieldElemTypePtr)MemHandleLock(hFieldElemArray);
   pCurrFieldElem = pFieldElemArray;
   for(nFieldIndex = 0; nFieldIndex < nNumFields; nFieldIndex++)
   {
      StrCopy(szBeginTag, "<");
      StrCat(szBeginTag, pCurrFieldElem->szName);
      StrCat(szBeginTag, ">");
      pszTemp = szBeginTag;
      pszTemp++;
      StrCopy(szEndTag, "</");
      StrCat(szEndTag, pszTemp);
      //Extract the data between the two tags
      MemSet(szData, MAX_DATA_LEN, 0);
      nResult = ExtractData(pszStartDelim, szBeginTag, szEndTag,
                            MAX_DATA_LEN-1, szData);
      if(nResult != errNone)
         return nResult;
```

At the beginning of the loop, we format the begin and end tags for the particular element of interest. We then extract the data between the tags with a call to
ExtractData.

Once we have the data, we determine its size, and store the result in the nDataLen
member of the array element.

```
   switch(pCurrFieldElem->nType)
   {
      case F_TYPE_STR:   //Char
         pCurrFieldElem->nDataLen = StrLen(szData) + 1;
```

```
            break;

        case F_TYPE_INT:    //Int16
            pCurrFieldElem->nDataLen = sizeof(Int16);
        break;

        case F_TYPE_LONG:   //Int32
            pCurrFieldElem->nDataLen = sizeof(Int32);
         break;

        default:
            return dbsLibErrParse;
         break;
    }

    *pnRecLen += pCurrFieldElem->nDataLen;
```

For our library, we only support F_TYPE_STR, F_TYPE_INT, and F_TYPE_LONG values. We keep a running total of the record's length in the pnRecLen argument.

Next, we create the memory for the tag's data and enter another switch statement to assign it.

```
pCurrFieldElem->hData = MemHandleNew(pCurrFieldElem->nDataLen);
if(pCurrFieldElem->hData == NULL)
    return dbsLibErrMemory;

switch(pCurrFieldElem->nType)
{
    case F_TYPE_STR:    //Char
    {
        Char* pData = (Char *)MemHandleLock(pCurrFieldElem->hData);
        if(pData == NULL)
            return dbsLibErrMemory;

        MemSet(pData, pCurrFieldElem->nDataLen, 0);
        StrCopy(pData, szData);
        MemPtrUnlock(pData);
    }
    break;

    case F_TYPE_INT:    //Int16
    {
        Int16* pData = (Int16 *)MemHandleLock(pCurrFieldElem->hData);
        if(pData == NULL)
            return dbsLibErrMemory;

        MemSet(pData, pCurrFieldElem->nDataLen, 0);
        *pData = StrAToI(szData);
        MemPtrUnlock(pData);
    }
}
```

```
        break;

    case F_TYPE_LONG:  //Int32
    {
        Int32* pData = (Int32 *)MemHandleLock(pCurrFieldElem->hData);
        if(pData == NULL)
            return dbsLibErrMemory;

        MemSet(pData, pCurrFieldElem->nDataLen, 0);
        *pData = StrAToI(szData);
        MemPtrUnlock(pData);

    }
    break;

    default:
        return dbsLibErrParse;
    break;
}
```

We use a second `switch` statement to increase code clarity, instead of combining this logic with the previous code. At the end of the loop, we move to the next element in the array. After exiting the loop, we unlock the field element array and return.

```
        pCurrFieldElem++;
    }

    MemPtrUnlock(pFieldElemArray);
    return errNone;
}
```

CreateSchema

To create our database's schema from the XML string, *CreateSchema* concatenates the Num, Type, and Len elements of each field into a string with the following format:

```
"Num1 Type1 Len1 Num2 Type2 Len2 ..."
```

Applications can then parse this string to determine how each record in the database is formatted. We will see how this schema can by used by an AppForge application later in this chapter.

CreateSchema uses a `for` loop to iterate through each item in the field element array.

```
Err CreateSchema(MemHandle hFieldElemArray, Int16 nNumElements, Char *pszSchema)
{
    DBSLibFieldElemTypePtr pFieldElemArray, pCurrFieldElem;
    Int16 nFieldIndex;
    Char szTemp[16];
    Int16 nSchemaLen;

    pFieldElemArray = (DBSLibFieldElemTypePtr)MemHandleLock(hFieldElemArray);
    pCurrFieldElem = pFieldElemArray;
    nSchemaLen = 0;
```

```
    for(nFieldIndex = 0; nFieldIndex < nNumElements; nFieldIndex++)
    {
        StrPrintF(szTemp, "%ld %d %ld ",
                        pCurrFieldElem->nNum,
                        pCurrFieldElem->nType,
                        pCurrFieldElem->nLength);
        nSchemaLen += StrLen(szTemp);
        if(nSchemaLen > DB_SCHEMA_LEN)
        {
            MemPtrUnlock(pFieldElemArray);
            return dbsLibErrParse;
        }
        StrCat(pszSchema, szTemp);
        pCurrFieldElem++;
    }

    return errNone;
}
```

We form the schema string by appending each element's Num, Type, and Len members to the pszSchema argument.

FreeFieldElemArrayData and FreeFieldElemArray

These helper functions assist with freeing the memory associated with the field element array. *FreeFieldElemArrayData* frees the data associated with each element in the field element array.

```
void FreeFieldElemArrayData(MemHandle hFieldElemArray, Int16 nNumElements)
{
    DBSLibFieldElemTypePtr pFieldElemArray, pCurrFieldElem;
    Int16 nIndex;
    pFieldElemArray = (DBSLibFieldElemTypePtr)MemHandleLock(hFieldElemArray);
    pCurrFieldElem = pFieldElemArray;
    for (nIndex = 0; nIndex < nNumElements; nIndex++)
    {
        if(pCurrFieldElem->hData != NULL)
            MemHandleFree(pCurrFieldElem->hData);
        pCurrFieldElem->hData = NULL;
        pCurrFieldElem++;
    }
     MemPtrUnlock(pFieldElemArray);
}
```

We loop through the field element array, calling *MemHandleFree* to free each element's hData member.

FreeFieldElemArray calls *FreeFieldElemArrayData* before freeing the array itself.

```
void FreeFieldElemArray(MemHandle hFieldElemArray, Int16 nNumElements)
{
    FreeFieldElemArrayData(hFieldElemArray, nNumElements);
    MemHandleFree(hFieldElemArray);
}
```

CountItems

This function parses a string, counting the number of XML tag pairs in the string.

```
Int16 CountItems(Char *pszStartDelim, Char* pszBeginTag, Char *pszEndTag)
{
   Char *pszStart = pszStartDelim, *pszEnd;
   Int16 nCount = 0;
   Boolean bContinue = true;

   while(bContinue == true)
   {
      pszStart = StrStr(pszStart, pszBeginTag);   //Find the begin tag
      if(pszStart != NULL)                         //Find the end tag
         pszEnd = StrStr(pszStart, pszEndTag);
      if(pszStart == NULL || pszEnd == NULL)  //Assume no more tag pairs
         bContinue = false;
      else
      {
         pszStart += StrLen(pszBeginTag);   //Skip past the begin tag
         nCount++;                          //Increment the count
      }
   }
   return nCount;
}
```

We continue searching the string for tag pairs in a while loop until there are no more.

ExtractData

As its name implies, *ExtractData* extracts characters in a string between a start and end delimiter.

```
Err ExtractData(Char *pszString, Char *pszStartDelim, Char* pszEndDelim,
                Int16 nMaxLen, Char *pszResult)
{
   Char *pszStart, *pszEnd;
   Int16 nIndex;

   pszStart = StrStr(pszString, pszStartDelim);   //find beginning delimiter
   if(pszStart == NULL)
      return dbsLibErrParse;
   pszStart += StrLen(pszStartDelim);   //increment past start delim
   pszEnd = StrStr(pszStart, pszEndDelim);
   if(pszEnd == NULL)
      return dbsLibErrParse;

   nIndex = 0;
   while(StrNCompare(pszStart, pszEndDelim, StrLen(pszEndDelim)) != 0)
   {
      pszResult[nIndex] = *pszStart;
      nIndex++;
```

```
        pszStart++;

        if(nIndex > nMaxLen)
            return dbsLibErrParse;
    }
    return errNone;
}
```

We verify the existence of the start and end delimiters. Next, we step through the string in a while loop, extracting characters until we reach the end delimiter or exceed the maximum length.

We have now discussed global and client memory management techniques and the functions that the DBSLib library implements. We have all of the pieces in place for our library except for one crucial element—the dispatch table.

Dispatch Table

A dispatch table is a lookup table that the Palm OS uses to find a library's public functions. Without it, a shared library will not function. Here is a brief overview of the dispatch table for our library.

 We use the dispatch table from the SampleLib project that comes with the Palm OS SDK as a template. The SampleLib code contains additional detailed comments.

Traps and custom function declarations

The Palm OS uses *system traps* to determine which custom functions in our library to call. Each trap is an index into our library's dispatch table. We declare traps for each custom function using the following defines.

```
#define dbsLibTrapAPIVersion sysLibTrapCustom
#define dbsLibTrapParseSchema dbsLibTrapAPIVersion + 1
#define dbsLibTrapGetSchema dbsLibTrapAPIVersion + 2
#define dbsLibTrapLast dbsLibTrapAPIVersion + 3
```

The OS has already defined traps for the required functions: *Open*, *Close*, and *Wake*. We initialize our first custom trap—dbsLibTrapAPIVersion—to sysLibTrapCustom, the first trap immediately following the required traps.

Next, we modify the library's custom function declarations to reference these traps. We add the OS SDK-defined SYS_TRAP macro to each declaration.

```
extern Err DBSLibOpen(UInt16 refNum, UInt32 * clientContextPtr)
            SYS_TRAP(sysLibTrapOpen);

extern Err DBSLibClose(UInt16 refNum, UInt32 clientContext)
            SYS_TRAP(sysLibTrapClose);
```

```
extern Err DBSLibSleep(UInt16 refNum)
            SYS_TRAP(sysLibTrapSleep);

extern Err DBSLibWake(UInt16 refNum)
            SYS_TRAP(sysLibTrapWake);

extern Err DBSLibGetAPIVersion(UInt16 refNum, UInt32 *pVer)
            SYS_TRAP(dbsLibTrapAPIVersion);

extern Err DBSLibParseSchema(UInt16 refNum, UInt32 clientContext,
                    Char* pszXMLSchema, Boolean bDeleteDB)
            SYS_TRAP(dbsLibTrapParseSchema);

extern Err DBSLibGetDBInfo(UInt16 refNum, UInt32 clientContext,
                    Char* pszName, Int16 *pnNumRecs,
                    Int16 *pnNumFields, Char* pszSchema)
            SYS_TRAP(dbsLibTrapGetSchema);
```

The SYS_TRAP macro takes each function's trap number as its argument and produces assembly language that results in the proper function getting called.

Dispatch table implementation

The implementation file for our dispatch table starts with the following declarations. Precompiled headers are turned off, and __PALMOS_TRAPS__ is set to zero. Then we include *PalmOS.h* and our library's header files.

```
#ifndef PILOT_PRECOMPILED_HEADERS_OFF
#define PILOT_PRECOMPILED_HEADERS_OFF
#endif

#if __PALMOS_TRAPS__
  #define EMULATION_LEVEL EMULATION_NONE // building Pilot executable
#endif

#undef __PALMOS_TRAPS__
#define __PALMOS_TRAPS__ 0
#define USE_TRAPS 0

#include <PalmOS.h>
#include "DBSLib.h"     //our library's custom declarations
#include "DBSLibMem.h"  //our library's memory management functions
```

Next are the declarations for our library's installation entry point and dispatch table. We omit the implementation of *DBSLibInstall* for brevity; we discuss this function in the next section.

```
#define DBSLibInstall __Startup__

Err DBSLibInstall(UInt16 refNum, SysLibTblEntryPtr entryP); //entry point
static MemPtr   asm DBSLibDispatchTable(void);              //dispatch table
```

```
Err DBSLibInstall(UInt16 refNum, SysLibTblEntryPtr entryP)
{
    ...detail omitted for brevity...
}
```

The actual dispatch table is implemented as a function—*DBSLibDispatchTable*—with inline assembly language. *DBSLibDispatchTable* uses the following definitions.

```
#define prvJmpSize        4
#define libDispatchEntry(index)        (kOffset+((index)*prvJmpSize))
#define numFunctions    8    //number of functions (0-based index)
#define    kOffset    (2*numFunctions)
```

numFunctions is the most important parameter from a developer's perspective. This parameter is set to the number of custom functions in the library plus one for the library's name.

Here is the declaration and initialization for *DBSLibDispatchTable*.

```
static MemPtr    asm DBSLibDispatchTable(void)
{
    LEA        @Table, A0    // table ptr
    RTS

@Table:
    DC.W        @Name  //Offset to library name
```

Next come the library's trap dispatch entries.

```
// Standard traps
DC.W        libDispatchEntry(0)    // Open
DC.W        libDispatchEntry(1)    // Close
DC.W        libDispatchEntry(2)    // Sleep
DC.W        libDispatchEntry(3)    // Wake

// Start of the Custom traps
DC.W        libDispatchEntry(4)    //GetAPIVersion
DC.W        libDispatchEntry(5)    //ParseSchema
DC.W        libDispatchEntry(6)    //GetDBInfo
```

Each entry makes use of the previously defined libDispatchEntry macro, which takes an index as its argument. This index must be numbered sequentially, starting with zero.

You will need to modify this list of traps to reflect the functions in your shared library. Remember, the first four traps are mandatory!

Next come the jump statements to each of the library's functions.

```
// Standard library function handlers
@GotoOpen:
    JMP        DBSLibOpen
@GotoClose:
    JMP        DBSLibClose
```

```
@GotoSleep:
    JMP         DBSLibSleep
@GotoWake:
    JMP         DBSLibWake

// Custom library function handlers
@GotoGetAPIVersion:
    JMP         DBSLibGetAPIVersion
@GotoParseSchema:
    JMP         DBSLibParseSchema
@GotoGetDBInfo:
    JMP         DBSLibGetDBInfo
```

Note that the @GoTo labels do not have to match the function's name. To add jump statements for your library, modify and/or add entries to this list. Be careful to make sure that the order of jumps and trap dispatch entries are identical.

The last entry before leaving the function is for the library's name. You must end your dispatch table with this entry.

```
@Name:
    DC.B        dbsLibName
}
```

We set the name to dbsLibName, which was previously defined as follows.

```
#define dbsLibName      "DBSLib.lib"
```

Applications use dbsLibName in a call to *SysLibFind* to see if the DBSLib library is loaded.

Dispatch table assignment

The first time a shared library is loaded, the Palm OS calls the mandatory __Startup__ function. Here is DBSLib's startup function, which we have seen before.

```
#define DBSLibInstall __Startup__
Err DBSLibInstall(UInt16 refNum, SysLibTblEntryPtr entryP)
{
    entryP->dispatchTblP = (MemPtr*)DBSLibDispatchTable();
    entryP->globalsP = NULL;
    return errNone;
}
```

We initialize the dispatch table pointer to our custom trap table with a call to *DBSLibDispatchTable*. As a result, the OS can now call our library functions through this pointer.

DBSLib Driver Application

In this section, we show how to use the shared library from a conventional Palm application. We assume you are familiar with developing C/C++ Palm applications using CodeWarrior, so we focus on the code used to access the shared library.

Our driver application is called *DBSLibFuser*, because we expect to eventually turn it into an AppForge fuser. The main screen for our driver is shown in Figure 8-1.

Figure 8-1. DBSLib driver application

The main screen consists of three buttons that make calls into the DBSLib shared library. GetAPI retrieves the API version of our library by calling *DBSLibGetAPIVersion*. CreateDB calls *DBSLibParseSchema* with a hardcoded XML string to create a fictitious Employee database. GetDBInfo calls *DBSLibGetDBInfo* to retrieve metadata for the newly created Employee database.

An application using a shared library performs five basic operations, as shown in Table 8-5.

Table 8-5. Library operations

Operation	Description
Load	Finds and loads the library.
Open	Opens the library for use. This step is required before calling the library's functions.
Use	Makes calls into the library.
Close	Closes the library when done.
Unload	Unloads the library if you are the only one using it.

Load and Open

We use the following structure to track information about the shared library we are loading.

```
typedef struct ShLibInfoType
{
   UInt16 nLibRefNum;
   Boolean bLibWasPreloaded;
   UInt32 nClientContext;
} ShLibInfoType;
typedef ShLibInfoType *ShLibInfoTypePtr;

static MemHandle g_hShLibInfo;
```

We do this to provide a convenient way to access and release library functions and resources. We also declare g_hSlLibInfo as a global MemHandle so we can access the ShLibInfoType structure throughout our program. Table 8-6 describes each item of this structure.

Table 8-6. ShLibInfoType items

Item	Description
nLibRefNum	Reference number for the shared library we have loaded
bLibWasPreloaded	true if library was loaded by another application; false if not
nClientContext	Client context for our memory in the shared library

Here is the function for loading the shared library.

```
Err LoadShLib(Char *pszLibName, UInt32 nDBType, UInt32 nDBCreator, MemHandle
*phShLibInfo)
{
    Err retVal;

    MemHandle hShLibInfo;
    ShLibInfoTypePtr pShLibInfo;

    hShLibInfo = MemHandleNew(sizeof(ShLibInfoType));
    if(hShLibInfo == NULL)
        return dbsLibFuserErrMemory;

    pShLibInfo = (ShLibInfoTypePtr)MemHandleLock(hShLibInfo);
    retVal = SysLibFind(pszLibName, &(pShLibInfo->nLibRefNum));

    if(retVal == errNone)
        pShLibInfo->bLibWasPreloaded = true;
    else
    {
        pShLibInfo->bLibWasPreloaded = false;
        retVal = SysLibLoad(nDBType, nDBCreator, &(pShLibInfo->nLibRefNum));
    }
```

We create memory for a ShLibInfoType structure and lock it for modification. Then we call *SysLibFind* to see if another application has loaded the library. If the library has not been loaded, we call *SysLibLoad*, which loads the library and returns a reference to it. In either case, we set the bLibWasPreloaded member of the ShLibInfoType structure accordingly.

Next, we store the handle to the ShLibInfoType structure in the pShLibInfo argument, unlock the structure, and return.

```
    *phShLibInfo = hShLibInfo;

    MemPtrUnlock(pShLibInfo);
    return retVal;
}
```

We call *LoadShLib* to load and open the DBSLib shared library in our application's *AppStart* function:

```
retVal = LoadShLib(dbsLibName, dbsLibTypeID, dbsLibCreatorID,
                   &g_hShLibInfo);

if(retVal != errNone)
    return retVal;

pShLibInfo = (ShLibInfoTypePtr)MemHandleLock(g_hShLibInfo);

retVal = DBSLibOpen(pShLibInfo->nLibRefNum, &(pShLibInfo->nClientContext));
MemPtrUnlock(pShLibInfo);
```

Use

Let's see how to use the functions provided by DBSLib. Like most conventional Palm applications, events from the main form are handled in the application's *MainFormHandleEvent* function.

Here is the event handler for clicking the GetAPI button.

```
case MainGetAPIButton:
{
    Err retVal;
    Char szTemp[256];
    UInt32 nVersion;
    ShLibInfoTypePtr pShLibInfo;

    pShLibInfo = (ShLibInfoTypePtr)MemHandleLock(g_hShLibInfo);
    retVal = DBSLibGetAPIVersion(pShLibInfo->nLibRefNum, &nVersion);
    MemPtrUnlock(pShLibInfo);

    if(retVal == errNone)
    {
        StrPrintF(szTemp, "Lib version = %d.%d",
                         sysGetROMVerMajor(nVersion),
                          sysGetROMVerMinor(nVersion));
    }
    else
        StrCopy(szTemp, "Call to GetDBAPIVersion failed!");

    FrmCustomAlert(InfoAlert, szTemp, "", "");
}
break;
```

After calling *DBSLibGetAPIVersion*, we use the sysGetROMVerMajor and sysGetROMVerMinor macros to format the result. We display the library version using a custom alert dialog, as shown in Figure 8-2.

Figure 8-2. Library version alert dialog

Here is the event handler for clicking the CreateDB button.

```
case MainCreateDBButton:
{
   Err retVal;
   Char* pszXML = XML_STRING;
   ShLibInfoTypePtr pShLibInfo;

   pShLibInfo = (ShLibInfoTypePtr)MemHandleLock(g_hShLibInfo);
   retVal = DBSLibParseSchema(pShLibInfo->nLibRefNum,
                              pShLibInfo->nClientContext, pszXML, true);
   MemPtrUnlock(pShLibInfo);

   if(retVal == errNone)
      FrmCustomAlert(InfoAlert, "DBSLibParseSchema succeeded.", "", "");
   else
      FrmCustomAlert(InfoAlert, "DBSLibParseSchema failed.", "", "");

   handled = true;
}
break;
```

We call *DBSLibParseSchema*, and report success or failure accordingly, as shown in Figure 8-3.

Figure 8-3. Successful parse dialog

XML_STRING is a sample string representing a fictitious Employee database.

```
#define XML_STRING "<Database Name=Employee Type=DATA Creator=AFLD>" \
                      "<Schema>" \
                        "<Field>" \
                          "<Num>0</Num>" \
                          "<Name>FirstName</Name>" \
                          "<Type>6</Type>" \
                          "<Length>0</Length>" \
                        "</Field>" \

                        ... detail omitted for brevity ...

                        "<Record>" \
                          "<FirstName>Jane</FirstName>" \
                          "<LastName>Williams</LastName>" \
                          "<Phone>(703) 222-5151</Phone>" \
                          "<Email>janew@company.com</Email>" \
                          "<ID>23</ID>" \
                        "</Record>" \
                      "</Data>" \
                    "</Database>"
```

Here is the event handler for clicking the GetDBInfo button.

```
case MainGetDBInfoButton:
{
    Char szDBName[DB_NAME_LEN];
    Char szSchema[DB_SCHEMA_LEN];
    Int16 nNumRecords;
    Int16 nNumFields;
    Err retVal;
    ShLibInfoTypePtr pShLibInfo;

    pShLibInfo = (ShLibInfoTypePtr)MemHandleLock(g_hShLibInfo);
    retVal = DBSLibGetDBInfo(pShLibInfo->nLibRefNum, pShLibInfo->nClientContext,
                        szDBName, &nNumRecords, &nNumFields, szSchema);
    MemPtrUnlock(pShLibInfo);
    {
        char szResult[128];
        char szTemp[128];

        if(retVal == errNone)
        {
            StrPrintF(szTemp, "Num recs = %d\n", nNumRecords);
            StrCopy(szResult, szTemp);
            StrPrintF(szTemp, "Num fields = %d\n", nNumFields);
            StrCat(szResult, szTemp);
            StrPrintF(szTemp, "Schema = %s\n", szSchema);
            StrCat(szResult, szTemp);
        }
        else
            StrCopy(szResult, "DBSLibGetDBInfo failed.");

        FrmCustomAlert(InfoAlert, szResult, "", "");
```

```
    }
  }
  break;
```

After calling *DBSLibGetDBInfo*, we format and display the results using a custom
alert dialog, as shown in Figure 8-4.

Figure 8-4. Database info dialog

Close and Unload

We close the DBSLib shared library and unload it in our application's *AppStop* function as follows:

```
pShLibInfo = (ShLibInfoTypePtr)MemHandleLock(g_hShLibInfo);
DBSLibClose(pShLibInfo->nLibRefNum, pShLibInfo->nClientContext);
MemPtrUnlock(pShLibInfo);

UnloadShLib(g_hShLibInfo);
```

After closing the library with a call to *DBSLibClose*, we call *UnloadShLib*, an internal
function, to unload it. *UnloadShLib* handles the chore of releasing the library.

```
Err UnloadShLib(MemHandle hShLibInfo)
{
   Err retVal = errNone;
   ShLibInfoTypePtr pShLibInfo;

   pShLibInfo = (ShLibInfoTypePtr)MemHandleLock(hShLibInfo);
   if(pShLibInfo->bLibWasPreloaded == false &&
                 pShLibInfo->nLibRefNum != sysInvalidRefNum)
   {
      retVal = SysLibRemove(pShLibInfo->nLibRefNum);
      ErrFatalDisplayIf(retVal != errNone,
                    "DBSLibDriver: Error uninstalling DBSLib.");
      pShLibInfo->nLibRefNum = sysInvalidRefNum;
```

```
        }
    MemPtrFree(pShLibInfo);
    return retVal;
}
```

We verify that the library was not already loaded by another application and that the reference number is valid. If we are the last client using the library, we call *SysLibRemove* to unload the library.

DBSLib Fuser

In this section, we modify the DBSLib driver application and create an AppForge fuser. This allows an AppForge VB application to access the shared library.

To convert the driver application to a fuser, you need to change its database type to FUSR. You must also set the structure alignment to 68K 4-byte in the 68K Processor panel of the project's settings. Make sure to recompile the project after making these changes.

Data Types

For use as a fuser, we define the following launch codes.

```
#define dbsFuserAppLaunchGetAPI    32767
#define dbsFuserAppLaunchCreateDB  32768
```

The dbsFuserAppLaunchGetAPI launch code corresponds to *DBSLibGetAPI*. To marshal data for this launch code, we use the following structure.

```
typedef struct DBSLibAPIStruct
{
  Int16  nMajor;      /* OUT */
  Int16  nMinor;      /* OUT */
  UInt32 nResult;     /* OUT */
} DBSLibAPIStruct;
```

We receive the IN items from the AppForge application and we pass the OUT items back to it. Here we only have OUT items. nMajor and nMinor are the major and minor numbers, respectively, of our library's version. nResult is the result of processing this launch code. 0 means success, 1 means failure.

We then combine *CreateDatabase* and *GetDBInfo* into one launch code— dbsFuserAppLaunchCreateDB. Since a fuser's global data is not generally available while processing a launch code, we must open and close the library each time.* This makes it difficult to maintain state between launch codes. Thus, we combine these two functions into one launch code.

We use the following structure to marshal data from the dbsFuserAppLaunchCreateDB launch code:

```
typedef struct CreateDBStruct
{
    UInt32 XMLString;    /* IN  */
    Boolean bDeleteDB;   /* IN  */
    UInt32 dbName;       /* OUT */
    Int16 nNumRecords;   /* OUT */
    Int16 nNumFields;    /* OUT */
    UInt32 Schema;       /* OUT */
    UInt32 nResult;      /* OUT */
} CreateDBStruct;
```

Table 8-7 describes each item.

Table 8-7. CreateDBStruct items

Item	Direction	Description
XMLString	IN	XML string containing database schema and records.
bDeleteDB	IN	If true, delete any existing database processing. If false, do not delete the database before processing.
dbName	OUT	Name of database.
nNumRecords	OUT	Number of records added to the database from the XML string.
nNumFields	OUT	Number of fields per database record.
Schema	OUT	String containing schema in a format suitable for parsing.
nResult	OUT	Result of processing launch code. 0 means success, 1 means failure.

Implementation

Our fuser responds to launch codes in *StarterPalmMain*. Here is the event handler for the dbsFuserAppLaunchGetAPI launch code.

```
case dbsFuserAppLaunchGetAPI:
{
    MemHandle hShLibInfo;
    UInt32 nVersion;
    ShLibInfoTypePtr pShLibInfo;

    errVal = LoadShLib(dbsLibName, dbsLibTypeID, dbsLibCreatorID, &hShLibInfo);

    if(errVal == errNone)
```

---

* Using a database or feature memory—memory that persists between application invocations—are two ways around this hurdle. We do not discuss either approach in this chapter.

```
    {
        pShLibInfo = (ShLibInfoTypePtr)MemHandleLock(hShLibInfo);
        errVal = DBSLibGetAPIVersion(pShLibInfo->nLibRefNum, &nVersion);
        MemPtrUnlock(pShLibInfo);

        if(errVal == errNone)
        {
          ((DBSLibAPIStruct *)cmdPBP)->nMajor = sysGetROMVerMajor(nVersion);
          ((DBSLibAPIStruct *)cmdPBP)->nMinor = sysGetROMVerMinor(nVersion);

          ((DBSLibAPIStruct *)cmdPBP)->nResult = 0;

        }
        else
          ((DBSLibAPIStruct *)cmdPBP)->nResult = 1;   //GetAPIVersion failed

        UnloadShLib(hShLibInfo);

    }
    else
        ((DBSLibAPIStruct *)cmdPBP)->nResult = 1;   //LoadShLib failed

    errVal = errNone; //Reset the error - afPalmOS.CallApp succeeded
}
break;
```

Once we load the shared library, we call to *DBSLibGetAPIVersion*, and store the results in the corresponding parameters of the cmdPBP argument.

It may seem unusual to assign a result of 0 or 1 to nResult, and to reset errVal to errNone. This is because errVal is returned to AppForge as a result of the *afPalmOS.CallApp* method, and nResult is the return value specific to the request being made—dbsFuserAppLaunch, in this case. We reset errVal to errNone to indicate the *afPalmOS.CallApp* method succeeded.

Upon successful return, the AppForge application examines the nResult value to determine if the specific dbsFuserAppLaunch call succeeded.

Here is the event handler for the dbsFuserAppLaunchCreateDB launch code.

```
case dbsFuserAppLaunchCreateDB:
{
  MemHandle hXMLString;
  Boolean bDeleteDB;
  MemHandle hdbName;
  Int16 nNumRecords;
  Int16 nNumFields;
  MemHandle hSchema;

  MemHandle hShLibInfo;
  ShLibInfoTypePtr pShLibInfo;
  Char *pXMLString;
  Char *pdbName;
```

```
Char *pSchema;
Char szDBName[DB_NAME_LEN];
Char szSchema[DB_SCHEMA_LEN];

errVal = LoadShLib(dbsLibName, dbsLibTypeID, dbsLibCreatorID, &hShLibInfo);

if(errVal == errNone)
{
  pShLibInfo = (ShLibInfoTypePtr)MemHandleLock(hShLibInfo);

  //Open the library
  errVal = DBSLibOpen(pShLibInfo->nLibRefNum, &(pShLibInfo->nClientContext));

  if(errVal == errNone)
  {
    hXMLString = NULL;
    hXMLString = AFStringToMemHandle(((CreateDBStruct *)cmdPBP)->XMLString);

    if(hXMLString != NULL)
      pXMLString = (Char *)MemHandleLock(hXMLString);

    bDeleteDB = ((CreateDBStruct *)cmdPBP)->bDeleteDB;

    if(bDeleteDB)
      bDeleteDB = true;
    else
      bDeleteDB = false;
```

After declaring several variables, we load and open DBSLib. We check and reassign the value of bDeleteDB to ensure that it is uniquely true (decimal 1 or 0x01) or false (decimal 0 or 0x00). In Visual Basic, a Boolean True is stored as −1, and False is stored as 0. Since a Boolean in the Palm OS is a typedef for an unsigned char, −1 gets marshaled as decimal 255, or 0xFF, and 0 gets marshaled as decimal 0, or 0x00. Our test ensures that bDeleteDB is properly initialized to true or false.

Next, we call *DBSLibParseSchema*. If this call succeeds, we call *DBSLibGetDBInfo*.

```
    errVal = DBSLibParseSchema(pShLibInfo->nLibRefNum,
                               pShLibInfo->nClientContext,
                               pXMLString, bDeleteDB);

  MemPtrUnlock(pXMLString);

if(errVal == errNone)
    errVal = DBSLibGetDBInfo(pShLibInfo->nLibRefNum,
                             pShLibInfo->nClientContext,
                             szDBName, &nNumRecords,
                             &nNumFields, szSchema);
```

We are ready to assign the corresponding *OUT* parameters for the AppForge application. First, we assign the database name and schema string parameters.

```
if(errVal == errNone)
    {
        // --- Assign the database name ---
        //Remove old string
        hdbName = AFStringToMemHandle((((CreateDBStruct *)cmdPBP)->dbName);
        if(hdbName != NULL)
            MemHandleFree(hdbName);

        hdbName = MemHandleNew(DB_NAME_LEN);
        pdbName = MemHandleLock(hdbName);
        StrCopy(pdbName, szDBName);

        //Assign new string
        errVal = MemHandleToAFString(hdbName,
                            &(((CreateDBStruct *)cmdPBP)->dbName));
        MemPtrUnlock(pdbName);


        // --- Assign the database schema ---
        //Remove old string
        hSchema = AFStringToMemHandle((((CreateDBStruct *)cmdPBP)->Schema);
        if(hSchema != NULL)
            MemHandleFree(hSchema);

        hSchema = MemHandleNew(DB_SCHEMA_LEN);
        pSchema = MemHandleLock(hSchema);
        StrCopy(pSchema, szSchema);

        //Assign new string
        errVal = MemHandleToAFString(hSchema,
                            &(((CreateDBStruct *)cmdPBP)->Schema));
        MemPtrUnlock(pSchema);
```

We call *AFStringToMemHandle* to obtain the strings passed in from VB, and to free them if they are allocated. This ensures the VB strings have the proper length when the fuser returns control to the AppForge application. Next, we allocate memory for each string, and store the result in the corresponding VB string with a call to *MemHandleToAFString*.

Next, we assign the number of records and fields. Finally, we update the result to indicate success or failure, and close the library.

```
        // --- Assign the number of records ---
        ((CreateDBStruct *)cmdPBP)->nNumRecords = nNumRecords;


        // --- Assign the number of fields ---
        ((CreateDBStruct *)cmdPBP)->nNumFields = nNumFields;
```

```
            //DBSLibParseSchema & DBSLibDBGetInfo succeeded
            ((CreateDBStruct *)cmdPBP)->nResult = 0;

          }
          else
          {
            ((CreateDBStruct *)cmdPBP)->nResult = 1; //DBSLibParseSchema or
                                                     //DBSLibDBGetInfo failed
          }

          // Close the library
          DBSLibClose(pShLibInfo->nLibRefNum, pShLibInfo->nClientContext);
```

We close with a series of else clauses that indicate failure of the library load or open calls.

```
          }
          else
            ((CreateDBStruct *)cmdPBP)->nResult = 1;  //DBSLibOpen failed

          MemPtrUnlock(pShLibInfo);
          UnloadShLib(hShLibInfo);
        }
        else
         ((CreateDBStruct *)cmdPBP)->nResult = 1;  //LoadShLib failed

        //Reset the error - afPalmOS.CallApp succeeded
        errVal = errNone;
      }
      break;
```

AppForge Driver Application

In this section, we show you how to integrate the DBSLibFuser into a simple App-Forge application to create a database and to populate a grid view control with the results. This application is similar to our driver application.

The main screen for the AppForge *AFLibDriver* application is shown in Figure 8-5, and appears similar to the *DBSLib* driver application.

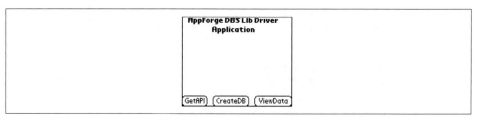

Figure 8-5. AFLibDriver application

The main screen consists of three buttons. GetAPI retrieves the API version of the library by passing the dbsFuserAppLaunchGetAPI launch code to our fuser. CreateDB creates the database and retrieves its metadata (name, number of records, schema, etc.) by passing the dbsFuserAppLaunchCreateDB launch code. ViewData does not use the fuser at all. When this button is clicked, we format an AppForge schema for the database, retrieve the records from the database, and display them in a grid view control, as shown in Figure 8-6.

Figure 8-6. AFLibDriver grid view

Fuser Data Types

In order to call into the fuser, we use the following commands, or launch codes.

```
Public Const cmdGetAPI As Long    = 32767
Public Const cmdCreateDB As Long = 32768
```

We use the following type for marshaling data with the *cmdCreateDB* command. Each item corresponds to those listed in Table 8-7. We pass the OUT items down to the fuser, and receive the IN items from it.

```
Public Type CreateDBStruct
    XMLString As String      ' OUT
    bDeleteDB As Boolean     ' OUT
    dbName As String         ' IN
    nNumRecords As Integer   ' IN
    nNumFields As Integer    ' IN
    Schema As String         ' IN
    nResult As Long          ' IN
End Type
```

For the *cmdGetAPI* command, we use the following type.

```
Public Type LibAPIStruct
    nMajor As Integer   ' OUT
    nMinor As Integer   ' OUT
    nResult As Long     ' OUT
End Type
```

All of these OUT parameters will contain values supplied by the fuser. nMajor and nMajor are the major and minor numbers, respectively, of the shared library's version. nResult serves the same purpose as it does for the CreateDBStruct type.

We declare the following two instances of these types, which are passed to the fuser via the *afPalmOS.CallApp* method.

```
Public g_DBAPIStruct As LibAPIStruct
Public g_DBStruct As CreateDBStruct
```

Database Types

The following global constants correspond to a field's <Num></Num> tag pair in the XML string.

```
Global Const LNG_EMP_FIRSTNAME As Long = 0
Global Const LNG_EMP_LASTNAME  As Long = 1
Global Const LNG_EMP_PHONE     As Long = 2
Global Const LNG_EMP_EMAIL     As Long = 3
Global Const LNG_EMP_ID        As Long = 4
```

AppForge uses these numbers to distinguish one field from another when defining a database schema. We discussed AppForge database schemas in Chapter 3. One plus to this approach is that if we want to add an additional field to our schema, we can increment this number and add the new field without impacting existing applications. As long as the original field numbers do not change, older applications will still work properly.

The next set of global constants correspond to a field's <Type></Type> tag pair in the XML string.

```
Global Const DBS_TYPE_BOOL  As Long = 0
Global Const DBS_TYPE_BYTE  As Long = 1
Global Const DBS_TYPE_DATE  As Long = 2
Global Const DBS_TYPE_FLOAT As Long = 3
Global Const DBS_TYPE_INT   As Long = 4
Global Const DBS_TYPE_LONG  As Long = 5
Global Const DBS_TYPE_STR   As Long = 6
```

The last declarations are for two variables.

```
Public g_lDB As Long
Public g_bDBCreated As Boolean
```

g_lDB is a handle to a database, and is used when we populate the grid view with the database's records. g_bDBCreated is used to track the database creation status. If this variable is True, the database was created successfully. If it is False, database creation failed.

Implementation

Now, let's take a look at the code behind each button of our application.

GetAPI

Here is the event handler for clicking the GetAPI button.

```
Private Sub btnGetAPI_Click()

    If afPalmOS.CallApp("DBSLibFuser", cmdGetAPI,
                        VarPtr(g_DBAPIStruct)) = False Then
        MsgBox "Call to DBSLibFuser failed.", vbOKOnly
    Else
        If g_DBStruct.nResult = 1 Then
            MsgBox "Could not get API version."
        Else
            MsgBox "API version = " + CStr(g_DBAPIStruct.nMajor) + "." + _
                CStr(g_DBAPIStruct.nMinor)
        End If
    End If
End Sub
```

We call *afPalmOS.CallApp* with g_DBAPIStruct as the argument to *VarPtr*. If this call succeeds, the fuser has populated the nMajor and nMinor OUT parameters. We extract them and display the results.

CreateDB

Here is the event handler for clicking the CreateDB button.

```
Private Sub btnCreateDB_Click()
    Dim bResult As Boolean

    g_bDBCreated = False
    g_DBStruct.bDeleteDB = True
    g_DBStruct.XMLString = ... detail omitted for brevity ...

    bResult = afPalmOS.CallApp("DBSLibFuser", cmdCreateDB, VarPtr(g_DBStruct))

    If bResult = False Then
        MsgBox "Call to DBSLibFuser failed."
    Else
        If g_DBStruct.nResult = 0 Then
            MsgBox "Create DB succeeded."
            g_bDBCreated = True
        Else
            MsgBox "Create DB failed."
        End If
    End If

End Sub
```

We initialize the global variable g_bDBCreated as False. Next, we initialize the bDeleteDB and XMLString OUT parameters of g_DBStruct. We indicate that we want the database to be deleted before records are added. The XMLString contains information for a fictitious employee database. We have omitted the details for brevity's sake.

If the call to *afPalmOS.CallApp* succeeds, we then examine the nResult member of g_DBStruct to determine if the *cmdCreateDB* command succeeded. If the database has been created, we update g_DBCreated accordingly. The fuser has also populated the dbName, nNumRecords, nNumFields, and Schema OUT parameters.

ViewData

Here is the event handler for clicking the ViewData button.

```
Private Sub btnViewData_Click()

    If g_bDBCreated = False Then
        MsgBox "Must create the database first."
        Exit Sub
    End If

    'load the data into the data view's grid that
    Call frmViewData.LoadData
    'hide this form and show the category form
    frmMain.Hide
    frmViewData.Show

End Sub
```

After verifying that the database has been created, we call *LoadData* to populate and display the grid view with employee data.

```
Public Sub LoadData()
    Dim nFieldNum As Long
    Dim nFieldType As Long
    Dim nFieldLen As Long

    Dim nFieldDefIndex As Integer
    Dim sFieldDef As String
    Dim lFieldDefOffset As Long
    Dim lFieldDefLen As Long
    Dim afFieldType As tFieldTypes
    lFieldDefLen = 6

    Dim strLastName As String
    Dim strFirstName As String
    Dim strPhone As String
    Dim strEmail As String
    Dim nID As Long
    Dim nRows As Integer
```

The variable declarations for *LoadData* fall into three categories. The first category is variables to identify the components of a field—number, type, and length. The next category is variables for parsing the schema string. The third category is for the items that are displayed in the grid view control.

Let's revisit the formatted schema string that the fuser returns. For a schema containing three fields, the fuser returns the following string.

```
"Num1 Type1 Len1 Num2 Type2 Len2 Num3 Type3 Len3"
```

An example with actual data might look like the following:

```
"0 6 0 1 6 0 2 5 0"
```

In this example, each field's definition takes up six character positions, including the trailing space. The lFieldDefLen variable is set to 6 for this reason.

After declaring the variables, we check to see if the database has been created.

```
g_lDB = PDBOpen(Byfilename, g_DBStruct.dbName, 0, 0, 0, 0, 0)

If g_lDB = 0 Then
    MsgBox "Could not open database " + g_DBStruct.dbName
    Exit Sub
End If
```

Defining the database schema involves telling AppForge how many and what type of fields make up each record in our database. We do this by looping on the number of fields.

```
For nFieldDefIndex = 1 To g_DBStruct.nNumFields

  lFieldDefOffset = (nFieldDefIndex - 1) * lFieldDefLen + 1

  'Field definition in the form: num, type, len
  sFieldDef = Mid(g_DBStruct.Schema, lFieldDefOffset, lFieldDefLen)

  'Pick off the field number
  nFieldNum = CLng(Mid(sFieldDef, 1, 1))

  'Pick off the field type
  nFieldType = CLng(Mid(sFieldDef, 3, 1))

  'Pick off the field length
  nFieldLen = CLng(Mid(sFieldDef, 5, 1))
```

We calculate the offset to the beginning of the field's definition in the schema string and assign it to lFieldDefOffset. We call *Mid* once to extract the field's definition, and then three more times to extract the field's number, type, and length.

We must map the field's type to the corresponding AppForge type. We do this using the following Select Case statement.

```
Select Case (nFieldType)
    Case DBS_TYPE_BOOL
        afFieldType = eBooleanField

    Case DBS_TYPE_BYTE
        afFieldType = eByteField

    Case DBS_TYPE_DATE
        afFieldType = eDateField

    Case DBS_TYPE_FLOAT
        afFieldType = eFloatField

    Case DBS_TYPE_INT
        afFieldType = eIntegerField

    Case DBS_TYPE_LONG
        afFieldType = eLongField

    Case DBS_TYPE_STR
        afFieldType = eStringField

    Case Else
        MsgBox "Invalid field type!"

End Select
```

Now we have all the information we need to set the field's type.

```
        PDBSetFieldType g_lDB, nFieldNum, afFieldType, nFieldLen
    Next
```

We simply call *PDBSetFieldType* with the corresponding parameters and iterate to the next field. Next, we perform some housekeeping in preparation for adding data to the grid view.

```
PDBSetSortFields g_lDB, LNG_EMP_LASTNAME

nRows = grdView.Rows
grdView.Visible = False

While Not (grdView.Rows = 0)
    grdView.RemoveItem (0)
    grdView.Refresh
    nRows = grdView.Rows
Wend

grdView.ColWidth(0) = 200
grdView.Col = 0
```

We sort the database by last name with a call to *PDBSetSortFields*. Next, we determine the number of rows in the grid and remove them. We also hide the grid to speed up drawing. We then set the grid's column width, and target the left column for setting cell tag properties. We are ready to populate the grid view with records from the database.

```
PDBMoveFirst g_lDB

While Not (PDBEOF(g_lDB) = True)
```

We move to the first record in the database with a call to *PDBMoveFirst*, and loop through each record.

We retrieve the employee's last and first name with calls to *PDBGetField*.

```
PDBGetField g_lDB, LNG_EMP_LASTNAME, strLastName

PDBGetField g_lDB, LNG_EMP_FIRSTNAME, strFirstName

grdView.AddItem strLastName + ", " + strFirstName, -1

grdView.Row = (grdView.Rows - 1)

grdView.RowHeight(grdView.Row) = 15
```

After adding this information to the grid view, we select the row just added, and set its height to 15.

We follow similar steps to add rows for the employee's phone, email, and ID.

```
PDBGetField g_lDB, LNG_EMP_PHONE, strPhone
grdView.AddItem "      " + strPhone, -1
    grdView.Row = (grdView.Rows - 1)
    grdView.RowHeight(grdView.Row) = 15

    PDBGetField g_lDB, LNG_EMP_EMAIL, strEmail
    grdView.AddItem "      " + strEmail, -1
    grdView.Row = (grdView.Rows - 1)
    grdView.RowHeight(grdView.Row) = 15

    PDBGetField g_lDB, LNG_EMP_ID, nID
    grdView.AddItem "      " + "ID: " + CStr(nID), -1
    grdView.Row = (grdView.Rows - 1)
    grdView.RowHeight(grdView.Row) = 15
```

At the end of the loop, we set the cell's font to 1 and move to the next record with a call to *PDBMoveNext*.

```
    grdView.FontStyle = 1
    PDBMoveNext g_lDB
Wend
```

We have now added all of the records to the grid view. We set it as visible and close the database before leaving the function.

```
    grdView.Visible = True
    PDBClose (g_lDB)
End Sub
```

This function results in displaying the employee information as shown earlier in Figure 8-6.

CHAPTER 9
Piedmont

In this chapter, we look at the AppForge *Piedmont* Framework (henceforth referred to as Piedmont), a component SDK for Windows and handheld devices. Piedmont uses a component-based architecture to bring portable component-oriented programming to the PDA.* As powerful as COM is for Windows platforms, it is useless on the PDA, since so much of COM relies on support from the Windows operating system. AppForge bridges this gap on the Palm through *BoosterPlus*, which provides the registration and runtime support services associated with COM.

Piedmont is portable in a number of ways, which is useful in development, integration, and deployment. Piedmont object development is started with Microsoft's Visual C++ environment. From there, the developer can continue to develop in Visual C++, debugging and testing his/her component from within Windows. At some point, the component is integrated into a Visual Basic AppForge project, or deployed on the handheld for Piedmont clients to use. Deploying the component involves compiling it with MetroWerks CodeWarrior, installing it on the Palm, and registering it with the Booster.

This chapter provides an overview of the Piedmont internals by creating a sample server component. We then show how to integrate the component with an App-Forge Visual Basic project.

Piedmont's extensive framework makes it difficult to cover all aspects of Piedmont in one chapter. In this chapter, we focus on the internals, since developers will want a taste of what it is like to develop with Piedmont. From a larger perspective, though, Piedmont is exciting and compelling for many reasons. See the "Ingots" sidebar later in this chapter for just one of the reasons why you should consider Piedmont for developing handheld-based components.

---

* Although Piedmont is targeted for different PDAs, including the Pocket PC, we focus on its use for the Palm. We refer to component-oriented instead of object-oriented programming, in keeping with COM's programming model and nomenclature.

We assume you are familiar with ATL-based COM development, interface definition language (IDL), and Palm application development using Metrowerks CodeWarrior for Windows.

Obtaining Piedmont

The Piedmont SDK must be obtained as part of AppForge's Technology Licensing program. Piedmont also requires the use of the BoosterPlus runtime. BoosterPlus is backward-compatible with Booster and includes enhanced capabilities for running applications containing Piedmont-based components. For details regarding App-Forge's Technology Licensing program, visit their web site at *http://www.appforge.net.*

Ingots

An ingot is a special type of Piedmont component that defines dual behaviors. An ingot's design-time behavior defines how it interacts within Visual Basic when added as a component to an AppForge project. Within Visual Basic, you access an ingot's properties just as you would with any standard VB control. An ingot's runtime behavior determines how it appears (if intended for display) and how it operates within Visual Basic or when deployed on the Palm. An ingot supports this dual nature by defining an outer ActiveX-compliant component that satisfies Visual Basic's design-time expectations of it and an inner component that satisfies Piedmont's runtime expectations of the ingot.

Thus, Visual Basic sees the ingot as an ActiveX control, while the ingot's inner component operates entirely within the Piedmont environment. This powerful duality means that a mobile developer can design and implement an ingot within Visual Basic and deploy it on any Piedmont-enabled platform, without requiring extensive modifications.

Architecture Overview

Piedmont is AppForge's SDK for extending its flagship product by creating component-based objects. As with COM on Windows, one or more Piedmont components can be housed within a module. On Windows, a module typically consists of an in-process dynamic link library (DLL) or an out-of-process executable (EXE). A Piedmont module consists of an in-process DLL on Windows, and a shared library on the Palm.

From a developer's perspective, Piedmont's architecture resembles the approach taken with ATL COM development. Much of the low-level work associated with COM (IUnknown implementation, reference counting, class factories, object creation, and module registration) is delegated to Piedmont-generated subclasses, which inherit from your class. In this way, Piedmont uses your class as a base class, and never instantiates it directly.* This keeps the focus on implementing interfaces in your class, while delegating the housekeeping portions of COM to the derived classes. The same is true for the module code. A virtual module class allows you to override some virtual methods if desired. Otherwise, all object creation, module registration, and other housekeeping is performed by the derived class implementation.

We will see the details of this architecture unfold as we proceed with an example of our own.

Module and Interface Definition

In this section, we define a Piedmont module and interfaces for our example TagParse component. TagParse parses data from within tag pairs of the following form:

```
<TAG>Optional Tag Data</TAG>
```

Similar to XML, an end tag differs from its start tag in that it contains an additional forward slash. Example 9-1 shows a contrived set of tags for a database definition.

Example 9-1. Sample database tags with data

```
<Database>
  <Schema>
    <Field>
      Data for field 1
    </Field>
  </Schema>
  <Data>
    <Record>
      Data for record 1
    </Record>
    <Record>
      Data for record 2
    </Record>
  </Data>
</Database>
```

Start by creating a directory called *TagParse*, with the subfolders shown in Figure 9-1.

Module and interface definitions are described using Piedmont's interface definition language (PIDL). PIDL uses XML syntax to describe the elements and attributes that

---

* We will see later how Piedmont deviates from this approach, using the PUSH_IUNKNOWN_IMPL_UP directive, but this is the default implementation.

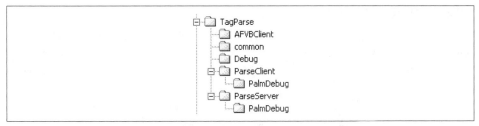

Figure 9-1. TagParse component directories

make up a module, interfaces, and the classes that implement interfaces. Each Piedmont component contains a module definition (MDX) file and one or more interface definition (IDX) files.

The Piedmont SDK comes with *ClassForge*, a GUI-based utility for setting up these files. We will use ClassForge to define the module, interfaces, and implementation class for the TagParse component. Note, however, that you may create module and interface definition files from scratch, using any text or XML editor.

Module Declaration

When ClassForge starts, you are presented with the properties for an empty module (see Figure 9-2).

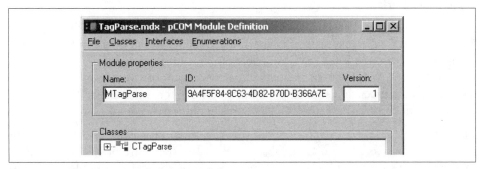

Figure 9-2. ClassForge module definition dialog

As with traditional COM development, all modules, interfaces, and classes are assigned globally unique IDs, or GUIDs. ClassForge automatically generates new GUIDs for each of these elements as they are added. The module ID is shown in the ID field. Type **MTagParse** in the Name field. After typing in the name, save the file as *TagParse.mdx* in the *ParseServer* directory you created previously. Do this by clicking on File → Save Module As.

Interface Declaration

We define the *ITagParse* interface for our module. This interface contains the methods for parsing tag pairs and extracting data between tag pairs. Add this interface by clicking `Interfaces` → `Add Interface` to bring up the `Interface Design` dialog in Figure 9-3.

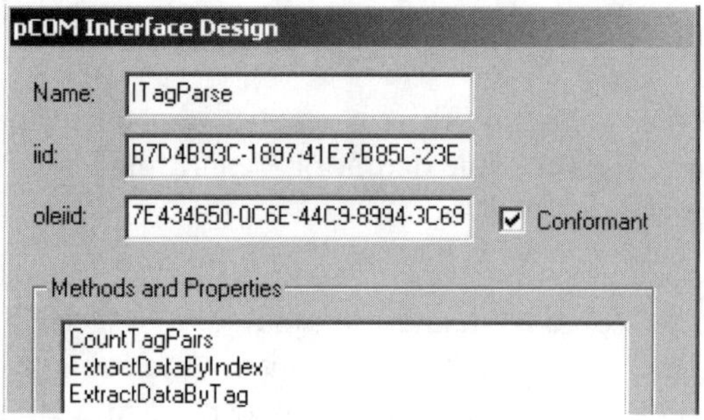

Figure 9-3. Interface Design dialog

Type **ITagParse** into the `Name` field. Notice that an interface ID (IID) is automatically generated and added to the `iid` field.

Conformant interfaces

The `oleiid` field and `Conformant` checkbox are for conformant interfaces. The App-Forge Booster runtime consists of a virtual machine (VM) that interprets a compiled byte-code version of a Visual Basic application. For a Piedmont component to interoperate with the VM, its interface method parameters and return types are limited to a subset of data types that are compatible with OLE automation under Windows. An interface containing such methods is said to be conformant.

In Piedmont, all conformant methods must return an HRESULT. Conformant parameter types correspond to a subset of Visual Basic data types. (A conformant method may also take conformant interfaces such as ICanvas, for example, as parameters. We do not discuss conformant interface parameters in this chapter.) Table 9-1 lists the conformant parameter types and their Visual Basic description.

Table 9-1. Conformant parameter types

Conformant parameter type	Visual Basic description
Integer	Integer value
String	Character string value
Boolean	Boolean value; True or False
Byte	Byte value
Long	Long integer value

Table 9-1. Conformant parameter types (continued)

Conformant parameter type	Visual Basic description
Date	Date or time value
Single	Single-precision floating-point value
Double	Double-precision floating-point value
Currency	Currency value

In some cases, the underlying representations of these types differ between Piedmont and Visual Basic. For example, a Visual Basic string is stored as a BSTR, a pointer to a Unicode character array, prefixed with a header that contains the length of the string.* In contrast, Piedmont uses the IString interface to work with string data between Piedmont interfaces.

When an interface is declared as conformant, the PIDL generates the necessary code to convert data between Piedmont primitives and Visual Basic. We will see how this is done later in this chapter. For now, check the Conformant checkbox, since we will be integrating our component into an AppForge application.

 Your component's interfaces must be conformant if you want the AppForge VM to access them from within Visual Basic.

The ITagParse interface has the following methods.

ExtractDataByTag
   Extracts data between a tag pair

ExtractDataByIndex
   Extracts data from a string given a start index and length

CountTagPairs
   Counts the number of occurrences of a particular tag pair within a string

The parameters for *ExtractDataByTag* are shown in Table 9-2.

Table 9-2. Parameters to ExtractDataByTag

Parameter	Type/attribute	Purpose
searchStr	String [IN]	String to search
startTag	String [IN]	First of tag pair
endTag	String [IN]	Second of tag pair
maxChar	Integer [IN]	Maximum number of characters to extract between tags
resultStr	String [OUT, RETVAL]	Extracted data

---

* BSTR is commonly used to refer to the header and Unicode character array as one. Strictly speaking, however, a BSTR is the pointer to the Unicode array.

At first glance, declaring resultStr's attribute as [OUT, RETVAL] seems to conflict with Piedmont's convention that all interface methods return an HRESULT. As we will see, the implementation for *ExtractDataByTag* does indeed return an HRESULT. A type library, however, wraps this function so that Visual Basic clients see resultStr as the return value. We will revisit type libraries when we integrate the ITagParse component into a Visual Basic project.

To add this method to the ITagParse interface, click the Add button, which brings up the Method/Property Definition dialog, as shown in Figure 9-4.

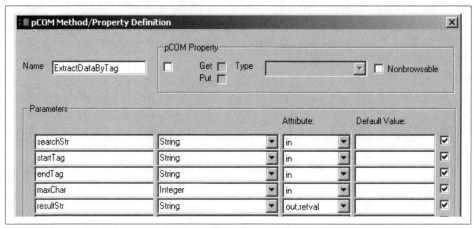

Figure 9-4. Method/Property Definition dialog

Type **ExtractDataByTag** in the name field. The purpose of the pCOM Property group box is to establish component properties. The TagParse component does not expose any of its members as properties, so you can ignore this area. Add each parameter from Table 9-2 to the dialog by checking the rightmost boxes and adding the corresponding information. Notice that the list box for selecting the parameter type (Integer, String, Boolean, etc) only contains options for the conformant data types. Click OK to add the method to the ITagParse interface.

Continue in this manner, adding the *ExtractDataByIndex* and *CountTagPairs* methods, as defined in Table 9-3 and Table 9-4.

Table 9-3. Parameters to ExtractDataByIndex

Parameter	Type/direction	Purpose
searchStr	String [IN]	String to search
fromIndex	Long [IN]	Character index at which to begin searching
fromCount	Long [IN]	Number of characters to extract
resultStr	String [OUT,RETVAL]	Extracted data

Table 9-4. Parameters to CountTagPairs

Parameter	Type/direction	Purpose
searchStr	String [IN]	String to search
startTag	String [IN]	First of tag pair
endTag	String [IN]	Second of tag pair
numItems	Long [OUT,RETVAL]	Number of tag pairs found

When you have added these methods, click OK in the Interface Design dialog. The Module Definition dialog now appears with the new unsaved interface listed under Interfaces and Enumerations as *UNSAVED IDX*. Select this interface and click Interfaces → Save Interface Collection As. Save the interface definition in the *ParseServer* directory as *TagParse.idx*.

Event Interface Declaration

The TagParse component also supports an event interface. An event interface is a contract between a client and a server component, in which the server sources, or sends, events and the client sinks, or receives, them. The client must register a callback interface with the server component to receive events, and it must revoke the callback interface to notify the server component to stop sending it events. Piedmont's event source/sink model is shown in Figure 9-5.

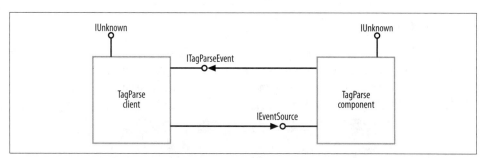

Figure 9-5. Event source/sink paradigm

The TagParse component exposes the IEventSource interface, which consists of the *Advise* and *Unadvise* methods. The component also defines the ITagParseEvent interface and associated event methods. The TagParse client implements this interface. When the client wants to receive (or sink) events, it queries for the IEventSource interface on the component and calls *Advise,* passing in its callback interface. In the *Advise* method, the component records the client's ITagParseEvent callback interface. When the component sinks an event, it calls the corresponding method on the ITagParseEvent interface. When the client no longer wishes to receive events, it calls We declare the ITagParseEvent interface, which includes two event sinks (methods) for propagating errors.

InvalidTagPair
> This event is sourced when an invalid tag pair is passed into one of the `ITagParse`
> methods. An invalid tag pair consists of a malformed pair, such as the following:
> `<Record></Recordd>`.

TagNotFound
> This event is sourced if the second tag of a given pair is not found.

The parameters for these methods are shown in Table 9-5 and Table 9-6.

Table 9-5. Parameters to InvalidTagPair

Parameter	Attribute/direction	Purpose
startTag	*String [IN]*	First of tag pair
endTag	*String [IN]*	Second of tag pair

Table 9-6. Parameters to TagNotFound

Parameter	Attribute/direction	Purpose
tag	*String [IN]*	Missing tag

You create the `ITagParseEvent` interface and methods just like we did for the
`ITagParse`. Don't forget to make the interface conformant! Save the `ITagParseEvent`
declaration in the *ParseServer* directory to a file called *TagParseEvent.idx*.

Class Declaration

So far, we have declared the `MTagParse` module and the `ITagParse` interface that it
supports. To declare the class that implements the `ITagParse` interface, simply click
`Classes → Add Class`. The `Class Information` dialog appears (see Figure 9-6).

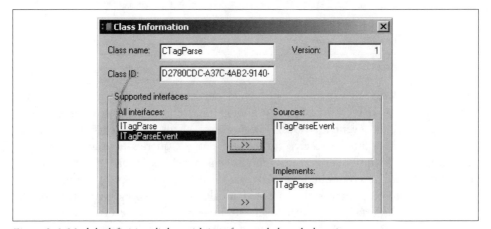

Figure 9-6. Module definition dialog with interface and class declarations

Type **CTagParse** in the Class name field. The CTagParse class implements the methods of the ITagParse interface and sources events of the ITagParseEvent interface. Select each of these interfaces from the left, and add them to the corresponding list box on the right. Add ITagParseEvent to the Sources list box, and add ITagParse to the Implements list box. Then click OK.

Save the module by clicking File → Save Module. You may exit ClassForge.

File Details

In this section, we examine the MDX and IDX files that ClassForge created for the TagParse component. We discuss these files to show how the XML elements tie to what we just declared using the ClassForge utility. We also manually add some PIDL code to complete the MDX file.

As you become proficient with writing your own Piedmont components, you may wish to explore more of the capabilities that PIDL provides. In some cases, you may need to create your MDX or IDX files from scratch, especially if you use a feature of PIDL that ClassForge does not support.

Module definition file

Here is the *TagParse.mdx* file produced by ClassForge.

```
<module name="MTagParse"
        modid="9A4F5F84-8C63-4D82-B70D-B366A7EE842E"
        version="1"
        xmlns:xsi="http://www.w3.org/2000/10/XMLSchema-instance"
xsi:noNamespaceSchemaLocation="http://frog.appforge.com/std/1/pidl_schemas.xsd">
  <import src="TagParseEvent.idx"/>
  <import src="TagParse.idx"/>
  <class name="CTagParse"
         version="1"
         clsid="D2780CDC-A37C-4AB2-9140-E93A71F418E7">
    <implements name="ITagParse"/>
    <implements name="IEventSource"/>
    <sources name="ITagParseEvent"/>
  </class>
</module>
```

Manually add the bolded implements element to the file. (The IEventSource interface may be added to the CTagParse class in ClassForge by dragging the interface onto the CTagParse class. We perform this step manually, since it is more straightforward.) The IEventSource interface must be implemented, since the TagParse component sources events.

The *name*, *modid*, and *version* attributes of the module element are taken from the ClassForge Module Definition dialog. ClassForge automatically generates two additional module attributes: an XML namespace and an associated schema instance.

These attributes are typically referenced by XML schema validation utilities. PIDL ignores these attributes when compiling the file.

The import elements reference the files for the interfaces that this module supports. The class element indicates that this module contains a class called CTagParse. This element contains the implements and sources subelements, which indicate that this class implements the ITagParse interface and sources ITagParseEvent events.

Interface definition file

Here is the *TagParse.idx* file produced by *ClassForge*.

```
<interfaces xmlns:xsi="http://www.w3.org/2000/10/XMLSchema-instance"
xsi:noNamespaceSchemaLocation="http://frog.appforge.com/std/1/pidl_schemas.xsd">
  <import src="pcom.idx"/>
  <interface name="ITagParse"
             iid="B7D4B93C-1897-41E7-B85C-23E158205DDF"
             oleiid="7E434650-0C6E-44C9-8994-3C6972F213CF">
    <method name="ExtractDataByTag">
      <param name="searchStr" type="String" attr="in"/>
      <param name="startTag"  type="String" attr="in"/>
      <param name="endTag"    type="String" attr="in"/>
      <param name="maxChar"   type="Integer" attr="in"/>
      <param name="resultStr" type="String" attr="out,retval"/>
    </method>
    <method name="ExtractDataByIndex">
      <param name="searchStr" type="String" attr="in"/>
      <param name="fromIndex" type="Long" attr="in"/>
      <param name="fromCount" type="Long" attr="in"/>
      <param name="resultStr" type="String" attr="out,retval"/>
    </method>
    <method name="CountTagPairs">
      <param name="searchStr" type="String" attr="in"/>
      <param name="startTag"  type="String" attr="in"/>
      <param name="endTag"    type="String" attr="in"/>
      <param name="numItems"  type="Long" attr="out,retval"/>
    </method>
  </interface>
</interfaces>
```

Interface definition files begin with the interfaces element and associated attributes. The import element at the beginning of the file references the *pCOM.idx* file. This file is part of the Piedmont SDK and contains a number of base interfaces, including those that the MTagParse module and TagParse component must implement: IModule, IUnknown, and IEventSource.

Next comes the interface element for the ITagParse interface. The *name* attribute is the name of this interface and iid is the GUID associated with this interface. The *oleiid* attribute specifies an additional GUID for use with conformant interfaces. We will see how this attribute is used later.

The method element, and corresponding param subelements, define the methods of the ITagParse interface. Each method is identified by its *name* attribute, and each parameter is identified by its *name*, *type*, and *attr* attributes.

Event interface definition file

Here is the *TagParseEvent.idx* file produced by ClassForge.

```
<interfaces xmlns:xsi="http://www.w3.org/2000/10/XMLSchema-instance"
xsi:noNamespaceSchemaLocation="http://frog.appforge.com/std/1/pidl_schemas.xsd">
  <import src="pcom.idx"/>
  <interface name="ITagParseEvent"
             iid="BA615D49-D31B-4F7F-AE46-F773363378B2"
             oleiid="8C003256-48A4-4692-B27E-75989733B05E">
    <method name="InvalidTagPair">
      <param name="startTag" type="String" attr="in"/>
      <param name="endTag" type="String" attr="in"/>
    </method>
    <method name="TagNotFound">
      <param name="tag" type="String" attr="in"/>
    </method>
  </interface>
</interfaces>
```

This file structure is similar to that of *TagParse.idx*, and contains the two event methods associated with the ITagParseEvent interface.

Component Code Generation

We can now use the PIDL compiler to generate C++ skeleton module and component code from the MDX and IDX files we created previously. From the skeleton code, we can compile either a Windows DLL, using Visual C++, or a PRC file, using Metrowerks' CodeWarrior.

With a DLL, you can write a simple Visual C++ driver program to test on Windows before deploying it to the Palm as a PRC file. More importantly, you can incorporate your component into an AppForge Visual Basic application and test it on Windows before deploying the component and the application to the Palm. Piedmont's dual DLL/PRC nature is what makes it such a powerful SDK.

In this section, we use the PIDL compiler to generate the skeleton code for the TagParse component and compile it as a Windows DLL. Before getting started, configure Visual C++ so it can find the various files associated with the Piedmont SDK. From the Visual C++ main menu, select Tools → Options to bring up the Options dialog. Click on the Directories tab. Assuming the Piedmont SDK is installed in *C:\Program Files\AppForge\SDK*, add the directories shown in Table 9-7.

Table 9-7. Visual C++ Piedmont SDK directories

File type	Directories
Include files	*C:\Program Files\AppForge\SDK\include*
	C:\Program Files\AppForge\SDK\include\Win32
Library files	*C:\Program Files\ AppForge \SDK\lib\Win32\MSVC60*
Executable files	*C:\ Program Files \ AppForge \SDK\bin*

Next, create a Win32 DLL project called `ParseServer` in the *ParseServer* directory where the IDX and MDX files are located (see Figure 9-1, shown earlier in this chapter). When prompted for the type of DLL to create, select `An empty DLL project`. From the Visual C++ main menu, select `Project → Settings`. From the `Project Settings` dialog, select the `MIDL` tab. Make sure the `MkTypLib compatible` checkbox is not checked. MkTypeLib is a compiler for creating type libraries from scripts written in object description language (ODL). Using MkTypeLib conflicts with the IDL output that PIDL produces. Click `OK` to accept the changes.

Add the MDX and IDX files from the *ParseServer* directory to the project. Right-click on the *TagParse.mdx* file and select `Settings` to set up a custom build step. Select the `Custom Build` tab and fill in the fields according to Table 9-8.

Table 9-8. TagParse module custom build settings

Field	Input
Description	`Generating module code...`
Commands	`pidl /I "C:\Program Files\AppForge\SDK\include" $(InputPath)`

Outputs	`MTagParse_GUID.h`
	`_CTagParse.inc`
	`_MTagParse.inc`
	`TagParseServer_tlb.idl`

Again, this assumes that the Piedmont SDK is installed in the default location. Add a post-build step to register the `TagParse` component with Windows. From the `Project Settings` dialog, select the TagParse project and then the `Post-build step` tab. Type in **regsvr32 $(TargetPath)** as the post-build command.

Click `OK` to accept these new project settings. Compile *TagParse.mdx* by right-clicking on it and selecting `Compile TagParse.mdx`. Table 9-9 lists the C++ files that PIDL produces for the `TagParse` component.

Table 9-9. PIDL-generated files

Source file	Output file	Description
TagParse.idx	*TagParse.h*	Defines the `TagParse` component interfaces and assigns interface GUIDs
TagParseEvent.idx		
TagParseEvent.mdx	*_CTagParse.inc*	Base class that derives from `CTagParse`; contains `IUnknown` implementation and class creation function

Table 9-9. PIDL-generated files (continued)

Source file	Output file	Description
	CTagParse.h	Class files; implement the `ITagParse` and `IEventSource` interfaces
	CTagParse.cpp	
	_MTagParse.inc	Base class that derives from `MTagParse`; contains `IUnknown` and partial `IModule` implementation, as well as module creation function
	MTagParse_module.h	Contains `CCustomIUnknown` and partial `IModule` implementation
	MTagParse_module.cpp	
	MTagParse_GUID.h	Contains module ID and class IDs
	TagParse_tlb.idl	IDL file that is subsequently compiled with Microsoft's MIDL compiler
	TagParse.def	Contains DLL export statements

Let's look at each file in more detail. Our coverage touches only on the salient features of each file and is not exhaustive.

TagParse.h

This file begins by including *pCOM.h*.

```
#include <pCOM.h>
```

pCOM.h declares several standard interfaces used throughout Piedmont, including `IUnknown`, `IModule`, and `IEventSource`, among others. Next are some forward declarations for the interfaces in *TagParse.h*.

```
typedef struct ITagParse ITagParse;
typedef struct ITagParseEvent ITagParseEvent;
typedef struct IShim_ITagParse IShim_ITagParse;
typedef struct IShim_ITagParseEvent IShim_ITagParseEvent;
```

We know about `ITagParseEvent` and `ITagParse`, but we haven't seen the `IShim_*` interfaces before. These interfaces are stand-in interfaces, used for conformant interfaces. When an interface is declared as conformant via the *oleiid* attribute, PIDL generates a stand-in interface that converts between native Piedmont data types and VB types. Stand-in interfaces are only required for Windows COM compliance. They are conditionally compiled out for the Palm.

For example, comparing the declarations for *ExtractDataByTag* and *_IShim_ ITagParse_ExtractDataByTag* (listed in Example 9-2 and Example 9-3) shows how the `IString` and `S32` parameters are converted to a `BSTR` and `short`, respectively. We will discuss the implementation of *ExtractDataByTag* later in this chapter.

Example 9-2. ExtractDataByTag method declaration

```
STDMETHOD(ExtractDataByTag)(
    /* in */ IString* searchStr,
    /* in */ IString* startTag,
    /* in */ IString* endTag,
```

Example 9-2. ExtractDataByTag method declaration (continued)

```
/* in */ S32 maxChar,
/* out,retval */ IString*& resultStr
)=0;
```

Example 9-3. IShim_ITagParse_ExtractDataByTag method declaration

```
STDMETHOD(_IShim_ITagParse_ExtractDataByTag)(
    /* in */ BSTR searchStr,
    /* in */ BSTR startTag,
    /* in */ BSTR endTag,
    /* in */ short maxChar,
    /* out,retval */ BSTR& resultStr
    )=0;
```

Further down in the file are the declarations for each interface.

```
interface ITagParse: public IUnknown
{
    . . .
}
interface ITagParseEvent: public IUnknown
{
    . . .
}
interface IShim_ITagParse: public IDispatch
{
    . . .
}
interface IShim_ITagParseEvent: public IDispatch
{
    . . .
}
```

The public interfaces that the TagParse component exposes—ITagParse and ITagParseEvent—inherit from IUnknown as you would expect.

CTagParse.h and CTagParse.cpp

These files contain the IEventSource and ITagParse interface method declarations and stubs for the CTagParse class. Here is the partial listing for *CTagParse.h*.

```
#include "MTagParse_module.h"

class MTagParse;

class CTagParse:
    public ITagParse,
    public IEventSource
{
public:
    CTagParse(MTagParse* module);
    ~CTagParse();
```

```
#ifdef PUSH_IUNKNOWN_IMPL_UP
    // IUnknown
    STDMETHOD(QueryInterface)(/* in */ REFIID iid,/* out */ void** object);
    STDMETHOD_(U32,AddRef)( );
    STDMETHOD_(U32,Release)( );
#endif // #ifdef PUSH_IUNKNOWN_IMPL_UP

    // Interface IEventSource

    /* Establishes a source/sink interface */
    STDMETHOD(Advise)(REFIID iid, void* sinkIntf);

    /* Breaks an existing source/sink relationship */
    STDMETHOD(Unadvise)(void* sinkIntf);

    // Interface ITagParse
    STDMETHOD(ExtractDataByTag)(IString* searchStr, IString* startTag, IString*
endTag, S32 maxChar, IString*& resultStr);
    STDMETHOD(ExtractDataByIndex)(IString* searchStr, S32 fromIndex, S32 fromCount,
IString*& resultStr);
    STDMETHOD(CountTagPairs)(IString* searchStr, IString* startTag, IString* endTag,
S32& numItems);

protected:
    MTagParse* m_module; // required, do not remove
#ifdef PUSH_IUNKNOWN_IMPL_UP
    U32 m_CTagParse_refCount;
#endif // #ifdef PUSH_IUNKNOWN_IMPL_UP
};
```

The PUSH_IUNKNOWN_IMPL_UP directive encapsulates the three IUnknown interface
method declarations. By default, this directive is not defined, and CTagParse does not
declare or implement IUnknown. CTagParse's corresponding IUnknown implementation
is not contained in *CTagParse.cpp*, as you might expect. We will see where it is
located in the next section of this chapter.

All stub implementations in *CTagParse.cpp* are identical. Example 9-4 shows the
stub for the IEventSource *Advise* method.

Example 9-4. IEventSource Advise stub implementation

```
STDMETHODIMP CTagParse::Advise(REFIID iid, void* sinkIntf)
{
    USE_CONTEXT;
    // TODO: Place your implementation here
    return E_NOTIMPL;
}
```

On Windows, the USE_CONTEXT context macro has no use and expands to nothing.
On the Palm, this macro is used to account for the Palm's lack of a conventional
model for global variables. Global variables are accessed via a pointer, or context,

which is maintained in the A5 register. Since the value of this register is not maintained across calls that span modules, it must be restored each time a module or component accesses global variables.* We will see how this is done when we discuss the MTagParse module.

The last line of the *CTagParse.cpp* file includes the class implementation derived from *_CTagParse.inc*.

```
#include "_CTagParse.inc"
```

_CTagParse.inc

This file contains the declaration and implementation for the _CTagParse class. After some introductory comments, the definition for CTagParse's implementation of the IUnknown interface appears, encapsulated by the PUSH_IUNKNOWN_IMPL_UP directive. (We have left the details out for the sake of brevity.)

```
#ifdef PUSH_IUNKNOWN_IMPL_UP
    . . .
STDMETHODIMP CTagParse::QueryInterface(REFIID riid, void** object)
{
    . . .
}
STDMETHODIMP_ (U32) CTagParse::AddRef( )
{
    . . .
}
STDMETHODIMP_ (U32) CTagParse::Release( )
{
    . . .
}
#endif // #ifdef PUSH_IUNKNOWN_IMPL_UP
```

As we mentioned previously, this implementation is compiled away by default. Examining the implementation of _CTagParse will shed more light on the role that the PUSH_IUNKNOWN_IMPL_UP directive plays.

Here is the start of the declaration for _CTagParse.

```
#ifndef PUSH_IUNKNOWN_IMPL_UP
class _CTagParse:
    public CTagParse
#ifdef AFWIN32
    ,public IShim_ITagParse
    ,public ISupportErrorInfo
    ,public IConnectionPointContainer
#endif // #ifdef AFWIN32
{
```

---

* Since modules are implemented as shared libraries on the Palm, the same issues regarding global memory that were outlined in Chapter 8 apply.

Consider the default case, where PUSH_IUNKNOWN_IMPL_UP is not defined. _CTagParse implements IUnknown, since it inherits from CTagParse. On Windows, _CTagParse also inherits and implements the three interfaces encapsulated by the AFWIN32 directive—these interfaces are required for COM compliance. However, on the Palm, these interfaces are compiled away, and Piedmont provides equivalent functionality.

Now, consider the case where PUSH_IUNKNOWN_IMPL_UP is defined. We know already that CTagParse implements IUnknown, so this interface is accounted for. However, the entire _CTagParse class goes away altogether. Thus, the case where PUSH_IUNKNOWN_IMPL_UP is defined only applies to the Palm, where the _CTagParse class and its Windows-only interfaces are not used at all.

You may wish to define this directive when you compile a Piedmont component using CodeWarrior, since it will reduce the component's footprint and overhead. The use of this directive shows the lengths to which AppForge has gone in order to make the Piedmont code as small and efficient as possible when compiled for the Palm.

On Windows, IShim_ITagParse is a stand-in interface, which we discussed previously. ISupportErrorInfo allows the TagParse component to return rich error information to clients, and Example 9-5 shows how this function works. IConnectionPointContainer is required for events.

CTagParse.inc also includes a function that the module calls to create _CTagParse objects. Example 9-5 shows how this function works.

Example 9-5. Create_CTagParse Function

```
HRESULT Create_CTagParse(MTagParse* module, IUnknown* outer, REFIID iid,
                         void** object, CTagParse** actual)
{
    if (outer)
    {
        return CLASS_E_NOAGGREGATION;
    }

#ifndef PUSH_IUNKNOWN_IMPL_UP
    if (_CTagParse* s = new _CTagParse(module))
#else
    if (CTagParse* s = new CTagParse(module))
#endif // #ifdef PUSH_IUNKNOWN_IMPL_UP
    {

        HRESULT hr;
#ifdef USE_CUSTOM_POSTCONSTRUCT
        hr = static_cast<CCustomIUnknown*>(s)->CustomPostConstruct();
        if (SUCCEEDED(hr))
#endif
            hr = s->QueryInterface(iid,object);
```

Example 9-5. Create_CTagParse Function (continued)

```
#ifdef USE_CUSTOM_POSTCONSTRUCT
    else
            pCoDebugTraceAnsi("CustomPostConstruct failed for CTagParse.");
#endif

    if (FAILED(hr))
    {
        delete s;
        return hr;
    }
    if (actual)
    {
        *actual = s;
    }
#ifdef PUSH_IUNKNOWN_IMPL_UP
    static_cast<IModule *>(module)->AddRef( );
#endif // #ifdef PUSH_IUNKNOWN_IMPL_UP
    return S_OK;
    }
    else
    {
    return E_OUTOFMEMORY;
    }
}
```

When the `PUSH_IUNKNOWN_IMPL_UP` directive is defined, `CTagParse` objects are created directly, instead of indirectly through the derived `_CTagParse` object. Thus, on Windows, `_CTagParse` objects are always created, whereas on the Palm, either object may be created, depending on how this directive is set.

The *Create_CTagParse* function also serves another useful purpose. If the `USE_CUSTOM_POSTCONSTRUCT` flag is defined, this function calls the virtual *CustomPostConstruct* method of the `CCustomIUnknown` class. We will see where `CCustomIUnknown` is implemented later in this chapter. This call allows us to perform custom initialization or to call virtual functions on the `_CTagParse` object, and return gracefully if initialization fails. Returning any unsuccessful `HRESULT` from this function results in the `_CTagParse` object not being created.

_MTagParse.inc

This file contains the implementation for the `_MTagParse` class, which inherits from the `MTagParse` base class. `_MtagParse` implements `IUnknown`, shielding `MTagParse` from the details of this interface.

A module must also implement the `IModule` interface and its associated methods: *CreateInstance*, *Register*, *EnumDependencies*, and *GetClassObject*. *CreateInstance* is where the module calls *Create_CTagParse* to create `CTagParse` objects. Example 9-6 shows how this function works.

Example 9-6. IModule CreateInstance method

```
STDMETHODIMP CreateInstance(REFCLSID clsid, IUnknown* outer, REFIID iid,
                            void** object)
    {
        USE_CONTEXT_SPEC(m_context);
        if (clsid == MODID_MTagParse)
        {
            return QueryInterface(iid,object);
        }
        else if (clsid == CLSID_CTagParse)
        {
            return Create_CTagParse(this, outer, iid, object, 0);
        }
        return CLASS_E_CLASSNOTAVAILABLE;
    }
```

We will discuss the USE_CONTEXT_SPEC context macro in the next section. _MTagParse makes use of the IHost interface in the *Register* method to register itself and its components. Example 9-7 shows how the *Register* method works.

Example 9-7. IModule Register method

```
STDMETHODIMP_(U32) Register()
    {
        USE_CONTEXT_SPEC(m_context);
        const CHAR16 sMOD[] = {'M','T','a','g','P','a','r','s','e','\0'};
        m_host->RegisterModule(this, MODID_MTagParse, 1, sMOD);
        static const CHAR16 sCLS_CTagParse[] = {'C','T','a','g','P','a','r','s','e','\0'};
        m_host->RegisterClass(this, CLSID_CTagParse, 1, sCLS_CTagParse);
        return 1;
    }
```

_MTagParse leaves the implementation of the two remaining IModule interface methods, *EnumDependencies* and *GetClassObject*, to the parent MTagParse class. *_MTagParse.inc* also includes the implementation for *CreateModule*, a C-style function for creating the module so it can serve up its components.

MTagParse_module.h and MTagParse_module.cpp

These files contain the implementation for the MTagParse base class. The PIDL compiler generates stub implementations for the two remaining IModule interface methods, *GetClassObject* and *EnumDependencies*. Example 9-8 shows the *GetClassObject* method.

Example 9-8. IModule GetClassObject method

```
STDMETHODIMP MTagParse::GetClassObject(REFCLSID clsid, REFIID riid, void** object)
{
    // If you wish to implement class factories, do so here.
    // If you return E_NOTIMPL, the system will emulate class factories for you.
    return E_NOTIMPL;
}
```

Example 9-8. IModule GetClassObject method (continued)

```
STDMETHODIMP_(U32) MTagParse::EnumDependencies()
{
    // TODO: Identify any external classes that this module depends on.

    // The easiest way to find out your dependencies is to search your
    // source code for CreateInstance calls, then add one call to
    // IHost::RegisterDependency() for each of tehm.

    // The second parameter to IHost::RegistryDependency() is the name users
    // will see if dependency checking fails, so you can set it to whatever
    // is most descriptive.

    // m_host->RegisterDependency(this, L"CSomeClass",  CLSID_CSomeClass,
SomeClassVersion);
    return 0;
}
```

You use *GetClassObject* to implement a custom class factory for a particular class. Custom class factories are useful if, for example, you want to provide multiple ways of creating a particular class that differ in their initialization parameters.

You use *EnumDependencies* to register component dependencies. This method is useful for managing the packaging, installation, and removal of interdependent Piedmont modules and components. We don't use these functions in our example.

MTagParse_module.h includes the declaration for CCustomIUnknown, a class with virtual methods that allows you to provide custom IUnknown behavior for any class within the module. Your class inherits from this class and overrides its methods to provide custom behavior.

In addition to the standard IUnknown methods, CCustomIUnknown contains two methods for providing custom initialization and shutdown of a class object—*CustomPostConstruct* and *CustomPreDestruct*. Your class can use the *CustomPostConstruct* method to perform custom initialization or to call its virtual functions just after it is created.

```
// Override this if you need to call virtual functions on the object as it is
created.
// #define USE_CUSTOM_POSTCONSTRUCT before including the .inc file
// Returning any non-successful HRESULT will cancel object creation.
virtual HRESULT CustomPostConstruct()
{ return S_OK;
```

If any of these operations fail, you can return control to the calling application. You may recall from our coverage of the _CTagParse class that *CustomPostConstruct* is called just after the class instance has been created.

```
// You can provide object shutdown code here.
// #define USE_CUSTOM_PREDESTRUCT before including the .inc file
virtual void CustomPreDestruct()
{ return; }
```

Your class can use this method to perform custom cleanup and to call any virtual functions before being destroyed. This function is called from the IUnknown *Release* method in *_CTagParse.inc* just before the object is deleted.

The MTagParse module constructor contains the third context macro—GET_CONTEXT—that we have seen thus far.

```
MTagParse::MTagParse(IHost* host): m_host(host)
{
    m_context = GET_CONTEXT;
    // Put your startup code here
}
```

Piedmont uses three context macros and a class to maintain the global pointer, or context, across module boundaries.

```
#define USE_CONTEXT CContext    __context__(m_module->m_context)
#define USE_CONTEXT_SPEC(x)    CContext __context__((x))
#define GET_CONTEXT            GetA5()
#define DO_NOT_USE_CONTEXT

class CContext
{
public:
    inline CContext(U32 newContext)
        { oldContext = GetA5(); SetA5(newContext); }
    inline ~CContext()
        { SetA5(oldContext); }

private:
    U32 oldContext;
};
```

GetA5 and *SetA5* are functions that contain equivalent assembly instructions for manipulating the A5 register.

```
static long GetA5(void) = 0x200D;        /* move.l a5,d0 */

inline void SetA5(unsigned long newA5)
{
    __asm {
        move.l newA5, a5
    }
}
```

The module stores the context from the A5 register in its constructor, using the GET_CONTEXT macro. Recall from Example 9-3, shown earlier in this chapter, that each component interface method starts with the USE_CONTEXT macro. This macro declares a local instance of a CContext object, which reinstates the module's context upon entering the interface method, and restores it upon leaving the method. In this way, the context is automatically restored across module boundaries. The *MTagParse_module.cpp* file ends by including the _MTagParse-derived class implementation.

```
#include "_MTagParse.inc"
```

MTagParse_GUID.h

This file defines the module ID and class IDs. These IDs are defined using the DEFINE_GUID macro.

```
// MODID_MTagParse {9A4F5F84_8C63_4D82_B70D_B366A7EE842E}
DEFINE_GUID(MODID_MTagParse,0x9A4F5F84, 0x8C63, 0x4D82, 0xB7, 0x0D, 0xB3, 0x66, 0xA7,
    0xEE, 0x84, 0x2E);


// CLSID_CTagParse {D2780CDC-A37C-4AB2-9140-E93A71F418E7}
DEFINE_GUID(CLSID_CTagParse,0xD2780CDC, 0xA37C, 0x4AB2, 0x91, 0x40, 0xE9, 0x3A, 0x71,
    0xF4, 0x18, 0xE7);
```

TagParse_tlb.idl

This file contains the IDL definition of the ITagParse and ITagParseEvent interfaces and the MTagParse module. *TagParse_tlb.idl* is compiled with Microsoft's MIDL compiler to produce a number of files, including a type library. You use the type library when integrating the TagParse component into a Visual Basic application.

TagParse.def

This file contains the export statements for the ParseServer DLL.

```
EXPORTS
    DllRegisterServer      @1    PRIVATE
    DllUnregisterServer    @2     PRIVATE
    _CreateModule          @3    PRIVATE
    _GetModuleInfo         @4     PRIVATE
```

Windows Component Implementation

We now have stub code for the TagParse component. In this section, we show how to fill in the method stubs and compile this code into a Windows DLL. Add the output files listed earlier in Table 9-9 to the ParseServer project.

 It is a good idea to verify that the stub component successfully compiles before proceeding.

Smart Pointer

We use the IPtr smart pointer interface template in the implementation of the CTagParse class and ITagParse interface.* A smart pointer automatically releases the interface to which it points when it goes out of scope. This alleviates some of the messy code that can accompany COM programming when an error occurs in the middle of a method, and existing interfaces need to be released before returning.

For example, in the code below, if bSuccess is set to false, we need to make sure and call *Release* on pMyString before returning. Otherwise, we will have a memory leak.

```
HRESULT MyMethod( )
{
    IString* pMyString;
    pCoCreateString(L"MyString", &pMyString);
    bool bSuccess = true;
    //...Processing ...
    if(bSuccess == false)
    {
        pMyString->Release( );
        return E_FAIL;
    }
    return S_OK;
}
```

Contrast this approach with using a smart pointer.

```
HRESULT MyMethod( )
{
    IPtr<IString, &IID_IString> spMyString;
    pCoCreateString(L"MyString", &spMyString);
    bool bSuccess = true;
    //...Processing ...
    if(bSuccess == false)
        return E_FAIL;
    return S_OK;
}
```

Here, we can simply return E_FAIL. The smart pointer automatically calls *Release* on its interface when it goes out of scope. The smart pointer implementation is in a file called *sptr.h* in the common directory (see Figure 9-1, earlier in this chapter), along with this chapter's sample code.

Debugging

The Piedmont SDK provides two functions for sending debug output to the Palm Reporter.

---

* The IPtr template is taken from Chapter 9 of "Inside Com" by Dale Rogerson. Piedmont's AUTORELEASE macro provides similar functionality. We do not discuss this macro in this chapter.

void pCoTrace(IString* msg)
> Sends the content of an IString to the Palm Reporter

void pCoTraceAnsi(const CHAR08* msg)
> Sends an ANSI style string to the Palm Reporter

However, these functions don't exist on Windows. We provide four conditionally compiled debug functions that send output to the console (and to an optional file) under Windows, and to the Palm Reporter on the POSE.

void Debug(IString *msg)
> On Windows, sends the content of an IString to the console and a file. On the Palm, same as *pCoTrace*.

void Debugln(IString *msg)
> On Windows, same as *Debug*, but appends a line feed to the output. On the Palm, same as *pCoTrace*.

void Debug(char *format, ...)
> On Windows, sends formatted, variable argument output to the console and an optional file. On the Palm, formats variable output into a string and calls *pCoTrace*.

void Debugln(char *format, ...)
> On Windows, same as variable argument *Debug*, but appends a line feed to the output. On the Palm, same as variable argument *Debug*.

In release mode, these functions are declared as inline, and are optimized away by the compiler.

On Windows, you must define DEBUG_FILE to send output to a file in addition to the console.

```
//Comment out this #define if you don't want to write to a file
#define DEBUG_FILE "C:\\Develop\\TagParse\\debug.txt"
```

We use the _DEBUG directive to enable debug and release modes. In Visual C++, this tracks the conventional debug and release modes. In CodeWarrior, you must manually enable and disable the _DEBUG directive before compiling the component.

You can find the implementation of the *Debug(ln)* functions in *debug.h* and *debug.cpp* in the *common* directory (see Figure 9-1, shown earlier in this chapter), along with this chapter's sample code.

CTagParse Methods

The methods for the CTagParse class consist of the *IEventSource* and *ITagParse* interface methods, and one internal method for verifying tags.

IEventSource

CTagParse implements the IEventSource interface, which contains the *Advise* and *Unadvise* methods. For our component, we only keep track of a single event sink. Add the member declaration for m_ITagParseEventSink to the class declaration for CTagParse.

```
protected:
    MTagParse* m_module; // required, do not remove
    ITagParseEvent *m_ITagParseEventSink;
```

m_ITagParseEventSink is initialized to NULL in the CTagParse constructor.

```
CTagParse::CTagParse(MTagParse* module): m_module(module)
#ifdef PUSH_IUNKNOWN_IMPL_UP
    ,m_CTagParse_refCount(0)
#endif // #ifdef PUSH_IUNKNOWN_IMPL_UP
{
    m_ITagParseEventSink = NULL;
}
```

The modifications to *Advise* and *Unadvise* are straightforward.

```
STDMETHODIMP CTagParse::Advise(REFIID iid, void* sinkIntf)
{
    USE_CONTEXT;
    m_ITagParseEventSink = (ITagParseEvent*)sinkIntf;
    return S_OK;
}

STDMETHODIMP CTagParse::Unadvise(void* sinkIntf)
{
    USE_CONTEXT;
    m_ITagParseEventSink = NULL;
    return S_OK;
}
```

We assign the m_ITagParseEventSink to the callback interface passed into the *Advise* method, and set it back to NULL in the *Unadvise* method.

The CTagParse class contains four methods.

VerifyTags
Internal, protected method for verifying given tag pair

ExtractDataByIndex
ITagParse interface method; extracts data from a string, given a start index and length

ExtractDataByTag
ITagParse interface method; extracts data between a tag pair

CountTagPairs
ITagParse interface method; counts the number of occurrences of a particular tag pair within a string

VerifyTags

We add the declaration for this protected method to *CTagParse.h*.

```
STDMETHOD_(BOOL08,VerifyTags)(IString *startTag, IString *endTag);
```

At the top of *CTagParse.cpp*, we add an include statement for the smart pointer and define the minimum lengths for one-character start and end tags.

```
#include "sptr.h"

#define MIN_START_TAG_LEN 3  //ex: <A>
#define MIN_END_TAG_LEN   4  //ex:</A>
```

VerifyTags uses a simple algorithm to verify that a tag pair is formatted properly.

```
STDMETHODIMP_(BOOL08) CTagParse::VerifyTags(IString *startTag, IString *endTag)
{
   IPtr<IString, &IID_IString> spTempEndTag;
   U32 foundIndex = 0;
   HRESULT hr;

   pCoCreateString(L"", &spTempEndTag);

   if(startTag->GetLength( ) < MIN_START_TAG_LEN ||
      endTag->GetLength( ) < MIN_END_TAG_LEN)
      return FALSE;

   hr = startTag->FindFirstOf(L"<", 0, -1, &foundIndex);
   if(hr == S_FALSE)
      return FALSE;

   hr = startTag->FindFirstOf(L"<", 1, -1, &foundIndex);
   if(hr == S_OK)
      return FALSE;

   hr = startTag->FindFirstOf(L">", 0, -1, &foundIndex);
   if(hr == S_FALSE)  //If the '>' character doesn't exist, return FALSE
      return FALSE;
   else
   {
      //if a '>' character occurs before the end, return FALSE
      if(foundIndex < (startTag->GetLength( )-1))
         return FALSE;
   }

   spTempEndTag->Append(endTag, 0, 1);
   spTempEndTag->Append(endTag, 2, endTag->GetLength( )-2);

   if(startTag->Compare(spTempEndTag, -1) != 0)
      return FALSE;

   return TRUE;
}
```

After declaring some local variables, we check to make sure each tag meets the minimum length requirement. Next we verify the format of the start tag. First we make sure the tag begins with the < character. We then verify there are no other < characters in the tag, and that it ends with the > character. To verify the end tag, we make a temporary copy, skipping the forward slash (/) character. Then we compare the end tag to the start tag to see if it matches. If we have successfully reached the end of the method, we return TRUE.

ExtractDataByIndex

This method extracts data from a string based on a starting index and character count. Although similar to IString's *Extract* and *ExtractAnsi* functions, *ExtractDataByIndex* extracts data into an IString instead of a character buffer. This method might be used, for example, to extract some string data and convert it to another type, such as an integer based on the context in which the data is extracted.

```
STDMETHODIMP CTagParse::ExtractDataByIndex(IString* searchStr, S32 fromIndex, S32
fromCount, IString*& resultStr)
{
    USE_CONTEXT;

    HRESULT hr;
    S32 lExtractCount;
    CHAR16 *pData;
    IPtr<IHost, &IID_IHost> spHost;

    resultStr = NULL;
    pCoGetHost(&spHost);

    if(fromIndex < 0 || (fromIndex > (S32)(searchStr->GetLength() - 1)))
        return E_FAIL;

    S32 countAvail = (searchStr->GetLength() - fromIndex);
    fromCount = (fromCount <= countAvail) ? fromCount : countAvail;

    U32 ulBytesReq = fromCount*(sizeof(CHAR16)) + sizeof(CHAR16);
    if(FAILED(hr = spHost->MemAlloc((void **)&pData, ulBytesReq)))
        return hr;
    spHost->MemSet(pData, 0, ulBytesReq);

    if(FAILED(hr = searchStr->Extract(pData, fromIndex,
                                fromCount, &lExtractCount)))
    {
        spHost->MemFree((void **)&pData);
        return hr;
    }

    if(FAILED(hr = pCoCreateString(pData, &resultStr)))
    {
        spHost->MemFree((void **)&pData);
```

```
        return hr;
    }

    spHost->MemFree((void **)&pData);
    return S_OK;
}
```

We begin by declaring variables and verifying the range of the starting index. We recalculate the fromCount parameter to ensure it does not exceed the search string's length. Next, we allocate enough memory for the result, and initialize it. We fill the data buffer with a call to the search string's *Extract* method. Finally, we copy the results into the return parameter. *pCoCreateString* performs both the allocation and copying in one call. We free the pData buffer before returning.

ExtractDataByTag

This method extracts data between two tags within a string. For example, if a string contains:

```
<Data>My data</Data>,
```

then *ExtractDataByTag* can be called to extract "My data" between the two tags. As with *ExtractDataByIndex*, the result can be converted to another type if desired.

```
STDMETHODIMP CTagParse::ExtractDataByTag(IString* searchStr, IString* startTag,
IString* endTag, S32 maxChar, IString*& resultStr)
{
    USE_CONTEXT;
    U32 ulStartIndex = 0;
    U32 ulEndIndex = 0;
    HRESULT hr;

    if(VerifyTags(startTag, endTag) == FALSE)
    {
        if(m_ITagParseEventSink != NULL)
            m_ITagParseEventSink->InvalidTagPair(startTag, endTag);
        return E_INVALIDARG;
    }

    hr = searchStr->FindSubstr(startTag, ulStartIndex, -1, &ulStartIndex);
    if(hr == S_OK)
    {
        ulStartIndex += startTag->GetLength( );

        hr = searchStr->FindSubstr(endTag, ulStartIndex, -1, &ulEndIndex);

        if(hr == S_OK)
        {
            if(ulEndIndex-ulStartIndex <= (U32)maxChar)
                return ExtractDataByIndex(searchStr, ulStartIndex,
                                          ulEndIndex - ulStartIndex, resultStr);
            else
```

```
            return E_FAIL;
        }
        else
            return E_FAIL;
    }
    else
        return E_FAIL;

    return S_OK;
}
```

First, we call to *VerifyTags* to verify the start and end tags. If this call fails, we source the InvalidTagPair event if a client has registered to receive events. We then return E_INVALIDARG. It is important to return an error code, since a client may not have registered to receive events on the ITagParseEvent interface. Next, we call the search string's *FindSubstr* method to find the start tag. If this succeeds, we skip past the start tag and call *FindSubstr* again to find the end tag. If we find both tags, we call *ExtractDataByIndex* to retrieve the data for the caller. If we don't find the tags, we return E_FAIL.

CountTagPairs

This method counts the number of matching pairs within a string. This function can be used to determine how many elements of a certain kind are in the string.

```
STDMETHODIMP CTagParse::CountTagPairs(IString* searchStr, IString* startTag, IString*
endTag, S32& numItems)
{
    USE_CONTEXT;
    HRESULT hr;
    numItems = 0;
    BOOLO8 bContinue = TRUE;
    U32 ulFoundIndex = 0;
    U32 ulStartIndex = 0;

    if(VerifyTags(startTag, endTag) == FALSE)
    {
        if(m_ITagParseEventSink != NULL)
            m_ITagParseEventSink->InvalidTagPair(startTag, endTag);
        return S_OK;
    }
    while(bContinue == TRUE)
    {
        hr = searchStr->FindSubstr(startTag, ulFoundIndex, -1, &ulFoundIndex);
        if(hr == S_OK)
        {
            ulFoundIndex += startTag->GetLength();  //increment past start tag

            hr = searchStr->FindSubstr(endTag, ulFoundIndex, -1, &ulFoundIndex);
            if(hr == S_OK)
            {
                numItems++; //found both start and end tags
```

```
                ulFoundIndex += endTag->GetLength( );  //increment past end tag
            }
            else  //did not find corresponding end tag
            {
                bContinue = FALSE;
                if(m_ITagParseEventSink != NULL)
                    m_ITagParseEventSink->TagNotFound(endTag);
            }
        }
        else  //There are no (more) tag pairs
            bContinue = FALSE;
    }
    return S_OK;
}
```

We first call *VerifyTags* to verify the start and end tags. Next, we enter a while loop
to look for matching tag pairs. We call *FindSubStr* twice to find the start and end
tags. If we find both tags, we increment numItems.

If we don't find the corresponding end tag, we source a TagNotFound event if a client
is registered to receive events. Note, however, that we don't return an error code as
we do for *VerifyTags*. We want to notify a client of this case, but since we don't add
mismatched tags to numItems, we simply set bContinue to FALSE and break out of the
while loop.

We continue looking for tag pairs in this manner until we do not find another start
tag. We then set bContinue to FALSE to break out of the while loop, and return S_OK.

This completes the TagParse component for windows. You should compile the
ParseServer project before proceeding. In the next two sections, we show how to
compile the component for the Palm, and how to integrate it into an AppForge
Visual Basic application.

> The sample code for this chapter includes a client driver application to
> test the TagParse component on Windows and the Palm. The test
> driver code is based on and, in some cases, copied from, examples
> provided with the Piedmont SDK. The code for this driver is in the
> ParseClient directory (see Figure 9-1, shown earlier in this chapter).
> We do not discuss the driver application in this chapter.

Palm Component Implementation

A Piedmont component is compiled as a shared library with the type set to zpco. Create an empty CodeWarrior project, called ParseServer in the *ParseServer* directory
you created earlier (see Figure 9-1, earlier in this chapter). Change the project settings to correspond with those listed. We assume the default Piedmont SDK and
Metrowerks compiler installations. These settings may vary based on your installation.

Target Settings panel

> *Target name*
>> `ParseServer`
>
> *Linker*
>> `MacOS 68 Linker`
>
> *Post Linker*
>> `PalmRez Post Linker`
>
> *Output directory*
>> `{Project}PalmDebug`

Access Paths Panel

> *User paths*
>> `{Project}`
>>
>> `C:\Program Files\AppForge\SDK\lib\PalmOS\DragonBall\CWPALM70`
>>
>> `{Project}..\common`
>
> *System paths*
>> `{Compiler}Palm OS 3.5 Support`
>>
>> `C:\Program Files\AppForge\SDK\include`
>>
>> `C:\Program Files\AppForge\SDK\include\PalmOS`

68K Target panel

> *Project type*
>> `PalmOS Application`
>
> *Filename*
>> `ParseServer.tmp`

C/C++ Language panel
>> *Checked items (check additional options depending on your development needs)*
>>
>> `Activate C++ Compiler`

68K Processor panel

> *Floating Point*
>> `PalmOS`
>
> *Checked items*
>> `4-Byte Ints`
>>
>> `PC Relative Strings`

PalmRez Post Linker panel

> *Mac Resource files*
>> `ParseServer.tmp`

Output file
    ParseServer.prc
Type
    zpco
Creator
    TAGS
Transliteration
    Palm OS 3.1 and later

Add the same files to this project as you did for the Windows ParseServer project except for the IDX, MDX, DEF, INC, and IDL files. You will also need to add the appropriate Piedmont libraries. These libraries can be found in the *lib\PalmOS\ DragonBall\CWPALM70* subdirectory of the Piedmont SDK directory. Add *pCOMd.lib* and *pCOMServerD.lib* for debug builds, or *pCOM.lib* and *pCOMServer.lib* for release builds. Of course, you also need to add the standard runtime library, for example, *MSL Runtime Palm OS (4i).Lib*.

When you compile the project, you will receive a warning that *__Startup__* in *PalmOS_Startup.c* is previously defined. You can ignore this warning, since Piedmont provides its own startup code.

AppForge VM Integration

In this section, we integrate the TagParse component into an AppForge project in Visual Basic. We write a simple driver application in Visual Basic and then install it on the Palm.

Create a new AppForge project for the Palm called AFVBClient in the *AFVBClient* directory (see Figure 9-1, earlier in the chapter). Name the form frmTagParse and add three AFButton controls with the properties from Table 9-10. Figure 9-7 shows how the form should look.

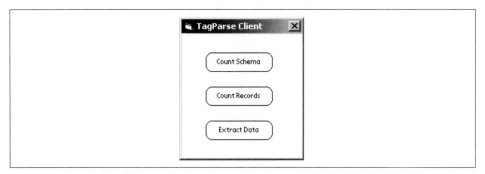

Figure 9-7. AFVBClient form

Table 9-10. AFButton control properties

Name	Caption
btnCountSchema	Count schema
btnCountRecs	Count records
btnExtractData	Extract data

Add a reference for the TagParse to the AFVBClient project. Select Project → References from the main menu and browse to the *TagParse_tlb.tlb* type library in the *ParseServer\Debug* directory. The MTagParseLib module reference should now appear as shown in Figure 9-8. Click OK to close this window.

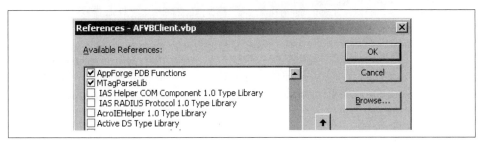

Figure 9-8. AFVBClient project references

Start the form by adding the following initialization code to frmTagParse.

```
Option Explicit

Dim WithEvents tagParse As CTagParse
```

In declaring the tagParse variable, we use the WithEvents keyword to indicate that we want to sink events from it.

Next, declare the two event sink methods.

```
'sink invalid tag pair event
Private Sub tagParse_InvalidTagPair(ByVal startTag As String,
                                    ByVal endTag As String)
   MsgBox "Invalid tag pair:" + startTag + ", " + endTag
End Sub

'sink tag not found event
Private Sub tagParse_TagNotFound(ByVal tag As String)
   MsgBox "Tag not found: " + tag
End Sub
```

With Automation in Visual Basic, the event method consists of the variable name, followed by an underscore and the event name. We simply display each method's arguments in a message box.

Let's look at the code for the buttons listed previously in Table 9-10. Here is the code for the btnCountSchema click event.

```
Private Sub btnCountSchema_Click()
    Dim numItems As Long
    Dim tagParseStr As String

    tagParseStr = "<Database><Data>" & _
            "<Record>Record data 1</Record>" & _
            "<Record>Record data 2</Record>" & _
            "<Record>Record data 3<Record>" & _
            "</Data></Database>"

    Set tagParse = New CTagParse
    numItems = tagParse.CountTagPairs(tagParseStr, "<Schema>", "</Schema>>")
    MsgBox "Num schemas: " + CStr(numItems)
End Sub
```

After creating a new CTagParse object, we call *CountTagPairs* with the malformed tag pair <Schema></Schema>>. When this method runs, we will receive the InvalidTagPair event (see Figure 9-9). This is followed by a message box with the number of schemas (see Figure 9-10). There will be zero schemas, since the tag pair could not be found.

Figure 9-9. InvalidTagPair event

Figure 9-10. Number of schemas

Here is the code for the btnCountRecs click event.

```
Private Sub btnCountRecs_Click()
    Dim numItems As Long
    Dim tagParseStr As String

    tagParseStr = "<Database><Data>" & _
            "<Record>Record data 1</Record>" & _
            "<Record>Record data 2</Record>" & _
```

```
            "<Record>Record data 3<Record>" & _
            "</Data></Database>"

    Set tagParse = New CTagParse
    numItems = tagParse.CountTagPairs(tagParseStr, "<Record>", "</Record>")
    MsgBox "Num records: " + CStr(numItems)
End Sub
```

This time, we pass in a valid tag pair to count the number of records, but we pass in a malformed record set (the third record has an invalid end tag). When this method runs, we will receive the TagNotFound event, as shown in Figure 9-11. This is followed by a message box with the number of records, as shown in Figure 9-12. The number of records is 2, since the last malformed tag pair is not counted.

Figure 9-11. TagNotFound event

Figure 9-12. Number of records

Here is the code for the btnExtractData click event.

```
    Private Sub btnExtractData_Click()
        Set tagParse = New CTagParse
        Dim resultStr As String
        Dim tagParseStr As String

        tagParseStr = "<Database><Data>" & _
                "<Record>Record data 1</Record>" & _
                "<Record>Record data 2</Record>" & _
                "<Record>Record data 3</Record>" & _
                "</Data></Database>"

        resultStr = tagParse.ExtractDataByTag(tagParseStr, "<Data>", "</Data>", 512)
        MsgBox "Record data: " + resultStr
    End Sub
```

This event shows how to successfully parse and extract data. We call *ExtractDataByTag* to extract the record data between the <Data></Data> tag pair and to display the result in a message box.

In Figure 9-13, we show the results as they appear on the Palm, instead of from within VB. Of course, this is what you would expect with Piedmont. The TagParse component behaves identically within VB as it does on the Palm. As we mentioned previously, this is what makes Piedmont such a powerful architecture for developing and testing components on the desktop and deploying them to the Palm.

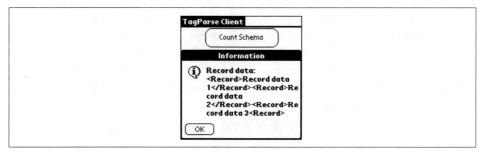

Figure 9-13. Record data

Our goal in this chapter was to give you a broad overview of AppForge's Piedmont SDK for extending their flagship product. Although we covered quite a bit of ground in our example, we hope you can see how powerful Piedmont is. It brings true component-based development and support to the desktop and the handheld in a seamless fashion.

Debugging

In this chapter, we look at some techniques for debugging an AppForge application on the POSE and the Palm handheld. These techniques are important, since you cannot step through an AppForge application or set breakpoints after it is installed on POSE or the handheld. We show how to use AppForge's *Debug* module in conjunction with the Palm Reporter and the Palm's buttons in POSE to obtain trace output at various points in an AppForge program. We also show how to send debug output to a Palm database, which can be used on both POSE and the handheld.

These techniques are only a starting point, however. You will undoubtedly expand these or develop techniques of your own to suit your needs.

Conditional Compilation

Conditional compilation is a part of Visual Basic, and allows you to compile out certain parts of your code for release versus debug versions, for example. Consider the *Form_Load* subroutine shown in Example 10-1.

Example 10-1. Conditional compilation example

```
#Const AFDEBUG = 1

Private Sub Form_Load( )

    'Form initialization ...
    txtFlow.Text = 150

#If AFDEBUG Then
    MsgBox "txtFlow.Text = " + txtFlow.Text
#End If

End Sub
```

After the form is initialized, the contents of the txtFlow component are displayed in a message box. The #If...#End If block is a conditional compilation block. If the

AFDEBUG argument is 1, Visual Basic includes this code block, and displays the results. If AFDEBUG is 0, this block is excluded from the program, and the results are not displayed.

You may assign conditional compilation arguments for an individual module, or for the entire project. You assign arguments for individual modules with the #Const statement at the beginning of the module. You assign arguments for a project in the Make tab of the project's properties, as shown in Figure 10-1.

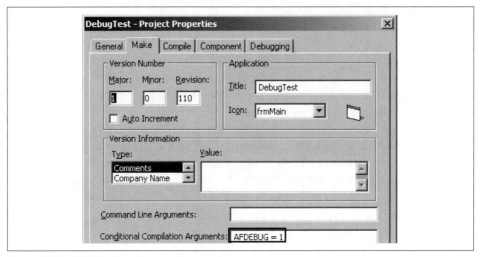

Figure 10-1. Visual Basic project make properties

In the next two sections, we show how to use conditional compilation in conjunction with the Palm Reporter and the keys on the Palm to obtain trace output.

Palm Reporter

The Palm Reporter is a standalone trace utility that can be used to display real-time trace output from the Palm OS Emulator (POSE).* The Reporter is especially important since you cannot execute Visual Basic code step by step, or set breakpoints, after compiling the code and installing it on the Palm. To use the Reporter, you simply run it and POSE at the same time. With the Reporter installed, you may configure POSE to send trace output to a file or to the Reporter application.

AppForge's *Debug* module includes a *Print* method, which sends its output to the *Immediate* window in Visual Basic and to the Reporter on POSE. Example 10-2 contains the code from Example 10-1, modified to use this method.

---

* The Palm Reporter can be downloaded freely from the same site where POSE is obtained. We do not cover the installation and use of the Reporter in this chapter.

Example 10-2. Conditional compilation example

```
#Const AFDEBUG = 1

Private Sub Form_Load( )

   'Form initialization ...
   txtFlow.Text = 150

#If AFDEBUG Then
   Debug.Print "txtFlow.Text = " + txtFlow.Text
#End If

End Sub
```

Palm Buttons

The Palm's buttons can also be captured and used to trigger debugging statements or functions. You might use this technique to asynchronously trace a program's state information at various points in its execution. The most common Palm buttons are shown in Figure 10-2.

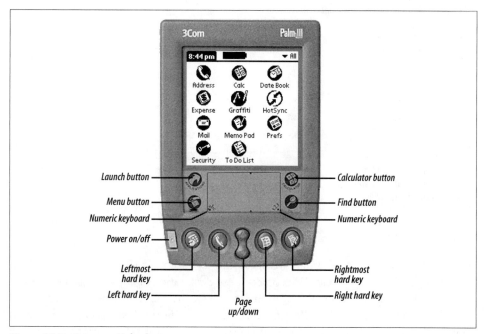

Figure 10-2. Common Palm buttons

The AppForge system library contains two functions that allow your program to register and release the keycode associated with a button.

RegisterKeyCode
> Registers a keycode for a corresponding button

ReleaseKeyCode
> Releases the keycode for a corresponding button

In addition to registering a keycode, you must set the active form's KeyPreview property to True. Registered keys are then received as a *Form_KeyDown* event within your program. Example 10-3 shows how this works in code.

Example 10-3. Key registration and release

```
Public Const vchrHard1 = &H204        ' Leftmost hard key
Public Const vchrHard2 = &H205        ' Center-left hard key
Public Const vchrHard3 = &H206        ' Center-right hard key
Public Const vchrHard4 = &H207        ' Rightmost hard key

Private Sub Form_Load()

#If AFDEBUG Then
  RegisterKeyCode vchrHard1
  RegisterKeyCode vchrHard2
  RegisterKeyCode vchrHard3
  RegisterKeyCode vchrHard4
#End If

End Sub

Private Sub Form_Unload(Cancel As Integer)

#If AFDEBUG Then
   ReleaseKeyCode vchrHard1
   ReleaseKeyCode vchrHard2
   ReleaseKeyCode vchrHard3
   ReleaseKeyCode vchrHard4
#End If

End Sub
```

We start by declaring constants corresponding to the four round buttons along the bottom of the Palm handheld. We copied these declarations from the AppForge documentation, which provides declarations for all of the Palm's buttons. We register these keycodes with a call to *RegisterKeyCode* in the *Form_Load* event and release them with a call to *ReleaseKeyCode* in the *Form_Unload* event. Keep in mind that these keycodes are tied up while the form is active. If you do not want to tie up the buttons this way, you might consider using menu options to trigger calls to the keycode registration and release functions.

In the form's *Form_KeyDown* event, shown in Example 10-4, we store the name of the key in the key variable and call *Debug_Key* to print the value.

Example 10-4. Form_KeyDown event

```
Private Sub Form_KeyDown(KeyCode As Integer, Shift As Integer)

#If AFDEBUG Then

  Dim key As String

  Select Case KeyCode

  Case vchrHard1
     key = "vchrHard1"

  Case vchrHard2
     key = "vchrHard2"

  Case vchrHard3
     key = "vchrHard3"

  Case vchrHard4
     key = "vchrHard4"

  End Select

  Debug_Key (key)

#End If

End Sub

#If AFDEBUG Then
Private Sub Debug_Key(key As String)
   Debug.Print ("You pressed the " + key + " key.")
End Sub
```

You can extend this technique to perhaps call different functions depending on which key is pressed. Again, this technique is especially useful for asynchronously examining the state of your program at various points of execution.

Debug Database

The previous debugging techniques involve POSE and the Palm Reporter. In this section, we show how to send debug information to a database on POSE or the Palm handheld. This technique is especially useful for debugging applications where the Reporter may not or cannot be used.

We encapsulate debug functionality in a module called *modDebugDB*, which can be accessed by other components in our application. This module contains four functions for logging messages to a database.

DebugDatabase
> This public subroutine logs a message to the debug database.

OpenDebugDatabase
> This private subroutine creates the debug database, if necessary, and opens it.

WriteDebugRecord
> This private function writes a record to the debug database.

DeleteDebugDatabase
> This public subroutine deletes the debug database.

PalmIDtoLong(PalmID As String) As Long
> This private helper function converts a Palm ID String to a Long. It is copied from the PDBTutorial project that comes with AppForge. We do not discuss this function in this chapter.

We begin the module by declaring variables for a database handle and record type.

```
Option Explicit

' Use this global to store the database handle
Private dbDebug As Long

Public Type tDebugRecord
        Message As String
End Type
```

Here, we simply store a message String in each record. This is the listing for *DebugDatabase*.

```
Public Sub DebugDatabase(msg As String)
    Dim debugRecord As tDebugRecord
    OpenDebugDatabase

    If dbDebug <> 0 Then
       'We successfully opened the database
       debugRecord.Message = msg
       WriteDebugRecord debugRecord
       PDBClose dbDebug
    Else
       MsgBox "Could not open the debug database."
    End If

End Sub
```

After declaring a record in which to store the message, we call *OpenDebugDatabase* to open the database. We store the message in the database record and pass its record to the *WriteDebugRecord* subroutine.

Here is the listing for *OpenDebugDatabase*.

```
Private Sub OpenDebugDatabase( )

    ' Try and open the database
    #If APPFORGE Then
    dbDebug = PDBOpen(ByTypeCreator, "afdebug", 0, 0, PalmIDtoLong("DATA"), _
                    PalmIDtoLong("DBUG"), afModeReadWrite)
    #Else
    dbDebug = PDBOpen(ByTypeCreator, App.Path & "\afdebug", 0, 0, _
                    PalmIDtoLong("DATA"), PalmIDtoLong("DBUG"), _
                    afModeReadWrite)
    #End If

    If dbDebug = 0 Then
      'Assume the database does not exist and attempt to create it
      #If APPFORGE Then
        'Create new database (if on the device)
        dbDebug = PDBCreateDatabase("afdebug", PalmIDtoLong("DATA"), _
                                PalmIDtoLong("DBUG"))
      #Else
        'Create new database (if on the PC)
        dbDebug = PDBCreateDatabase(App.Path & "\afdebug", _
                                PalmIDtoLong("DATA"), _
                                PalmIDtoLong("DBUG"))
      #End If

      If dbDebug <> 0 Then
       'Create the debug table
       PDBCreateTable dbDebug, "DebugTable", "Message String"
      Else
         MsgBox "Could not create database."
      End If

    End If

End Sub
```

If the call to *PDBOpen* fails, we assume the database does not exist. We then call *PDBCreateDatabase* to create the database. After creating the database, we call *PDBCreateTable* to create the database schema.

Here is the listing for *WriteDebugRecord*.

```
Private Function WriteDebugRecord(dbRecord As tDebugRecord) As Boolean

        'Create a new record in dbDebug using the schema.
        PDBCreateRecordBySchema dbDebug

        'Write the data to the new record.
        WriteDebugRecord = PDBWriteRecord(dbDebug, VarPtr(dbRecord))

        'Update the new record.
        PDBUpdateRecord dbDebug
End Function
```

After creating a new record with a call to *PDBCreateRecordBySchema*, we call *PDBWriteRecord* to write the record to the database. Finally, we call *PDBUpdateRecord* to commit the results to the database.

Here is the listing for *DeleteDebugDatabase*.

```
Public Function DeleteDebugDatabase() As Boolean
    Dim bResult As Boolean
    #If APPFORGE Then
      'Delete the database (if on the device)
      bResult = PDBDeleteDatabase("afdebug", 0, 0)
    #Else
      'Delete the database (if on the PC)
      bResult = PDBDeleteDatabase(App.Path & "\afdebug", 0, 0)
    #End If

    DeleteDebugDatabase = bResult

End Function
```

Here, we simply call *PDBDeleteDatabase* and return the result. This function can be called, for example, by an application upon initialization, or it can be tied to a button press on the Palm to selectively delete the database as desired. AppForge comes with a PDB Database Viewer, which is a handy utility for viewing the debug database. Of course, you will need to export the database from POSE or the Palm handheld onto the PC for viewing.

You can add conditionally compiled calls to this module at any point in your application:

```
Private Sub Form_Load()

#If AFDEBUG Then
  DebugDatabase ("Form_Load: IN")
#End If

#If AFDEBUG Then
  DebugDatabase ("Processing...")
#End If

'... Load processing

#If AFDEBUG Then
    DebugDatabase ("Form_Load: OUT")
#End If

End Sub
```

Using conditional compilation in conjunction with the Palm Reporter, Palm buttons, and the Debug Database module are just some of the approaches you can take when debugging Visual Basic applications using AppForge.

Appendixes

Ingot and Enumeration Summary

This appendix provides a convenient reference to the current set of AppForge ingots' supported properties, methods, and events. It also includes the major enumerations and constants used by the AppForge ingots and libraries.

Basic Ingot Components

Command Button Ingot

Properties
Alignment, Appearance, BackColor, Caption, Enabled, FontName, FontSize, FontStyle, ForeColor, Height, Index, Left, Tag, Top, Visible, Width

Methods
Move, Refresh, SetFocus, ZOrder

Events
Click

CheckBox Ingot

Properties
Alignment, AllowGrayState, Appearance, BackColor, Caption, Enabled, Font-Name, FontSize, FontStyle, ForeColor, Height, Index, Left, Tag, Top, Value, Visible, Width

Methods
Move, Refresh, SetFocus, ZOrder

Events
Click

ComboBox Ingot

Properties
Alignment, Appearance, BackColor, Enabled, FontName, FontSize, FontStyle, ForeColor, Height, Index, ItemData, Left, List, ListCount, ListIndex, Locked, NewIndex, SelLength, SelStart, SelText, Sorted, Style, Tag, Text, Top, TopIndex, Visible, Width

Methods
AddItem, Clear, Move, Refresh, RemoveItem, SetFocus, ZOrder

Events
Change, Click, SelectItem

Label Ingot

Properties
Alignment, BackColor, BorderStyle, Caption, Enabled, FontName, FontSize, FontStyle, ForeColor, Height, Index, Left, Tag, Top, Visible, Width

Methods
Move, Refresh, SetFocus, ZOrder

Events
Change, Click

ListBox Ingot

Properties
Alignment, Appearance, BackColor, Border, Enabled, FontName, FontSize, FontStyle, ForeColor, Height, Index, ItemData, Left, List, ListCount, ListIndex, MultiSelect, NewIndex, SelCount, Selected, Sorted, Style, Tag, Text, Top, TopIndex, Visible, Width

Methods
AddItem, Clear, Move, Refresh, RemoveItem, SetFocus, ZOrder

Events
Change, Click, SelectItem

Radio Button Ingot

Properties
Alignment, Appearance, BackColor, Caption, Enabled, FontName, FontSize, FontStyle, ForeColor, GroupID, Height, Index, Left, Tag, Top, Value, Visible, Width

Methods
   Move, Refresh, SetFocus, ZOrder
Event
   Click

Shape Ingot

Properties
   BackColor, BorderColor, BorderStyle, BorderWidth, Enabled, FillColor, Fill-Style, Height, Index, Left, Shape, Tag, Top, Visible, Width
Methods
   Move, Refresh, SetFocus, ZOrder

TextBox Ingot

Properties
   Alignment, Appearance, BackColor, BorderStyle, DisplayableLines, Enabled, FontName, FontSize, FontStyle, ForeColor, Height, Index, Left, Locked, Max-Length, MultiLine, PasswordChar, ScrollBars, SelLength, SelStart, SelText, Tag, Text, Top, TopLine, TotalLines, UnderlineStyle, Visible, Width
Methods
   Move, Refresh, SetFocus, ZOrder
Events
   Change, Click

Timer Ingot

Properties
   Enabled, Height, Index, Interval, Left, Tag, Top, Visible, Width
Methods
   Move, SetFocus, ZOrder
Event
   Timer

AppForge Form

The form is listed here because it's part of *BasicIngots.prc,* which all applications must have deployed to the device.

Properties
   BackColor, Caption, Enabled, ForeColor, Height, KeyPreview, Left, Scale-Height, ScaleLeft, ScaleTop, ScaleWidth, StartUpPosition, Tag, Top, Visible, Width

Methods
    Hide, Move, Refresh, Show, ZOrder

Events
    Activate, Click, Deactivate, Initialize, KeyDown, KeyPress, KeyUp, Load, QueryUnload, Resize, Terminate, Unload

Enhanced Ingots

Graphic Ingot

Properties
    BackColor, Enabled, Height, Index, Left, Picture, Tag, Top, Visible, Width

Methods
    Cls, DrawCircle, DrawLine, DrawRectangle, DrawText, Invert, InvertArea, Move, PaintPicture, Refresh, SetFocus, SetPixel, ZOrder

Events
    Click, MouseDown, MouseMove

Graphic Button Ingot

Properties
    Alignment, BackColor, DisabledPicture, DownPicture, Enabled, FocusPicture, Height, Index, Left, NoFocusPicture, Tag, Top, Visible, Width

Methods
    Move, Refresh, SetFocus, ZOrder

Events
    Click

Grid Ingot

Properties
    Appearance, BackColor, BorderStyle, Col, ColAlignment, ColIsVisible, Cols, ColWidth, Enabled, FontName, FontSize, FontStyle, ForeColor, GridLines, Height, Index, ItemData, Left, LeftCol, NewRow, Row, RowHeight, RowIsVisible, Rows, SelectionType, Tag, Text, TextMatrix, Top, TopRow, Visible, Width

Methods
    AddItem, Move, Refresh, RemoveItem, SetFocus, ZOrder

Events
    Click, SelectCell

Horizontal Scroll Ingot

Properties
> Appearance, BackColor, Enabled, Height, Index, LargeChange, Left, Min, Max, SmallChange, Tag, ThumbColor, Top, Value, Visible, Width

Methods
> Move, Refresh, SetFocus, ZOrder

Event
> Change

Slider Ingot

Properties
> Appearance, Enabled, Height, Index, LargeChange, Left, Max, Min, ShowTicks, SmallChange, Tag, ThumbBackColor, ThumbForeColor, TickFrequency, Top, TrackBackColor, TrackForeColor, Value, Visible, Width

Methods
> Move, Refresh, SetFocus, ZOrder

Event
> SliderMoved

Vertical Scroll Ingot

Properties
> Appearance, BackColor, Enabled, Height, Index, LargeChange, Left, Min, Max, SmallChange, Tag, ThumbColor, Top, Value, Visible, Width

Methods
> Move, Refresh, SetFocus, ZOrder

Event
> Change

Multimedia Ingots

Movie Ingot

Properties
> CurrentFrame, Enabled, FileName, FramesPerSec, Height, Index, Left, LoopMovie, Tag, Top, TotalFrames, Visible, Width

Methods
> Move, Play, Refresh, SetFocus, Stop, ZOrder

Event
> End

FilmStrip Ingot

Properties
> AnimationStyle, Enabled, Frame, FrameCount, FrameFile, FrameIndex, Frames, Height, Index, Interval, Left, Tag, Top, Visible, Width

Methods
> AddFrame, ClearFrames, Play, Refresh, RemoveFrame, SetFocus, Stop, ZOrder

Events
> Click, LastFrame

Tone Ingot

Properties
> Duration, Enabled, Height, Index, Left, Pitch, Tag, Top, Visible, Width

Methods
> Move, Refresh, SetFocus, ZOrder

Events
> None

Data Communication Ingots

Signature Capture Ingot

Properties
> BackColor, BackPicture, BorderStyle, Enabled, Height, Index, Left, PenColor, PenWidth, SignatureData, Tag, Top, Visible, Width

Methods
> Clear, Move, Refresh, SetFocus, ZOrder

Events
> None

ClientSocket Ingot

Properties
> Height, Index, Left, Protocol, RemoteHostIP, RemotePort, Tag, Top, Visible, Width

Methods
> Close, Connect, GetByte, GetInteger, GetLong, GetString, Move, ResolveHost-Name, SendByte, SendInteger, SendLong, SendString, SetFocus, ZOrder

Events
> DataWaiting, Error

INetHTTP Ingot

Properties

Configuration, ConnectionAvailable, ContentType, Conversion, DeviceID, Document, Height, Index, Left, RequestTimeout, ResponseCode, ResponseInfo, StillExecuting, SystemError, Tag, Top, URL, Visible, Width

Methods

Clear, Execute, GetChunk, GetHeader, Move, SetFocus, URLEncodeString, ZOrder

Events

Error, ReceivedData, StateChanged

Serial Ingot

Properties

Break, CommEvent, CommPort, CTSHolding, DSRHolding, Handshaking, Height, InBufferCount, InBufferSize, Index, Input, InputLen, Left, Output, PortOpen, RThreshold, Settings, Tag, Top, Visible, Width

Methods

Move, ReadInputB, SetFocus, WriteOutputB, ZOrder

Event

OnComm

Scanner Ingot

Properties

AimDuration, Angle, AssertParamsOnOpen, BeepAfterGoodDecode, BidirectionalRedundancy, CodebarParams, Code128Params, Code39Params, Code93Params, D2of5Params, ErrorCode, Height, I2of5Params, Index, LEDOnDuration, LEDState, Left, LinearCodeTypeSecurityLevel, MSIPlesseyParams, PointerMode, ScanEnabled, ScannedBarCodeType, ScannerOpen, ScanTimeOut, Tag, Top, TransmitCodeIDCharacter, TriggerMode, UPCEANParams, Visible, Width

Methods

DoScan, GetDecoderVersion, GetPortDriverVersion, GetScanManagerVersion, SetDefaultParams, StopScan

Events

ScanError, ScanReceived, ScanTimedOut

AFTone Ingot Pitch values

The following table provides values for the *Pitch* property. This property will reproduce the desired note, as indicated:

Note	1st octave	2nd octave	3rd octave	4th octave	5th octave
C	262	523	1047	2093	4186
CS	277	554	1108	2218	
D	295	587	1175	2349	
DS	311	622	1245	2489	
E	330	659	1319	2637	
F	349	699	1397	2794	
FS	370	740	1480	2960	
G	392	784	1568	3136	
GS	415	831	1661	3322	
A	440	880	1760	3520	
AS	466	932	1864	3729	
B	494	988	1976	3951	

Database Error Codes

The following table lists errors that are returned from calls to the method *PDBGetLastError*. Note that some of these "errors" are, in reality, simply status codes and not true errors that are reported after unsuccessful database operations.

Constant	Value	Description
ErrNone	0	No errors have occurred.
ErrMemError	−1	A memory error occurred.
ErrIndexOutOfRange	−2	The designated index is out of range.
ErrInvalidParam	−3	The parameter specified is not valid.
ErrReadOnly	−4	An attempt has been made to modify a database that is in read-only mode.
ErrDatabaseOpen	−5	The previous action could not be performed, and the database is open.
ErrCantOpen	−6	The database could not be opened.
ErrCantFind	−7	Can't find the desired resource.
ErrRecordInWrongCard	−8	An attempt to attach a record has been made when the database and record reside on different memory cards.
ErrCorruptDatabase	−9	The database is corrupted.
ErrRecordDeleted	−10	The specified record has been deleted.

Constant	Value	Description
ErrRecordArchived	−11	The record being acted on is an archived record, and the action requires a non-archived record.
ErrNotRecordDB	−12	A record function has been attempted on a resource database.
ErrROMBased	−13	There was an attempt to modify a ROM-based database.
ErrRecordBusy	−14	The record being acted on is busy.
ErrNoOpenDatabase	−15	No databases are currently open.
ErrInvalidCategory	−16	The specified category is not valid.
ErrNotValidRecord	−17	The record handle used is not valid.
ErrWriteOutOfBounds	−18	A write method has surpassed the bounds of the record.
ErrSeekFailed	−19	The last attempted seek has failed.
ErrAlreadyOpenForWrites	−20	The database is already open in write mode.
ErrOpenedByAnotherTask	−21	The specified database is already opened by another task.
ErrUniqueIDNotFound	−22	A record with the designated unique ID was not found.
ErrAlreadyExists	−23	A database with the same name already exists in RAM.
ErrInvalidDatabaseName	−24	The name designated for the database is not valid.
ErrDatabaseProtected	−25	The database is protected.
ErrInvalidVarType	−26	The type specified for a variable is not valid.
ErrFieldMisMatch	−27	The specified field type does not match the return field type.
ErrNoFieldsDefined	−28	No fields have been defined for the specified database.
ErrInvalidFieldNum	−29	The field number specified is not valid.
ErrInvalidFieldType	−30	The field type specified is not valid.
ErrRecordNotInEditableState	−31	The record cannot be edited.
ErrNoRecordSelected	−32	No record is selected.
ErrEmptyDatabase	−33	The database is empty.
ErrDatabaseNotOpenedForReading	−34	The database cannot be read.
ErrDatabaseNotOpenedForWriting	−35	The database cannot be written to.
ErrNoSchemaDefined	−36	A schema has not been defined.
ErrInvalidFieldName	−37	The field name is invalid.
ErrNoSortDefined	−38	A sorting method has not been specified.
ErrUnableToCreateSortInfo	−39	Unable to create the sort information.
ErrUnableToCreateSortIndex	−40	Unable to create a sort index.
ErrReadOutOfBounds	−41	The database read out of bounds.
ErrCouldNotDeleteRecord	−42	Unable to delete the record.
ErrCouldNotConvertString	−43	Unable to convert the string to another type.
ErrCannotOverwriteAppInfo	−44	The information cannot be overwritten.
ErrInvalidCategoryBlock	−45	The category block is invalid.
ErrNoCategoryInfo	−46	There is no category information.

Constant	Value	Description
ErrCategoryNameTooLong	−47	The name of the category is too long.
ErrCouldNotAttachAppInfo	−48	Unable to attach the AppInfo.
ErrInvalidDeleteMode	−49	The delete mode is invalid.
ErrReservedCategory	−50	This category is reserved.
ErrUnsupportedOperation	−51	This operation is unsupported.
ErrUnknown	−1000	An unknown error has occurred.

Palm OS system preference settings

The following list provides the AppForge constant and actual values for getting and changing the Palm OS preference settings, using the *GetSystemPreference* and *SetSystemPreference* methods from the AppForge Extended Function library.

Constant	Value	Description
afExtLibSysPrefAlarmSoundLevelV20	10	Specifies whether sound alarms are enabled or disabled.
afExtLibSysPrefAlarmSoundVolume	32	The sound level for alarms.
afExtLibSysPrefAllowEasterEggs	16	If true, mysterious things happen.
afExtLibSysPrefAnimationLevel	29	
afExtLibSysPrefAntennaCharAppCreator	39	The Creator ID of the application to launch when the antenna is raised (used only for devices with built-in antennas). Available with preferences version 6 or greater.
afExtLibSysPrefAutoOffDuration	7	Minutes of user idle time before the device powers off. The default value for this preference is specified in defaultAutoOffDuration. In preferences version 8, this preference was replaced by autoOffDurationSecs.
afExtLibSysPrefBeamReceive	33	If true, the device can receive beams from other devices. If false, the device cannot receive beams, but can still send them.
afExtLibSysPrefCalcCharAppCreator	24	The Creator ID of the application to be launched by the Calculator silkscreen button.
afExtLibSysPrefCalibrateDigitizerAtReset	34	If true, the user must recalibrate the digitizer after a soft reset. The default is false.
afExtLibSysPrefCountry	1	The country for which the device was built.
afExtLibSysPrefDateFormat	2	The short format used to display dates.
afExtLibSysPrefDefSerialPlugIn	36	The Creator ID of the default serial plug-in database.
afExtLibSysPrefDeviceLocked	12	If true, the device is locked. When the device is locked, it remains so until the user enters the password.

Constant	Value	Description
afExtLibSysPrefGameSoundLevelV20	9	Specifies whether game sound effects are enabled or disabled.
afExtLibSysPrefGameSoundVolume	31	The sound level for game sounds.
afExtLibSysPrefHard1CharAppCreator	20	The Creator ID of the application to be launched by the leftmost hard key (the Date Book button by default).
afExtLibSysPrefHard2CharAppCreator	21	The Creator ID of the application to be launched by the second hard key from the left (the Address button by default).
afExtLibSysPrefHard3CharAppCreator	22	The Creator ID of the application to be launched by the second hard key from the right (the To Do List button by default).
afExtLibSysPrefHard4CharAppCreator	23	The Creator ID of the application to be launched by the rightmost hard key (the Memo Pad button by default).
afExtLibSysPrefHardCradle2CharAppCreator	28	The Creator ID of the application to be launched by the HotSync button on the modem.
afExtLibSysPrefHardCradleCharAppCreator	25	The Creator ID of the application to be launched by the hard key on the HotSync cradle.
afExtLibSysPrefHidePrivateRecordsV33	11	If true, applications should not display database records that have the secret attribute bit set.
afExtLibSysPrefLauncherAppCreator	26	The Creator ID of the application to be launched by the Applications silkscreen button.
afExtLibSysPrefLocalSyncRequiresPassword	13	If true, the user must enter a password before a HotSync(r) operation can be performed.
afExtLibSysPrefLongDateFormat	3	The long format used to display dates.
afExtLibSysPrefMeasurementSystem	40	The system of measurement to use. Available with preferences version 7 or greater.
afExtLibSysPrefMinutesWestOfGMT	17	The time zone given as minutes EAST of Greenwich Mean Time (GMT). For preferences version 9, use timeZone instead.
afExtLibSysPrefNumberFormat	6	The format used for numbers, with regard to the thousands separator and the decimal point.
afExtLibSysPrefRemoteSyncRequiresPassword	14	If true, the user must enter a password on the desktop computer before a HotSync(r) operation can be performed.
afExtLibSysPrefRonamaticChar	19	The virtual character generated when the user enters the ronamatic stroke. The ronamatic stroke is dragging the pen from the Graffiti(r) area to the top of the screen.
afExtLibSysPrefStayLitWhenPluggedIn	38	If this constant is true and if afExtLibSysPrefStayOnWhenPluggedIn is true, the device stays lit when it is in its cradle.
afExtLibSysPrefStayOnWhenPluggedIn	37	If true, the device stays powered on when it is in the cradle.

Constant	Value	Description
afExtLibSysPrefSysBatteryKind	15	The type of batteries installed.
afExtLibSysPrefSysPrefFlags	27	
afExtLibSysPrefSysSoundLevelV20	8	Specifies whether system sounds are enabled or disabled.
afExtLibSysPrefSysSoundVolume	30	The sound level for system sounds, such as taps and beeps.
afExtLibSysPrefSystemKeyboardID	35	The Resource ID of the keyboard panel.
afExtLibSysPrefTimeFormat	5	The format used to display time values.
afExtLibSysPrefVersion	0	The preferences version number.
afExtLibSysPrefWeekStartDay	4	The first day of the week (Sunday or Monday). Days of the week are numbered from 0 to 6, starting with Sunday = 0.
Available with Version 8 or greater		
afExtLibSysPrefShowPrivateRecords	41	If `true`, applications should show a gray rectangle in place of database records that have the secret attribute bit set. If `hideSecretRecords` is `false`, this value is ignored.
Available with Version 9 or greater		
afExtLibSysPrefLanguage	48	The language that the device should use.
afExtLibSysPrefLocale	49	Locale for the country selected via the `Setup app /Formats` panel.
afExtLibSysPrefTimeZone	43	The time zone given as minutes east of Greenwich Mean Time (GMT).
afExtLibSysPrefTimeZoneCountry	50	The country selected to specify what the time zone is.
afExtLibSysPrefDaylightSavingAdjustment	44	The number of minutes to add to the current time for daylight savings time.
afExtLibSysPrefDaylightSavings	18	The type of daylight savings correction. For preferences version 9, instead use `daylightSavingAdjustment`.
afExtLibSysPrefDefaultAppCreator	52	Creator ID of the application that is launched after a reset.
afExtLibSysPrefAttentionFlags	51	The user's preferences for receiving attention signals.
afExtLibSysPrefAutoLockTime	46	The date at which the system locks itself. If `afExtLibSysPrefAutoLockType` is after `PresetDelay`, this is the number of seconds until the system should lock itself.
afExtLibSysPrefAutoLockTimeFlag	47	If `true`, `afExtLibSysPrefAutoLockTime` is given in minutes. If `false`, the time is given in hours.
afExtLibSysPrefAutoLockType	45	Specifies when the auto-locking feature should take effect.

DBSLib Sample Project Setup

In this appendix, we show you how to create and configure the DBSLib shared library project using Metrowerks CodeWarrior 7 for Windows (IDE version 4.1.0.2 Build 0646). Creating a shared library in CodeWarrior is analogous to generating a library on the Windows platform, with an additional post linker step. After your source code is compiled into objects, CodeWarrior creates a temporary file (TMP file) that is then run through the PalmRez Post Linker. The post linker creates a resource database (PRC file) that is ready to run on the Palm PDA. These steps are transparent to you as a developer, allowing you to focus your efforts on the task at hand.

The PalmOS SDK comes with a sample shared library project called SampleLib. The settings shown in this appendix are largely based on this project. Although you can copy this project and modify its settings to meet your needs, we thought it would be helpful to know how to create a shared library from scratch. (CodeWarrior 8 has a shared library wizard, which simplifies these steps.)

To start the project for the shared library, select File → New from the main menu. From the Project tab in this dialog, select Empty Project as shown in Figure B-1, and enter **DBSLib** for the name of your project.

Upon creating an empty project, you will be presented with the project dialog, as shown in Figure B-2. To better organize our files by type, create the *Incs* (include files), *Obj* (object files), and *Src* (source files) subdirectories under the parent *DBSLib* directory, as shown in Figure B-3.

 CodeWarrior creates the *DBSLib_Data* directory. You can ignore it for the most part.

Bring up the project settings and modify the following settings panels. Only the panels relevant to the DBSLib project are discussed.

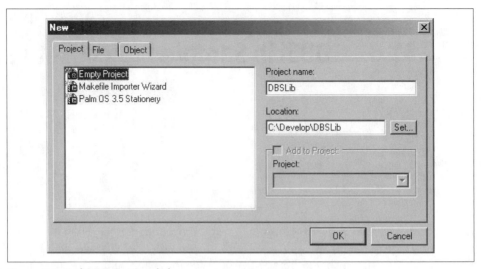

Figure B-1. CodeWarrior New dialog

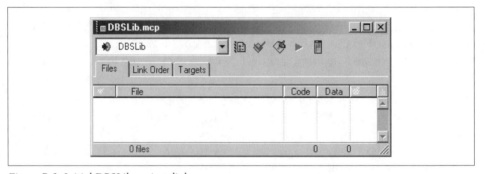

Figure B-2. Initial DBSLib project dialog

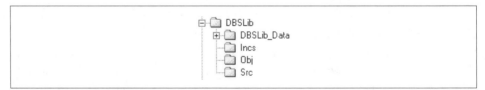

Figure B-3. DBSLib subdirectories

Target Settings

The Target Settings panel is shown in Figure B-4. The Target Name field specifies the name of our project's build target. Enter **DBSLib** in this field.

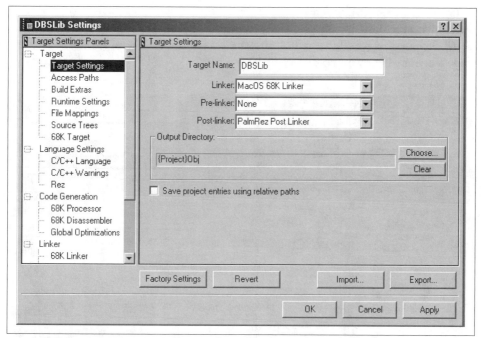

Figure B-4. Target Settings panel

The name you enter in the Target Name field is not the name of the final resource database file, which resides on the Palm PDA. It is an internal name you assign as your project's build target. The name of the resource database file is set in the Output File field of the PalmRez Post Linker panel.

The Linker drop-down specifies the type of linker to use. Select MacOS 68K Linker, since it is the standard for the Palm OS. The Output Directory field specifies the directory where the final, linked output file—*DBSLib.prc*, in our case—will be placed. Click the Choose button; select the Obj subdirectory you created previously.

Access Paths

Access paths are directories that the CodeWarrior IDE searches to locate files when compiling and linking your project. The Access Paths panel is shown in Figure B-5, with the System Paths radio button selected. Initially, {Compiler} is the only path listed under System Paths. Modify this path by clicking the Change button and selecting the Palm OS 3.5 Support directory from the access path selection dialog (see

Figure B-6). Make sure to leave Path Type set to Compiler Relative. Now, add the DBSLib project path by clicking the Add button. Select Project Relative for Path Type. Browse to and select the DBSLib parent directory for the project and click OK. CodeWarrior will now be able to locate your project files and the Palm OS SDK files.

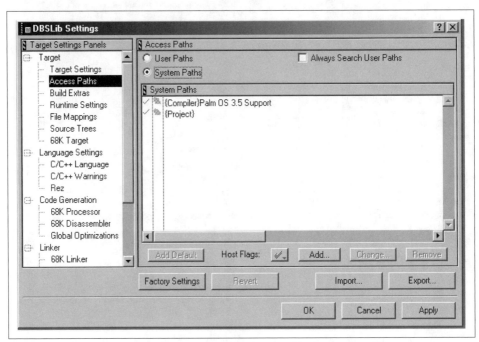

Figure B-5. Access Paths panel

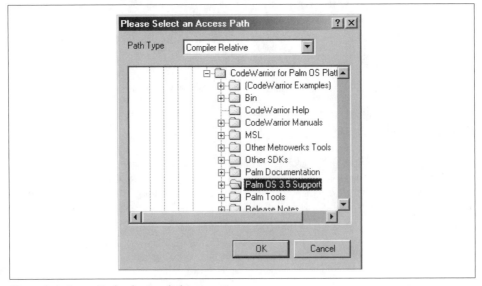

Figure B-6. Access Path selection dialog

68K Target

The 68K Target options panel (see Figure B-7) is where you set the type of project you want to create. The options on this panel vary, depending on the type of project selected. In the Project Type drop-down list, select PalmOS Code Resource.

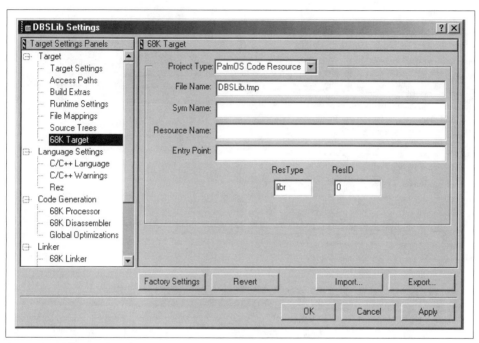

Figure B-7. K Target panel

The File Name field specifies the name of the intermediate file, which the CodeWarrior project will generate. This file is then converted by the PalmRez Post Linker into a resource database ready to run on the Palm PDA. Enter **DBSLib.tmp** into this field.

The ResType field specifies the type of resource database we are creating. To the Palm OS, a shared library is simply a resource database with its type set to libr. Enter **libr** in this field as shown.

C/C++, Processor, and Global Optimizations Settings

Figures B-8 through B-11 show various options panels you will need to modify. Select these panels and modify their settings to correspond with those shown.

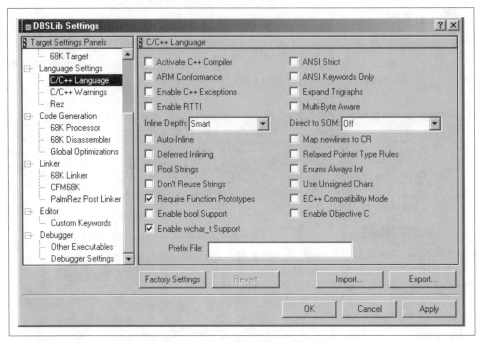

Figure B-8. C/C++ Language panel

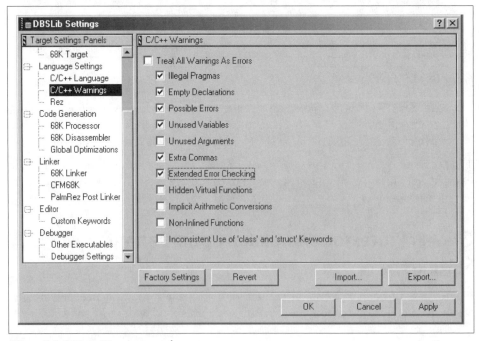

Figure B-9. C/C++ Warnings panel

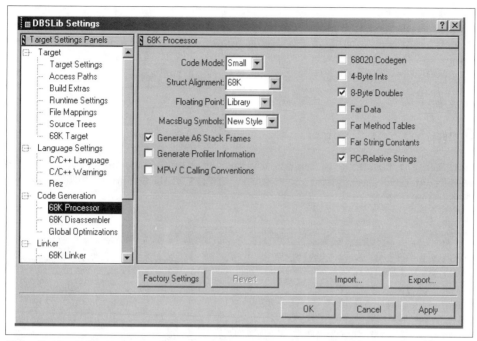

Figure B-10. 68K Processor panel

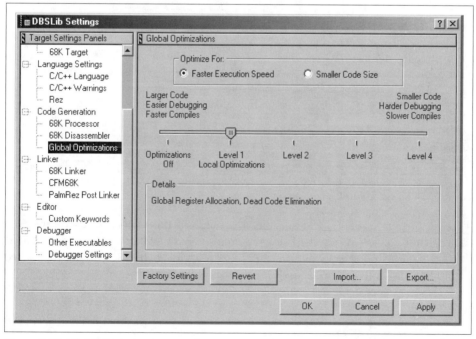

Figure B-11. Global Optimizations panel

As you develop more applications for the Palm PDA, you will want to explore the different settings and modify them to meet the unique needs of your project. CodeWarrior comes with a number of useful online references that cover these panel options in detail. The *C Compilers Reference* covers the C/C++ Language and Warnings panels, *Targeting the Palm OS Platform* covers the 68K Processor panel, and the *IDE Users Guide* covers Global Optimizations.

PalmRez Post Linker

The PalmRez Post Linker converts the file generated by the project into a Palm resource database, ready to run on the Palm PDA. This option panel is shown in Figure B-12.

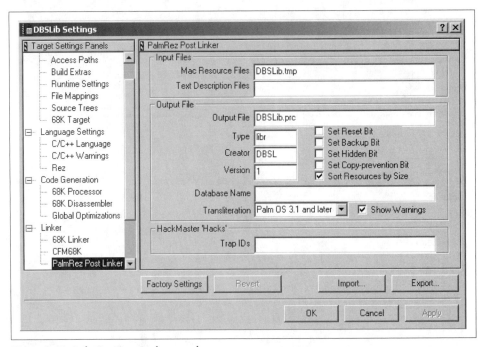

Figure B-12. PalmRez Post Linker panel

The Mac Resource Files field specifies the name of the file generated by the 68K linker that is converted into the Palm resource database, which represents our shared library. This field corresponds to the File Name field of the 68K Target panel (see Figure B-7, earlier in this appendix). Enter **DBSLib.tmp** in this field.

The Output File field specifies the name of the Palm resource database that will be generated and will ultimately reside on the Palm PDA. Enter **DBSLib.prc** in this field.

The Type field specifies the type of Palm application that is being created, and corresponds to the ResType field on the 68K Target Panel. Since this project is for a library resource database, enter **libr** in this field.

The Creator field specifies a four-character Creator ID to uniquely identify our library. See "The Palm Creator ID" sidebar in Chapter 1 for more details regarding Palm Creator IDs. Enter **DBSL** in this field.

You now know how to configure the settings for the DBSLib project. Notice that the DBSLib project dialog now appears as shown in Figure B-13, with a Segments tab instead of a Link Order tab (compare with Figure B-2, shown earlier in this chapter).

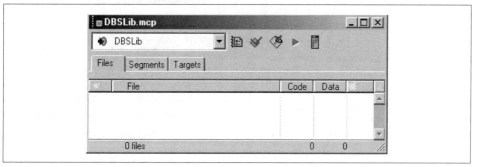

Figure B-13. Updated DBSLib project dialog

Configuring and Adding Files

Now, we need to create and organize our files within the DBSLib project. Under the Files tab in the DBSLib project dialog, create a group called Source. Select Project → Create Group from the main menu and enter **Source** as the group name. Under the Segments tab in the DBSLib project dialog, double-click on First Segment and change the segment's name to **AppSource**. Do not change any of the other settings.

To create the *DBSLib.c* source file for the project, start with the Files tab selected in the DBSLib project dialog. Select File → New from the main menu, which brings up the New dialog (see Figure B-14). Select the File tab and click the Set button. Browse to the *Src* subdirectory for the project, type in **DBSLib.c** for the filename, and click Save. Check Add to Project, and check DBSLib under the Targets list. Your dialog should look like that shown in Figure B-14.

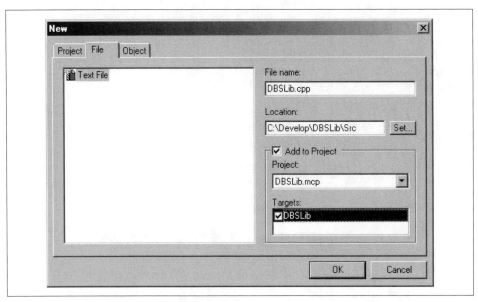

Figure B-14. CodeWarrior New file dialog

Click OK to create and add *DBSLib.c* to your project. Perform these steps again to create the following additional files: *DBSLib.h*, *DBSLibMem.h*, *DBSLibMem.c*, *DBSLibDispatch.h*, and *Debug.h*.

Your have now configured the DBSLib project, and you are ready to begin coding.

Index

We'd like to hear your suggestions for improving our indexes. Send email to *index@oreilly.com*.

P

X

XML (extensible markup language)
    database schema, 265
    parsing, 279–284
    PIDL and, 320

Z

zero-based field numbers, 95
ZOrder method, ingot position, 43

About the Authors

Matthew Holmes has been developing computer software for 15 years. He cherishes his liberal arts degree in foreign affairs from the University of Virginia, and he also holds a graduate degree in computer science from George Mason University. Matthew has been using and programming the Palm handheld, mostly in C++, since 1999. He has developed for every version of VB since its initial release, and for VBScript and Active Server Pages since the beta stages of those products. His most recent commercial project was the Palm VII wireless interface for a major online storage vendor.

Patrick Burton has been developing software for 10 years. He holds a bachelor of science degree in electrical engineering from Virginia Polytechnic Institute and State University (Virginia Tech) and a master of science degree in electrical engineering from George Washington University. Pat has been programming in C/C++ for most of his career. His experience includes algorithm development for embedded satellite receivers, Linux system programming, and Windows programming using the Win32 API and Microsoft Found Classes (MFC). His recent experience includes writing COM-based plug-ins to extend the capabilities of RealPlayer and RealServer.

Roger Knoell is a software developer with over 10 years of experience in designing and developing Internet-based and multitiered object-oriented applications, leveraging high-level language development tools and environments. He initially developed software using three releases of PowerSoft's PowerBuilder. He moved (permanently) to using Visual Basic when Version 4.0 was released. He later began exploring AppForge, which he first saw at VBITS 2000. He is especially fond of AppForge's direct integration into the VB development environment, as well as its cross-platform capabilities. He holds a bachelor's degree in computer science from Embry-Riddle Aeronautical University and a master's degree in computer science from the University of Idaho.

Colophon

Our look is the result of reader comments, our own experimentation, and feedback from distribution channels. Distinctive covers complement our distinctive approach to technical topics, breathing personality and life into potentially dry subjects.

The animals on the cover of *Programming Visual Basic for Palm OS* are flying fish. The 40 species of flying fish (the common name of the family Exocoetidae) can be found in warm ocean waters all over the world. They range in length from 7 to 12 inches. They have pectoral fins similar to bird wings and unevenly forked tails.

Flying fish are so called because of their method for escaping predators. They glide on their tails, which act as propellers, for up to 14 miles, reaching speeds up to 30 miles per hour. Their velocity builds to a point where they can launch themselves into the air and flap their "wings" to hold them up. Gusts of wind aid the flying fish in their flight, sometimes causing them to land on the decks of passing ships.

Claire Cloutier was the production editor and proofreader for *Programming Visual Basic for Palm OS*. Ann Schirmer provided proofreading assistance. Tatiana Apandi Diaz, Sarah Sherman, and Jeffrey Holcomb performed quality control checks. The index was written by Johnna VanHoose Dinse and revised by Brenda Miller and Judy Hoer. Claire Cloutier, Sarah Sherman, Jeffrey Holcomb, David Chu, Julie Flanagan, Sue Willing, and Phil Dangler were the compositors.

Ellie Volckhausen designed the cover of this book, based on a series design by Edie Freedman. The cover image is a 19th-century engraving from the Dover Pictorial Archive. Emma Colby produced the cover layout with QuarkXPress 4.1 using Adobe's ITC Garamond font.

Melanie Wang designed the interior layout, based on a series design by David Futato. Mihaela Maier converted the files from Microsoft Word to FrameMaker 5.5.6 using tools created by Mike Sierra. The text font is Linotype Birka; the heading font is Adobe Myriad Condensed; and the code font is LucasFont's TheSans Mono Condensed. The illustrations that appear in the book were produced by Robert Romano and Jessamyn Read using Macromedia FreeHand 9 and Adobe Photoshop 6. The tip and warning icons were drawn by Christopher Bing. This colophon was written by Linley Dolby.

 # More Titles from O'Reilly

Visual Basic 6.0 Programming

Access Cookbook

By Ken Getz, Paul Litwin & Andy Baron
1st Edition February 2002
718 pages, ISBN 0-596-00084-7,

Access Cookbook provides solutions to practical user interface and programming problems for the Microsoft Access power user or programmer who is running up against some of the apparent limits of the software. The book contains a comprehensive collection of problems, solutions, and practical examples for Access power users and programmers at all levels, from the relatively inexperienced to the most sophisticated.

COM+ Programming with Visual Basic

By Jose Mojica
1st Edition June 2001
304 pages, ISBN 1-56592-840-7

There's simply no other documentation available for much of what's in *COM+ Programming with Visual Basic*; this book draws from the author's wide experience as a COM+ developer and instructor. The first part delivers information that's indispensable for creating robust, efficient, high-performance COM+ applications. The second focuses on incorporating individual COM+ services, like transaction support, security, and asynchronous operations, into applications.

VB & VBA in a Nutshell: The Language

By Paul Lomax
1st Edition October 1998
656 pages, ISBN 1-56592-358-8

For Visual Basic and VBA programmers, this book boils down the essentials of the VB and VBA languages into a single volume, including undocumented and little-documented areas essential to everyday programming. The convenient alphabetical reference to all functions, procedures, statements, and keywords allows programmers to use this book both as a standard reference guide and as a tool for troubleshooting and identifying programming problems.

VBScript in a Nutshell

By Paul Lomax, Matt Childs & Ron Petrusha
1st Edition May 2000
512 pages, ISBN 1-56592-720-6

Whether you're using VBScript to create client-side scripts, ASP applications, WSH scripts, or programmable Outlook forms, *VBScript in a Nutshell* is the only book you'll need by your side—a complete and easy-to-use language reference.

Access Database Design & Programming, 3rd Edition

By Steven Roman
3rd Edition January 2002
448 pages, ISBN 0-59600-273-4

When using GUI-based software, we often focus so much on the interface that we forget about the general concepts required to use the software effectively. *Access Database Design & Programming* takes you behind the details of the interface, focusing on the general knowledge necessary for Access power users or developers to create effective database applications. The main sections of this book include: database design, queries, and programming.

MCSD in a Nutshell: The Visual Basic Exams

By James Foxall, MCSD
1st Edition October 2000
632 pages, ISBN 1-56592-752-4

Programmers tend to be specialists—they often do the same kind of programming over and over. The MCSD exam is targeted at technical generalists—developers familiar with a broad array of Microsoft technologies and development approaches. With its comprehensive overview of core technology areas, *MCSD in a Nutshell* is the perfect study guide and resource to help developers master the technologies that are less familiar to them.

O'REILLY®

TO ORDER: **800-998-9938** • **order@oreilly.com** • **www.oreilly.com**
ONLINE EDITIONS OF MOST O'REILLY TITLES ARE AVAILABLE BY SUBSCRIPTION AT **safari.oreilly.com**
ALSO AVAILABLE AT MOST RETAIL AND ONLINE BOOKSTORES

Visual Basic 6.0 Programming

ASP in a Nutshell, 2nd Edition

By A. Keyton Weissinger
2nd Edition July 2000
492 pages, ISBN 1-56592-843-1

ASP in a Nutshell, 2nd Edition, provides the high-quality reference documentation that web application developers really need to create effective Active Server Pages. It focuses on how features are used in a real application and highlights little-known or undocumented features.

Subclassing & Hooking with Visual Basic

By Stephen Teilhet
1st Edition June 2001
704 pages, ISBN 0-596-00118-5

Subclassing and the Windows hooking mechanism ("hooks") allow developers to manipulate, modify, or even discard messages bound for other objects within the operating system, in the process changing the way in which the system behaves. This book opens up a wealth of possibilities to the Visual Basic developer—possibilities that ordinarily are completely unavailable, or at least not easy to implement.

Developing ASP Components, 2nd Edition

By Shelley Powers
2nd Edition March 2001
832 pages, ISBN 1-56592-750-8

Microsoft's Active Server Pages (ASP) continue to grow in popularity with web developers—especially as web applications replace web pages. *Developing ASP Components*, 2nd Edition, provides developers with the information and real world examples they need to create custom ASP components.

Win32 API Programming with Visual Basic

By Steve Roman
1st Edition November 1999
534 pages, Includes CD-ROM
ISBN 1-56592-631-5

This book provides the missing documentation for VB programmers who want to harness the power of accessing the Win32 API within Visual Basic. It shows how to create powerful and unique applications without needing a background in Visual C++ or Win32 API programming.

ADO: ActiveX Data Objects

By Jason T. Roff
1st Edition May 2001
618 pages, ISBN 1-56592-415-0

The architecture of ADO, Microsoft's newest form of database communication, is simple, concise, and efficient. This indispensable reference takes a comprehensive look at every object, collection, method, and property of ADO for developers who want to get a leg up on this exciting new technology.

VBScript Pocket Reference

By Paul Lomax, Matt Childs & Ron Petrusha
1st Edition January 2001
126 pages, ISBN 0-596-00126-6

Based on the bestselling *VBScript in a Nutshell*, this small book details every VBScript language element—every statement, function, and object—both in VBScript itself and in the Microsoft Scripting Runtime Library. Entries are arranged alphabetically by topic. In addition, appendixes list VBScript operators and VBScript intrinsic constants.

O'REILLY®

TO ORDER: **800-998-9938** • **order@oreilly.com** • **www.oreilly.com**
ONLINE EDITIONS OF MOST O'REILLY TITLES ARE AVAILABLE BY SUBSCRIPTION AT **safari.oreilly.com**
ALSO AVAILABLE AT MOST RETAIL AND ONLINE BOOKSTORES

Hand-held Computing

Palm OS Cookbook for Programmers

By Jaron Rubinstein
1st Edition October 2002 (est.)
500 pages (est.), ISBN 0-596-00199-1

Palm OS Cookbook for Programmers is a comprehensive collection of problems, solutions, and practical examples for anyone developing for the Palm OS. Topics range from Graphics Manipulation and Animation to Bluetooth, to Web Clipping Applications. This book provides answers to beginners' questions on techniques that even the most experienced Palm developer will learn from.

Palm OS Programming: The Developer's Guide, 2nd Edition

By Neil Rhodes & Julie McKeehan
2nd Edition October 2001
702 pages, ISBN 1-56592-856-3

Palm OS Programming: The Developer's Guide, Second Edition shows intermediate to experienced C and C++ programmers how to build a Palm application from the ground up. The book follows up the success of our best-selling first edition with expanded coverage of the Palm OS, up to and including the latest version, 4.0. This book will set the standard for the next generation of Palm developers.

PalmPilot: The Ultimate Guide, 2nd Edition

By David Pogue
2nd Edition June 1999
624 pages, Includes CD-ROM
ISBN 1-56592-600-5

This new edition of O'Reilly's runaway best-seller is densely packed with previously undocumented information. The bible for users of Palm VII and all other Palm models, it contains hundreds of timesaving tips and surprising tricks, plus an all-new CD-ROM (for Windows 9x, NT, or Macintosh) containing over 3,100 PalmPilot programs from the collection of palmcentral.com, the Internet's largest Palm software site.

Programming Visual Basic for the Palm OS

By Roger Knoell, Matthew Holmes & Patrick Burton
1st Edition April 2002 (est.)
375 pages (est.), ISBN 0-596-00200-9

Programming Visual Basic for the Palm OS is the only book designed to help the Visual Basic desktop programmer to break into the Palm market. With Programming Visual Basic for the Palm OS, Visual Basic programmers can become Palm programmers almost over night.

Palm OS Network Programming

By Greg Winton
1st Edition September 2001
400 pages, ISBN 0-596-00005-7

Palm OS Network Programming is the complete guide to the hot new field of network applications development for the Palm computing platform. All the major concepts needed to develop in the Palm networking environment are here, as well as the inside tips on the many Palm OS nuances that will put developers ahead of the curve. Anyone serious about Palm developing will want to buy this book.

How to stay in touch with O'Reilly

1. Visit Our Award-Winning Web Site

http://www.oreilly.com/

★ "Top 100 Sites on the Web" —PC Magazine
★ CIO Magazine's Web Business 50 Awards

Our web site contains a library of comprehensive product information (including book excerpts and tables of contents), downloadable software, background articles, interviews with technology leaders, links to relevant sites, book cover art, and more. File us in your bookmarks or favorites!

2. Join Our Email Mailing Lists

Sign up to get email announcements of new books and conferences, special offers, and O'Reilly Network technology newsletters at:
elists.oreilly.com.
It's easy to customize your free elists subscription so you'll get exactly the O'Reilly news you want.

3. Get Examples from Our Books

To find example files for a book, go to:
http://www.oreilly.com/catalog
select the book, and follow the "Examples" link.

4. Contact Us via Email

order@oreilly.com
For answers to problems regarding your order or our products. To place a book order online visit:
http://www.oreilly.com/order_new/

catalog@oreilly.com
To request a copy of our latest catalog.

booktech@oreilly.com
For book content technical questions or corrections.

proposals@oreilly.com
To submit new book proposals to our editors and product managers.

international@oreilly.com
For information about our international distributors or translation queries. For a list of our distributors outside of North America check out:
http://international.oreilly.com/distributors.html

5. Work with Us

Check out our web site for current employment opportunites:
http://jobs.oreilly.com/

6. Register your book

Register your book at:
http://register.oreilly.com

O'Reilly & Associates, Inc.
1005 Gravenstein Hwy North
Sebastopol, CA 95472 USA
TEL 707-827-7000 or 800-998-9938
(6am to 5pm PST)
FAX 707-829-0104

International Distributors

http://international.oreilly.com/distributors.html • international@oreilly.com

UK, EUROPE, MIDDLE EAST, AND AFRICA (EXCEPT FRANCE, GERMANY, AUSTRIA, SWITZERLAND, LUXEMBOURG, AND LIECHTENSTEIN)

INQUIRIES
O'Reilly UK Limited
4 Castle Street
Farnham
Surrey, GU9 7HS
United Kingdom
Telephone: 44-1252-711776
Fax: 44-1252-734211
Email: information@oreilly.co.uk

ORDERS
Wiley Distribution Services Ltd.
1 Oldlands Way
Bognor Regis
West Sussex PO22 9SA
United Kingdom
Telephone: 44-1243-843294
UK Freephone: 0800-243207
Fax: 44-1243-843302 (Europe/EU orders)
or 44-1243-843274 (Middle East/Africa)
Email: cs-books@wiley.co.uk

FRANCE

INQUIRIES & ORDERS
Éditions O'Reilly
18 rue Séguier
75006 Paris, France
Tel: 33-1-40-51-71-89
Fax: 33-1-40-51-72-26
Email: france@oreilly.fr

GERMANY, SWITZERLAND, AUSTRIA, LUXEMBOURG, AND LIECHTENSTEIN

INQUIRIES & ORDERS
O'Reilly Verlag
Balthasarstr. 81
D-50670 Köln, Germany
Telephone: 49-221-973160-91
Fax: 49-221-973160-8
Email: anfragen@oreilly.de (inquiries)
Email: order@oreilly.de (orders)

CANADA
(FRENCH LANGUAGE BOOKS)
Les Éditions Flammarion ltée
375, Avenue Laurier Ouest
Montréal, QC H2V 2K3 Canada
Tel: 1-514-277-8807
Fax: 1-514-278-2085
Email: info@flammarion.qc.ca

HONG KONG
City Discount Subscription Service, Ltd.
Unit A, 6th Floor, Yan's Tower
27 Wong Chuk Hang Road
Aberdeen, Hong Kong
Tel: 852-2580-3539
Fax: 852-2580-6463
Email: citydis@ppn.com.hk

KOREA
Hanbit Media, Inc.
Chungmu Bldg. 210
Yonnam-dong 568-33
Mapo-gu
Seoul, Korea
Tel: 822-325-0397
Fax: 822-325-9697
Email: hant93@chollian.dacom.co.kr

PHILIPPINES
Global Publishing
G/F Benavides Garden
1186 Benavides Street
Manila, Philippines
Tel: 632-254-8949/632-252-2582
Fax: 632-734-5060/632-252-2733
Email: globalp@pacific.net.ph

TAIWAN
O'Reilly Taiwan
1st Floor, No. 21, Lane 295
Section 1, Fu-Shing South Road
Taipei, 106 Taiwan
Tel: 886-2-27099669
Fax: 886-2-27038802
Email: mori@oreilly.com

INDIA
Shroff Publishers & Distributors PVT. LTD.
C-103, MIDC, TTC Pawane
Navi Mumbai 400 701
India
Tel: (91-22) 763 4290, 763 4293
Fax: (91-22) 768 3337
Email: spdorders@shroffpublishers.com

CHINA
O'Reilly Beijing
SIGMA Building, Suite B809
No. 49 Zhichun Road
Haidian District
Beijing, China PR 100080
Tel: 86-10-8809-7475
Fax: 86-10-8809-7463
Email: beijing@oreilly.com

JAPAN
O'Reilly Japan, Inc.
Yotsuya Y's Building
7 Banch 6, Honshio-cho
Shinjuku-ku
Tokyo 160-0003 Japan
Tel: 81-3-3356-5227
Fax: 81-3-3356-5261
Email: japan@oreilly.com

SINGAPORE, INDONESIA, MALAYSIA, AND THAILAND
TransQuest Publishers Pte Ltd
30 Old Toh Tuck Road #05-02
Sembawang Kimtrans Logistics Centre
Singapore 597654
Tel: 65-4623112
Fax: 65-4625761
Email: wendiw@transquest.com.sg

AUSTRALIA
Woodslane Pty., Ltd.
7/5 Vuko Place
Warriewood NSW 2102
Australia
Tel: 61-2-9970-5111
Fax: 61-2-9970-5002
Email: info@woodslane.com.au

NEW ZEALAND
Woodslane New Zealand, Ltd.
21 Cooks Street (P.O. Box 575)
Waganui, New Zealand
Tel: 64-6-347-6543
Fax: 64-6-345-4840
Email: info@woodslane.com.au

ARGENTINA
Distribuidora Cuspide
Suipacha 764
1008 Buenos Aires
Argentina
Phone: 54-11-4322-8868
Fax: 54-11-4322-3456
Email: libros@cuspide.com

ALL OTHER COUNTRIES
O'Reilly & Associates, Inc.
1005 Gravenstein Hwy North
Sebastopol, CA 95472 USA
Tel: 707-827-7000
Fax: 707-829-0104
Email: order@oreilly.com

O'REILLY®

TO ORDER: **800-998-9938** • **order@oreilly.com** • **www.oreilly.com**
ONLINE EDITIONS OF MOST O'REILLY TITLES ARE AVAILABLE BY SUBSCRIPTION AT **safari.oreilly.com**
ALSO AVAILABLE AT MOST RETAIL AND ONLINE BOOKSTORES